Family Treatment in Social Work Practice

Family Treatment in Social Work Practice

Third Edition

Curtis Janzen

Oliver Harris

both Emeritus, University of Maryland at Baltimore

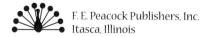 F. E. Peacock Publishers, Inc.
Itasca, Illinois

Cover image:
The Family, by Diana Ong. Private collection/Diana Ong/SuperStock.

Contents

Preface

This edition is intended to expand and strengthen the emphases of earlier editions, which had a primary focus on the internal operations of the family. How the family functions as a system is still a central theme, but this volume brings, on the one hand, added consideration of the individual and, on the other hand, the good, bad, and sufficient or insufficient connections to society for more complete understanding of individual and family difficulty. Building the understanding of social workers in family systems thinking has been a primary goal through all editions, but we are pleased now to draw the reader's attention to the ways in which the family therapy field has broadened to include more of the person-in-situation thinking that is at the core of social work practice.

For example, Erickson (1988) argues that limitations are placed on family treatment thinking by looking only at current system operations and by thinking of families as closed systems—a "synchronic" view. This neglects individual histories, which bring in a "diachronic" view and are important to understanding.

Steinglass (1991) comes to this emphasis on the individual in the family from the standpoint of individual differences that have been highlighted in studies in genetics. Here the question is "Why is it that, within the same family, children turn out to be so different?" Individual differences in temperament, genetically based, have a profound impact—not only on the individual, but on the family as a whole.

Steinglass's questioning is based on research reported by Dunn and Plomin (1991). While they draw attention to genetic differences, they also say that "with the current trend towards 'biologizing' the behavioral sciences, it is important to emphasize that there is behavioral evidence for the importance of nurture as well as nature," and that "the finding is this: environmental factors important to development are those that two children in the family experience differently."

Erickson says further that the concentration on the internal functioning system also neglects the networks of which family systems are a part and which impact in significant ways in individual and family behavior. The concept of network is also diachronic since a historical account of any current state is necessary.

Our revisions in this edition seek to restore attention to a greater extent to both of these aspects of professional understanding and practice. We will draw attention to how the thinking on the part of social work and non–social work family therapists now emphasizes the importance of history, individual development in the family, and the impact of the social and ethnic systems beyond the family's boundaries. These emphases, added to a deepened understanding of internal family operations, provide a broader, stronger base for family treatment.

Within the broad frame of theory just mentioned is another aspect of the social context of which we have taken note. Goldner (1985) points to the concept circularity in family systems thinking and how it implies interchangeability of positions and equal responsibility for family events and interaction. This appears to feminists like blaming the victim for what happens—especially, as we will note, in the case of family violence. Family therapists have focused on transactions within the family but have neglected to look at the ways the social structure enforces the division of labor and power positions of males and females. The social structure has cast women into a socio-emotional role and males into the instrumental role. Both role definitions leave women in a lesser power position than that of men.

In this edition Part I, the theory section, is enlarged. Theories upon which we draw are seen as relevant to understanding of all types of family members, such as those discussed in Part II, and not only the traditional, married, heterosexual, two-parent couple with children.

Chapters 1 and 2 have been expanded to give broader exposure to the different theories of family treatment. Chapter 1 includes a look at classifications of differing approaches and serves to draw attention to categories of difference and sameness. Chapter 2 includes reference to theories used in social work practice that we see as useful but which are not made explicit in previous editions; we give more attention than previously to the means of treatment. Chapter 3 attends to aspects of treatment common to numerous approaches and not limited to one specific approach.

Chapters 4 and 5 address matters of prominence at the beginning of contact with the family. Assessment of a family should include answers to two questions: What kind of problem do they have, and what is their problem in solving the problem? A third question has to do with how the therapist needs to work at the beginning of contact to obtain answers to the first two questions and how to come to agreement to work with the family on the problems presented. Several ways of working at beginning have been added to the discussion.

Part II has been expanded in a number of ways. New chapters on single-parent families (6) and on gay and lesbian families (9) focus on family types that are known to social workers and are increasingly common in practice situations. Though much of general treatment theory is relevant to them, the chapters should help in understanding the special aspects of these family situations.

A further expansion in this volume is in relation to the varieties of family problems. One new chapter (11) looks at family treatment in mental illness situations, particularly schizophrenia. It includes use of a psycho-educational approach with families, which is proving useful with other family problems as well.

Chapter 12 on AIDS as a chronic/terminal illness provides the opportunity to look both at features shared by families dealing with various types of chronic illness as well as at many aspects that are special to the AIDS situation.

A third kind of expansion in Part II broadens the content of chapters included in the previous editions. Chapter 7 is no longer limited to discussion of African American families and introduces Asian and Hispanic/Latino families as well. Chapter 13 on child abuse now shows more connections to violence throughout the family. Chapter 14 is broadened by reference to substance abuse, not only to alcohol abuse, and by its attention to the situation in which the abuser is one of the children rather than a parent.

Clearly, we believe that families are important in good times as well as in all of life's difficulties. We share a viewpoint from Whitehead (1993) who says

> within the culture, a shift is beginning to take place. It is a shift away from an ethos of expressive individualism and toward an ethos of family obligation and commitment. It is a shift away from the assertion of individual rights...and toward a recognition of individual responsibility. It is a shift away from a preoccupation with adult needs and toward a greater attention to children's needs. It is a shift away from a calculus of happiness based on individual fulfillment and toward a calculus of happiness based on the well-being of the family as a whole. pp. 61–62

Although current events do not readily bear out the reality of such a shift in thinking, this is an expression of values that we can heartily support. It is in this light that we frame our thinking and our practice.

REFERENCES

Erickson, Gerald. 1988. "Against the Grain: Decentering Family Theraphy." *Journal of Marital and Family Therapy* 14(3):225–36.

Dunn, Judy, and Plomin, Robert. 1991. "Why Are Siblings So Different? The Significance of Differences in Sibling Experiences Within the Family." *Family Process* 30:271–83.

Goldner, Virginia. 1985. "Feminism and Family Therapy." *Family Process* 24: 31–47.

Steinglass, Peter. 1991. "An Editorial: Finding a Place for the Individual in Family Therapy." *Family Process* 30(3):267–69.

Whitehead, Barbara. 1993. "The New Family Values." *Utne Reader* No. 57, May–June 1993, 61–65.

Part I

Theoretical Framework

The purpose of Part I is to introduce the field of family treatment and some of the most widely accepted support for the study and treatment of the family. No single theoretical structure for treating families has yet been developed, and we draw on several approaches to family treatment. All these approaches, however, use systems concepts to understand how the family operates to achieve growth and resolve problems. It is in this context that this part of the book has been written. Each of the chapters contributes to building an understanding of family functioning and suggests ways to plan appropriate strategies for changing interactional patterns when families become dysfunctional.

The first chapter gives a broad overview of family treatment in social work practice and of contributions by other professions. Chapter 2 develops in greater depth key concepts for understanding families and approaches to treatment and is centered on the communications, structural, strategic, and social learning approaches. Chapter 3 makes explicit strategies implicit in the specific approaches of Chapter 2 but emphasizes their usefulness in any of them.

Chapter 4 continues the task of building a framework for the study and treatment of families by examining the impact of various problems on the organization and functioning of the family, making extensive use of crisis theory as a framework for understanding problems as critical transitions in the life of the family. It also emphasizes the kinds of realignments and changes necessary to resolve problems when they occur. Meeting the material needs of the family, adapting to role changes, resolving conflict between family goals and individual goals, and communication and negotiation around changed circumstances are among the issues discussed in this chapter. The interrelatedness of a family's problems and its problem-solving efforts is demonstrated, with examples of the intimate relationship between the persistence of family problems and the effectiveness of problem-solving methods.

Chapter 5 completes our suggested framework for assessing family functioning and planning intervention. This chapter moves into the social worker's process of intervention with families. The ways in which the system's view of the family affects the beginning of treatment and engaging the family are delineated. The use of conjoint sessions with families, the task of actually engaging the family, procedures for beginning with the family, the social worker's role in treatment, and contracting with the family are among the topics discussed. A major emphasis is the worker's concurrent efforts in solving the problems presented by the family and changing the way in which the family goes about solving these problems.

CHAPTER 1

Introduction to Family Treatment

The idea of involving the entire family in resolving a problem expressed by one of its members is still relatively new when compared with other well-established modes of intervention. Prior to the advent of treating the family as a client system, most therapists, including social workers, approached problem solving from the viewpoint of changing the individual who by reason of his or her behavior was identified as the change target. It was believed that the cause of the maladaptive behavior was within the individual and it was necessary to deal with the psychic aspects of the personality if problem-solving efforts were to be effective. This was supported by psychoanalytic theory and the prevailing emphasis on individual treatment.

These beliefs were largely discounted as therapists began to work with more than one member of the family. Social workers in public and private agencies were among those involved in this new movement that began in the early 1950s and was usually referred to in social work circles as *multiple-client interviewing*. At this time only limited knowledge was available regarding the process and outcome of this mode of problem solving; yet, many practitioners were engaged in exploring this dimension of practice. Interviews usually involved two members of the nuclear family, most often the parents seen together. New information not previously furnished by individuals when seen alone became available, and differences in the way family members perceived the same problem situation were revealed. This caused social workers and other professionals working with more than one member of the family to seek better ways to understand these observations, and they began to pay more attention to the way family members were experiencing each other in their various encounters. This signaled the beginning of a new way of thinking about problem configuration and the ways of intervening with those involved in family conflict. The client was no longer identified as an individual with symptoms, but a family with a problem.

FROM INDIVIDUAL TO FAMILY TREATMENT

The movement away from the traditional approach of treating an individual with a problem to treatment of the family as a unit has been a gradual process. Though family treatment as a mode of practice was formally introduced in the 1950s, some of the underlying ideas and observations that support this process appeared in social work literature as early as the first quarter of the century. Mary Richmond addressed the components of problem assessment in her book *Social Diagnosis* (1917), which in many ways reflected the beginning of a family orientation in casework practice. In discussing the caseworker's activity in diagnosing problem situations, she noted the importance of knowing the main "drift" of the family's life as a key to understanding what might be troubling the individual family member. In other words, she was emphasizing the importance of family history in delivering casework services to individuals. Richmond also recognized the importance of family unity and suggested that it would be useful to learn of the difference between the power of cohesion in stable and unstable families. She believed the caseworker should inquire about the family's interest, its hope and ambition, and the activities its members engaged in together.

While Richmond stopped short of suggesting family interviews, she moved closer to this a few years later. In commenting on the development of casework, she suggested, "The next stage in development is to bring the client and those to whom he is socially related together…and then to observe the relationship in being, instead of merely gathering a report of it second hand" (Richmond, 1922, p. 138). This also hints at the importance of family interaction, which is accepted as the "centerpiece" of contemporary work with families.

It is fair to say that Richmond's perception of the caseworker's activity in providing services to clients is reflected in contemporary family treatment. Her vision of involving family members in change efforts takes on additional significance when we consider the fact that it occurred at a time when psychoanalytic theory and individual treatment formed the prevailing base of social work practice.

Further development of the observations set forth by Richmond and others continued over the years and culminated in a thrust toward working with families. This movement to family treatment was widely reflected in the literature through the writings of a number of social workers who viewed the interactions of family members as an appropriate area of attention. Scherz (1953) in writing about family-centered casework saw the individual as a part of the family constellation and suggested this individual "could not be adequately understood or helped in isolation from persons with whom he had close emotional ties" (p. 343). She also emphasized the value of seeing more than one family member when exploring family difficulties. By seeing more than one member, knowledge of family interaction and the role of each participant in this process could be obtained. The move toward treating the family was also supported by Siporin (1956), who recognized the importance of the role theory and small group theory in the conceptualization of theory and practice relative to changing the behavior of the family group. He was among those who initially visualized the necessity of understanding family structure and viewing the family as a social system.

Gomberg (1958) pointed up the limitations implicit in relying solely on individual psychology for an understanding of human problems and stressed the need to include social factors and the family in order to encompass the larger whole. He cautioned that we should not choose between a concept of the family and a psychology of the individual, but should seek a balanced understanding of the interrelatedness between the two. Gomberg was aware of the growing importance of such phenomena as complementarity, role reciprocity, and the congruence of relationships in understanding the family. He further recognized the need to understand "the nature of family equilibrium, social roles, and role expectations characteristic between husband and wife, parent and child, siblings, and within the family group as a whole" (p. 75).

About the same time that Gomberg was reporting on the limitations of individual psychology as the single theoretical base for intervention, Sherman (1959) was writing about the growing trend of seeing two or more family members in an interview, which he defined as joint interviewing. This reflected a shift from viewing the distress of the individual as the problem to recognizing this distress as symptomatic of a family problem or as pathology in the whole family. Sherman also saw a connection between individual treatment and family treatment and suggested "sometimes the best treatment for the individual is treatment of his family" (p. 22).

Coyle (1962), like Siporin, advanced the idea of the applicability of small group theory in helping the family. She emphasized group structure and dynamics as relevant to family organization and the distribution of power and authority. Coyle also likened the emergence of subgroups within the group process to subsystems in the family, each with specific roles and responsibilities for achieving the goals of their respective organizations.

Pollak and Brieland (1961), reporting on the Midwest Seminars on Family Diagnosis and Treatment, recognized the importance of understanding breakdown in interpersonal relationships within the family. They found that relationships became more complicated as family size increased and additional subsystems came into being. The interrelatedness of the subsystems was such that deterioration in one was likely to cause deterioration in others. Focusing on the whole family was strongly supported, including concern for the development stage of the problem family and viewing the family group in its natural habitat through home visits and partaking of a meal or other hospitality in the home as a way of better understanding family interactions. This was quite a departure from the traditional hour with an individual in the caseworker's office.

Scherz (1962), continuing the move from individual to family treatment, stressed the necessity of focusing on the whole family in order to gain sufficient understanding to diagnose and treat the problems expressed by individual family members. She recognized that this way of dealing with family interactional processes introduced more complications and placed more demands on the caseworker than would be experienced in working with an individual client. In spite of her acceptance of the contributions of multiple-client interviewing, she did not see this as something to be used exclusively, suggesting that both multiple-client and individual interviews should be used in some cases. She wrote, for example, "The emergence of strong dependency needs that cannot be sufficiently gratified in a group treatment process is an indication that individual treatment should supplement family group treatment" (p. 123).

Klein (1963), writing about the systemic aspects of the family, recognized the difference in treating the family as a system instead of treating the individual. He viewed the family group as a medium through which individual change is realized. In other words, he proposed that a change in family interactional patterns would produce change in the way the individual interacted with others within and outside of the family.

Hollis (1981), a much read authority on a psychodynamic approach to social work treatment with individuals, expanded the attention she gave to family work in the 1981 edition of her book. A fourth edition (Woods and Hollis, 1990) expanded the emphasis on family work even more. The view of the family as a system, which we elaborate in Chapter 2, is increasingly adopted by social work authors. The eco-systems perspective (Meyer, 1988) utilizes systems concepts that locate the family as a subsystem in the context of the multiplicity of systems with which family members have to deal. These developments can be seen as bringing a shift in emphasis from individual to family functioning and a shift from individual treatment to family group methods of treatment. We fully agree with Sherman that this is not just a shift in intensity but represents a basic shift in the way problems of individual and family functioning are conceptualized. While the field at the time was clearly trying to find a new way and many of the concepts were in early stages of definition, it is clear that core concepts were identified. These concepts have been developed over the last couple of decades and are currently in use, both by social workers and other family therapists.

To summarize the current status of family treatment, the social worker working with families cannot be solely concerned about what one person is doing, but must think in terms of two or more people interacting and influencing each other. For example, if a child is experiencing problems at school or is involved in negative peer group behavior outside the home, the problem should not be viewed solely as the child's. It must be remembered that the child is a member of a family system that includes others, such as parents and siblings, and experiences a relationship which is influenced by the behavior of those with whom he or she is interacting. Therefore, it becomes necessary to acquire a different perspective of problem formation and problem solution when treating the family as a unit than when working with an individual.

It might be helpful to remind social workers making the transition from work with individual clients to work with families that breaking old patterns of behavior is not always easy. It is not uncommon for the new family therapists to approach the task by interviewing individuals in the presence of other family members. This is to say that the social worker may carry on a dialogue with one family member at a time, which can result in an overemphasis on changing individual behavior rather than focusing on changing the way family members relate to each other. In this case the family's participation as a unit is limited, and the opportunity to assess family interactional patterns will be impaired. This is not to suggest that attention should never be focused on the individual in family treatment. It may indeed be necessary at times to focus on an individual in certain situations, such as when the family should listen to a member who is seldom heard or to give support to a family member who needs help in gaining or maintaining a sense of individuation.

To illustrate the change in therapeutic considerations between the traditional one-to-one approach and the family treatment perspective, consider an adolescent client who is truant and has difficulty in school. In the traditional approach, therapeutic efforts would likely focus on the client's fears, feelings of inadequacy, and so on. The objective would be to help the client develop insight into the cause of the problem, which would pave the way for a change in behavior. The involvement of parents and siblings would most likely be peripheral. The parents might be asked to provide some information about the problem; contacts with them would likely be separate from those with the child, and neither they nor other children would be given more than minimum responsibility for the problem.

Conceptualization of the problem is quite different in the family treatment method. The family member whose behavior is in question is thought of as the symptom bearer of a family problem. Among the objectives of the social worker is the shifting of attention from the symptom bearer to the family and involving other members in working toward necessary changes. Seeing family members together is useful because it provides an opportunity to observe various family patterns as members interact around the problem, and this reveals a more complete picture of the issue to be addressed. The therapist who sees only one family member gets only that person's view of the problem, which represents the way it is experienced from the unique position held in the family by that individual.

Take the case of a child in treatment who reveals a reluctance to play with other children in the neighborhood. The mother responds to the child's remarks by saying she realizes this isn't good, but the playgrounds are unsafe and she is fearful that the child might get hurt if allowed outside to play. The mother's comment gives the social worker and the child a different idea about the problem. The child experiences a conflicting message with regard to the inappropriateness of staying in the house and the danger of going outside to play. And the worker now has a notion about the mother's role in the child's behavior. If they had not been seen together, the manner in which the mother impacts on the child's behavior might never have been connected in this way.

To understand the way people interact and perform as members of a family, it is necessary to be aware of conceptualizations about the family as a functioning unit. For example, some notion of family structure and the processes in which the family engages as it maintains its existence is necessary. In the remainder of this chapter we will present some of the essential concepts used in family treatment. We also broaden the definition of family beyond the usual conception of the isolated nuclear family, doing so to underscore our position that the framework we present is applicable to a variety of family types. Presentation of these concepts will lay the groundwork for theoretical framework for understanding the dynamics of the family as a complex interactive system, and this will be developed further in Chapter 2.

OTHER PROFESSIONAL CONTRIBUTIONS

Men and women from different professions have contributed a great deal to the development of family treatment. Included among the earlier originators were Gregory Bateson, Don Jackson, Jay Haley, John Weakland (Bateson, Jackson, Haley, and Weakland, 1963), and Virginia Satir (1964), sometimes known as the Palo Alto group and known for their development of communications theory. Coming from a base in psychoanalysis in his work with schizophrenic patients was Murray Bowen (1978). Nathan Ackerman (1958) and Carl Whitaker, as well, moved from individual to family treatment with psychiatric patients. Also among the early developers were Ivan Boszormenji-Nagy (1965), James Framo (1970), and Gerald Zuk (1971) in the Philadelphia area, as well as Salvador Minuchin (1974) and the Child Guidance Center.

Developments within social work as well as in the broader mental health field have led to a proliferation of theories of family treatment. The various theories set forth a variety of concepts in promoting the understanding of individual and family functioning, and of what goes wrong and needs to be righted. Upon closer examination, some similarities are obscured by differences in emphasis on one or another aspect of family structure or process, or in the language used to describe them. Theorists also differ in their thinking about the goals and means of treatment. We will note that while the frameworks differ in the above ways, they turn out to be neither mutually exclusive nor limited to a theoretical approach. Space allows us neither to introduce nor provide a detailed understanding of all of them. The following discussion will introduce core ideas, principles, and richness of thinking available, drawing attention to similarities and differences among some of them, specifying the concepts we have drawn upon in developing the framework we wish to present to you.

As many as 17 different approaches to family treatment have been identified, described, and compared (Horne and Passmore, 1991). These include approaches that are derivatives or other therapies and attempts to integrate several approaches. Other writers have seen fewer types (Nichols, 1984). Still other authors have made efforts to classify approaches according to the followers of a particular theorist (Hoffman, 1981), basic belief systems, or similarities of thinking about the goals and methods of change. Kolevson and Green (1985) review all such efforts at classification in preparing their research efforts to identify the differences in what the avowed practitioners of several approaches actually think and do.

Efforts to identify areas of overlap and similarity, as well as areas of difference and uniqueness, have resulted in a variety of classifications of treatment approaches. In one of the earlier efforts Madanes and Haley (1977) grouped them in relation to six aspects: (1) whether the emphasis was on past or present functioning; (2) whether method was consistent for all families or adjusted to specific family problems; (3) whether interpretation of behavior or promotion of behavioral change had priority in the method; (4) whether the goal was personal growth of family members or the solution of the presenting problem; (5) whether the therapist thinks of the family in terms of individuals, dyads, triads/triangles, or other groupings; and (6) whether all family members are seen as equal or related in a hierarchial manner to each other.

We will use three of Madanes and Haley's categories, (1), (3), and (4), for the dual purposes of illustrating the kinds and range of differences in family treatment approaches and beginning to identify aspects of different approaches that we will later develop in defining our own. We have constructed Table 1-1 to draw attention to similarities and differences in various approaches as well as to introduce several subsequent attempts to classify them. Each of these has a slightly different basis for classification. The entries in each column of the table do not necessarily refer to identical conceptions of the approaches, though there are similarities and overlap which, in our thinking, justify placement in a given column. Each label derives from the particular author's basis for classification.

Past Versus Present Orientation

Some approaches to family treatment are based on the idea that past experiences determine present individual and family behavior and that becoming aware of and understanding them is important in changing behavior. Approaches classified as historical and psychoanalytic later in Table 1-1 are congruent with such an emphasis. There is little disagreement among all treatment approaches that the past—experience in the family of origin—has been influential in the problems and behavior of the individual and the family. But the way in which the past is dealt with differs greatly among approaches. Those based on psychoanalytic therapy elicit the individual's past negative experience with parents or siblings or family events. Friedman (1980) notes that psychoanalytic and object relations (Scharff and Scharff, 1991) theories allow a focus on learning about, and surfacing feelings about, the past that adds depth to the understanding of each individual family member. Friedman integrates this understanding with techniques that attend primarily to here-

TABLE 1-1
Classifications of Treatment Approaches

Past vs Present	Interpretation vs Behavior Change		Growth vs Problem Solution
(a) Historical	Structure/Process		Experiential
(b)	Structural Strategic Social Learning		Experiential
(c) Psychoanalytic	Systems (Bowen)	Behavioral	Humanistic
(d) Rationality	——Activity——		Emotionality

(a) Levant (1980)
(b) Olson, Russell, and Sprenkle (1980)
(c) Hansen and L'Abate (1982)
(d) L'Abate and Frey (1981)

and-now interactions between family members to promote changed behavior and that minimize the necessity of awareness and understanding. In his work with couples, Framo (1970) has family of origin relationships constantly in mind, but works on resolving or renewing ties by bringing in family of origin members primarily at a later phase of treatment.

Bowen's (1978) systems approach, while somewhat psychodynamically based in its emphasis on family of orientation, sees problematic individuals and families as being overinvolved and emotional about their families of origin. Two or three generations of family history play into present difficulties. The goal of treatment is for individuals to be less tied to, but not cut off from, family of origin. One of the means is through cognitive understanding, acquired through a dispassionate search for information from members of the extended family. This (systems) approach directs attention to achieving a more objective (rational) view of relationships among all family members over several generations. Relationships within a generation affect and are affected by those across generational lines, and understanding and interpretation of these relationships is a major focus of treatment. On the other hand, treatment does not necessarily draw in all family members. One person's change as a result of family-focused treatment can effect changes in the entire system. Rationality, a L'Abate and Frey category, is valued over emotionality in relating to family and achieving change.

At the other end of this past/present continuum are approaches that inquire little or not at all about the past, forgoing interpretation and insight, and focusing on present interactions between family members and the structure or organization of the current family. Some treatment approaches make no effort to learn specifics of the past, looking only at the present problem and what keeps the family functioning in a problem-perpetuating manner. Madanes (1981), in the strategic approach, would be an example. This focus on the here-and-now generally characterizes the approaches named in the next column.

Interpretation Versus Behavior Change

Here the distinction between approaches is on the means of bringing about change in the family. As indicated in the previous section, psychodynamic approaches assume that talking and developing awareness of the origin of the problem provide the basis for change.

The approaches in the second column of Table 1-1 focus primarily on the here-and-now of family relationships, on promoting changed behavior more than on understanding, and on restructuring the role network. Structural practitioners (Minuchin, 1974) hold images of how families need to be organized in order to solve the problems of the family and its individual members. Role definitions for husbands and wives, mothers and fathers, and parents and children, as well as clarity about who is in charge, the importance of generational distinctions and boundaries, and clarity about rules for behavior all need to be understood and corrected. Parents are helped to be parental, and children to be children; males and females have specific roles to perform. In developing their image of the properly structured family, therapists need to be aware of the ways in which their image of the well-functioning family is shaped by their experience in their family of origin and its religious and ethnic environment. A sexist bias is seen by some therapists to be inherent in the structural approach.

Seeing family members together in order to observe how they deal with each other, the reenactment of family events, giving direction to change unhelpful responses, suggesting new responses in the interview, and assigning tasks to be carried out between interviews are also among the primary methods of promoting change. Recurring sequences of interaction are seen as made of helpful or unhelpful actions in solving the family's problems; responses reward or discourage desirable behavior or problem solution.

Differences between the approaches to behavior change also lie in the degree to which the family is involved in producing a problem solution and the level of responsibility taken by the therapist. In strategic approaches (Madanes, 1981)—in some ways similar to a structural approach—the therapist might unilaterally determine which family members would be seen, how to frame the problem, and the number of steps needed to solve it. This might occur without any effort to develop the family's understanding of causation or reasons for perpetuation of the problem. Directions are given for things to do between sessions. The emphasis is clearly on problem solution and not on giving family members the opportunity for personal growth or an emotional experience with each other.

Social learning approaches promote behavior change by developing a detailed understanding of which actions by family members reward or discourage desirable behavior and what new behaviors need to be acquired in order to promote the desired behavior. Family members are instructed to instrument new behaviors that will encourage desired responses from others and to eliminate behaviors that encourage undesired responses.

Growth Versus Problem Solution

Several categories of contrasts are included in the labels in this column. The main distinction in this dichotomy is whether the primary goal of treatment is individual growth and change or solution of the presenting problem. In one sense, solution of the presenting problem may result from growth of family members as autonomous persons. Helping them to experience themselves as separate and whole persons helps them and the family to function better. Alternately, solution of the problem may occur through change in family roles, alliances or other aspects of structure. Such changes allow as well for generally better relationships and ongoing problem solution.

Several aspects of treatment are included in the label of "experiential." As implied above, the intent is to allow during the sessions for clarification of relationships and expression of feelings between family members, to enable them to experience and understand each other in new ways, as separate and unique, different but valued. The means for achieving this may be through verbal exchange or through physical means such as decreasing or increasing distance, or having persons face each other or change the seating arrangement during a treatment session.

A second aspect of the experiential approaches is the use of the therapist's own emotional response to the family to enable family members to become "real people" in their own right. In context of supportive actions that are clearly directed to such a goal, the therapist fosters emotional intensity, spontaneity, and genuineness, by direct, sometimes provocative, response to the family or individual behavior. Such therapist behavior serves as a model for the family but requires therapists who are themselves mature, open, spontaneous, and self-aware and aware of how far the family can be "pushed" on this experiential level.

Emotionality—Rationality—Activity

The classification of L'Abate and Frey is a cross-classification and draws attention to another basis for difference between approaches. It picks up Bowen's concern about emotional overinvolvement. We have put L'Abate and Frey's term, "rationality," in the past versus present column because of the emphases in these approaches on achieving rational understanding of the problems and dealing with them in a rational rather than emotionally based manner. They argue that the dominant emphasis in the field has been on the family as a system, resulting in neglect of the affective component and the experience of the individual in the family. The approaches they group as attending to emotional aspects are those in the other classifications labeled as experiential and individual-growth oriented.

Systems and Communication

Aspects of systems theory are inherent in all of the approaches to family treatment in the social work profession. Bowen's approach, just referred to, is identified in the second column of the table and tends to focus more on interpretation than behavior change. Other mental health approaches, whether psychodynamic, behavioral, client centered, gestalt, among others, address the family as social system. Individuals in the family come over in time to have a particular role within the system. Change for better or worse in individual functioning and performance requires change in the functioning and role performance of other members of the system. Likewise, changes in membership, role demands, communicative processes, or other events in the family necessitate change in individual functioning. The functioning of any individual may thus be seen as both an effect or cause of the functioning of other parts or whole of the family system. The various approaches differ in the degree to which they are explicit in developing such ideas and in the extent of family membership included.

Inherent also in family treatment theories is more or less explicit emphasis on the need for, and modes of communication between, family members in the promotion and maintenance of family health and in family problem solving. Persons cannot *not communicate* since nonverbal behavior communicates just as do words. Communication modes and problems can be separately assessed, but they are in fact inherent in family structure and role divisions. Family rules and structure are evident in the freedom or lack of it in expressing doubt or difference, and in who can say what to whom and when. Communication conveys how much each family member is valued and who has power in the system.

A PERSPECTIVE LOOK AHEAD

It should be clear from this brief overview of different approaches to treatment of the family that there are many variations in ways of conceptualizing the problems of the family or the individual in it, in the methods of treatment, and in the goals to be achieved. Similar ways of defining the problem may lead to different methods of treatment, and different problem definitions may use similar methods of treatment. See our discussion of Sturkie's (1986) classification of treatment procedures in Chapter 3 for illustration and elaboration. Goals may be achieved by more than one method and, conversely, similar methods may achieve different or several ends.

While identifying them, we have given only a sketchy picture of the different approaches. In the following chapters we define our own understandings of the family and the means and goals of treatment, and we will demonstrate where our approach draws from the ones we have already mentioned. Our elaboration will convey that we are clearly in favor of individual growth and overall family well-being, but that solution of the presenting problem is our priority. Our method is more focused on changing behavior and relationships than on interpretation and acquisition of understanding by family members. At the same time, we actively involve family members in developing problem solutions, seeing ourselves more responsible for the conduct of treatment sessions and less directive in determining the steps the family needs to take to change. And while we see history and past relationships with extended family as significant and useful in developing our understanding, our approach focuses more on the set of present relationships.

Not accounted for in the preceding classification of approaches is the great emphasis on a different understanding of sex roles brought by feminist thinkers and therapists. Their look at aspects of the different approaches leads to a different understanding of the male and female roles in and accountability for events and transactions in the family. Two separate critiques (Dienhart and Avis, 1990; Ault-Riche, 1986) from a feminist point of view of five of the major approaches to family treatment introduce feminist concerns and suggest modifications to accommodate their concerns. Further reference to feminist thinking will be made in subsequent chapters.

Before embarking on the more detailed exposition of our theoretical understanding of families and approach to treatment, it is important to draw attention to several broad themes that are significant in our overall exposition.

We want to be clear about our conception of what is, and who is in, a family. The theory to be set forth is relevant to the structure, process, and situation of all kinds of families. The image of family that first comes to mind may not be the same for all readers and is likely formed out of one's own experience as much as out of a scientific definition. Different images will reflect the fact not all families are the same—not all fit into the category of "typical nuclear family" with two parents and two children. In fact, other family types are more likely to be encountered in social work practice, including unmarried partners, remarried persons and their children, single-parent households, gay or lesbian partners— any of whom may include significant other extended family members or nonrelative others. Beyond the differences in family membership, it is obvious that families differ according to the culture, class, or ethnic group of which they are a part and the life circumstances with which they have had to cope.

While we devote separate chapters to some of these different types, our theory in the sections that follow attempts to outline a framework for looking at the structure and process of families that allows for understanding the sameness among them as well as the obvious differences.

Our approach thus far has examined mainly the internal operations of families, and has not put the family system into the larger social context—the community or communities in which the family resides or of which it is a part. Families acquire values and standards and modes of operation not only from their families or origin, but also from the ethnic and religious communities to which they are attached. Therapeutic involvement requires attention to the physical environment in which the family resides as well as to the institutional communities—the work and school environments—that ordinarily impinge on family functioning and to the systems offering services to the family in need of help.

SUMMARY

We have tracked a transition in social work practice from a primary focus on work with individuals to work with the family as a group. A similar course has been identified in psychiatry and the mental health professions, generally. In doing so we have both noted the existence of a variety of conceptions of the family and modes of treatment and offered a way of classifying them. The constructs and theories introduced will be elaborated in the following chapters to fill out our framework for understanding and treating families.

REFERENCES

Ackerman, N.W. 1958. *The Psychodynamics of Family Life*. New York: Basic Books.

Ault-Riche, Marianne. 1986. "A Feminist Critique of Five Schools of Family Therapy." In *Women and Family Therapy*, ed. Marianne Ault-Riche. Rockville, MD: Aspen Systems Corporation.

Bateson, G., Jackson, D.D., Haley, J., and Weakland, J.H. 1963. "Toward a Theory of Schizophrenia." *Behavioral Science* 1:251–54.

Boszormeny-Nagy, I., and Framo, J.L. (eds.). 1965. *Intensive Family Therapy*. New York: Harper & Row.

Bowen, M. 1978. *Family Therapy in Clinical Practice*. New York: Jason Aronson.

Coyle, Grace L. 1962. "Concepts Relevant to Helping the Family as a Group." *Social Casework* 43:347–54.

Dienhart, Anna, and Avis, Judith. 1990. "Men in Therapy: Exploring Feminist Informed Alternatives." In *Feminist Approaches for Men in Family Therapy*, ed. Michelle Bograd. Binghamton, NY: Harrington Park Press.

Framo, J.L. 1970. "Symptoms From a Family Transactional View Point." In *Family Therapy in Transition*, ed. N.W. Ackerman. Boston: Little, Brown.

Friedman, L.J. 1980. Integrating Psychoanalytic Object-Relations Understanding with Family and Systems Intervention in Couples Therapy." In *Family Therapy*, eds. J. Pierce and L.J. Friedman. New York: Grune and Stratton.

Gomberg, Robert M. 1958. "Trends in Theory and Practice." *Social Casework* 39:73–83.

Hansen, J.C., and L'Abate, L. 1982. *Approaches to Family Therapy*. New York: Macmillan.

Hoffman, L. 1981. *Foundations of Family Therapy*. New York: Basic Books.

Hollis, F. 1981. *Casework: A Psychosocial Therapy*. New York: Random House.

Horne, Arthur, and Passmore, J. Laurence. 1991. *Family Counseling and Therapy*. Itasca, IL: F.E. Peacock Publishers.

Klein, Alan. 1963. "Exploring Family Group Counseling." *Social Work* 8:23–29.

Knudson-Martin, C. 1994. "The Female Voice: Applications to Bowen's Family Systems Theory." *Journal of Marital and Family Therapy* 20(1):35–46.

Kolevson, Michael, and Green, Robert. 1985. *Family Therapy Models*. New York: Springer Publishing Co.

L'Abate, L., and Frey, J. 1981. "The E-R-A Model: The Role of Feelings in Family Therapy Reconsidered: Implications for a Classification of Theories of Family Therapy." *Journal of Marital and Family Therapy* 7:143–150.

Levant, R.F. 1980. "A Classification of Family Therapy: A Review of Prior At-tempts and a New Paradigmatic Model. *American Journal of Family Therapy* 8:3–16.

Madanes, C. 1981. *Strategic Family Therapy.* San Francisco: Jossey-Bass.

Madanes, C., and Haley, J. 1977. "Dimensions of Family Therapy." *Journal of Nervous and Mental Disease* 165:88–97.

Meyer, C. 1988. "The Eco-Systems Perspective." In *Paradigms of Clinical Social Work*, ed. R. Dorfman. New York: Brunner/Mazel Publishers.

Minuchin, S. 1974. *Families and Family Therapy.* Cambridge, MA: Harvard University Press.

Nichols, Michael. 1984. *Family Therapy: Concepts and Methods.* New York: Gardner Press.

Olson, D., Russell, C.S., and Sprenkle, D.H. 1980. "Marital and Family Therapy." *Journal of Marriage and the Family* 42:973–94.

Pollak, Otto, and Brieland, Donald. 1961. "The Midwest Seminar on Family Diagnosis and Treatment." *Social Casework* 42:319–24.

Richmond, Mary E. 1917. *Social Diagnosis.* New York: Russell Sage Foundation.

_____. 1922. *What Is Social Casework?* New York: Russell Sage Foundation.

Satir, V. 1964. *Conjoint Family Therapy.* Palo Alto, CA: Science and Behavior Books.

Scharff, David, and Scharff, Jill. 1991. *Object Relations Family Therapy.* New York: Jason Aronson.

Scherz, Frances H. 1953. "What Is Family-Centered Casework?" *Social Casework* 34:343–49.

_____. 1962. "Multiple-Client Interviewing: Treatment Implications." *Social Casework* 43:120–24.

Sherman, Sanford N. 1959. "Joint Interviews in Casework Practice." *Social Work* 4:20–28.

Siporin, Max. 1956. "Family Centered Casework in a Psychiatric Setting." *Social Casework* 37:167–74.

Sturkie, Kinly. 1986. "Framework for Comparing Approaches to Family Therapy." *Social Casework* 67:613–21.

Whitehead, Barbara. 1993. "The New Family Values." *UTNE Reader* No. 57, May-June, 61–65.

Woods, M., and Hollis, F. 1991. *Casework: A Psychosocial Therapy.* New York: McGraw-Hill.

Zuk, G.H. 1971. "Family Therapy: 1964–1970." *Psychotherapy: Theory, Research and Practice* 8:90–97.

CHAPTER 2

Systems and Theoretical Approaches to Family Treatment

Understanding the family as a system and planning intervention require both knowledge of concepts that help explain the interaction of family members within the system as well as theoretical approaches designed to intervene in case of family dysfunction. First we will focus on some systemic aspects of family functioning and follow with selected theoretical approaches.

SYSTEMIC CONCEPTS

The systemic concepts we will discuss include social roles and the function of homeostasis, triangulation, family rules, and family myths, all of which are important considerations for social workers and other professionals engaged in treating families.

Social Role

The concept of role within the context of family functioning may be viewed as a prescription for interpersonal behavior, associated with individuals as actors and the status of positions. We agree with Heiss (1976) that role requirements are learned in the process of social interaction and the occupants of a role see it as carrying a specific status for the occupant and for others with whom the occupant interacts. Learning the behaviors expected in various roles involves both observation and teaching.

Learning role expectations by observation may be realized through *role-taking*. Role-taking is essentially imagining oneself to be in the position of another person. This occurs through the process of observing and initiating the behavior of one who is perceived as a person whose behavior is accepted by the role-taker. In the best of all worlds, this would reflect that which is good and supportive of positive interaction. However, it should be kept in mind that the behavior taken on by the role taker is not always that which society considers positive. This is because the individual's behavior that is admired and accepted by the role-taker is often brought on by negative experiences of a hostile environment, including discrimination, poverty and crime. As a result, social roles do not always make positive impressions or support that which is considered ideal in contemporary society.

In the case of role-teaching, information about the role is conveyed by direct communication through which a set of expectations is given to the role occupant by others, thus transmitting what is expected of the occupant of the position. For example, through the process of interaction people learn what is expected in their respective roles. If one partner does not make decisions and repeatedly refers all family matters to the other partner, this behavior communicates the expectation that this person is to be the decision maker. As this person continues to make decisions, it reinforces the behavior and defines the dependency of the other partner with regard to making decisions. In the meantime, the role of decision maker is established, and it is expected that this person will behave in this way.

If both partners are satisfied with their respective role behaviors, this indicates that they have harmonized their interpersonal roles around this independent-dependent relationship and role complementarity exists between them. In this case, the complementary needs of both are fulfilled by this independent-dependent interaction. And in spite of the appearance of an unequal relationship, this couple may function satisfactorily due to a congruence of roles.

Their relationships would be quite different if an incongruity of roles existed, as would be indicated if the couple did not agree on the appropriate behavior to be associated with the roles they are to fill. For example, if one partner expects to make all decisions about family matters, but is denied this opportunity by the other partner, who also wishes to share in decision making, this will result in role conflict, and an incongruity of roles will exist.

It should not be assumed that a lack of congruence in the relationships means there is also disagreement. Since an individual takes on a series of roles in the process of identifying and developing a self, a lack of congruence might arise as a result of inconsistencies between identities that surface in response to situations experienced by the role occupant. This can be seen when the occupant interacts with various others where existing relationships call forth incompatible identities, as in the case of a superior interacting with a subordinate who is also a friend (Heiss, 1976). The identity compatible with exchanges between friends is usually characterized by a *symmetrical relationship*, where both communicators behave equally. In the case of communication between superiors and subordinates, the participants exchange different types of behaviors with one (the superior) giving and the other (the subordinate) receiving, as is common in a *complementary relationship* (Okun and Rappaport, 1982). While disagreement regarding appropriate behaviors is not involved in this exchange, incongruence develops from the incompatible identities called forth by one actor being in a superior position to the other, who is also a friend. In other words, congruence cannot occur when both equal and unequal behaviors are required simultaneously.

To this point we have been concerned primarily with role as related to various role images. Finally, we will focus on roles from an intrafamilial perspective. Since the parent role is invested with the responsibility for the family system, it represents a logical point at which to begin the intrafamilial focus, which will be followed by discussion of the role of children in the family.

Assimilation into the role of parent, as well as the role of child, occurs in the same manner as previously described—that is, through the learning process. The role of parent does not automatically begin with the union of two people whose roles may carry different responsibilities. The role prescription for parent requires the exercise of authority in the interest of the development of children, while at the same time providing the opportunity for growth as reflected in separation and individuation. Preferred behaviors for the parent role can be learned through teaching as exemplified in parent effectiveness training. Nevertheless, the first and perhaps most important learning of role behavior comes through observation and role-taking. This is to say that the child learns parenting behavior from his or her relationship with parents as they move through the life cycle. And much of the behavior demonstrated by parents in association with their children becomes the behavior that the child will demonstrate in the future when he or she becomes a parent. For example, several studies have found that children who are abused by their parents also abuse their children when they become parents. Positive qualities will likewise be transferred to the future parent role.

The role of the child comes with the birth of the infant, and much of the early role behavior is characterized as instinctive and dependent. However, the infant's behavior is also influenced by the responses of the parents in their effort to meet the child's needs. If the child is provided appropriate physical and emotional comfort by the parents and given food when hungry, he or she is likely to respond in ways that reflect contentment. The child's contented behavior pleases the parents and elicits more of the parental responses that produced this behavior, thus defining expected role behavior for both parents and child. The parent role is to provide appropriate nourishment for the child, while the child is to behave in ways that reflect happiness and contentment. Even at this early stage of life, role behavior is learned through the process of interacting with others.

As the child grows, he or she learns expected role behavior from a number of associations and experiences including siblings, peers, and various adults. One of the most influential sources of learning from adults other than parents is experienced when the child enters school and takes on the role of student. This is a new role, and the child must learn how to behave as a student whose primary objective is to gain specific knowledge designed to facilitate movement through various stages of life. Teaching and observation are again the primary vehicles for communicating what is required of the child in the student role. The teacher communicates specific information and requires the child to demonstrate the extent to which this information is understood and integrated into an orderly body of knowledge commensurate with the child's level of development. In addition to providing information and guiding the child's quest for knowledge, the teacher almost always becomes a role model for the child and thereby enhances the role-taking process through which role expectations are learned. This interaction defines how the child should behave as a student: That is, that he or she should acquire knowledge under the guidance of the teacher and be able to demonstrate this achievement in communication with others. Understanding various role sets as experienced by family members and the way in which these roles are defined will greatly assist social workers and other professionals in determining appropriate strategies for intervening in family conflict.

Family Homeostasis

All systems have a self-regulatory mechanism through which a state of equilibrium is maintained. They seek to maintain a steady state, or a desired balance in their existence, through an error-activated feedback process. In regard to maintaining balance in relationships, if one person shows a change in relationships to another person, that person will react in a manner designed to modify and decrease the impact of that change. In the case of the family, homeostasis implies that the family acts so as to achieve a balance in relationships. This means that all parts of the system function in such a way that change is unnecessary for realization of family goals.

Most but not all families maintain a balance in relationships through wholesome growth-producing transactions. This implies that permeable boundaries facilitate feedback, and the feedback process promotes adjustments to life cycle developments, which maintain the desired balance. However, family homeostasis may be achieved in a variety of ways. For example, as early as the 1950s, study of schizophrenic patients and their families revealed that in some of these families there was a vested interest in the patient's illness. In this case, when the patient began to improve, family members exerted pressure to maintain the illness. In other situations when the patient got well, someone else in the family became symptomatic. This behavior suggests the need for a symptom bearer in the family in order to maintain the established pattern of relationships.

In such cases, the family, in its efforts to maintain a homeostatic state, may not always serve the best interests of all its members. Therefore, the worker should keep in mind that in maintaining its emotional balance, the family may try to prevent unwanted change in the system by encouraging role performance that is destructive for the role occupant. Yet, much of the behavior that maintains the status quo within the family is accepted by its members as a legitimate part of the family's operation. This supports the suggestion that someone outside of the family is most often the first to identify such behavior as deviant and to send out the call for help. For example, the school is often the first to call attention to the deviant behavior exhibited by the child. The family fails to recognize this behavior as deviant because it serves the function of maintaining equilibrium within the family.

To further illustrate the homeostatic process, consider the case of parents who fight in the presence of a child and frequently threaten to separate. The child fears loss of the parents and reacts to prevent this loss by displaying behavior that claims the parents' attention. When the parents focus their attention on the child, they must discontinue their fighting. The threat of loss for the child subsides, and the family remains intact. As this transaction is repeated, it becomes a pattern of behavior in the family; the parents fight and the child acts out to keep them together.

Family Triangulation

A number of theorists have contributed to the development of the concept of triangulation in family relations. In keeping with this concept it is accepted that the formation of a unit of three as a way of relating is a process common to all emotional systems. Knowledge of this process is essential to understanding the family as it struggles to maintain itself as a viable system. The triangle, as most commonly perceived, involves three persons (for example, parents and a child) or two persons and an issue (for example, a couple and alcohol). The two-person system has difficulty maintaining its stability under the pressure of anxiety and tension. When this system experiences intolerable frustration, it triangulates a third person or an issue in the hope of reducing the level of tension. The social worker engaged in family treatment is also a likely object of triangulation, especially when dealing with a two-person system. In a triangle situation the third operative—person or issue—becomes the object of attention for at least one of the original two, and sometimes both engage in a struggle for the advantages offered by the third component of the triangle.

The concept of triangles in human relationships is most often applied as a way of describing the relations of a unit of three. However, more than three persons, or a combination of persons and issues, may be involved, as demonstrated in the family where two or more children alternate as the triangulated family member. In other families, more than one child may be brought into the relationship struggle between parents at the same time. As an example, consider the parent whose actions convey to the children that the other parent is not interested in the welfare of the family. This encourages the children to join with the first parent to ensure survival. It creates a situation in which at least three have come together against one, and at least four people are actively involved in the triangulation process.

It is important to recognize the existence of a perverse triangle within the process of family relating. This triangle is potentially pathological and can lead to conflict and possible dissolution of the system. In describing the perverse triangle, Haley (1987) suggests that one member is of a different generation (such as parent and child). These two people of different generations form a coalition against the peer of one of the members (for example, one parent and child against the other parent) but deny the presence of the coalition, in spite of behavior that confirms its existence. If the coalition continues and the denial of its existence is repeatly offered, this pattern of relating is established and a pathological situation exists.

The concept of the triangle in human relationships provides the social worker with a way of viewing the patterns of relating within the family. To illustrate the working of this concept as it is frequently observed in family treatment, a case example from our experience is the H family:

Mr. and Mrs. H were both 31 years of age. He was a successful executive and she was a housewife and mother. They were married at 21, when both were in their last year of college. Their first and only child was a son, D, who was born one year after the marriage. D had just celebrated his ninth birthday when the family came for treatment.

The parents were very articulate, and Mr. H's skills in public relations and sales, areas in which he had been quite successful, were readily observed in the early sessions. He explained the family's route to therapy as a mutual decision, coming after D's increasing show of dependent behavior. In school he was demanding more attention, and the teachers thought he was showing signs of insecurity. At home his behavior was somewhat confusing to the parents, as he demanded more attention, yet at times he withdrew from their efforts to engage with him.

It was learned during the course of treatment that the beginning of this behavior followed closely what Mrs. H described as "rather serious" misunderstandings between her and Mr. H. For the past five years Mr. H had advanced steadily with his company and, about one year ago, was promoted to a position of increased responsibility. This position required travel and a good deal of entertaining, which forced curtailment of many activities the family had previously enjoyed. Mrs. H was feeling left out of her husband's life, and as both she and the job demanded more and more of Mr. H's time, anxiety and tension developed. In commenting on this Mrs. H stated "the job seemed to be winning" and they had more than once discussed divorce. As a result of the increasing anxiety Mrs. H experienced, she began to do more things with her son, shared her loneliness with him, and in various ways conveyed abandonment by Mr. H and their need to be together. This led to a coalition between mother and son, as the son was triangulated by the mother to help in dealing with her relationship with her husband. Nevertheless, this was an uneasy coalition, as D was very fond of his father. When the father also bid for D's attention, D withdrew out of fear of hurting one of his parents. The burden this placed on D was too great to be contained within the family relationship and spilled over into his relationship within the school system.

The family triangle does not necessarily involve the same third person or object throughout the triangulation process, and usually a number of alternatives are available to complete it. In the H case, for example, Mrs. H might also have chosen to attach herself to her parents to help in dealing with her husband or attempted a coalition with the therapist for the same purpose.

It should also be noted that triangulation is not always an indication of pathology in the family. For example, either parent may develop an interest in an outside activity such as volunteer work as a way of spreading out the tension that usually develops in intense intimate relating. It is not likely that bringing this third component into the relationship will become problematic, as long as it does not replace the other principal participant in the relationship. By redirecting some of the energy that otherwise goes into the buildup of tension, both partners are better able to carry out normal functions. In summary, triangulation is a predictable way in which human systems handle problems in relating as they seek to relieve the buildup of tension. While it can, under certain circumstances, contribute to family dysfunctioning, it can also be an alternative that leaves the participants in an intimate relationship somewhat more free to function effectively.

Family Rules

Family rules are essentially relationship agreements that influence family behavior. Some rules are explicit and established along the lines of specific roles and expectations of family members. With these rules what is desired is likely to be discussed, which opens the rules to the possibility of negotiation and change. The most powerful family rules, however, are those that are implicit, having been established over time by repeated family transaction. For example, consider the case of a family in which one parent is involved in an extramarital love affair. This affair has generated repeated experiences through which family members have come to realize that the extramarital relationship exists. The parents never openly talk about the relationship themselves or entertain discussion of it by the children. As this scenario is repeated, it becomes an established rule that the family will not talk about the parent's affair. The strength of this rule lies in the fact that, without discussion, relevant information about the experience is not processed. When discussion does not occur, the family is less likely to take actions to alter the status quo. The self-perpetuating mechanisms within the family system take over and reinforce the implicit rule, which continues unchanged among family members.

Families also have different ways of enforcing rules in treatment. For example, if the social worker seems to be getting too close to a family secret in an interchange with one family member, someone else may enter the discussion with a different idea that changes the flow of information. In another situation, especially where children are involved, a child may suddenly display some form of disruptive behavior. This claims the attention of the group, taking the focus away from the possible revelation of the secret as awareness turns to this new and unexpected activity.

Some families also have rules governing communication around valued areas of family life such as sexual behavior and family illness. Whatever the governing mechanism, when it interferes with the effective course of treatment, preventive measures should be taken.

The Family Myth

The family myth essentially consists of family members' shared beliefs and expectations of each other and their relationships (Ferreira, 1977). It is characterized by unquestioned sharing of beliefs and expectations by all family members, which results in automatic agreement on the myth without further thought by any member. Ferreira gives this example:

> The wife in a family of 16 years' duration did not drive an automobile, nor did she care to learn. It was necessary for the husband to drive her everywhere she wished to go, which he did at whatever personal sacrifice it required. The wife explained her position by saying she was not "mechanically inclined." The husband immediately agreed with his wife and corroborated her statement by adding that she often let things fall from her hands around the house, and had always been that way. He further reported that she also did not trust cab drivers, while the wife nodded her approval. (p. 51)

The husband so completely shared the belief that his wife was not mechanically inclined and needed his assistance that he not only agreed with her statement but supported the belief by offering an example of her awkwardness. He obviously had no thought of questioning her position.

It is also important to keep in mind that, in spite of the irrationality often apparent in the existence of a family myth, it is perceived by family members as an emotionally indispensable and necessary part of their reality. As such, it not only determines the behavior of all family members but also reveals something about family relationships. It implies the existence of reciprocal roles in the family, which is to say, if the myth is around something someone in the family cannot do, it implies that it can be done by someone else in the family. As further emphasis on the myth in family relating, consider the central characters, George and Martha, in the drama *Who's Afraid of Virginia Wolf?* Much of the discussion between the characters in this drama centers around the existence of an imaginary son. Although the son does not exist, both Martha and George believe him to be real and repeatedly express agreement on matters pertaining to him. Myths may also serve a homeostatic function within the family and are likely to surface at times of extreme tension that threaten to disrupt family relationships. The myth prevents change in relationships, as do all balancing mechanisms, enabling the family to continue functioning in its customary manner.

Separateness and Connectedness

It is important that family members act both in concert with others and individually. Human relationships are characterized by a process of being together and being apart from one another. Two strong emotional forces are at work in this process: the need for emotional closeness, which brings people together; and the desire for individuality and autonomy, which moves the individual away from the control of others.

The family is characterized by a connectedness between members and also separateness of members from one another. This duality is reflected in the situation surrounding the newborn infant. Although coming from the parents, the infant is physically a separate individual and must remain so. Returning to the womb is impossible, and the child's psychobiological individuality will exist despite experience with the socialization process. The parents must maintain their psychobiological individuality regardless of their emotional closeness. The infant also exemplifies connectedness among family members. The newborn must depend on parents for nurturance in order to survive and therefore cannot sever this connection. And if the parents are to fulfill the infant's needs, they must come together and accommodate each other in the parenting role.

The other side of being separate and connected involves emotional issues. Fusion and differentiation behavior among family members are essential elements in their coming together and being able to separate. Fusion behavior is an adaptation of speech and actions designed to establish a system of feeling and responses that is in keeping with the family's preferred pattern of behavior. Differentiation behavior is the opposite of fusion behavior, in that the individual develops speech and actions that will disengage his or her own feelings and responses from a pattern of automatic compliance with what is preferred by others. This means that the individual seeks freedom from control by others, freedom to be different from others, and freedom to be apart from others.

Maintaining connectedness to others creates a sense of belonging, which satisfies the basic human need for closeness and identification. Yet, we must keep in mind that excessive closeness minimizes the opportunity for separateness; and if this condition exists enmeshment and loss of identity may result. Separateness has a similar quality in that it contributes to individuality and autonomy, but when carried to the extreme, it can produce loneliness and isolation. Therefore, a balance must be sought that will allow family members to come together to share and support, but also to separate and follow individual pathways to fulfillment and satisfaction.

The ways in which family members want to be together and the ways they want to be apart are reflected in the family's patterns of behavior. Some families develop around an excessive need for emotional closeness, while other families place great emphasis on separateness as shown in autonomy of behavior. If the need for closeness is too great, fusion within family relationships is likely to result. And when fusion occurs, family members will not be able to express themselves in a manner other than what is preferred by the family. If the drive for individuality and self-determination exceeds all other interests, the ability of family members to be close and supportive in relationships with one another is lessened. Extremes in either case contribute to family dysfunction.

The pattern of relating within a family is not the result of an accidental process. It is influenced by the patterns established in the parents' families of origin. If the parents were never given permission to separate from their own families of origin they will experience difficulty in establishing separate ego boundaries between themselves. The new parents will then transmit this need for togetherness to their children, who will also have difficulty separating from them. The implicit obligation in this type of family is to remain devoted to the families of origin. Individuation is not encouraged among family members, and the avenues through which this might take place are frequently blocked. This blocking behavior is often subtle. It can be seen in the family that permits members to transcend its boundaries but systematically rejects all feedback from such encounters. A typical example is the adolescent who is allowed to interact with systems outside the family but is denied the opportunity to use this experience for personal growth. Families accomplish this denial in various ways. Sometimes they discourage differentiation indirectly by disqualifying the child's attempts at new behavior or expressing fear that great danger is associated with his or her wish to be different at such a tender age. In this way the avenue to differentiation is blocked, and the family goal of maintaining the devotion of its members is supported.

The experience of separateness in relationship is not entirely a physical phenomenon. Boszormenyi-Nagy and Sparks (1973) suggest that actual physical separation is not necessary for one to attain the individuation implied in being separate from the other. Instead, the ability to be separate is realized through the formation of a psychic boundary.

With this boundary established, one is not always a product of and dependent upon the family but becomes a separate entity by reason of psychic emancipation. This type of boundary formation is reflected in the work of Laqueur, Labrut, and Morong (1971), who report that as the child develops, primary objects of attachment are gradually replaced. This occurs when the child learns to transfer energies from these primary objects to a widening circle of outside figures, interests, and tasks. As this is accepted by other family members and they assist the child in this growth process, a psychic boundary is formed that facilitates the achievement of a sense of belonging and a sense of being separate.

We believe that one of the most important developments within the family as it passes through its life cycle is the determination of what it will do about closeness and separation in family relations. Most families are able to establish a workable balance in how its members will come together and support each other and how they will be different and able to be apart from each other. The extent to which this balance is achieved is crucial, and social workers may often find this a necessary target area for their change efforts.

THEORETICAL APPROACHES

There are several approaches to family treatment. While we will concentrate on only four specific ones, many of the concepts and techniques we discuss will be applicable to other theoretical approaches. We believe the presentation of these approaches, together with the concepts and techniques they embrace, will help professionals working with families to better understand the dynamics of the family as a complex interactive system amenable to intervention and change. The following are the approaches we will discuss: (1) the structural approach, (2) the communications approach, (3) the strategic approach, and (4) the social learning approach.

The Structural Approach

The structural approach to therapeutic intervention with families emphasizes the importance of family structure, family subsystems, and boundaries around the family, its individual members, and its subsystems. Although reference to these concepts will appear at other points in this book, it is here that we hope to provide a definition and fully describe the functions of each. Our discussion will reflect our experiences as well as the thinking of others, including Minuchin and Nichols.

Family Structure

Minuchin (1974) defines family structure as "The invisible set of functional demands that organizes the ways in which family members interact. Repeated transactions establish patterns of how, when, and to whom to relate and these patterns underpin the system" (p. 51). For example, one parent tells the child to stop playing and go to bed. When the child refuses, the other parent becomes infuriated by this display of disobedience and yells at the child, after which the child complies with the wish of the other parent and goes to bed. Repetition of this way of dealing with the child establishes a transactional pattern and creates a structure in which the parent who first gave the child the order to go to bed is viewed as an incompetent disciplinarian and the parent who enforced the order is considered competent.

Another aspect of family structure is the rules that govern family organization and transactions within the family. Such rules are often recognized in the way various family members protect each other. If the parents cannot handle intimacy and closeness in their relationship, the child behaves in such a way as to demand their attention and thereby prevent the necessity of the parents having to relate to each other on an intimate level. Nichols (1984) suggests that family structure is also shaped by universal and idiosyncratic constraints. This involves a power hierarchy in which parents and children have different levels of authority. A complementarity of functions is also necessary, with both parents accepting an interdependency of functioning and supporting each other as a team.

Family Subsystems

The second component of structural family therapy is *family subsystems*. Subsystems are created by family members joining together to carry out various functions. Coming together in this way may be centered around age (generation), gender function, or common interest. Among the natural groupings that form subsystems are adult couples, siblings, and parent and child. There are many roles to be filled in the family, and each member may play several roles in a number of subgroups. One parent may be at different times a father, son, or nephew, while the other may be a mother, daughter, or niece depending on time, place, and circumstances. Among the basic underpinnings of the structural approach to family treatment is the belief that the family is a system that functions through the support of subsystems. The major subsystems that develop over time within the nuclear family structure are the *couple subsystem*, the *parental subsystem*, the *sibling subsystem*, and the *parent-child subsystem*. It should be noted that the adults involved in the couple subsystem, the parental subsystem, and the parent-child subsystem are not always a married couple. These parent roles are sometimes filled by extended family members, including grandparents, uncles, aunts, or other relatives who assume responsibility for the child. The role of parent may also be filled by the significant other of the child's responsible relative.

Couple Subsystem.   The couple subsystem is the first to emerge and comes into being when two adults come together with the desire to exist as a unit, sharing and accommodating to each other. Complementarity and accommodation are the primary components of a successful couple subsystem. This means that each partner should develop patterns of behavior that lend support to effective functioning of the other. In carrying this out, a kind of joining and cooperating takes place. Yet, the ability to be and act separately is also essential to effective functioning of the couple subsystem. Therefore, the two people involved must seek a balance between being close and supportive, and maintaining the individuality necessary for independent action.

Thus the couple subsystem, like all subsystems, is characterized by a boundary within a boundary structure. The inner boundary maintains the individuality of the participants, while the outer boundary defines the subsystem and protects it from the intrusion of outside forces. The outer boundary that surrounds the couple subsystem also differentiates it from other family systems and provides a turf over which these two participants are the rulers. When the boundary is appropriately in place, the couple subsystem is clearly separated from families of origin, and extended family interference is controlled. At the same time, the individual boundaries provide the partners turf over which each can rule within the subsystem boundary, as exemplified by the ability of each to act without complete support and validation from the other. This also allows a self to be identified and responsibility to be taken for individual action. When children come into the family, the couple subsystem boundary also protects against the children's intrusion into the couple's domain. This does not mean the couple subsystem is isolated from other systems. However, it symbolizes the right of the couple subsystem to engage in its own internal processes without interference from outside its boundary.

In spite of the boundary's objective of safeguarding the integrity of the system, boundary violations do occur. Take the case of a newly formed couple whose parents are consistently interfering with the new relationship by invading its psychosocial space—which is a serious threat to the boundary around this subsystem. If the new couple accepts the efforts of these relatives to control their lives, these two subsystems become diffuse, and the identity of two separate systems does not exist. In the case of such encroachment, it is not uncommon to find a coalition existing between two principals of different generations. For example, one partner may join with a parent in a coalition against the other partner of the newly formed couple. This is a generational boundary violation that reflects the lack of a clear boundary between the partner and the parent, and this contributes to dysfunctioning in both couple and parent systems. While the parent is involved with the kinship partner against the other partner of the couple, it is likely that the parent's relationship will be neglected, giving rise to yet another relationship problem.

Parental Subsystem. Until the arrival of the first child by birth, adoption, or custody proceedings the partners are viewed as a couple subsystem reflecting primary concern for their roles as partners. With the arrival of the first child (or children), three new subsystems come into being that must be recognized in considering family functioning. The new family units are the parental subsystem, composed of two adults; the sibling subsystem, which may be one child or two or more children; and the parent-child subsystem, which comes into existence as a functional unit when the parents individually or collectively interact with a child.

The parental subsystem is largely child-focused and has executive responsibility for the entire family system. This responsibility is rooted in the hierarchical position accorded the parents, who provide the leadership and authority necessary for family growth and development. If parents do not demonstrate leadership and authority, the family system, including wholesome development of their children, is placed at risk. Parents who do not direct and lead children leave them on their own to find appropriate role models and authority figures by trial and error, which can be devastating for a child. A problem is also presented in cases where one part of the hierarchical system is absent. This creates a void into which a child may be elevated for a number of reasons. For example, a lonely and distraught parent may turn to a child to replace the affections of the absent parent and thereby create a closeness in the parent-child relationship that denies the child the opportunity to develop autonomy. At the same time, this closeness may tie the two participants together so closely that one cannot function without the other. If this occurs, a symbiotic relationship can develop that seriously impairs the adjustment of parent and child. In order to perform effectively as a parental subsystem, parents must be flexible and maintain a delicate balance between exercising control over their children and promoting their independence. Unlike the couple subsystem, which is protected from the intrusion of children, the parental subsystem operates differently where children are concerned. The boundary of the parental subsystem permits free movement of children back and forth across the perimeters of the system. This new role of parent carries with it responsibility for the rearing of children. One of the first things parents must do is give up some of what they previously shared exclusively when occupying only the role of partner in the couple relationship.

In systems theory, a change in one part of the system requires change in other parts. With the introduction of a child (or children) into the couple system, the partners in this system become parents. The additional member(s) impacts the relationship and sets a change process in motion. The previous balance in relationship enjoyed by the parents is disrupted, and a new boundary must be established around themselves and the child (or children). This boundary expansion presents the parents with new responsibilities as children must be nurtured. This nurturing requires parents to restructure their own need-meeting activities in order to meet the physical and emotional needs of their children.

Sometimes changing to include a child is difficult for new parents. Before the introduction of children into the system, parents are primarily concerned with their own and each other's needs and expectations, in an intimate and personal relationship. When they become parents, there is likely to be less time for enjoying each other. Leisure time may have to be spent differently, or recreational activities may be sharply curtailed in the interest of child care. If parents are unable to make these adjustments by redefining the manner in which they interact within their own life space, functioning as a family is likely to be problematic.

These role adjustments must be repeated with each addition of another child to the family. The older children also become involved in the sharing and need-meeting process as it relates to each new member. For example, when a younger child joins the family by birth, adoption, or through the exercise of parental custody, it affects the next oldest child, who must give up the role of "baby" in the family and relinquish some of the closeness previously shared with parents. The parents must extend the nurturing role to include the new member, and by so doing alter their relationship with the other children. Physical accommodations must also be made for the new child that may affect the other children's play activities, sleeping arrangements, and so on. Sometimes these changes will impact negatively on the older children, who may react with such behavior as withdrawing, thumb sucking, or bed-wetting. Such behavior is usually temporary if parents are able to demonstrate caring for the older children. However, the role of parents can become more difficult as the children grow and seek increased individuality. This places great demand on the control and permission functions of the parental subsystem. Maintaining a balance between these functions in a manner that supports autonomy, while exercising the necessary control at appropriate points in the developmental process, can be a difficult task for parents. The difficulty is enhanced by our changing society, in which values are continuously tested and disagreements are evidenced in many areas.

We believe conflict is inherent in the parenting role, and this should be kept in mind when working with families, especially around problems involving adolescents. This is the time at which parents attempt to guide and protect children and it may include measures that are controlling and restricting. And children who are striving to grow and become individuated may reject their parents' efforts to guide them in this direction. This presents a difficult problem for parents and children and a challenging situation for social workers intervening with families unable to cope with these interlocking conflicts.

Sibling Subsystem. In order to grow and develop individuality, children need their own turf—where experimentation and learning can take place without interference from adults. This makes the sibling subsystem a very important part of the family organization. It is in this subgroup that children learn how to relate to each other, including how to share, disagree, make friends, bargain, and protect themselves from the down position of a complementary relationship. Also, this experience serves as a shield of protection for the child in encounters with other systems. The first use of this experience may be seen as the child interacts with the parents and learns to adjust to a relationship of unequal power. Although the young child does not master the skill of negotiation and compromise from the sibling subgroup experience, alternative behaviors in personal encounters are likely to be learned and will be further tested with elders in the future. In this way the child establishes and broadens patterns of relating. This is not to imply that the child learns only within the conflicts of the sibling subsystem experience. Much is also learned from interacting with parents and later with extrafamilial systems. However, experiences in this subsystem remain among the most important for the child, as they provide one of the earliest opportunities to test behavior and to learn from trial and error. And this type of learning is essential for the child's growth and development.

Like other subsystems, the sibling subsystem has a boundary that protects the system from instrusion by adults. Nevertheless, the boundary is permeable. This allows parents to move back and forth across it but gives children the right to privacy without parental interference when the need arises. For example, children need the opportunity to have their own special interests, try out their own thinking in specific areas, and offer their own kind of support to each other in times of stress, without direct guidance from parents. Some adjustment becomes necessary in this system as a result of the growth and development of children. With this growth and age differential come different interests, privileges, and responsibilities. At this point the subsystem is usually divided into two groups, along the lines of teenagers and subteenagers. Such a division ensures more effective functioning of the system, while at the same time it protects the integrity of the system as it relates to the life cycle of participants.

If a permeable boundary exists around the family, children should be able to interact freely with extrafamilial systems involving age-appropriate activities. The children will make inputs into the family system from these experiences, and if the substance of these inputs seriously threatens the way the family wishes to operate, the boundary around the family may become inappropriately rigid. For example, consider the teenage daughter who shares with her parents the desire to spend a weekend camping with her boyfriend, as others among her peer group are doing. The parents are very much opposed to such association between boys and girls and disapprove not only of the weekend camping but also of the daughter's association with the peer group. This reflects increasing rigidity in the family boundary and may well interfere with the daughter's separation from the family.

Parent-Child Subsystem. In the parent-child subsystem, parent(s) and child or parent(s) and children interact as a functional unit within a boundary. It is different from the three subsystems previously discussed in that at least one of the persons composing it is of a different generation. While a subsystem composed of different generations can become dysfunctional, this is not an automatic outcome. For example, a parent and young child may be closely involved in an interactional process that forms a subsystem of two different generations, but as long as the boundary around this system is not inappropriately rigid and permits crossing by other family members, it is not likely to become pathological. If, on the other hand, one parent and a child should become aligned in such a way as to exclude the other parent from entering the system, it would then be dysfunctional. Minuchin (1974) suggests that the clarity of boundaries surrounding a subsystem is more important than who makes up the subsystem. Take the case of a single-parent family, in which the parent is employed and depends on the oldest child to help with the care of younger children. This places them in a boundary together with shared responsibility. However, this boundary will remain functional as long as the limits of authority and responsibility placed with the child are clearly defined and the hierarchy is maintained. In other words, if the parent tells the child that overseeing the behavior of younger children is to be done only in the parent's absence, and that when at home the parent will be in charge of the family, the system can function smoothly.

Difficulty will develop when the lines of authority are not clear and the child becomes locked in a rigid boundary with the parent. In this case the individual boundaries around parent and child become diffused, and the child's authority will not be limited by the parent's presence. The child then becomes a "parental-child" and may act indiscriminately as an extension of the parent where younger children are concerned. This denies the other children free access to the parent and may result in problem behavior for these children.

Boundaries

The third component of structural family therapy is boundaries. Boundaries are "invisible barriers which surround individuals and subsystems, regulating the amount of contact with others" (Nichols, 1984, p. 474). The function of boundaries is to safeguard the differentiation and autonomy of the family and its subsystems. For example, if a parent restricts a child's play to the immediate neighborhood and this is accepted, a boundary is established that protects the child from wandering far from home and perhaps becoming lost. Boundaries may vary from being rigid to being diffuse. Rigid boundaries allow little contact with outside systems, which promotes disengagement and isolates the individuals and subsystems involved. While this permits growth and independence, it also limits warmth, affection, and mutual support. Diffuse boundaries produce enmeshment, which is characterized by extreme closeness. Enmeshed subsystems promote a heightened sense of mutual support, but lack independence and autonomy. Children who are enmeshed with their parents are likely to be uncomfortable when left by themselves and may have difficulty relating to people outside the family (Nichols, 1984). Other boundary characteristics have been presented in our discussion of the couple and sibling subsystems and will not be repeated here. (For details, see those sections.)

In structural family therapy the family is conceptualized as an open system and as such is influenced by and impacts the surrounding environment. The family is also perceived as being in constant transformation, and over time transactional rules evolve as each family group negotiates arrangements that are syntonic and effective for a given period. This evolution is influenced by the interplay of homeostasis and change (Colapinto, 1991). Homeostasis serves as a balancing mechanism whenever the family system is threatened. And change is seen as the family system's adjustment to a different set of environmental circumstances or to essential developmental needs. In moments of crisis, homeostasis plays a role in maintaining equilibrium.

Structural family therapy focuses on the current relationship between system and problem behavior and accepts that the knowledge of the origin of a problem is largely irrelevant to the process of therapeutic change (Minuchin and Fishman, 1981). This approach also holds that problems brought to therapy are essentially dysfunctions of the family's structure, and efforts are focused on changing the structure, which means change in the relative positions of family members. For example, the therapist may need to bring the executive branch of the family closer together or provide for more distance between a parent and child. Structural therapy perceives change as the process of helping families outgrow their stereotyped pattern of behavior. And this is done by releasing underutilized resources that keep the family functioning at an adequate level, and this release will create a climate for system change.

Role of the Therapist

The structural family therapist must enter the system that needs to be changed by accommodating to the rules of the system and joining with the family. The therapist brings to the family encounter a series of hypotheses that are tested, expanded, and corrected when necessary (Colapinto, 1991). Mobility on the part of the therapist is required as he or she moves from one role to another and forms alliances with different family members while maintaining a focus that connects all of this activity to the presenting problem.

This approach prescribes activity, initiative, and directiveness for the therapist who organizes and starts family interaction but refrains from becoming too central in order to allow the family to display its limitations and potentialities. In summary, "the role of the therapist is to move around within the system, blocking existing stereotyped patterns of transactions and fostering the development of more flexible ones" (Colapinto, 1991, p. 91).

Techniques

Structural family therapists have developed a number of techniques, some of which are applicable to other approaches and demonstrated in other chapters in this book. The following are some of the techniques frequently used in restructuring families.

Confirmation.   This technique may be employed by the therapist who is giving a sympathetic response to a family member's affective presentation of himself or herself, for example, "You seem to be worried." Confirmation can also be executed by describing an obviously negative characteristic of the client, followed immediately by a statement that removes blame for the behavior, for example, the therapist may say to the wife, "You are very critical of your husband. What does he do to make you unhappy?"

Reversal.   This technique is operationalized by the therapist directing a family member to reverse his or her attitude or behavior regarding a crucial issue that elicits a paradoxical response from another member. For example, Minuchin and Fishman (1981) report a situation in which the wife resented her husband's overly close relationship with his mother. The therapist instructed the wife (in private) to reverse her attitude regarding the relationship. Instead of opposing it, she should praise the beauty of the devotion between mother and son and encourage her husband to spend more time with his mother. The husband did not appreciate his wife telling him what he should do and defied her instructions by becoming less involved with his mother (p. 248). This technique is used when one family member is cooperative and will follow advice while another member will resist it. The person on the receiving end should not be present when the reversal is given, as success depends on that individual's being surprised by the change in attitude of the other person and, therefore, reacting spontaneously to the unexpected change. Reversals can also be used effectively in helping parents manage rebellious children (Minuchin and Fishman, 1981).

Boundary Making.   Boundary making occurs when the therapist defines an area of interaction as being open to some family members but closed to others (Colapinto, 1991). When the mother who is overinvolved with the children is asked to leave her seat between the children and take a seat next to her husband, this is a beginning effort on the part of the therapist to establish appropriate boundaries around both the parental and sibling subsystems.

Joining. The technique of joining is letting the family know that the therapist understands them and is working with and for them (Minuchin and Fishman, 1981). Joining is realized when the therapist becomes accepted as such by the family and the therapist understands the family's organization and style and blends with them. Joining is facilitated as the therapist listens to and speaks the family's language and views the problem through the family's eyes, making comments and asking questions where necessary, but always with sufficient distance to claim and maintain leadership throughout the course of therapy. Joining between the therapist and one family member may also occur during the treatment process. For example, the therapist may support the father in revealing his experiences in the family; followed by support of the mother in explaining her frustration in trying to cope with family disorganization; and later join with the children as they describe how difficult it is for them to know what to expect and how to behave. By joining with the family in this way the therapist is positioning himself or herself to be able to move the family toward positive change, which is the goal of therapy.

The Communications Approach

The communications approach to the study and treatment of the family developed largely from the work of the Palo Alto Medical Research Foundation Project. The focus of this project was on treating families of schizophrenic patients. Among those who were connected with it and contributed to the basic concepts of the communication approach were Gregory Bateson, Jay Haley, Don Jackson, and Virginia Satir. It is accepted in this approach to family treatment that all behavior has communication value and conveys several messages on different levels. The family is seen as a living system that maintains a relationship with the environment through communication, which involves the sending and receiving of messages and a feedback process. As a result, family relationships are products of communication. Family members establish rules that regulate the ways they relate to each other and to the outside world. Once these rules are established, the family seeks to maintain the status quo. In other words, the family is viewed as a rule-governed, complex, interactive system, with communication patterns playing a primary role in family functioning. Communication is defined as all verbal and nonverbal behavior within a social context. This speaks to the complexity of the process of communication. We can readily imagine a simultaneous sending and receiving of messages by gesture, manner of dress, tone of voice, facial expression, body posture, and so on.

In order to understand dysfunction in the family, the communication process operating within family relationships must also be understood. It is important to realize that the way a family communicates, member to member and member to the outside world, reflects the way the family perceives itself and how it will function. The way members of a family communicate with each other shapes the view they have of themselves and others. This in turn influences the way members report themselves to others, including those outside the family. For example, if the family perceives a member's behavior as good and in keeping with the way it views itself, and it repeatedly communicates satisfaction with this behavior, the response will impact on the individual. This member's perception of self will likely be one of value, and this perception will be manifested in transactions with others. If, however, family feedback to a member is constantly negative, the reverse will most likely happen.

If the family decides it is best to rely on its own internal processes for validation of its functioning and it intensifies interaction between members, the freedom to communicate across family boundaries will be restricted. This encourages more communication within the family and more dependence upon one another. If the family is successful in establishing this pattern of behavior, communications from family members will reflect a sameness, and family functioning will likely be characterized by enmeshment.

The existence of one person in the presence of another sets the stage for communication and, at the same time, assures that the process will take place. This obviously makes possible the act of verbal exchange, which is the most widely understood form of communication. However, both persons may choose to remain silent, and communication will still take place. Messages are conveyed by silence and inactivity as well as by language and activity. The silence of a person who refrains from talking in the presence of another conveys a message to the other, who in turn responds to this silence. Communication has taken place. For example, if the message sent by silence is interpreted as a desire not to engage with the receiver, who respects the wish by also remaining silent, the communication cycle has been completed. The message has been sent, received, and interpreted, and the receiver has responded by the conscious decision to remain silent. And if these two people remain in an interactional situation, despite their silence, they will continue the communication process, with each being aware of the other and through body language, if nothing more, conveying messages one to the other. In other words, one cannot refrain from communicating when in the presence of another.

The content and relationship of messages provide additional material for social workers in understanding human communication. Bateson, Haley, Jackson, and Satir, of the Palo Alto project, suggest that every communication carries many levels of information. One of these levels is concerned with the relationship in which the communication occurs; people in communication with each other are constantly attempting to define their positions in this relationship. There are two types of relationships, complementary and symmetrical. In the complementary relationship the communication involves two people of unequal status. The behavior of each participant identifies his or her status in the relationship. For example: In a complementary relationship one person initiates action and the other person follows that action, which indicates that these individuals complement each other. The opposite exists in the case of a symmetrical relationship, where two individuals react to each other from positions of equal status. This means each person exercises the right to initiate action, offer advice, and criticize the other.

Double-Binding Communication

The existence of a paradox in human communication, represented by the double-bind phenomenon, may be observed in some families. The exchange of communication in these families is characterized by the sending of incongruent messages, usually within the boundary of a complementary relationship. The incongruency of the double message is reflected in its request that the receiver obey and disobey the message simultaneously. This, of course, cannot be done, and if this type of communication is used repeatedly, paradoxical behavior will result. To further illustrate double-binding communication, take the case of an adolescent who wishes to spend the night with a friend. As he and his mother talk this over, she remarks after much discussion, "You know I want you to go and be with your friend; don't worry that I'll be here alone in this big house." This message tells the youngster to go, but at the same time it calls his loyalty to his mother into question and speaks to her fright in being alone, which also says "Don't go."

Incongruent messages may become a double-bind in certain relationships when a necessary set of conditions is present. The following conditions are set forth as the essential ingredients of double-bind communication by Watzlawick and Jackson (1967, p. 212):

1. There are two or more persons involved in an intense relationship that has a high degree of survival value for one or more of the participants.
2. In this context, messages are given that assert opposing commands, i.e., the assertions are always mutually exclusive, which means neither assertion can be obeyed without disobeying the other.
3. The recipient of the message is prevented from commenting on it or walking away from it.

Consider the case of the parent-child relationship. Here the relationship is likely to be intense and to have survival value for the child, who needs nourishment from the parent. This places the child in the position of being unable to comment on the opposing commands of the parent successfully or to walk away from them. As a result, the child is often exposed to the double-bind effect.

Double-bind communication is not peculiar to pathologic families. It may be observed to greater or lesser extent in a wide variety of families, most of whom do not require professional intervention. The issue of family pathology may be determined by whether or not the double-binding transaction is repeated sufficiently to become an established pattern in family communication. When this has occurred and the self-perpetuating force of the pathological system takes over, family dysfunctioning results. It should also be kept in mind that the double-bind process is not a unidirectional phenomenon. The paradoxical behavior that results from the double-binding message in turn creates a double bind for the sender of the message, thus creating and perpetuating pathologic communication.

Metacommunication

Metacommunication is an important part of the communication pattern observed in human interaction. Metacommunication may be defined as the sending of a message about a message, both of which are sent at the same time. The message conveys to the receiver how the sender wishes it to be received and how the receiver should react to it. Metacommunication also comments on the nature of the relationship between the persons involved, indicating the way the sender perceives the receiver and the attitude the sender has toward the message and toward self. The content of the message, tone of voice, facial expression, body posture, and so on serve to shape and define further what is verbalized by the sender. This adds to the complexity of the communication process and forces the receiver of metacommunicative messages to assess not only the content but also the content within the context of the message.

For example, consider an interchange between husband and wife in which the husband comments, "The children really keep you busy." The literal content of the message is that the children are claiming the wife's attention in such a way that she spends a good ideal of time responding. However, this seemingly simple statement may carry a number of messages on a metacommunicative level. First, the context within which the message is sent will help the receiver define it. If it occurs in a relaxed conversation after dinner and in a tone of voice that recognizes the wife's many responsibilities, it may convey the message, "I value you and I appreciate your accomplishments as a wife and mother." Here the sender's attitude toward the message, the receiver, and himself is one of friendliness. On the other hand, if the same comment is made in a sarcastic manner as the husband restlessly awaits his wife's preparation of dinner, it may well carry the message, "I want you to give greater priority to preparing meals on time." The sender's attitude in this case would likely be, "I am not friendly, you are not treating me in a friendly manner, and the message is a warning to be heeded."

Metacommunication can also be sent on a verbal level. Satir (1967, pp. 76–77) suggests that this occurs when the sender verbally explains the message being sent. This, too, can occur at various levels of abstraction. For example,

1. It may involve labeling the kind of message sent and telling the receiver how the sender wishes it to be received—"It was a joke" (laugh at it).
2. The sender can verbalize the reason for sending the message by referring to a previous perception from the other—"You hit me. So I hit you back." "I thought you were tired and wanted my help."

The combination of verbal and nonverbal metacommunication creates for the receiver a complex situation from which to determine the meaning of messages received. Making this determination usually requires more attention to the context of the message and the nonverbal metacommunication than to the verbal aspects, as the latter is more explicit. Satir (1967) observes, in her discussion of human communication, "Whenever a person communicates he is also asking something of the receiver and trying to influence the receiver to give him what he wants" (p. 78). Since such requests are not always expressed verbally, those on the receiving end of messages must rely on metacommunication to understand what is asked of them and to determine how they will respond.

Accepted Principles

The communications approach to family therapy does not emphasize the internal structure of family members but concentrates on their communication in order to determine what is cause and what is effect. This model accepts communication as having both a report and a command function. Information is conveyed through the report function while the command function defines relationships. This is demonstrated when one family member speaks to another member and by so doing delivers a message. At the same time, a statement is also made about how the deliverer of the message views both himself (or herself) and the receiver of the message. For example, when a child in tears reports to a parent that he or she has been mistreated by a sibling, the message carries information but also delivers a command to the parent—who is viewed as an authority figure—to do something about it.

This model of family therapy assumes that functional families are characterized by a set of properties that includes equality in relationships, includes an appreciation for similarities and differences, is open to change, and maintains congruent communication. In this family, only a few rules are observed, but these rules are consistently applied. The dysfunctional family has rigid rules that are inconsistently applied. Family communication is also used to gain access to family rules and clarify coping styles within the family.

Role of the Therapist

In the communications model of family therapy the therapist identifies the symptom to be changed as a communicative message (Nichols, 1984). In the first contact with the family the therapist focuses attention on each family member and demonstrates a readiness to listen and to touch and be touched. It is not unusual for the therapist to hold the hand of a family member during the therapeutic encounter. This reflects the therapist's humanness and establishes the foundation for trust in his or her leadership to guide the family through the process of change. In the role of leadership the personhood and humanness of the therapist is more important than any set of skills he or she might possess (Satir and Bitter, 1991). The therapist must also model congruence and respond in a completely nonjudgmental manner to the communication and metacommunication of the family.

It is essential for the therapist to have faith in the ability of the family to grow and change. In addition, a therapeutic posture that includes humanness, a readiness to listen and respond appropriately to different modes of family communication, and the ability to assume leadership of the therapeutic process must be maintained at every stage of treatment.

Techniques

The communications approach to treating families has developed a number of techniques that have been used successfully in changing undesirable behaviors. Most of these techniques involve teaching rules of clear communication, and manipulating family interactions (Nichols, 1984). We will not attempt to discuss all of these techniques, but following are two that are frequently used by communication therapists.

Sculpting. A family sculpture is created by arranging family members or objects in such a way as to symbolize the family's emotional relationships. Each member's perceived position in the family system is identified. As sculpting takes place, each family member may be asked to create a live family portrait by placing members together with reference to their posture and spatial relationships, depicting both action and feelings. In this way a visual picture of each member's experience in the family is placed in evidence (Sherman and Fredman, 1986). Sculpting helps the therapist handle excessive verbalization, defensiveness, projection of blame, and so forth by removing the family's familiar ways of communicating and forcing them to communicate with each other in a new and different way.

Family sculpting may be operationalized at any time during the therapeutic process by explaining it as a useful way to see how it feels to be a member of the family. Each family member is asked to take turns in arranging the family in a way that defines his or her position in the family. After each member has shown, through sculpting, how he or she currently experiences the family, they may be asked to rearrange the positions of members to reflect the family as they would like it to be.

Sculpting can be used in different ways. Some therapists may ask the sculptor to assign a word or phrase to each member that describes that member's behavior, for example, "supportive" or "controlling." The therapist may also intervene during the sculpting process by suggesting possibilities or coaching the sculptor in order to enhance or clarify the family portraits. Questions may be asked of family members regarding their feelings about occupying the position given to them by the sculptor: For example, do they agree with this portrait of the family? Some therapists may choose not to engage in a discussion of the family sculpting, and may allow them to integrate the experience on their own (Sherman and Fredman, 1986).

Metaphor. "A metaphor is a statement about one thing that resembles something else. It is the analogous relationship of one thing to another" (Haley, 1976, p. 65.) In other words, it is a symbolic and non-threatening way of communicating with the family. A metaphor may be used to convey an idea or feeling, to each, or suggest options that are not readily apparent" (Satir and Bandwin, 1983, p. 245). To demonstrate the use of this technique we borrow an example from Erickson's work with a couple experiencing difficulty in sexual relations. The experience of eating together is introduced and discussion developed concerning the conditions surrounding the meal. The therapist may ask if there are times when they have dinner without the children present, then move to talk about some aspect of eating that resembles sexual relations. For example, the therapist may say that sometimes a wife may want to begin the meal slowly by having an appetizer before the main course is served, while her husband likes to receive the main course without delay. If the couple appears to be understanding the analogy, the therapist may return to some aspect of the dinner that does not relate so closely to sexual activity, such as commenting that some people like dinner by candlelight, while others like to eat with bright lights. At the end of the discussion the therapist may move toward assigning a task around dinner to be carried out as homework before the next appointment, with the hope that if the dinner is successful the mood will carry over to improved sexual relations.

The Strategic Approach

Strategic family therapy is a problem-focused strategy that is concerned with repeated sequences of behavior and dysfunctional hierarchies within the family. Jay Haley is perhaps the most well-known figure associated with the strategic approach to family treatment. While there are distinct differences between the various approaches to family therapy, there are also a number of similarities. This is especially so in the case of the structural, communications, and strategic approaches. This may be due in part to Haley's close association with the Palo Alto group of Bateson, Satir et al., who developed the communications approach, and also with Minuchin at the Philadelphia Child Guidance Clinic, where structural family therapy began. Among other things, all three approaches give some attention to family homeostasis, communication, boundaries, and triangles involved in family relationships.

These common characteristics have already been discussed as they relate to the structural and communication approaches and will not be repeated in our discussion of strategic family therapy. We will include the role of the therapist, the accepted principles of the approach, and the techniques used to solve family problems.

The theoretical support for strategic therapy is based on general systems theory and cybernetics (Nichols, 1984). The therapist is at the center of all activity and each family is seen as unique. Therefore, emphasis is placed on designed strategies to solve each family's specific problems rather than developing strategies for use with all families. Since the primary focus is problem solving and not the development of insight, restructuring the family system is not always required. "Therapy is typically accomplished by the therapist's assessing and understanding the family's life cycle stage of development, the hierarchical dysfunction, and the repetitive sequence or cycle of family interactions, then correcting the hierarchy and breaking the cycle through straightforward or paradoxical directives" (Schilson, 1991, p. 142).

Accepted Principles

Schilson suggests several tenets upon which strategic therapy is based. These tenets will serve as the basis for the principles we will develop as the cornerstone of the strategic therapist's work with families. As previously mentioned, strategic therapy and structural therapy embrace many common principles, some of which will be reflected in those we develop and list below.

1. Each family is seen as a unique entity with its own rules and its own set of identifying factors.
2. A functional family is seen as reflecting appropriate distribution of power within the family, with parents having more power than children.
3. Family problems are viewed not in terms of an identified patient, but as interaction between family members.
4. Strategic therapists are active in directing the therapy process, with much emphasis placed on giving directives to be carried out at home—sometimes referred to as homework.
5. In diagnosing dysfunctional families, the strategic therapist emphasizes the present rather than the past; the family life cycle; and the concepts of systems theory, i.e., coalitions, circularity, boundaries, etc.
6. The development of insight is not required for change in daily functioning. Emphasis is placed on relabeling or reframing, which is designed to give the family a different perception of the difficulty it is

experiencing, and this will increase the family's effectiveness in solving its problem.

7. Primary attention is given to the problem brought to the therapist's attention in the first interview. This reflects the symptom-focused, problem-solving emphasis of the strategic approach to family therapy.
8. The expression of feelings or emotions per se is not encouraged by strategic therapists, who see such expression as diverting attention from the interactional process within the family that needs to be changed.
9. The family system is seen as operating by repeated interactional patterns, and in dysfunctional families, problems are maintained by these ongoing interactional patterns.
10. The therapist is responsible for success in therapy, and if it fails the therapist is blamed for the failure. If it is successful, the therapist does not take credit for it but gives the credit to the family. In order to be considered successful, the therapeutic experience must produce beneficial change in the presenting problem.
11. The strategic approach supports the belief that triangulation is a part of family interaction. When the problem involving two family members becomes too stressful for these members to resolve, a third person is brought into the conflict.
12. When the presenting problem has been eliminated, the strategic therapist will likely discontinue therapy.

Haley (1980) suggests intense involvement and rapid disengagement following positive change. During the course of therapy the strategic therapist often works with individuals and subsystems of the family. Attention is given to four interrelated elements—symptoms, metaphors, hierarchy and power, and the life cycle development of the family (Schilson, 1991, p. 153).

Role of Therapist

The therapist must be in control of what happens in the therapy session. This includes being directive and persuasive, yet remaining sensitive to client concerns. The presenting problem is important to the strategic therapist and should be given a great deal of consideration in the initial interview and throughout treatment. The therapist's activity is pivotal in the initial interview, which is conducted in stages, with each stage having a specific purpose. (For details on conducting the first interview, see Chapter 5.) The therapist is considered the expert in his or her interaction with the family and should be comfortable with this role (Schilson, 1991).

In keeping with the emphasis placed on the hierarchy of the family in strategic therapy, the therapist must help the parents feel sufficiently empowered to appropriately carry out their executive function. With regard to the presenting problem, the elimination of which is of primary concern to the strategic therapist, he or she must reframe this problem in such a way that it is seen by the parents as a manageable task they are capable of handling within their executive capacity (Haley, 1976).

Techniques

Most strategic therapists believe common-sense solutions to problems experienced by dysfunctional families are usually ineffective because these families are unable to move far enough outside of their environment to see what maintains the problem (Nichols, 1984). As a result, what are often referred to as uncommon techniques are usually used. These techniques include "Directives and homework tasks, relabeling or reframing, empowerment, straightforward directives, and paradoxical directives" (Schilson, 1991, pp. 168–73).

Directives and Homework Tasks. A directive may be defined simply as the therapist telling someone what to do. For example, Haley (1976) suggests when the therapist addresses a specific question to the client "tell me more about that," he or she is giving a directive. When dealing with inappropriate sequences of behavior, the therapist may use directives or tasks to break through this behavior if other efforts are ineffective (Schilson, 1991). When a family is given directives or homework, it accomplishes three things. First, it provides new subjective experiences that change the family's pattern of behavior. Second, it keeps the family connected to the therapist and intensifies their relationship. Third, the way the family responds to the directive will provide the therapist with information about the family (Haley, 1976).

When selecting a task for the family, the therapist should choose one that changes the dysfunctional hierarchy and the behavioral sequence in the family. At the same time, a directive should be in keeping with what the family can afford in terms of time and resources. It should also be formulated on a level commensurate with the family's ability to accomplish and stated clearly in language that the family can understand. They should be made to understand that the directive is important, and congratulations should be offered by the therapist if it is successfully completed. If, however, the assigned tasks are not carried out, the reasons for this must be explored, and the family should not be excused without a valid reason.

Relabeling. Relabeling, sometimes referred to as reframing, is the therapist's way of giving a positive view to a family member's behavior, the objective of which is to alter the way the family views the presenting problem. This technique is demonstrated in the family where criticism, fighting, and bickering are always present. The therapist may relabel this behavior by telling the family this is their way of expressing affection for each other: There is lots of love and caring in the family, but this is the only way they know to show it. This gives the family a new way of looking at the problem and a new approach to changing their patterns of behavior.

Empowerment. This technique is used to help the family realize that their efforts to deal with the presenting problem have not been ineffective. They may be told they have done some things right, that if not, the problem would be worse. Also, they have within themselves the ability to improve their coping skills and redirect their efforts toward different objectives. This gives the family confidence and new energy with which to carry out directives from the therapist (Haley, 1976).

Straightforward Directives. These directives are given in a straightforward manner and are usually used with families that are cooperative and can use cognitive information. The straightforward directive or task is given with the expectation that family members will comply. These directives may consist of a straightforward task designed to change family interactional patterns (Papp, 1980). For example, in an interview, the therapist may tell the mother who continues to interrupt a discussion between the father and son that this is the father and son's time and she must not interrupt. She will have the opportunity to share her views later. The message here is clear and straightforward, and the therapist has no reason to think the mother will not follow the directive.

Paradoxical Directives. Paradoxical directives may be used when the family is uncooperative and resistive to the help being offered, when they are fighting among themselves with a lack of support for their members, and when parental guidance for children is lacking (Weeks and L'Abate, 1982). In these situations, the therapist, in giving the directive, actually instructs the family to do the exact opposite of what he or she would like them to do. In other words, the directive asks the family not to change but to continue the dysfunctional behavior for which they are seeking help. Paradoxical directives are based on the assumption that the resistive family will defy the therapist and discontinue their dysfunctional behavior, which produces the desired change.

As an example of a paradoxical directive, consider parents who have failed to provide guidance for their 14-year-old son and have resisted all efforts to change their behavior. The therapist tells the parents he or she has given their situation a good deal of thought and has decided they need to give the boy more freedom to do the things he likes to do because he is at a point where he needs to grow up and become more independent. And they should start by increasing his allowance to show their support for this growth and development. The therapist then tells the boy he should help his parents understand the progress he is making in becoming more mature by taking more responsibility for doing some of the things he likes, such as shopping at the mall. In order to do this he should ask his parents for a specific increase in his allowance sufficient to go shopping at least once each week to buy the clothes he likes. If he runs short of money, he should ask for more because he has reached the age where he needs to be concerned about the clothes he wears. If he and his parents cooperate in carrying out this task it should bring them much satisfaction. The parents will most likely resent the boy's increasing demands and show their resistance to the therapist by failing to follow the directive and begin setting limits on what the boy is allowed to do.

Sometimes when the family realizes positive behavior changes as a result of a directive, they may want to give credit to the therapist for their improvement. However, the therapist should not accept credit for the change. If credit is accepted and the family relapses and returns to their previous dysfunctional behavior, it will be considered the therapist's fault. The therapist can avoid the credit by saying he or she is surprised that the change occurred and is not sure it will last (Haley, 1976). This will also make the family work harder to maintain the improvement in order to prove to their therapist that it is real.

The Social Learning Approach

Social learning as applied to the treatment of families borrows much from behavioral therapy. While behavior therapy relates more to how specific behaviors are changed than it does to how families function, social learning therapy recognizes the importance of family functioning and accepts the mutual impact of interactions of family members, which is shared by a number of other approaches to family therapy. Horne (1991) defines social learning as an education in human relations that takes place within the social environment. Although there is a tendency to think of learning theory as primarily concerned with a group of techniques designed to change behaviors, this is no longer true. Social learning family therapy has evolved as a general set of principles that can be readily applied to a wide variety of human problems (Horne, 1991, p. 464). It transcends the idea of specific techniques and is currently "a method of inquiry for analyzing problems, designing intervention strategies and evaluating effectiveness" (Horne, 1991, p. 464).

There is no single individual associated with the development of social learning family therapy like, for example, Minuchin with the structural approach or Haley with strategic therapy. Instead, a number of individuals have made contributions including Boardman, Patterson, Falloon, and Stuart, to mention a few.

Early application of social learning theory to family therapy focused on parent training, the treatment of sexual dysfunctions, and behavioral marriage therapy. Families with aggressive children also received attention, with the focus on intervention placed on the child's dysfunctional behavior. Parents and others in the child's environment were trained to act as agents of change by using candy to reward the child for appropriate behavior. This was replaced by the use of a point system that gave the child points for good behavior, and when a given amount of points were received, the child could exchange the points for material things of his or her choosing. Time-out was used, which meant basically the child was ignored or isolated for misbehaving (Nichols, 1994). In planning intervention strategy, the social learning therapist obtains data with which to determine the conditions under which the behavior in question occurs and the frequency with which it occurs before attempting to change it. This is known as "baselining," and it enables the therapist to carry out one of the most important aspects of treatment—which is to measure the rate at which the undesirable behavior is extinguished.

The status of social learning family therapy is one of continuous development, with successful application to an increasing number of problems. For example, it is now used in work with developmentally disabled family members, anxiety disorder, depression, and alcoholism, among others (Horne, 1991). Systemic theory has also been incorporated to enable social learning therapists to consider more involved interactional patterns as a basis for change in behavior (p. 472).

Accepted Principles

Families usually come into therapy because of concern about the behavior of a family member who has been identified as disruptive to family functioning. At the beginning of treatment, this individual is the focus of attention. However, further exploration usually reveals that other family members are involved and, in some way—often unknowingly—contribute to the undesirable behavior of the identified disruptive member of the family usually referred to as the identified patient. The social learning family therapist believes, based on social learning theory, that members of the family behave in an interdependent manner (Horne and Sayger, 1990). These interdependencies are seen as reinforcers of various stimuli and cues provided by different members at different times. In other words, each family member impacts other members and, in turn, is also impacted by them. Therefore, the social learning therapist must understand the reinforcing stimuli provided by all family members and be aware that, to change one member, all members must be changed.

Social learning theory purports that behavior is not innate but instead is a learned activity. There are several ways behavior is learned, including positive reinforcement, negative reinforcement, and accidental learning.

Positive Reinforcement. Positive reinforcement occurs when particular behaviors are seen by family members as appealing and for this reason they are encouraged (Patterson, 1982).

Negative Reinforcement. When the stimulus to a behavior is stopped, which in turn leads to an increase in the frequency of that behavior, this is known as negative reinforcement. For example, a child cries because he wants candy, the mother provides the candy, and the crying stops. The mother is then reinforced by giving the child candy. However, the child has also been reinforced for the behavior (crying) that the mother wishes to stop, because the child has now learned that crying will lead to receiving candy from his mother and will most likely repeat this behavior when candy is again desired. The same negative reinforcing process also works for adults.

Accidental Learning. This type of learning occurs when behaviors develop as a result of unintentional reinforcement or unintentional punishment (Horne, 1991). The situation in which the child was given candy is an example of accidental learning by unintentional reinforcement.

Reciprocity and coercion are two social reinforcement mechanisms familiar to the social learning family therapist.

Reciprocity. This mechanism is indicative of a social interaction exchange in which two people reinforce each other at an equitable rate, with both maintaining the relationship through positive reinforcement (Horne, 1991, p. 475). In a reciprocal relationship, one partner will most likely receive a reward from the other partner, followed by the recipient's giving of a reward to the partner who gave the first reward.

Coercion. Coercion is shown when both persons exchange distasteful (aversive) stimuli that control the ensuing behavior, which results in negative reinforcement as the aversive reactions are terminated. Coercion in a relationship by one person causes a reciprocal use of coercion by the other person (Horne, 1991).

Companionship with other family members is reinforcing in nondistressed families and results in members being together and engaging in activities that bring them closer. In distressed families companionship is not reinforcing and results in members attempting to avoid each other (Jacobson and Margolin, 1979). Knowledge of the developmental stages of the family is important in social learning therapy. Also, understanding the function of reciprocity in reinforcement and punishment is helpful in determining the source of distress in troubled families.

Role of the Therapist

The social learning approach to work with families emphasizes analyzing problems, formulating strategies for intervention, and evaluating the change that takes place during the therapeutic process. The therapist who has the responsibility of carrying out the three steps in this process must have the necessary skill and training to execute this responsibility. This includes basic interpersonal relationship skills sufficient to establish a therapeutic environment within which family members are comfortable and can feel safe in discussing their most intimate feelings and concerns (Horne, 1991). The therapist must also be an empathic, genuine, caring, and supportive individual who can impart these qualities to family members.

One of the primary roles of the therapist is to define the family's problem in a way that is understandable and amenable to change. This requires a thorough assessment of the difficulties experienced by family members. Observational data can be collected from the family by having various members demonstrate during the interview the ways in which they handle problems and communicate with each other. Another source of information gathering by the social learning family therapist is standardized instruments such as the Marital Adjustment Scale (Locke and Wallace, 1959), the Spouse Observation Checklist (Weiss, Hops, and Patterson, 1973), and the Family Problem Solving Scale (Nickerson, Light, Blechman, and Gandelman, 1976).

Collecting baseline data is essential in assessing progress in social learning therapy. Here the therapist focuses on specific target areas with an exactness peculiar to behavioristic intervention. For example, the therapist may elicit from family members how many times an individual in question does or does not do what is desired in a given period of time. How many times does the child use vulgar language each day? How many times a week is the husband late for dinner? These data identify the extent of the problem and also establish the norm against which desirable or undesirable behavior is assessed. If, for example, the child uses vulgar language only twice a day compared to six times prior to therapy, this indicates progress toward eliminating the undesirable behavior. The possession of good relationship-building skills, an accurate assessment of the family problem, and effective use of baseline data will greatly assist the social learning family therapist in carrying out the responsibility with which he or she is charged.

Techniques

An important part of change efforts in social learning family therapy focuses on teaching parents how to change the behavior of children by using various techniques, including the use of discipline and reinforcement. The method of discipline taught to parents for use with children depends upon the behavior to be changed. The method usually falls into one of the six categories suggested by Horne (1991, p. 487).

- Withholding attention
- Grandma's law (Presnack Principle: Eat your peas, then you may have dessert)
- Natural and logical consequences
- Time-out
- Assigning extra work
- Taking away privileges

Sometimes more than one method of discipline may be used, depending on the nature of the behavior to be changed and the child's cooperation toward this end (Horne, 1991).

Behavioral Rehearsal. This is a technique drawn from learning theory and behavioral therapy. It teaches a client how to handle a specific interpersonal exchange for which he or she feels unprepared. The client rehearses or practices a specific behavior to be performed in a future interpersonal encounter (Sheafor, Horejsi, and Horejsi, 1988).

This is essentially a form of role playing in which the client practices what he or she will say to another person with the therapist, who assumes the role of the person in question. The therapist provides feedback to the client, offers suggestions and alternative ways of behaving, and in some cases may demonstrate the behavior that is later imitated by the client. Behavioral rehearsal helps reduce client anxiety and builds confidence.

Contingency Contracting. This technique is usually used with couples after they have been taught to communicate in ways that promote problem-solving. It means changing something contingent on changes being made by the other person involved in the relationship. There are two types of contract negotiation used in behavioral family therapy.

1. Quid pro quo contract (Knox, 1971). In this contract, one spouse agrees to make a change in behavior after a prior change is made by the other spouse. Each partner specifies the behavioral changes desired, after which a written list is made and signed by both partners.
2. Problem-solving training. This type of contracting is used when problems are too complicated for simple exchange agreements. Negotiations are preceded by a specific definition of problems. When agreement on the definition of a problem is reached, discussion of a solution begins by discussing one problem at a time. Each spouse paraphrases what the other has said and is taught to avoid making inferences about the other's motivation. Verbal abuse should also be avoided, and when defining a problem it is most effective to begin with a positive statement (Nichols, 1984).

Reinforcement. There are several methods of reinforcement that may be used in accordance with the child's needs and interest. For example, a token system may be used with younger children in which points or stars are given to reward them for appropriate behavior. When enough tokens are earned, the child may exchange them for a tangible reward such as a toy.

Time-out is also effective with children and may be operationalized by having the child discontinue the undesirable behavior and sit in a corner or be sent to his or her room. A *monetary allowance* system usually works well with adolescents. *Contracting* is another method of reinforcement in which one person agrees to do something after something is done by another person.

In cases of problematic marital relationships, the social learning family therapist completes an elaborate, structured assessment process. This usually includes interviews and standard marital assessment instruments such as the Lock and Wallace Marital Adjustment Scale (Locke and Wallace, 1959). This instrument consists of 23 questions regarding marital satisfaction. When the assessment is completed, the strengths and weaknesses of the marital relationship and the way rewards and punishments are exchanged between the couple are revealed to the therapist. A low rate of positive reinforcement exchanged is a major contributor to disturbed marital interaction. As a result, the early work with couples should focus on establishing positive behaviors and improving communication. This may be followed by teaching the couple the steps of problem solving as suggested by Baruth and Huber (1984):

- Discuss only one problem at a time.
- Paraphrase or clarify communications.
- Avoid abuse exchanges.
- Begin with positives.
- Be specific.
- Encourage expressions of feelings.
- Validate feelings.
- Own mutual responsibilities.
- Focus on finding solutions.
- Base final solutions on mutuality and compromise.
- Make final agreements specific. (pp. 102–04)

These steps should be monitored by the therapist while being incorporated by the couple. Marital therapy can be provided conjointly with parent-training/family therapy as indicated by Horne (1991, pp. 489–90).

A FEMINIST PERSPECTIVE

The feminist perspective in family treatment provides the therapist with a necessary reminder of the impact of gender difference in the helping process. We believe it is important to present this view in connection with theoretical and systems thinking as applied to family treatment. Both male and female therapists should be mindful of the feminist perspective as they engage with families in a mutual effort to improve family functioning.

Feminist therapists have drawn attention to several aspects of systems thinking that do not adequately represent the real position of women. The systems concepts that change in one part of the system affects other parts of the system, that a change in the definition of the male role and the functioning of male members affects the role definition and functioning of the female member of the system is not doubted. What feminists question is the view that the power to influence is as great from female to male as it is in the reverse direction. Therapists need to take into account society's patriarchal definitions of the male role as breadwinner and head of the family and how this has given males authority and power of decision over wife and children. Definition of the woman's role as confined to the family with responsibility as the nurturant and care-taking member leaves women relatively powerless. Structural therapists who assume equality in reciprocity only reenforce the limited role for wives and mothers.

In observation of family situations, therapists have sometimes noted that the male is peripherally involved in household and family operations, and his marginal involvement is seen as contributory to family malfunction. Interventions designed to move him back into a more central role are seen as degrading to the wife, reenforcing the traditional patriarchal view of her position and power in the family. A therapist who is aware of the traditional orientation may, even so, assess the family as needing more investment from the peripheral male but will intervene in a way that sees the wife as, and enables her to function as, an equally powerful partner. Interventions designed to expand the male role definition from its directive and authoritative aspects to include connecting and nurturing functions serve to improve family functioning without depreciating the woman's role, while also increasing male satisfaction.

The traditional view of the male role can be seen as limiting the male experience (Dienhart and Avis, 1991) by keeping him in the instrumental role. Feminist therapists would help males to move from their individualistic and competitive positions and encourage more mutuality and sharing from which they can profit and grow.

The achievement of separateness, individuality, and autonomy—or differentiation of self, as it is called in Bowen's systems theory—is seen in all therapeutic approaches as important to individual and family functioning. It results in giving members a feeling of competence and a sense of empowerment. It enables family members to see and relate to other members as individuals and not solely as someone to meet self's needs. From this emphasis on separateness, the nurturant activity of wives/mothers in fostering and regulating relatedness between family members has sometimes been seen as overinvolvement and denying of their separateness. On this point, feminists assert that women "develop a connected sense of self and define themselves through attachments to others" (Knudson-Martin, 1994, p. 36). Further, it is important to recognize that nurturance, connectedness, and involvement have been society's expectation for women; they have been socialized into a gender identity that expects them to do just that (Cosse, 1992). Their separateness and definition of self has come through engagement in relationships. The goal for themselves and their family is to develop their separateness while maintaining connectedness. By contrast, males' achievement of a sense of separateness is a "process of separating from the primary caregiver, who is almost always female. This separation process stresses differences rather than similarities. The process of separating from the primary caregiver typically leaves men with a deficit in the relational capacities and skills which their female counterparts have developed" (Dienhart and Avis, 1991, p. 27).

Feminist family therapists view attempts to help men and women to fit into traditional role definitions as being unhelpful and destructive. Therapists should take a "political position" as well as a therapeutic one that challenges "stereotyped sex roles, as well as sexist assumptions about family structure, society and culture... Neutrality in the conventional therapeutic sense is believed to reenforce the status quo (i.e., the socioeconomic oppression of women). The client is encouraged not only to develop insights about her role in maintaining the familial and societal contexts of which she is a part, but also to take responsibility for changing them" (Ault-Riche, 1986). Leeder (1994, p. 2) similarly advocates a feminist view of treatment that is "dedicated to overcoming and working with gender discrimination as a political and therapeutic goal."

SUMMARY

In this chapter we have discussed some systems constructs and theoretical approaches relative to family treatment. Family structure and various systemic aspects of family organization and function are emphasized, including roles, boundaries, homeostasis, triangulation, rules, myths, and the importance of separateness and connectedness in relating. The necessity of regulating distance between individuals and the subsystem as a means of balancing and maintaining wholesome family relationships is presented. The role of the therapist and some of the techniques applicable to changing dysfunctional families are brought clearly into view and discussed with regard to their use with different approaches to family treatment.

Attention is also given to a feminist view of working with families. Therapists are advised to be aware of the possible impact of some of the more traditional ways of thinking, as they relate to male and female roles, that might interfere with the therapeutic process, and to avoid activity that is likely to reinforce unequal role participation between male and female family members.

REFERENCES

Ault-Riche, Marianne. 1996. *Women and Family Therapy*. Chapter 1, "A Feminist Critique of Five Schools of Family Therapy." Rockville, MD: Aspen Systems Corporation.

Baruth, L., and Huber, C. 1984. *An Introduction to Marital Theory and Therapy*. Monterey, CA: Brooks/Cole.

Boszormenyi-Nagy, I., and Sparks, G. 1973. *Invisible Loyalties: Reciprocity in Intergenerational Family Therapy*. Hagerstown, MD: Harper & Row.

Colapinto, J. 1991. "Structural Family Therapy." In *Family Counseling and Therapy*, 2nd ed., eds. A. Horne and J. Passmore. Itasca, IL: F.E. Peacock Publishers.

Cosse, W.J. 1992. "Who's Who and What's What: The Effects of Gender on Development in Adolescence." In *Gender Issues Across the Life Cycle*, ed. Barbara Wainrib. New York: Springer Publishing Co.

Dienhart, Anna, and Avis, Judith. 1991. "Men in Therapy—Exploring Feminist-Informed Alternatives." In *Feminist Approaches to Men in Therapy*, ed. Michele Bograd. New York: Harrington Park Press.

Faloon, I. 1988. *Handbook on Behavioral Family Therapy*. New York: Guilford.

Ferreira, A.J. 1977. "Family Myths." In *The Interactional View*, ed. P. Watzlawick and J.H. Weakland. New York: W.W. Norton & Co.

Haley, J. 1976. *Problem Solving Therapy*. San Francisco: Jossey-Bass.

_____. 1980. *Leaving Home*. New York: McGraw-Hill.

Handel, G. 1985. *The Psychosocial Interior of the Family*, 3rd ed. New York: Aldine Publishing Co.

Heiss, Jerold, ed. 1976. *Family Roles and Interaction*. Chicago: Rand McNally.

Hess, R.D., and Handel, G. 1985. "The Family as Psychosocial Organization." In *The Psychosocial Interior of the Family*, 3rd ed., ed. G. Handel. Chicago: Aldine Publishing Co.

Horne, A.M. 1991. "Social Learning Family Therapy." In *Family Counseling and Therapy*, 2nd ed., eds. A. Horne and J. Passmore. Itasca, IL: F.E. Peacock Publishers.

Horne, A.M., and Passmore, J.L., eds. 1991. *Family Counseling and Therapy*, 2nd ed. Itasca, IL: F.E. Peacock Publishers.

Horne, A., and Sayger, T.V. 1990. *Treatment of Conduct and Oppositional Defiant Disorders of Children*. New York: Pergamon Press.

Jacobson, N., and Margolin, G. 1979. *Marital Therapy: Strategies Based on Social Learning and Behavior Exchange Principles*. New York: Brunner/Mazel Publishers.

Knox, D. 1971. *Marriage Happiness: A Behavioral Approach to Counseling*. Champaign, IL: Research Press.

Knudson-Martin, C. 1994. "The Female Voice: Applications to Bowen's Family System Theory." *Journal of Marital and Family Therapy* 20(1):35–46.

Laqueur, H.P., Labrut, H.A., and Morong, E. 1971. "Multiple Family Therapy: Further Developments." In *Changing Families*, ed. J. Haley. New York: Grune and Stratton.

Leeder, Elaine. 1994. *Treating Abuse in Families; A Feminist and Community Approach*. New York: Springer Publishing Co.

Locke, H.J., and Wallace, K.M. 1959. "Short-term Marital Adjustment and Predication Test: Their Reliability and Validity." *Journal of Marriage and Family Living* 21:251–55.

Minuchin, S. 1974. *Families and Family Therapy*. Cambridge, MA: Harvard University Press.

Minuchin, S., and Fishman, H.C. 1981. *Family Therapy Techniques*. Cambridge, MA: Harvard University Press.

Nichols, Michael. 1984. *Family Therapy: Concepts and Methods*. New York: Gardner Press.

Nickerson, M., Light, R., Blechman, E., and Gandelman, B. 1976. "Three Measures of Problem Solving Behavior: A Procedural Manual." *ISAS Catalog of Selected Documents in Psychology* (M51190), Winter.

Okun, Barbara F., and Rappaport, Louis J. 1982. *Working with Families: An Introduction to Family Therapy*. Belmont, CA: Duxbury Press.

Papero, D.V. 1991. "The Bowen Theory." In *Family Counseling and Therapy*, eds. A. Horne and J. Passmore. Itasca, IL: F.E. Peacock Publishers.

Papp, P. 1980. "The Greek Chorous and Other Techniques of Family Therapy." *Family Process* 19:45–47.

Patterson, G.R. 1975. *Families: Application of Social Learning Theory to Family Life*. Champaign, IL: Research Press.

_____. 1982. *Coercive Family Process*. Eugene, OR: Castalia.

Satir, V. 1967. *Conjoint Family Therapy*, rev. ed. Palo Alto, CA: Science and Behavior Books.

Satir, V., and Baldwin, M. 1983. *Satir: Step by Step*. Palo Alto, CA: Science and Behavior Books.

Satir, V., and Bitter, J. 1991. "The Therapist and Family Therapy: Satir's Human Validation Process Model." In *Family Counseling and Therapy*, 2nd ed., eds. A. Horne and J. Passmore. Itasca, IL: F.E. Peacock Publishers.

Schilson E. 1991. "Strategic Therapy." In *Family Counseling and Therapy*, 2nd ed., eds. A. Horne and J. Passmore. Itasca, IL: F.E. Peacock Publishers.

Sheafor, B.W., Horejsi, C.R., and Horejsi, G.A. 1988. *Techniques and Guidelines for Social Work Practice*. Boston: Allyn and Bacon.

Sherman, R., and Fredman, N. 1986. *Handbook of Structured Techniques in Marriage and Family Therapy*. New York: Brunner/Mazel Publishers.

Sluzki, C.E., and Beavin, J. 1977. "Symmetry and Complementarity: An Operational Definition and a Typology of Dyads." In *The New Interactional View*, eds. P. Watzlawick and J.H. Weakland. New York: W.W. Norton & Co.

Stuart, R. 1980. *Helping Couples Change*. New York: Guilford.

Watzlawick, P., and Beavin, J. 1977. "Some Formal Aspects of Communication." In *The New Interactional View*, eds. P. Watzlawick and J.H. Weakland. New York: W.W. Norton & Co.

Watzlawick, P., and Jackson, D.D. 1967. *Pragmatics of Human Communication*. New York: W.W. Norton & Co.

Weeks, G.R., and L'Abate, L. 1982. *Paradoxical Psychotherapy: Theory and Practice with Individuals, Couples and Families*. New York: Brunner/Mazel Publishers.

Weiss, R.L., Hops, H., and Patterson, G.R. 1973. "A Framework for Conceptualizing Marital Conflict, A Technology for Altering It. Some Data for Evaluating It." In *Behavioral Change: Methodology, Concepts and Practice*, eds. L. Hamerlynch, L. Handy, and E. Mash. Champaign, IL: Research Press.

CHAPTER **3**

Strategies and Goals in Family Treatment

Chapters 1 and 2 conveyed our overall framework for assessment of family functioning and the means and methods of treatment, identifying the different approaches to understanding and treatment that we have found useful. The present chapter makes more explicit some of our broad principles that are not tied to a specific approach yet are relevant and important for practice.

AN INVESTIGATIVE STANCE

Most theories about treatment emphasize the importance of information gathering during initial phases of contact. Indeed, some theories would seem to convey that information gathering is the only purpose at this phase and that treatment cannot properly begin until information is gathered, filtered, organized, and integrated for full and complete diagnosis. Clearly, the worker does need information about the way the family works. The process of gathering the information, the nature of the questions asked, and the kind of data sought are guided by hypotheses about what information is needed to understand the problem and the family's way of dealing with it. These hypotheses are the worker's frame of reference for problem solving, but they are not necessarily made explicit for the family. Information is sought from all family members; each person's view is considered valuable; images of family are elicited from different family members; sequences of member responses to each other become visible out of members' reporting of their behavior; feelings surface that may have been withheld. Information obtained can be about events, behavior, or feelings. It cannot help but alter the system in some way.

From the family members' response to the questioning, new information emerges and becomes available to all family members as well as to the worker. The information provides the worker with understanding needed to initiate and promote change. But it is also change for the members of the family (Hoffman, 1981). There is also in the worker's investigative stance an implicit reframing of the family's problem, a new metaphor for their situation, a new way of thinking, of perceiving reality, and of approaching problem solving. The respect the worker shows for each member's views and the information they produce prompt new images of other family members and their contributions. The connections the worker makes between bits of information, the tracing of sequences, and the determination of what is relevant all influence family understanding. Family members now see what others see and understand what others feel. They acquire new images of each other and of events and are prompted to act according to the new images that will in some way be different from previous behavior.

This happens without the worker's explicit expectation for family members to change. At a minimum, the new information and worker method may produce confusion or doubt, enough to prompt members' own questioning. It may challenge them to rethink their situation or to alter their behavior. At best they may begin to learn a new approach to problem solving. This is in itself the beginning of change. It is in this sense that assessment and treatment are concurrent. The change will vary in degree from one family situation to the next and in most situations will probably not be sufficient for the family's needs. The model for treatment and the problem-solving process is inherent in the investigative stance and will be repeated and reinforced for their learning throughout the treatment process.

It is important for the worker to retain this investigative stance throughout treatment and not to abandon it after the initial exploration of the family problem. There are several reasons for this. Families are complex organizations in themselves, and ties to systems outside immediate family boundaries are many. Workers need all the information and help they can get from cumulative information, not only about the immediate family, but also about the family's social context, some of which may not be revealed and may even be withheld in initial contacts. It is too easy for workers to come to feel that they know all they need to know in order to help. Continuing an investigative stance minimizes the possibility of forming premature conclusions. It may also serve to promote the family members' own curiosity about their situation.

A further reason for maintaining an investigative stance throughout treatment is that the family members should not come to feel that the worker needs them to change more than they themselves need or want to change. A worker position that pressures for unwanted change arouses unneeded opposition and keeps the family stuck in its unproductive ways. While family and worker both know that their reason for being together is that someone thought that something needs to change, family members and workers likely do not have the same ideas about the necessity of change. In this somewhat paradoxical condition, the worker seeks first to engage family members as allies in the exploratory efforts, hoping that their own discomfort and interest will propel them not only to new understanding of their situation, but prompt them to change on their own initiative.

Questions on what the family wants for itself and what it would hope to gain from contacts with the worker serve to minimize the sense of someone else's pressure for them to change. At the same time, they serve to convey willingness to help the family achieve its own goals. Our reference to the solution-focused approach in Chapter 14 will help to illustrate.

The worker also does not push specific kinds of change contrary to the family's wishes. He or she investigates what the family members want for themselves from worker and agency and how they want to solve the problems that brought them into treatment. The worker seeks to understand similarities and differences in individual members' views of the problem. Repeated clarification throughout treatment of problem definition and changes sought reinforces the worker's alliance with the family. Where worker and agency definitions of problems and required changes differ from those of the family, these need to be explicated and followed by exploring the possible consequences of their separate views.

Though there is a high degree of neutrality in the investigative stance, the family therapist's questions may well arise out of his or her way of understanding what can happen in families in combination with the facts known prior to the first interview. Responses could then confirm or disaffirm earlier data or preliminary assessments. This approach to questioning seems to us to be congruent with that of Selvini-Palazolli, Boscolo, Cecchin, and Prata (1980), who outline a form of circular questioning.

Also congruent with our thinking, Tomm (1987, 1988) notes the possibility of a dual intention in the asking of questions. On the one hand, questions may be intended primarily to provide information for the therapist. Or they may be intended to serve a treatment function. (Both uses are implied in the term "exploration," which has been much used by social workers.) Tomm's categorization of types of questions seems highly useful to us.

Though a general category of questions he calls "reflexive questions" are intended to further change or "healing," they do not imply a meta-communicational command to change and hence do not push the family to do so. But they do serve as stimuli or probes that may have particular meaning to the family or some of its members. It may get them to thinking in ways that lead to different behavior and interaction.

Several examples may serve to illustrate. The purpose of reflexive questions may be to get an observer perspective: "What do you think she is thinking when she talks about suicide?" or "When your father gets into an argument with your sister, what does your mother usually do?" Such questions asked in the presence of the other family members are likely to evoke a response and a basis for work on the issues.

An unexpected context-change question—What would life be like if once a week mom and dad had a night out by themselves?—provides a basis for envisioning other possibilities and includes an imbedded suggestion. Normative comparison questions—Do you think you disagree more or have more trouble reaching agreement than do other families?—can also be stimulus for further work. Penn (1985) emphasizes the value of another of Tomm's categories of questions: Those about the future—What do you think you will be doing differently a year from now?—have value in evoking a consideration of goals, implying that family members have goals for themselves or each other or will generate them. A future-oriented question can lead to discussion of what they want each of the members and the family to be like. Benson, Schindler-Zimmerman, and Martin (1991) show that the method is usable with children as young as age ten, or even younger, if some props such as pictures or role play are used in conjunction.

Question may be raised about the degree of neutrality implied in this approach to questioning. Selvini-Palazolli and associates suggested that no evaluation of responses and no directives be given. Tomm clearly suggests that the therapist's intent can be to influence thinking and behavior. And we agree with him that this is certainly not the only aspect of treatment, that there are times for the therapist to make statements, suggestions, and even directives. Willbach (1989) expresses concern about extreme neutrality in cases of spousal abuse, doubting both the wisdom and ethics.

EMPHASIS ON HERE-AND-NOW

Conjoint meetings of family members serve to convey a sense of the here and now of family interaction. We consider it important to be able to observe how family members relate to each other and prefer not to rely on members' reports about how they get along. We assume that what we can observe will give us a fuller view of actual relationships than one member's report of relationships. Though the worker's presence influences, even without trying to, how family members interact, we assume that what we can observe in our presence approximates what happens when we are not present, or will come to reveal critical features of their usual interaction patterns as they grow to feel accepted by the worker. Being there makes it possible for us to comment on the interactions and check out with the family whether what we are seeing is like what goes on at home. Family members are usually able to tell us, and that offers further understanding about what is wrong and what needs to be done.

Conjoint sessions make it more possible for family members themselves to be made aware of their responses to each other and offer an immediate forum for trying new ways to elicit the responses they want from each other. For example, a family member who has been naming all the things he or she thinks another family member does wrong can come to see that all the criticism is not producing the desired response. This family member may, on the spot, be able to use the worker's suggestion either to speak about himself or herself by talking about the hurt or pain experienced, or to say what he or she needs or wants or to identify positive attributes of the other member. The ability or inability of a family member to use the suggestions becomes immediately evident to worker and the family as do the responses of other family members. These leave the worker with a clear image of what works and what doesn't, what needs to be worked on, and what else might be tried.

Our focus is first of all on how people treat each other and on the possibilities of their treating each other in a more positive, less dysfunctional manner. We shift to exploring their reasons for treating each other that way only when they prove to be unable to follow worker directives or suggestions for new behavior. Here-and-now exploration in the presence of other family members is in itself enlightening and change producing for other family members, not only for the worker.

THE USES OF HISTORY

Our focus on the here and now does not preclude an interest in family history. In some instances, family members seem stuck in their current patterns of interaction, and suggestions, direction, or other worker interventions result in no change. History relevant to current behaviors can be useful in understanding blockages. It is not so much a matter of understanding the evolution of the current state of affairs as understanding the images of roles and patterns of interaction that have been brought to the present from families of origin and seeing how these are being replayed in the current family situation. If members are complaining about each other's behavior or telling each other how to behave, it seems useful in some instances for them and the worker to become aware of how their ideas about husbanding and wifing stem from patterns in families of origin, that their families were different in their patterns, that such difference does not mean that either of them is bad, and that perhaps they could now develop some new ideas of their own that fit better with their present situation. Patterns of mothering and fathering can benefit from similar investigation.

It is also useful to understand whether in the past there may have been significant events that have been transitions into states of lesser productive functioning in the family. The most immediate past transition would be the events that prompted the referral or application for treatment. A loss of a job or taking a new one, a death, a move to a new location, an illness, the arrival of a new family member, and all the attendant ramifications of these can often be identified as significant events in shifting family relationships. Often families are not able to identify any such events, but with some persistence on the part of the worker, it may be possible to ascertain that the meanings that family members attach to current events reflect lack of resolution of such events in the past. Viewing current behavior of other family members as threats of separation, may, for example, reflect unresolved grief. A tendency to view other family members as critical even when they are not may be attributed to an experience of loss of self-esteem consequent to a specific event or relationship in the past.

Included in the efforts to understand relevant history is what McGill (1992) calls learning the family's cultural story. This story refers to origin and identity of the ethnic or cultural group of which the family is a part. Workers need to learn, if they don't already know, how the client family's story differs from their own family story. The client family is helped to see how their story was shaped by and is similar to their respective culture's story and at the same time is unique to their own particular family.

Our principle guiding the acquisition and uses of history is one of selectivity rather than comprehensiveness. History should help to understand the specific interaction, problem, or difficulty being experienced and acted out in the family relationships at a given point in time. Needed and useful history relates little to complete chronology and more specifically to key events and relationships that bear upon the present problem. It does not attempt to answer the question of "who started this" but is focused on the meanings that past events have for present relationships. Such recall may evoke strong feelings about past events that have not been fully resolved, such as lingering grief over losses. Or recall may develop clearer images about old relationships in families of origin that are being reenacted in one's present family. Awareness of such old feelings and images can provide a basis for redirection of family behaviors. And, lest this sound completely like a foray in promoting individual insight, we emphasize the importance of developing this kind of history in the presence of other family members, so that all may gain from the information and expression of feeling that accompanies it, and participate in the reordering of family interaction that is warranted by it.

CHANGING FEELINGS AND CHANGING BEHAVIOR

The debate as to whether feelings about other family members have to change before one can change behavior toward them, or whether behavior change can occur without prior feelings change, is not an either/or proposition. Both routes can be helpful. In many instances, family members may be able to follow worker suggestions by trying new behaviors, given an awareness that present behaviors do not serve them well or, in the absence of such awareness, as an experiment to see how things go. These suggestions may range from a simple new behavior such as saying something differently to a more complex directive about tasks to undertake between sessions. When suggestions are not followed, new tasks may be suggested or it may be useful to explore the feelings that enter into the failure to try the new behavior. Often such feelings have to do with the anticipated responses of other family members. When these feelings are drawn out in the presence of other family members, the reactions and different feelings of others can immediately be noted. When new behaviors are tested, positive responses on the part of other family members can lead to change in feelings and attitude on the part of the members, which can in turn stimulate the trying of other new behaviors. Negative responses from other family members are of course possible, in which case worker suggestions to the responding member to try a different response may be the best route. In other situations the alternate route of exploring the reasons for the negative response and the initial actor's response to the negative response of the other would also be useful.

We are clearly focused on here-and-now feelings and are interested neither in unnecessarily stirring old disappointments and resentments nor in the catharsis of accumulated negative affect, particularly not in the presence of other family members. Such discharge of affect serves more to arouse defensiveness, blame, and counterhostility and only replays in the worker's presence the family's everyday experience. In some instances of intense emotion, separate sessions can be useful to drain negative affect and allow the worker to begin to structure a more positive approach to the relationship. A separate session may also enable a less defensive response and provide opportunity for the worker to help the member to act less defensively in subsequent conjoint sessions. In other instances, family members may be helped in dealing with negative feelings in conjoint sessions by reframing the feelings in a more positive way or by the use of other procedures that serve to regulate communication. And we are interested in making it possible for family members to express positive feelings about each other because they have often neglected to offer each other such self-affirming messages. These, too, are new behaviors and can stimulate new responses from other family members.

L'Abate and Frey (1981) argue for an approach to practice similar to ours that includes recognition and expression of emotions in addition to emphases on rationality and behavior change. They say it is in the awareness and expression of hurt, emptiness, loneliness, and pain that one can fully experience separateness and individuality and that this experience allows individuals to come together in a more complete relationship. Recognizing and working through feelings and acquiring a new way of thinking about the situation are both needed emphases in a thoroughgoing model of treatment. We can also affirm along with Bowen (1978) that where everything is so highly emotionally tinged and charged, there needs to be a strong emphasis on rationality. Both emphases are congruent with our approach to treatment.

Different methods may be used to change both feelings and behavior. Akin to our discussion of experiential approaches in Chapter 1, Sturkie (1986) notes that approaches to change can be through verbal exchange ("talking," in our earlier discussion) or through tasks and activities ("experiencing"). The goals of either of these method categories might be either systems change (problem solution) or enhanced awareness (personal growth). Though our terms in parentheses are not identical conceptually, Sturkie's categories are useful in developing our approach to treatment.

Among verbal techniques to enhance awareness would be efforts to facilitate discussion, define problems, elicit information, and express reactions and feelings. Among verbal techniques focused on change in the system and problem solution, Sturkie names such things as reframing the problem and attributing a positive intention to behavior being labeled as hostile. Tasks and activities to increase awareness and experience personal growth could include role playing, family sculpting (placing family members in physical positions that symbolize their relationships), writing a diary, or keeping a log of behavior. And, to promote system change, directives to engage in some new behavior toward the family outside the interview might be used.

Clearly, there is overlap in Sturkie's categories. There is also the likelihood, as we suggested earlier, that a given technique can simultaneously promote personal growth and systems change or problem solution; or that both talking and experiencing can serve similar ends.

PROBLEM-SOLVING ORIENTATION

We indicated in Chapter 1 that our primary goals in treatment have to do with resolving the problems brought by the family and with which they want help. Upon first meeting, it often seems that families or one or more family members don't see a problem, or see a different one than the one for which they were referred, or they have reservations about acknowledging difficulties of any kind or acknowledging a need for help. We also said, a few paragraphs ago, that we make an effort to avoid our seeming to want them to change more than they want to, or in a way they don't see as needed.

Given this apparent dilemma, a great deal of effort is devoted to arriving at a mutually agreed upon definition of "the problem to be worked." Family members often bring problems other than the ones they first presented or for which they were referred. The identified problem member—the substance abuser, the violence-prone parent or spouse—can, in the course of the worker's effort to understand the problem, often agree that she or he would like things to be different.

It then becomes important to understand how family members would like things to be different, where they got the idea that things could be different, whether they had ever experienced the difference they desire, and what had made its occurrence possible. Further exploration might reveal their having done something to make it happen. Such exploration implies the existence somewhere in family members of strengths to do something about their situation. "Better," as thus defined, becomes something to work for, and recognition of their own ability to contribute to the difference becomes a motivator. The focus of therapy shifts from defining what is wrong to defining what can be done to make it right.

Again, as we said in our introduction to various approaches to family treatment, it is possible to see personal growth in such problem-focused efforts.

STRENGTHENING FAMILY STRUCTURE

Elements of family structure are observable in the communication processes of the family. Who speaks to whom; who listens to whom; whose ideas are adopted; who gets put down, shut out, or ignored; and who seldom or never speaks are aspects of communications that tell of role, status, power, control, affection, and distance regulation in relationships. Communications contribute to the shaping of family structure, and family structure in turn serves to shape the pattern of communications. Other aspects of structure that need worker attention in the helping process are factors of stability and changeability, family hierarchy, family subsystems, and distance regulation.

Changeability

One concern about structure is that it should not be so rigid as to prohibit variability and change. At the same time it should be sufficiently stable, so that members can experience the family as dependable and predictable enough to provide some guidelines by which the individual members can be clear about what roles and behaviors are expected. On the other hand, structure should also not be so changeable as to be chaotic, with no clearly defined roles or rules for behavior, with only vaguely defined subsystems within the family and no sense of leadership and control. For individuals, subsystems, and the family as a whole to function properly, subsystem boundaries, roles for individuals, and rules of the system need to be clearly defined without being permanently fixed, subject to change as the needs and demands upon individual members and the system as a whole change. Achieving clarity about boundaries, roles, and rules in the interest of stability, and at the same time enabling the family to allow for needed change, is a central task in the treatment process.

Hierarchy and Subsystems

Family systems and individuals function best when the parents provide leadership, direction, and rules for behavior for the children, whether there is one parent or two in the home. Consider the mother who permits her oldest son to intervene repeatedly in correcting the behavior of his younger brother; he becomes an authority to the younger brother and creates a structure that defines the older brother as the disciplinarian and the mother as incompetent in controlling the behavior of her children.

The object of change in this situation is to restore the mother to her rightful place in the family hierarchy, which is the position of control of family operations. To realize this the social worker must find ways to help the mother define her role as it relates to the behavior of both of her sons. For example, she might be helped to tell the older son that she will correct his brother's behavior whenever she thinks it necessary, or direct him to inform her if he observes behavior that should be corrected and she will handle this with his younger brother. As this pattern of behavior is repeated, it will establish a new structure with mother and children having different levels of authority. Her adult partner's support in bringing this about will serve to ensure further the operation's success and the family's growth.

Consider also a situation in which the parents are constantly fighting when they are together. One spouse comes home and exchanges unpleasant greetings with the other, which signals distress, and the children intervene by misbehaving. This claims the parents' attention and prevents them from having to deal with each other, and everyone is protected from the open conflict of the parents. These sequences of events are structured within the family's transactional patterns and most likely will change only if the basic structure of the family is changed. Social workers may alter family structure by initiating alternative patterns of interaction. At such points the worker's attention is directed toward rebuilding and strengthening the relationship of the marital and parental pair. Encouraging the partners to spend time together in relaxing activity without the children or by asking them to plan together how to regulate the children's behavior may both serve the purpose.

In the example just given, our concern was to protect the boundaries around the parental subsystem from inappropriate cross-generational alliances or interference. Similarly, it is sometimes important to protect the subsystem of children from unneeded involvement by the older generation. This can be seen, for example, in repeated parental intervention in disagreements between children and making decisions for them regarding the issues involved. Such action does not allow children the opportunity to learn how to negotiate and settle disagreements within the boundary of the sibling subsystem. The parents' intrusion in this way is a violation of the subsystem boundary, which is supposed to protect the children from this kind of interference from parents. On the other hand, children are sometimes allowed to intrude into the domain of parents such as interrupting the parents' conversations or entering their bedroom and sleeping with them whenever they wish. In each case, the boundary around the subsystem is not functioning properly, as it does not prevent intrusion from outside the system.

Rules

Family transactions are also governed by a set of covert rules within the family structure. The manifestation of these rules can be observed in various ways depending on the family members involved and the context in which it occurs (Nichols, 1984). Such rules may focus on the dependence of family members upon each other or the joining of members to protect each other. For example, a teenage daughter is planning to do the shopping for a picnic and is offered transportation by a friend but does not accept because her father plans to go shopping and would also like her to go with him and help select a gift for her mother. In this instance, the unspoken rule is that family obligations take precedence over nonfamily relationships.

REGULATING DISTANCE

As indicated in Chapter 2, the balance between separateness and connectedness among family members is important as the family carries out its various functions. Boundaries surround not only the subsystems just discussed, but also the individuals within the subsystems and serve to regulate the distance between both individuals and subsystems.

Serious boundary problems are seen when distance between individual family members is not properly regulated by boundary protection. This most often takes the form of extreme closeness or extreme distance in interpersonal relating among family members. These extremes of boundary functioning are identified as *enmeshment* and *disengagement*. The presence of either of these conditions indicates difficulty in the way family members perform tasks and carry out responsibilities.

Enmeshment

Minuchin (1974) emphasizes the necessity of clear subsystem boundaries for proper family functioning. This means the boundary around a subsystem should be well defined, allowing subsystem members to perform necessary functions without interference from others. However, maintaining a clear boundary does not presume an impenetrable wall, but a state of permeability that allows members of a subsystem to have contact with others. When movement across boundaries is not allowed, closeness in relating within the subsystem becomes central, and enmeshment is likely to follow.

Consider the example of a mother and daughter who over time have turned to each other for emotional support and understanding, gradually shutting out the father and labeling him as an outsider. The boundary between mother and daughter becomes diffuse, with no clear separation of roles and identities and a loss of the ability to act individually. As this continues they become more and more dependent upon each other and increasingly unable to communicate across the boundary that surrounds them. This is an enmeshed state and also represents an intergenerational boundary violation, as both mother and daughter, different generations, are locked in a common boundary.

A state of enmeshment may also envelop the family system as a whole. Minuchin notes that some families center activities so much among their own members that they "develop their own microcosm" (1974, p. 54). This makes for increased communication within the family and decreases contact with others outside the family circle. As a result, members are drawn closer to each other and boundaries are blurred.

A major deficit associated with enmeshed subsystems or families is that, although there may be an increased sense of belonging shared by those involved, members also give up the ability to act alone. With this loss of autonomy, subsystems will not likely be able to explore, take chances, and solve problems that normally fall within their range of activity. Likewise, enmeshed families find it difficult to adjust to change under stressful circumstances (Minuchin, 1974).

Change efforts in cases of enmeshment may vary depending on the severity of closeness demonstrated and other circumstances surrounding the problem. However, the goal of change activity is to strengthen individual subsystem boundaries, as indicated, and restore autonomy. This will allow communication outside of the confines of the family and its subsystems and help to reverse the pattern of turning inward for all of the support needed for daily living.

Disengagement

In contrast to the diffuse boundaries of enmeshed families, disengaged families experience inappropriately rigid boundaries, and members become disengaged with regard to their patterns of interactions. These rigid boundaries make communication between subsystems difficult, counteracting the development of a sense of closeness and belonging. As a result, disengaged individuals and subsystems become isolated. Nevertheless, they may develop a strong sense of autonomy, which supports independent functioning.

Disengagement in families limits the normal protective functions of the family and sharply decreases feelings of loyalty and the capacity to share with other members and request help from them when needed (Minuchin, 1974). The emotional distance between family members does not allow the stresses experienced by one member to be shared by other members except in instances where stress is unusually high and persistent. In other words, the disengaged family is an individually oriented family, with each member being primarily concerned about his or her own interest.

When social workers encounter disengaged families, the primary objective is to restructure boundaries in such a way as to open them up to communication across subsystems. This will help to promote interdependent interaction between individuals and introduce the opportunity for increased closeness in relating.

Separation-Individuation

Distance in emotional relating within the family might also be viewed from a developmental perspective. While each family is primarily responsible for the way in which distance is regulated among its members, we would not overlook the fact that the parents as architects of the family bring to this task the experiences of development in their families of origin. And this experience will have some influence on the way differentiation takes place in the new family they create. If the developmental experience was one in which the parents were allowed to grow and move toward independence as children, chances are good that the climate for growth will be positive for their children. On the other hand, if they were subjected to experiences that discouraged their own efforts to effect emotional separation from their families of origin, it is likely that the situation will be less encouraging for children seeking to develop their own individuality.

It is useful to keep in mind that the separation-individuation process occurs gradually over time. At birth the infant is physically dependent upon the mother for existence but shows signs of wanting to experience separation as soon as he or she is able to crawl away from the mother to explore new territory. The distance of separation is not very far at this stage, and the child always returns to the mother. This perhaps provides the first test of how distance is to be regulated among family members. For example, a mother who must watch over and guide each move the child makes as he or she crawls around the room might not find it easy to allow more freedom later when walking could take the child out of her sight. This is not to minimize the importance of early attachment between mother and child, which is critical to healthy development in later stages of childhood and even into adulthood. Yet, there has to be a willingness to allow children to separate and explore the world around them, even in early childhood.

The regulation of emotional closeness and distance among family members surfaces in a more observable manner during late adolescence and early adulthood when confrontation is likely around conflicting issues. It is also at this point in family development that the determination is made regarding "how much of family life is to be regulated by considerations of authority" (Hess and Handel, 1985, p. 44). This must be answered by parents, who have to decide to what extent they will impose their wishes on the children. Flexibility on the part of parents as reflected in the ability to rethink their position and adjust their objective for the children in the interest of a wholesome balance in the separation process is an important factor.

When problems in regulating distance occur in relation to separation-individuation, social workers intervening in these situations must look for the way in which authority is used and explore the objectives parents have for their children. Do parents want the children to behave like adults or remain dependent and childish? Do they push the children toward desired objectives or restrain them from movement toward individuation? How do parents define themselves and the children? Understanding how the family functions in relation to promoting appropriate autonomy for its members will usually provide an acceptable point of entry for the introduction of change strategies.

Another factor that influences closeness and distance in family relationships is the extent to which there is a congruence of images among family members. In the process of living together, each individual develops an image of what other members are like. This image includes realistic and idealized components derived from the personalities of both the holder and object of the image. It involves experiences with each other and evaluations by parties outside of the dyadic relationship. In addition to the image each member holds about the other, each individual also has an image of the family. This image expresses the relationship of the image holder to the family and the impact the family has on the holder (Hess and Handel, 1985). For example, an adolescent may conceive of his or her family as an excellent environment in which to live and grow, or a prison that restrains and confines.

It is important to realize that a congruence of images among family members is not based on how similar they are to each other, but the extent to which differences and similarities are mutually acceptable (Hess and Handel, 1985). Consider a husband who does not allow his wife to carry any responsibility for the family: She perceives this as his concern for her welfare and recognizes his control as a strength, while he sees her passive contentment with his actions as support for the welfare of the family. The differences here are mutually accepted, and there is congruence of the images they hold of each other. We agree with Hess and Handel, who suggest that family relationships are shaped by the interlocking meanings derived from the perceived images that exist between its members, and these images determine in large measure the closeness and distance members will experience in relating.

REGULATING COMMUNICATION

Virginia Satir (1983) was the first of family therapists to detail the problems in family communication. We draw heavily from her thinking in out promotion of efforts to improve communications between family members, thereby enhancing relationships and the family's problem-solving ability.

Family communications must aid the process of problem solving rather than hinder it. The problem about communication is not that they do not occur, because "no communication" is not a possibility. The problem is that communications that do occur do not, for a variety of reasons, lead to problem solving. On the content level, verbalizations may not convey a clear understanding of what the person meant to say. Verbalizations may be confounded by dissonant body language. Tone of voice may accentuate difficulties by conveying heavy affect or great insistence on the rightness of what a person is saying and the necessity for all others to agree. Individuals may be interrupted by others before they are finished. They may not be heard because of the simultaneous talking of others. They may be responded to with a topic of change as though they were not heard. Some members' points of view never get aired, much less heard and taken into account. Consequently, topics are not pursued until they are understood, until differing points of view have been adequately aired, and until plans are made or disagreements have been resolved. And the family remains stuck in its dysfunctional state.

Given such a state of affairs, family relationships deteriorate. Individual members feel disrespected, misunderstood, and alone. They may respond by further withdrawal or greater insistence or heavier affect, escalating the unproductive cycle. Distance between family members may increase, and power struggles or physical conflict may ensue. Caring and investment in relationships is decreased.

The need for new patterns of communications thus becomes evident. Worker activity needs to ensure that individual points of view are heard, understood, and responded to relevantly; that family members get the help they need in saying what they intend to say; that they are enabled to say what they themselves need and want and to express positive feelings rather them only airing anger, criticism, and blame. Worker reregulation in the here and now of dysfunctional communication processes requires active, on-the-spot worker intervention and serves to promote problem solving as well as the development of more positive relationships between family members.

PROMOTING POSITIVE INTERACTION WITH THE FAMILY'S ENVIRONMENT

Of all professionals who work with families, social workers are probably most aware of the effects of extrafamilial forces on the internal functioning of families. It is repeatedly noted that dysfunctional families are under stress from lack of needed social supports and from material, social, or psychological burdens placed upon them by their environment. They may be isolated by lack of meaningful positive connectedness to important external systems such as kin networks, organized groups, social agencies, schools, and places of employment. At worst, external systems can create stress, and at best they often provide no relief, respite, or support. The family's lack of connectedness also leaves them isolated from the standards, guidance, and restraints that society offers and that could provide information and direction for structuring family life. Social workers' efforts to bring the resources of the community to bear upon the family in a constructive way are clearly needed to reduce stress, to provide positive support, and to promote family responsiveness to these outside sources of support and direction. Several examples will illustrate what we mean.

The availability of income, from whatever sources, or lack thereof has consequences for the family's survival as a body, for the esteem of the family in the eyes of the community and of the members themselves, and for the members' esteem for each other. In some instances, efforts to ensure income maintenance may do more for internal family operations than any other form of intervention. Restoring the breadwinner's role as breadwinner may restore not only his or her self-esteem but enhance capacity to provide the leadership and structure needed for effective functioning as parent and partner. The provision of services that restore health or increase capacity to handle disability may serve similar purposes.

Reconnection to relatives from whom the family has been distanced may open avenues for support that is badly needed for understanding and acceptance, for acquisition of new ideas, or for something as practical as relief from child-care responsibility. Kin networks are sometimes burdensome and controlling and need a social worker's intervention to interdict negative effects or to produce positive ones. Where, for example, the extended family has serious problems for which the present family has had to assume responsibility, such as serious illness of a parent or sibling, and where this has resulted in marital or parent-child discord, assistance in coping with extended family may be what helps most in resolving the marital discord. Or where overly close ties to the family of origin serve to interfere with the integrity of the family group, the worker may need to involve both families in working out a new accommodation.

Religious and ethnic connections can also have profound effects on family functioning, infusing not only the family's values but also the rules by which it operates. An ethnic or religious value that promotes strong paternal control and leadership, for example, can have the effect of overcontrol of spouse or children. A worker's effort to engage a religious leader or trusted friend with the family may do more to mitigate possible negative consequences or promote positive ones than if the worker sought to work only with the family.

In all the connection we have mentioned, it is important for the various extrafamily systems to provide support for the family to fulfill its functions to its members. Where that support is not forthcoming, worker interventions need to be directed at ensuring it. Conversely, the family needs to be open to feedback from the community about its operations and for information and direction relevant to its tasks. In their thinking, workers would seek to enable the family to maintain its separateness and integrity as a unit while at the same time ensuring a positive sense of relatedness and connectedness to the community.

In this latter regard we note the special situation of the multiproblem, multiagency family. Such families are so subject to multiple agency directives and influences that the sense of the family's own directedness is lost. While failure of self-directedness was most probably the initial reason for multiagency involvement, such families need worker assistance in sorting out multiple demands and taking control of their own destiny.

The means for dealing with the complexity of family–community relationships are many. A telephone call to or an in-person contact with a significant other that suggests contact of a directed kind with a family member may in some instance be useful. In other instances, the inclusion of various significant others in one or more conjoint sessions with the family may be needed. For the multiagency family, an interagency conference is necessary to reduce the contradictory and often overwhelming demands placed on the family. Such meetings may profitably include members of the family as well. These interventions with significant others, though time-consuming, are clearly necessary if the family is to be restored to adequate functioning. Worker purpose in these interventions is variously to activate natural helping systems, to minimize negative elements in the family's network of significant others, and to promote understanding of the family's situation and further cooperation on its behalf of all elements in its life space.

SUMMARY

Our emphasis on an investigative stance in treatment is in harmony with the social work principle of starting where the client is and with the need to involve the client family in the problem-solving process. Our clear preference for focus in treatment is on here-and-now behavior and feelings determined by a selective investigation of history, including both events and relationships often serving a useful purpose in the production of change. Since families live in a social context, we see that it is important to build effective linkages between family and other systems when other systems undermine or fail to support the family or when families fail to use the support and guidance of those systems.

Areas of focal attention in the treatment process are the family's communication patterns, its structure, and its regulation of interpersonal distance. Families and family subsystems need boundaries and a balance of leadership, direction, rules, hierarchy, separateness, and belonging for effective functioning, and constructive communication processes that clarify all of these for family members. In some cases, all these aspects of functioning may need work; in other cases, only some aspects will need improvement.

Families coming to the attention of social workers present a broad range of problems in functioning. The treatment approach which we have described draws on several treatment models and is, we think, broad enough to be applicable to a variety of family situations.

REFERENCES

Benson, Mark, Schindler-Zimmerman, Toni, and Martin, Doris. 1991. "Assessing Children's Perceptions of Their Family: Circular Questioning Revisited." *Journal of Marital and Family Therapy* 17(4):363–72.

Bowen, M. 1978. *Family Therapy in Clinical Practice*. New York: Jason Aronson.

Hess, R., and Handel, G. 1985. *The Psychosocial Interior of the Family*. New York: Aldine Publishing Co.

Hoffman, L. 1981. *Foundations of Family Therapy*. New York: Basic Books.

L'Abate, L., and Frey, J. III. 1981. "The E-R-A Model: The Role of Feelings in Family Therapy Reconsidered." *Journal of Marital and Family Therapy* 7(2): 143–50.

McGill, David. 1992. "The Cultural Story in Multicultural Family Therapy." *Families in Society* 73:339–49.

Minuchin, S. 1974. *Families and Family Therapy.* Cambridge, MA: Harvard University Press.

Nichols, M. 1984. *Family Therapy.* New York: Gardner Press.

Penn, Peggy. 1985. "Feed Forward: Future Questions, Future Maps." *Family Process* 24(3):299–310.

Satir, Virginia. 1983. *Conjoint Family Therapy,* rev. ed., 1st ed. 1965. Palo Alto, CA: Science and Behavior Books.

Selvini-Palazolli, M., Boscolo, L., Cecchin, G., and Prata, G. 1980. "Hypothesizing, Circularity, Neutrality: Three Guidelines for the Conductor of the Session." *Family Process* 19:3–12.

Sturkie, Kinly. 1986. "Framework for Comparing Approaches to Family Therapy." *Social Casework* 67:613–21.

Tomm, Karl. 1987. "Interventive Interviewing: Part II. Reflexive Questioning as a Means to Enable Self Healing." *Family Process* 26:167–83.

_____. 1988. "Interventive Interviewing: Part III. Intending to Ask Lineal, Circular, Strategic or Reflective Questions?" *Family Process* 27(1):1–15.

Willbach, Daniel. 1989. "Ethics and Family Therapy: The Case Management of Family Violence." *Journal of Marital and Family Therapy* 15(1):43–52.

CHAPTER **4**

Impact of Family Life Cycle and Family Development: Stressors on Family Functioning

Change is inevitable in family life. It may be due to the growth and development of individual family members with the passing of time; it may be demanded by events in the world outside the family or to the interaction between family members and the outside world. Whatever the stimulus for change may be, the family will have some response, as individuals and as a group. How they respond depends on the nature of the stimulus for change, its familiarity, how they have responded to earlier expectations for change, and the means for response that are available to them, as well as the meaning and significance the stimulus has for them. How well they have resolved the problems and issues demanded by earlier change events will also affect their response to the current situation. A positive resolution should facilitate action in the present. A less than adequate response will hamper individual and family development and the family's problem-solving capacity.

FAMILY STRESS AND CRISIS

Over the years, researchers have studied family response to hard times and disasters. Angell (1936) looked at the response to the economic depression; Hill (1949) studied the response to war separations; still others studied the response to disasters such as floods, fires, storms, and train wrecks. Efforts to define successful coping and the factors that made it possible led to the development of the ABCX formula and its revision, the double ABCX model (McCubbin and Figley, 1983). The ABCX model said simply that the stressful event (A) interacting with the family's crisis meeting resources (B) interacting with the family's definition of the situation (C) produce the crisis (X). The double model factors in also the compounding or mitigating effects of the family's initial response to the stressful situation.

In this model, the stressor does not by itself produce a crisis but does so only if family resources are not adequate for the situation and the definition of the situation is that it is overwhelming and hopeless. Failure to cope successfully with a given stressor only mires the family further, whereas success in coping restores or even improves its coping capacity and functioning. Or, to put it in our terminology, the family's problem-solving resources in combination with the meaning the family attaches to the problem may or may not serve to solve the problem.

Each of the different approaches to family treatment from which we draw our thinking assumes that families change over time. Therapies have at times been more attentive to the ways they maintain stability, given all the pressures to change (homeostasis or morphostasis), and at other times they have been more attentive to the goal directedness of family organization that prompts change over time (morphogenesis). Events in the family life cycle and other events in family development are stressors that create problems for the family to solve and with which the family must deal. Family life cycle, as distinguished from family development, refers to the aging and growth of family members and to additions and losses to family membership. Stages in the life cycle are identified with the recognition that each stage requires changes in roles and rules of family organization. Family development encompasses the life cycle but also includes any set of events, experiences, or circumstances that alter the life of the family. In combination, the life cycle and other aspects of development identify stressful points in the family experience. Falicov (1988) analyzes the specific ways in which the different family therapies have connected to studies of the family life cycle and family development.

In this chapter, we will review briefly both kinds of stressful events that produce expectations for change: those that occur naturally over the family life cycle and those resulting from events or circumstances outside the family, or the behavior of family members, or their interaction with the outside world. We will introduce the factors that enter into the family's response to the needed change. All demands for change are problems for solution in the sense that the family is called upon to make some kind of a response, and not only in the sense that it is stuck and may need help in coping with the situation.

Falicov's discussion notes that the literature on life cycle stages frequently is descriptive of the family during the various stages and dwells less often on the transition between stages. The transition is the point at which the family is most likely to be in need of help and therefore has been of greater interest to family therapists. Her focus—and ours, and that of crisis theory—is more on the transition, and on the available family resources to cope successfully with it. Similarly Golan (1981) draws from crisis intervention theory in relating to life cycle stages, and focuses on the transition as a teachable moment, a time at which problem solving can produce gains for the family.

THE FAMILY LIFE CYCLE

Stages of the family life cycle are largely specified by additions to family membership or by distancing or complete separations from the family. Their labels identify the focus of the family at that particular stage and distinguish it from an earlier stage. Change occurs gradually during each phase, some of it anticipatory of succeeding stages. Transitions between stages are generally more stressful periods of family life in that more change is required for adaptation to the new stage. At least six stages are readily identifiable in the natural course of events.

- **New Family Formation**—Two adults decide to form a new family. Task is to define new boundaries for self and for the couple, roles and rules, levels and kinds of intimacy for the relationship.
- **Birth of First Child**—This stage is a call for a shift from a system of two persons to one of three persons. Accommodation of the couple relationship to a new member, defining roles and rules for all. Additional children will be accommodated better if this transition is successful.
- **Child Reaching School Age**—A small separation from the family. Same for subsequent children.
- **Adolescence**—Similar to the prior stage in that it represents movement out of the family.
- **Adult Children**—This may refer to several kinds of further separations such as departure for college, move to separate housing, marriage.
- **Retirement and Old Age**—Further losses and separations.

The movement between closeness and separateness implied in all of the life cycle transitions is accompanied by changes in individual boundaries, subsystems, rules, and family organization. After taking note of other kinds of problems the family has to face, we will discuss the family tasks and resources involved in accomplishing changes in levels of closeness and the various aspects of family organization.

OTHER FAMILY DEVELOPMENT FACTORS

Most families do not go through the family life cycle without the intrusion of other factors, especially families known in social work practice. These other factors interact with the normal growth and development of individual members and include such events as job, school, or residence changes, and the awareness of forces and changes in the outside world and the need to adapt to them. Some of the demands for change are beyond the control of the family, such as job or income loss or change, and illness, both physical and mental. Others—marital conflict, including separation and divorce, parent-child or sibling conflict, addiction, delinquency and imprisonment—are brought about by the behavior of family members. These changes intrude into the usual family life cycle and generally complicate family life.

A CLASSIFICATION OF FAMILY PROBLEMS

Taken together, these life cycle stages, and the other family circumstances we have mentioned, can be grouped as a listing of family problems or crises, which we display in Table 4-1. It is an adaptation of a listing developed by Reuben Hill (1958), one of the early exponents of the concept of the family life cycle. This classification may be contrasted to three other types of classification that are in ways overlapping, relevant, and useful.

Olson (1988) has a classification of sixteen family types built out of categories of cohesion and adaptability. These factors will be described in greater detail on subsequent pages. Types differ in degree of malfunction as well as where they fall in terms of both dimensions. They may be flexible and connected—healthy families. They may be rigid and enmeshed, or chaotic and disengaged—types of severe malfunction. A recent social work classification, the *Person-in-Environment System* (Karls and Wandrei, 1994), including situations in our list, categorizes individuals and problems on a number of dimensions familiar to social workers, putting them in family context. A scale of a variety of life stresses developed by Holmes and Rahe (1967) includes events from our list like divorce and death and weights them according to perceived severity. They are evaluated in terms of their impact on the individual—increased number of stressors and increased weight being seen as deleterious to individual health.

While our list is not necessarily exhaustive it does cover a large variety of family circumstances known to social workers. The occurrence of any of these events or changes does not necessarily result in a referral

TABLE 4-1
A Classification of Family Crises

1. Accession to Membership
    Marriage or remarriage
    Pregnancy (wanted or unwanted) and parenthood
    Deserter or runaway returns
    Stepparent addition or remarried family combination
    War reunions
    Foster child addition, adoption, or other adult addition
    Restoration to health (e.g., terminated alcoholism)

2. Loss of Membership
    Death
    Hospitalization
    War or employment separation
    Child starting school, leaving home
    Wife starting employment

3. Demoralization
    Abuse, battering, violence
    Chronic illness or handicap
    Job problems, including job loss
    School problems
    Parent-child, sibling conflict
    Nonsupport or other income loss
    Infidelity or other marital conflict
    Alcoholism or other addiction
    Delinquency
    Community and neighborhood conditions

4. Demoralization Plus Accession or Loss
    Illegitimate or unwanted pregnancy
    Runaway or desertion
    Separation/divorce
    Imprisonment
    Suicide or homicide
    Hospitalization for mental illness

5. Changes of Status
    Sudden shift to poverty or wealth
    Move to new housing or neighborhood
    Maturation due to growth (e.g., adolescence, aging, therapy, or other
        sources of individual change)

Each event has consequences for:
    Individual adjustment both psychologically and behaviorally
    Family group adjustment, role relationships, tasks
    Family group relationship to the outside world

for help or a voluntary appeal from the family. Some families may adjust to the problem without external support. The concern is not whether the problem is definable as a crisis, but with the fact that the family appears in need of help.

There are five principal types of family difficulties that may be seen as stressful changes or events. Classified by nature of the difficulty, they are (1) accession to membership, (2) loss of membership, (3) demoralization, (4) demoralization plus accession or loss, and (5) changes of status.

These problems have consequences that affect individual adjustment, the family group's response to the outside world, and the family's own internal group adjustment through changes in role relationships, tasks, and communication efforts.

The following paragraphs on the major problem categories serve not only to describe the problem area, but also to specify the nature of the demands for change. They also serve to outline the kinds of resources needed by individual members and the family as a whole in order to cope with those demands. The problem definitions and the demands for change are not unique to four-person nuclear families, but are applicable to all family types. Social workers may need to look at specifics according to family type and ethnic background.

Family Accessions and Role Changes

In the individual, changing roles requires both an internal, psychological change and a change in overt behavior. As a part of role definition, images and feelings about self and others guide individual behavior. Role images include expectations about behavior related to the role of others (such as mother) and of self in relation to other. They develop in the interaction between family members as the result of members' attempts to regulate one another's behavior. They are, therefore, both consequence and cause of the overt behavior between members.

The addition of a family member requires both the redefinition of existing roles and a definition of the role of the new member. On an individual level, readiness to accommodate and connect to additional or new members must be achieved. A new self-image must incorporate a view of self in relation to the new person. If the incoming member is a child, infant or older, natural or foster, new or returning, the role definition for parent or parents will be enlarged or altered. When both parents are present in the home, the new role definition for Parent A should have the concurrence or consent of Parent B, and vice versa. Similarly, the roles and responsibilities of the added child member need a definition, varied according to the age and need of the child, which has the concurrence not only of the adult members, but of other children in the family. These role definitions are necessary if the enlarged system is to operate in a way that is gratifying to all members and avoids conflict resulting from incongruent role conceptions.

If the added member will occupy a parental role, a similar process is needed. A returning adult member may expect to move into the role as it was previously occupied. This is not likely to occur automatically without some readjustment on the part of the family members already in the system, since their role expectations will have shifted to account for the fact that the reentering member had not been participant in the ongoing activities of the family. The difficulty of reentry will vary according to the status of the individual. Jackson (1956) has detailed the difficulty alcoholics have in reentering the family system upon recovery from alcoholism, largely due to the fact that their participation, status, and esteem within the family had ebbed to an extremely low level. On the other hand, McCubbin, Dahl, Lester, Benson, and Robertson (1976) report that prisoner-of-war families who had maintained the expectancy of return and a clear definition of a husband-father role were likely to facilitate reintegration of the serviceman.

Remarried families are another example of the accession of family members. When two partial families are joined, it is not strictly a matter of adding one person to a family but rather of adding two families together. In order to attach successfully to these new relationships, each member must first grieve and detach from lost relationships. The two adults in the family are detaching from their ex-spouses and working out their relationship as new spouses and as parents. Simultaneously, the children are comparing the role-taking of the new adults with that of the now-separated parent. They are reflecting on their own positions vis-à-vis the new parent and their new siblings. In difficult situations, the two families may not become a family but remain as two sets of individuals within the same household. The degree to which they achieve solidarity or remain distant will be a function of the parents' ability to join constructively with each other and with each other's children (Duberman, 1975). More attention will be paid to the tasks of merging and joining such family groups in Chapters 15 and 16 on divorce and family reconstitution.

Another complexity in relation to accession of members arises in foster care situations. The child and the family have the task of connecting to each other while simultaneously being prepared for separation. In addition, each party to the new arrangement is likely to be dealing with separations from prior relationships, the child from his or her family of origin, the parents from a previous foster child. All participants now have to gain an image of themselves and of each of the others in relation to themselves. Meanwhile, the images of prior relationships continue to be real and to guide behavior, however appropriate or inappropriate those images may be to the new set of relationships. Thus both child and foster parents face a considerable adjustment task, one in which they often have little or no assistance. Their efforts meet with varying degrees of success.

There are two additional points in relation to the shifts in patterning of role relationships (both of which will be elaborated later). One is that changes in role relationships occur within and across the different family subsystems. They affect both the hierarchical, intergenerational relationships of parents and children and the relationships in the separate parental and child subsystems. The second point has to do with the communication processes by which these role relationships are altered. If the family has effective communication capability, these changes in family structure can be achieved in spite of tension and turmoil. If effective communication capability is lacking, new role relationships may not be clearly defined and may remain problematic.

Membership Losses or Separations and Role Changes

Similar considerations apply in the case of losses involving family membership. Even temporary losses like extended hospitalization or business trips require readjustment of the expectancies of all members. On an individual level elements of grief or loss come into play, and the relevant feelings need to be dealt with. In general, there is the expectation that remaining members will compensate in some way for the gaps left by the missing member. At the same time, however, the degree of role arrangement required upon loss or departure of a family member depends upon the position and status of the departing member. Fathers, for example, may expect older children to assume household responsibilities during mothers' illnesses. Wives, upon loss of husbands to extended illness or occupational duties, may rely upon children to assume parenting or even spouse roles. Children will look to the remaining parent to carry both parental roles. The departure of a child will have a different effect. The normal departure of a child would ordinarily not achieve problem status in a family, though it may if that child has assumed significant family responsibility. Rosenberg (1975) describes a case in which a daughter's separation from the family for college became problematic because of her role as a peacemaker between her parents.

None of these readjustments comes easily. Remaining family members may lack skills required in adding to their roles, or they may lack the willingness to undertake new responsibilities. Further, the readjustments may entail blurring of generational boundaries or previously adhered-to-sex-role definitions. Since there is an element of loss in the various types of separation, a grief reaction on the part of the remaining individuals may also be expected. In discussing losses in single-parent families, Fulmer (1983, p. 261) says that "They must mourn not only the loss of existing family members, but the loss of previous organization of family as well."

Fulmer also points out that normal mourning of losses may not occur because of additional demands placed on surviving members, the feeling that "if I start crying, I may not stop, so I'd better not start." And when a parent's mourning is thus inhibited, children's expressions of grief may be similarly submerged.

Family members may handle their individual reactions to each of these types of readjustment to loss or separations with varying degrees of speed or success. Compounding the individual variations in response is the fact that the readiness of one person to respond constructively may not concur in time with the readiness of others, so that not all members are at the same place at the same time in their readiness to adapt.

Some of the adaptive difficulties following loss or separation of a family member are illustrated in greater detail in the following case material (Deykin, Weissman, and Klerman, 1971). While the loss to the family is due to the psychological withdrawal of a depressive mother rather than physical absence, many of the problems are the same. Such psychological withdrawal may in itself be seen as a function of family operations, but it also affects the response to the family system.

> Even before hospitalization, many families have to deal with the discrepancy between the patient's former functioning and her depressed state. Some relatives are unprepared to cope with role reversals and may themselves become discouraged when their emotional needs are unfulfilled. While this reaction can be seen in any relatives, it is most evident in the patient's spouse. Many husbands develop symptoms similar to those of the patient's, especially somatization. In such marriages, it appeared that both the patient and spouse were vying for the position of the "sick" person....
>
> A spouse who has had to assume many household responsibilities may feel overwhelmed and resentful. Concentrated attention to the patient without any exploration or acknowledgement of the husband's position tends to entrench the spouse's feelings of burden and to diminish his ability to cope with these responsibilities. A simple acknowledgement of the spouse's difficulties may suffice to support him over his trying period. Occasionally, the caseworker has to initiate intensive work which may include helping the spouse to modify his existing living patterns.
>
> The interruption of the characteristic interpersonal family balance, whether it be between spouse and patient or between the patient and other relatives, may have repercussion on all other family relationships. (Deykin et al., 1971, p. 277)

The family's response to the depressive behavior also may serve to exacerbate the anger, despair, and hopelessness already inherent in the patient. The conflict between patient and spouse may reflect an effort to alter, or restore, a previously existent complementarity. Relief from depression might result if greater symmetry could be achieved.

Demoralization and Role Changes

Role and task adjustments are necessary in relation to demoralizing problems in much the same way they are with additions and losses to membership. Here, however, the basis for role reassignment may arise as much from the needs and feelings of family members about the demoralizing behavior as from the actual need for change in the performance of responsibilities and tasks. Role adjustments as a consequence of additions or losses are also accompanied by a great deal of feeling, but they are likely to be more intense if the presenting problem is a demoralizer.

A family dealing with alcoholism illustrates both the feeling intensity and the problems in changing roles. Denial, despair, and anger all make their appearance over time. Apologies give rise to hope, and further drinking brings disappointment, anger, accusations, blame, self-doubt, and feelings of abandonment and loss. Expressions of these feelings are shared, spread among family members, and give rise to further apology, or defensiveness, anger, and counteraccusations. Emotional intensity rises in the exchange.

Concurrently, while the alcoholic's failure to meet family responsibility has given rise to these feelings, things are left undone. Role-taking is affected. The "underfunctioning" on the part of the alcoholic requires compensatory behavior on the part of others and often prompts "overfunctioning" because of the feelings involved, in ways or areas in which compensation would not be necessary. Such overfunctioning reinforces and increases the underfunctioning of the alcoholic. Both the over- and underfunctioning feed the emotional intensity. How to interrupt this cycle needs to be worked out in each situation. Similar cycles can occur with other problems such as physical disabilities, which, though possibly less demoralizing, also require solution to the problem of how to compensate without overcompensating.

Demoralization Plus Accession or Loss

An example of family reaction to suicide serves to illustrate intensity as well as how different sets of feelings can foster conflict. Hajal (1977) describes the efforts of a ten-year-old girl to take over her father's role after his suicide so as to perpetuate an impression of his continuing presence in the family. Her constant denial put her into conflict with her mother, who had acknowledged her loss and experienced her anger, and was now ready to reorient her life and that of her family to what lay ahead. The daughter's internal resolution lagged but unquestionably needed to proceed. Here the intrapersonal and interpersonal are clearly linked.

When there is added intensity of feeling because of presenting problems in the demoralizer category, several factors are involved. One is the threat that the problem poses to the family's physical survival, as in the case of loss of support or the imprisonment of one of the adults. Additionally, the problem may represent deviations from the family's or society's value system. Infidelity or adolescent unwed pregnancy are examples. The problems are violations of the rules by which some family members thought the family was governed. Rejection of the rules may be experienced as a rejection of the family or of persons who made the rule. Or the problem may be seen as a threat to the image or esteem of the family or of individual members in the community.

For these and other reasons, feelings of threat, blame, anxiety, and anger arise when demoralizing problems are encountered. The family should have at its disposal a means to deal with the intense feelings and resolve the conflicts that arise.

Status Changes and New Roles

This category of family crisis is intended to reflect the fact that the world in which the family lives may change. Change here is less due to intrafamily events than to external conditions—a new neighborhood, a change in the job market, a promotion, new views about the role women evidenced in the outside world. Accessions or losses of membership are not part of the picture. The family nevertheless has the task of adapting to newness and difference. Upward mobility certainly is more to be desired than downward mobility, but in either case, changed circumstances require new images of self and of the family, and new role-taking to accommodate to the changed status. Family members need to relocate themselves in the social structure, to see where they fit with their new place in the world. There may be accompanying pride and self-esteem, new extrafamily contacts, or, as in the case of downward mobility, accompanying loss of self-esteem and pride. In some instances, like moves to a new neighborhood, all family members share a common task learning their way around and finding new contacts. The move may be fraught with eager anticipation or fear, or both as in the case of a move into a public housing project. Where the move is of some distance, mobility may have separated all members from close ties to friends and kin and left them bereft, at least until new ties are established. Some highly mobile families, such as military families or those in which job promotions mean moves to new cities, repeatedly face the tasks of dealing with the loss of old ties and establishing new ones. In other instances, such as educational achievement and the change that brings for the individual, other family members are required to adapt to the newness of the individual's role and status. That may be different for each separate member, but it may also require a whole family reorganization as in the case of the family in which advanced education has not been included in its picture of "what our family is like."

Even in those situations in which family members have a common task of adapting to a new social environment, the specifics of the task may be different for each individual member. For some, the task will automatically be facilitated by circumstances such as a good school or a highly evaluating employer. Some members may grieve longer for old relationships and invest themselves more slowly in the new situation. For others, new ways and new conditions are more difficult to accept. The situation of immigrant families offers many useful lessons in this regard. Differences in pace or degree of adaptation may give rise to conflict. Thus it becomes evident that while the family as a group has a common task in adapting to the changed outer circumstances, internal adaptations to each member's adaptation are also required if the family is to cope successfully with the circumstance.

Our discussion here is not exhaustive. We have focused more on some circumstances than others. Doubtless, our readers could identify other circumstances of importance that we have not mentioned. We are also aware of the "miscellaneous" nature of this category which makes principles or issues harder to define and which limits our ability to be exhaustive. In spite of these limits, we hope we have drawn enough attention to nonfamily sources of change to give our readers a basis for awareness of their implication for the family.

RESOURCES FOR FAMILY RESPONSE TO CHANGE

Whether the family accomplishes a successful transition through all the stages, crises, and problems will depend on the resources in the family system has developed and available. Some of the strengths and coping capacities of individual family members have become evident in the preceding pages. It is evident that the need for and ability to make role changes affects and is affected by others in the system. Four other categories of resources for change are properties of the family as a group: (1) family integration or cohesion—the value placed on the family group in contrast to the priority given to individuals; (2) family adaptability—the family's authority and leadership structure and rules; (3) communication—the member's ability to communicate and negotiate difference; and (4) ties to external systems.

The views and attitudes of individual family members will influence to varying degrees the level of cohesion, degree of adaptability, quality of communication, and the relatedness to the outside world. They will differ on where the family is on each of these dimensions and on where it needs to be. Some will be ready to move ahead, others wanting to stay put. Their views may vary, according to their role in the family and the family's stage of development.

Cohesion

Family ability to cope with change depends on family members' ability to work together in times of stress. Family cohesion has been conceptualized as a balancing of individual and family needs and goals. Our discussion in Chapter 2 on separateness and connectedness begins to suggest this need for balance. (See Olson, Sprenkel, and Russell, 1979, for further elaboration and review.) If unbalanced in favor of connectedness, cohesion becomes enmeshment of family members and loss of individuality and contribution of individual members. If cohesion is unbalanced in favor of separateness and individuality, members become disengaged, and the family as a group loses strength for its maintenance. Cohesion is manifest in such things as emotional bonding, mutual inclusiveness, exclusion of nonfamily persons, and shared time, space, friends, and interest on the one side and a complementary sense of independence from each other.

Levels of cohesion and separateness vary through the natural course of the family life cycle as well as with the nature of other family problems. The pull to connectedness is stronger earlier in the cycle. Distancing and separateness are clearly more evident by the stage of adolescence. Research by Olson, Lavee, and McCubbin (1988) documents the variation of cohesion and the next factor, adaptability, at specific points in the family life cycle.

Members vary in the commitment to the family. Some may see themselves as peripheral and prefer the pursuit of their own goals. Some may feel their own needs will be met by continuing family participation. Others may support or participate in family operations to the neglect of their own interests. These priorities may vary among individuals in the same family. They also vary among families. Where the family has seen the outside world as alien and hostile, as minority families often have had to, mutual support and "family first" may be emphasized, to the detriment of individual pursuits, though putting the family first need not be detrimental to individual growth. Josselyn (1953) reports on the importance for the development of individual identity of a widowed parent's effort to "keep the family together"—an effort in which the value of the family group was primary.

Families in which both individual and family group goals are important should be able to maintain some flexibility in movement to allow for the resolution of particular difficulties. Lacking this flexibility, they will have difficulty when problems arise.

Adaptability

Adaptability has also been further defined in recent research. It is manifest in assertiveness, leadership and control, discipline, negotiation, capacity to shift roles, and rules for behavior. As in the cohesion dimension, there may be too much or too little of each characteristic. Neither extreme is conducive to successful adaptation either of individual members or for the survival of the family as a group. One extreme is inflexibility and rigidity; the other is a complete lack of structure, irresponsibility, and chaos.

Along with the capacity for adaptation, the family also needs to maintain a sense of stability. In this regard Frazer (1984) comments that at "points of pattern change, existing couple or family system constructs are called to task. There is a need now to construe these new pattern variations in ways that both adapt to their new directions while assimilating them under some broad enough umbrella construction so as to maintain the system's general definition of itself as an on-going unit" (p. 369).

We focus specifically here on the elements of authority, leadership, roles, and rules. In some families the pattern is strong parental leadership and control; in others, children participate more actively in decision making. These patterns are derived from the way parents value and define adult and child roles, based on their own prior life experience. Strong parental leadership or control may have caused the problem. It also may exacerbate the problem, stand in the way of its solution, or contribute to its resolution. Similarly, depending on the ages of involved family members, *weak* parental participation and leadership may have caused the problem, may exacerbate it, or may stand in the way of solution.

As will be shown later in relation to adolescent substance abuse, the family's regulation and control, which is frequently reduced for adolescents, may need to be tightened in order to solve that problem, rather than following the usual loosening.

The abdication of a family role by one of the adult members, or his or her involvement in a demoralizing event, may well limit his or her capacity to provide leadership in the solution of problems. This allows the movement of other members, children in particular, into leadership or parental roles. Another aspect of family leadership is that adults may see a problem and the participation of others in problem solving as a threat to their leadership or authority within the family. Parental leadership which allows for the inputs of child members, however, can contribute significantly to problem resolution.

Closely related to the important leadership and role structure is the operational set of family rules. These serve to prescribe expected behaviors and give individual members a sense of what they can or need to do to alleviate stress and solve the current family problem. It is expected that members of the adult generation will be primarily responsible for setting rules. To the degree that they do so, rules may be many or few, rigid or flexible according to situation, defined with varying degrees of clarity, enforced consistently or irregularly. Here too it is evident that an optimum balance between extremes is desirable.

Communication

The third factor affecting family members' response to a particular problem is their ability to communicate about the changed circumstances and to negotiate about possible responses. In closed family systems, communications may not allow for the assimilation of new information and ideas and may dictate the "one right way" to think about or do things. Differing points of view may be poorly tolerated, even though the occurrence of the problem calls for new ideas and new solutions. Tallman (1970) says:

> What seems necessary is a structure which allows for the expression of a diversity of conflicting views, all of which are subject to evaluation and criticism. At the same time, the integrity of the individual must be protected. A structure which allows for creative problem solving, therefore, should maintain open channels of communication within an evaluative framework which provides for a critical examination of the ideas presented. (p. 95)

The value system must provide for the freedom to communicate differences and to evaluate the ideas presented by others, in order to solve the problems presented to it. In open family systems rules regulating communication allow for expression of intense feeling and different ideas, both of which are necessary for adequate crisis resolution. Members need freedom both to negotiate and to promote change in response to the problem. They also need effective mechanisms for negotiation. Some communications, such as denial, blaming, or withdrawal, are not particularly useful to a family in coping with the tasks at hand and solving the issues presented by a particular problem. Other strategies, such as efforts to understand each others' feelings, values, and goals, may be more useful but may not be available in the family, especially under present circumstances. Additional difficulties may arise if some members verbalize feelings and others wish to withdraw, or if some continue to blame while others seek reconciliation. Individuals respond on the basis of their own needs in the situation. Whether these conflicts are resolved depends on how the family has handled differences in the past and whether they can permit worker suggestions or directions to influence them to develop new responses.

Lacking effective modes of communication, family members may lose their investment in the system and their willingness to contribute to solution of its difficulties. They may attack the system, or fall silent or otherwise withdraw from it. Their potential inputs are lost to the system, as is the system's value to them. The relative value placed on family as over against the individual and the degree of freedom to communicate derive from the family value system, which is largely determined by the adult members.

Ties to External Systems

The family resources discussed thus far have been within the boundaries of the family system. Effective coping with all the stressors requires not only internal adaptation: Ability to relate beyond its boundaries is also required. The family system must not be so rigid and closed off to inputs from the outside world that it is isolated from help and direction, nor should it be so open and adaptable as to lose sense of its own control and integrity.

In times of stress, families may need external supports in order to survive and cope. Needed resources may be material, as we suggested at the outset of this chapter, or they may be more for emotional support, which can come from friends and extended family systems. To the extent that these existed prior to the current presenting problem they may be readily drawn upon and contribute to problem resolution. To the extent that they need to be found and developed, problem resolution may be delayed or forestalled.

SUMMARY

This chapter has given major attention to the renegotiation of roles as families experience the impact of increases or decreases in family membership, changes in family members or conditions, and demoralizing events. These events are seen as placing stress upon individuals within the family and upon the family as a whole. We noted that internal adaptation on the part of individual members is required. Individuals adapt not only to the stress but to each other's adaptation, thus making response an interpersonal and family event as well as an individual one.

A family's ability to survive such changes requires a great deal of flexibility in role definitions and role behavior. Rigid adherence to previously existent role definitions stands in the way of problem solution.

REFERENCES

Aldous, Joan, and Klein, David. 1988. "The Linkages Between Family Development and Family Stress." In *Social Stress and Family Development*, eds. David Klein and Joan Aldous. New York: Guilford.

Angell, R. 1936. *The Family Encounters the Depression*. New York: Scribners.

Bowen, M. 1981. *Family Therapy in Clinical Practice*. New York: Jason Aronson.

Deykin, E., Weissman, M., and Klerman, G. 1971. "Treatment of Depressed Women." *British Journal of Social Work* 1:277–91.

Duberman, L. 1975. *The Re-Constituted Family*. Chicago: Nelson-Hall.

Falicov, Celia. 1988. "Family Sociology and Family Therapy Contributions to the Family Development Framework; A Comparative Analysis and Thoughts on Future Trends. In *Family Transitions—Continuity and Change Over the Life Cycle*, ed. Celia Falicov. New York: Guilford.

Frazer, F.S. 1984. "Paradox and Orthodox: Folie a Dieux?" *Journal of Marital and Family Therapy* 10(4):361–72.

Fulmer, R.H. 1983. "A Structural Approach to Unresolved Mourning in Single Parent Family Systems." *Journal of Marital and Family Therapy* 9(3):259–69.

Golan, Naomi. 1981. *Passing Through Transitions*. New York: Free Press.

Hajal, F. 1977. "Post-Suicide Grief Work in Family Therapy." *Journal of Marriage and Family Counseling* 3(2):35–42.

Hill, R. 1949. *Families Under Stress*. New York: Harper and Bros.

_____. 1958. "Generic Features of Families under Stress." *Social Casework* 39:139–49.

Holmes, T.H., and Rahe, R.H. 1967. "The Social Adjustment Rating Scale." *Journal of Psychosomatic Research* 11:213–18.

Jackson, J.K. 1956. "Adjustment of the Family to Alcoholism." *Marriage and Family Living* 18:361–69.

Josselyn, I. 1953. "The Family as a Psychological Unit." *Social Casework* 34:336–43.

Karls, James, and Wandrei, Kirin. 1994. *Person-in-Environment System*. Annapolis Junction, MD: NASW Press.

McCubbin, H., Dahl, B., Lester, G., Benson, D., and Robertson, M. 1976. "Coping Repertoires of Families Adapting to Prolonged War-Induced Separations." *Journal of Marriage and the Family* 38(3):461–71.

McCubbin, Hamilton, and Figley, Charles. 1983. *Stress and the Family*, Vol. I. New York: Brunner/Mazel Publishers.

Olson, David. 1988. "Family Type, Family Stress, and Family Satisfaction: A Family Development Perspective." In *Family Transitions*, ed. Celia Falicov. New York: Guilford.

Olson, David, Lavee, Yoav, and McCubbin, Hamilton. 1988. "Types of Families and Family Response to Stress across the Family Life Cycle." In *Social Stress and Family Development*, eds. David Klein and Joan Aldous. New York: Guilford.

Olson, D., Sprenkel, D., and Russell, C. 1979. "Circumplex Model of Family Systems." *Family Process* 18(1):3–28.

Rosenberg, B. 1975. "Planned Short-Term Treatment in Developmental Crisis." *Social Casework* 56:195–204.

Tallman, I. 1970. "The Family as a Small Problem Solving Group." *Journal of Marriage and the Family* 32:94–104.

CHAPTER 5

Beginning Treatment

The theoretical framework for family treatment from a systems viewpoint is operationalized when it is put into practice by the social worker or practitioner. In making plans for intervention in a family problem situation, the worker must assess the way the family is organized and functions. The underlying issues of family structure and dynamics must be understood before decisions regarding change strategies can be made.

Given the assumption that the family as a group needs to find the means to solve the problem at hand, rather than simply having solutions promulgated by the social worker, one goal of the initial contacts between the worker and the family is to gain the participation of needed family members in the problem-solving process. In achieving this goal the worker must be clear about who the needed family members are and how they can be involved in the process.

Many questions come to mind in the preparation for meeting with a new family. Who are members of the family? How will they describe the problem? What do they expect in coming for help? Who should be present at my initial contact with them? What kind of information do I need in order to help? Do they really want help? How can I get their agreement to work with me to solve the problems? How do I get the information needed to understand the way the family works? How do I proceed in my first contact with them?

There is more than one way to proceed and to answer such questions. Different theoretical approaches suggest different ways. This chapter serves to define some of the considerations necessary prior to initial contact. It then describes at length a first-meeting approach taken from our here-and-now orientation, illustrating the kinds of information that come from this approach. In some instances, additional information about extended family or others in some way connected to the family may be needed. Ways of obtaining the desired information are offered by way of reference to beginnings illustrative of other approaches identified in Chapter 1. The usefulness of each approach to the worker and to the family will become evident.

TREATMENT FOR THE FAMILY OR FAMILY GROUP TREATMENT

Three separate but interrelated questions need to be addressed in planning treatment. The first is whether to involve family members in the treatment process; the second question is which of the family members to involve; the third asks the way in which they are to be connected to the treatment process.

The understanding of the family as a system implies that all family members are in some way connected to the problems or whatever happens in the family. Thus, involvement of one individual in treatment, even if intended to produce change only in that individual, is one way to intervene in a family. In that sense then, thinking "family systems" precedes the question of whether to involve other members, since the therapist will always keep in mind the effects of change in the person seen on others in the family. The question, then, is how much and what kind of help is needed from other family members by the individual being seen and how much and what kind of help is needed by other family members in accomplishing change. Ordinarily this will mean the involvement of other family members in the treatment process.

Family therapists have taken different positions on the totality and frequency of involvement of family members. One position taken was that all family members needed to be present in every session, and that if not all were present the interview would not be held. It was assumed that all member participation was needed to solve the problem and that the absence of persons undermined the treatment process. Rigid adherence to this position often resulted in dropouts from treatment. Other therapists took the position of working with family members most able to change, or most motivated, or whoever was willing to participate. In some instances this was not the presenting problem person, but this has in some instances been shown to result in the disappearance of the problem of that identified patient.

The emphasis is on the potential contribution of the family member to problem solution, as well as on the gain the family member may experience by participation. Family members often interpret the worker's efforts to involve them in treatment as blaming them for the problem. That is never the intent. While it may often be true that certain members have helped create the problem, there is no advantage to the establishment of blame or causation, and no efforts are expended in this direction. However, if causation is defined as an interactional sequence, it may usefully be understood. All members participate in that process, but this is not the same as ascribing blame.

Such reasoning might generally exclude young children from family sessions, and children, generally, if the parents' problems are focus of the treatment, though they might usefully be seen at some time during the life of the case. Thus, who is included may vary depending on problem focus at the time. Including young children and others is seen as an important part of family assessment to elicit their understanding and insights about the family's functioning and to provide opportunity to observe how family members relate to each other. As before, the definition of family is flexible enough to include relevant persons in the family network, whether they are related by blood, marriage, or presence in the home, or are in some other way significant to one or more family members.

Conjoint sessions have advantages that individual sessions cannot offer. Direct observation of family members together provides information that is not ordinarily produced in family members' telling of how the family operates. Problems in the family's problem solving and interactional sequences of which family members themselves are unaware appear during the session and can be immediately noted or addressed. This here-and-now approach also allows for family members to try out with each other new behaviors suggested by the therapist or to engage in discussion and solving of problems with the support and direction of the therapist. Conjoint sessions offer the therapist a greater degree of objectivity since there is strong pull from family members to take sides, and they minimize the distortion of information that frequently occurs. A similar advantage accrues to family members who may be distrustful of other family members and of the therapist. Conjoint sessions also reveal communication failures such as the lack of sharing of perceptions and information. Family members often hold differing and distorted images of themselves and of each other. Family events are often perceived differently by different members, and often these images and perceptions have not been shared. Conjoint sessions hold the possibility for sharing positive images and feelings along with negative ones, and members may find support along with the opposition they frequently experience. The exchange of perceptions of events can lead to new definitions and to changes in interpersonal behavior. With the worker's assistance, conjoint sessions can provide a sense of safety and can help reticent members express themselves to others when they have not been able to do so on their own. These sessions can also enable members to confront differences which have been denied or deemed unresolvable.

The net effect of such disordered communication processes is serious interference with the family's problem-solving ability. When problems are presented and responded to by distraction, opposition, silence, and distancing, they are never solved. Individual and family goals are not achieved. Tasks are not completed. The use of conjoint sessions enables the family to focus on the problem and to pursue meaningful verbal exchanges until the issues can be effectively addressed, to the satisfaction of all members.

Individual sessions may be utilized to free members for more involvement in the conjoint session, and occasionally to drain excessive emotion that interferes with the progress of the conjoint sessions. Separate sessions should be framed in advance in the context of the conjoint sessions in order to strengthen the individual to deal with content that will be later brought back into conjoint sessions. This is particularly important since requests by family members for separate sessions often result in revelations of material heretofor unknown to the therapist and to other family members.

Family members can be involved in treatment constellations other than conjoint sessions. Work on family problems can take place in parent groups, groups for husbands or wives when the identified problem person is one of the family adults, multiple-family groups, or multiple-couple groups. (These will be referred to at appropriate points in later chapters.)

ENGAGING THE FAMILY IN TREATMENT

The social worker's desire to include a number of family members in the diagnostic process, if not in treatment, influences the procedures used for the first contact. Certain actions at this time are facilitative and may be undertaken for the purpose of engaging needed members in the problem-solving process.

The process of engaging a family in treatment is both similar to and different from beginning individual or other group treatment.

An applicant for service in a social work agency is not yet a client. The person who initiates agency contact may be certain only about the need for help but not about the kind of help needed, or may have a specific kind of help in mind that is different from what the agency and the worker have to offer. Negotiation is needed to clarify how expectations of the applicant are or are not congruent with those of the worker or the agency. In case of the family there are, additionally, differences between family members about what is needed and sought. There are differing reactions to what is made available by the worker and the agency. Before family members willingly engage themselves in a treatment process, negotiations among themselves and with the worker as to the purposes, goals, means of treatment, and the nature of their participation are needed to enable the family to make the shift from applicant to client.

Strean (1974) notes that clients are simultaneously attempting to place workers in a role that reciprocates with their idea of their own role in the treatment process. This is immensely complicated in family work because each family member is attempting to place the worker in a role particularly advantageous to self, a position that may not be at all desirable to another family member. The worker is immediately sought as an ally by various individuals or coalitions of individuals in the family.

Elements of Resistance to Treatment

There are numerous obstacles in the path of engaging family members in treatment. One is the view held by family representatives that one of the members is the problem—not the family as a whole. It is a difficult obstacle to remove if the family has been encouraged in this view by the referring person. Whether such referral sources are inside one's own agency as in the case of a multidisciplinary agency, or are representatives of other agencies, family-oriented workers should educate referring workers to a family systems view of presenting problems. Such a view will put them in a better position to help families accept referrals. The worker also needs to take steps to gain acceptance of the need for family participation by the family member who is the contact initiator.

A second kind of obstacle to family participation in treatment is the view held by many referred families that no problem exists. They contact the family-oriented worker under compulsion from a school, a probation officer, or an employer. They profess no awareness of the reasons for referral, or they see only that others are creating problems for them. They do not know why the school sent them, or why the employer is upset with them. The individual identified as the problem may be willing to keep a proffered appointment to comply with the referring person, but only for that reason. He sees no need for the family to be involved. Or the family may agree to have the identified person come, but sees no need for their participation. The worker, however, may readily sense the need for treatment of the problem and sees the benefits of involvement of the family in treatment.

Families obviously have the right to refuse treatment and to take whatever consequences may come with their refusal. Our concern is to enable the family to establish and maintain contact with helping persons long enough for them to know what it is they are refusing and what the potential gain for them individually and collectively might be. They may or may not be aware of the consequences of refusal for their relationships with referral sources or other community systems.

Work with a family may begin under coercive circumstances. In some situations the agency or the workers may have the authority to force family members into treatment. Such use of authority may be useful in opening up other possibilities for the family or in considering the consequences of no effort to change. Procedures used by the worker in the initial phases of contact may enable the family to move from participation under a sense of coercion to voluntary participation, with an expectancy of personal and family gain (Cirillo and DiBlasio, 1992).

Because so many families known to social workers are of this type, we will devote considerable space to an explication of procedures that help in moving the family into the role of client. The procedures are directed not only at such scapegoating or denying families; they are useful with all types of families. The method described is the process of engagement by means of conjoint interviews. Other beginnings may be made with families, but the conjoint session has special value in the assessment of family functioning, and special usefulness in enabling all family members to see their parts in the family problem-solving process.

The Family Encounters the Workers

The therapeutic situation itself evokes certain responses by virtue of the fact that another person is added to the system. Family members calculate how to adjust their responses to account for the new person in the midst. Each family member has his or her own preferences about what to do and what is needed to cope with the problem. Since the conflicts about possible actions have not been resolved within the family process, there is a natural tendency to seek the support of the worker for one's own position, along with depreciation of the views of others.

These efforts are understandable both in relation to the need of each member to preserve individual integrity and esteem and in relation to the level of caring and trust among family members. There is the expectation that others will not appreciate one's own needs and therefore will not take them into account. There is the expectation that other members will take advantage of expressions of weakness and error. Efforts to blame and demand change in others are a defense arising out of this view of others. The exercise of these actions by family members is accompanied by efforts, observable in the family group interview, to enlist the support of other family members.

As these efforts become manifest to the worker, they are also interpretable as efforts to seek the worker as an ally, to strengthen one's own position vis-à-vis other family members. This is revealed with dramatic clarity in some situations when, in separate interviews, individual members are able to be less defensive and accept more responsibility for family problems than they can in conjoint sessions.

The worker, in response, attempts to establish a caring, understanding relationship with the family members and to value the contributions of each of them. These attempts serve to resist the family pressures to take sides. Family members are forced to take this resistance into account. Failure to take individual responsibility for action is gradually, more or less directly, confronted. Family members may counteract the worker's resistance to their usual routines by intensifying their previous efforts; new responses may be found and learned to take the place of the anger and blame.

Thus, while the behaviors that family members display during their contact with the worker are manifestations of familiar family routines, they are not fully interpretable in this light. They also should be understood as responsive to the worker's entry into the family system. It is important for the worker to become a part of the family system, while at the same time not becoming entangled in its usual routines. The family must be helped to accept the worker's entry into the system and to be responsive to the worker's inputs demanding change.

The Worker's Role with the Family

It has been said of family work that the social worker is in charge of the treatment, but the family members are in charge of their lives. The worker's task in treatment, especially in beginning treatment, is to provide the family with a structure that enables problem solving to take place. The worker actively takes charge of the procedures at this beginning stage. He or she has certain steps in mind for the session and asks the family to cooperate. Though the family may appear to have the initiative in the interview, this may be because the worker has asked the members to struggle with a problem in order to see how they go about solving problems. If problem solving does not succeed, the worker interrupts, either to facilitate or move on to other tasks. (While it is conceivable that a family's interaction may not be interruptable, the worker usually has means of gaining the family's attention and cooperation.)

The degree to which the worker is able to establish control over the process in the session is a measure of the worker's skill. It is also a measure of the family's ability to gain from participation in treatment, and it thus provides diagnostic information about the family's workability and flexibility.

The diagnostic and treatment efforts should help the family members take charge of their lives. In the sessions the worker requires them to talk about their concerns to the worker and to each other. While it is expected that talking can create new understanding and awareness and can generate ideas about what to do, awareness and understanding are only part of the help available. The worker's requirement that family members engage in different kinds of action in the conjoint sessions vis-à-vis each other sets up new ways of relating that are more productive in problem solving than were their old ways. We expect the family to see the usefulness of the new patterns, learn them, and appropriate them for regular use. But family members are free to accept and make use of, or reject, what they learn in the sessions about themselves, each other, and their interactions with each other.

The worker obviously is concerned about how family members run their lives and may at times offer specific suggestions or directions about what to do. In some institutional settings the worker may even be in a position to tell the family members how to manage their lives outside the sessions and may have some expectation that they will follow the suggestions. It may even be useful to propose courses of action in order to solve a problem or prevent the occurrence of one. The worker's principal task, however, is to structure treatment sessions so that constructive decision making about life issues is possible for the family. While it is important to solve a problem, the worker's goal is not necessarily to solve it for the family, but to make it possible for them to solve it. The beginning phase addresses both aspects. The decision about what to do is the family's.

OPENING PROCEDURES

The first goal of the initial contact is to acquire a firm understanding of the nature of the problem presented by the family and of the workings of the family system that serve to perpetuate the problem or prevent its solution—a picture of how the family is stuck. A second and equally important goal is to gain the family's agreement to participate in a problem-solving process, since the members do not necessarily come with the readiness to do so. A third goal is to set procedures for change in motion. Family members should be able to leave with beginning confidence that they have been understood, that something new is being offered, and that something positive can happen as a result of agency contact.

These goals are interrelated. As the worker acquires understanding, the worker's way of questioning, responding to, and understanding the family's situation provides a different frame of reference for the family. The new information, the new way of looking at things, and the steps that the worker asks family members to take in the initial sessions are themselves the beginnings of change.

Steps or phases in the process of engaging the family in treatment have been identified by both Haley (1978) and Solomon (1977). While there are differences between their approaches, both have elements that we use and have incorporated in our formulation of a procedure to be followed by the social worker in initiating contact with family treatment. As we have noted, these stages are similar to but more complex than the engagement and contracting efforts required in individual treatment.

The steps we outline are for an initial conjoint session, which includes as many family members as seem necessary to problem solution. Most family treatment begins through contact with one family member. The worker takes a position at first contact that the family needs to be involved. Starting with one person and waiting until later to insist on family participation results in lost time and requires a second start. In the initial contact, whether in person or on the telephone, the worker seeks to learn who the family members are. There is enough exploration of the problem to give the worker some sense of agency appropriateness and family relatedness. But the exploration is brief for two reasons. The problem cannot be adequately understood from one person's reporting, and the image of an alliance between the initiator and the worker needs to be particularly avoided in this phase.

Attention therefore shifts rather quickly to the need to engage both the initiator of the contact and other family members in the treatment process. The caller is requested to ask other family members to come and to bring them along to an initial session. The value of the information they can provide and of the suggestions they might offer is emphasized. Family members are frequently responsive to this emphasis on the importance of their contributions to problem solving. If they are not responsive, the worker's efforts must focus on the resistance, rather than on the problem presented by the family. If the problem presenter in the initial contact seems resistant, the resistance should be explored. If the problem presenter attributes resistance to other family members, their anticipated reasons and the presenter's intended means for handling their responses can be explored.

If the presenter's means for handling the resistance of other family members seem inadequate, alternative responses may be suggested. The suggestions are, in effect, new inputs into the family system. If the suggestions are adopted, both the behavior of the initial problem presenter and family processes are thereby altered. Treatment of the family has begun. If the resistance is not strong, family members may recognize that each family member's view of the problem is important if it is to be fully understood, and they may respond to the request that all family members participate at least in the initial exploratory session.

Stage 1: Relieving Initial Anxiety

Once the social worker has succeeded in arranging an in-person meeting with the needed family members, his or her first task in the initial session is to relate to each family member's feelings about having to be there. Family members may have arrived at the appointment with different understandings of what is to take place and what is expected of them. They may be fearful of revealing secrets or expect undesirable changes to be demanded. They may fear blame, punishment, removal from the home, or shock treatment. They may expect helpers to take sides against them.

The worker's overall objective (as in individual treatment) is to establish a safe, nonthreatening relationship with all persons present. The worker inquires about conversations the family members may have had with each other about the appointment, how it has been explained to them, and how they felt about what they had been told prior to coming. This procedure has both communicative and metacommunicative value. On the communicative level it elicits information regarding their anxieties about meeting the worker, airing family problems, asking for help, and revealing themselves to other family members. It provides data about the way family members view both the relationship with the worker and relationships within the family. Family members may have communicated little or much about coming. Clear communication may have gone to some members but not to others. They may feel free to speak in the session or wait for cues from others. The procedure's metacommunicative value to the family is that it conveys the worker's intention to regard each person's view as important and permits it to be heard and valued. The individuality and separateness of family members is emphasized, while their value to the problem-solving effort is affirmed. The procedure allows for each family member to be heard by other family members. If family members do not spontaneously comment, the worker may ask them if they are aware of each other's point of view or solicit comments on what has been said.

Stage 2: Eliciting Problem Definitions—Questioning That Confuses

After the family members' anxieties about the interview have been re- duced, the social worker can proceed to elicit from each one a state- ment about the problem or problems that have brought the family to the session. There will likely be differences in statements of the problem. For some families this may be the first time that different views have been expressed and heard. The worker's presence may create a toler- ance for these differences that was not present in the family's own ef- forts to deal with the problem. The extent of the members' ability to wait for one another's expressions will offer the worker some begin- ning cues as to the family's ability to listen and to learn. If they are able to convey appreciation for having heard something from others that they have not heard before, the worker will have an even greater sense of their treatability.

This is not often the case, however. Frequently family members single out one of their number as "the problem." The worker gets the clear impression that the identified person is blamed and isolated and finds little support in the family. The worker may sense little tolerance for the position that the views of each family member are important where the identified problem person is concerned. Such rigidity offers little to sup- port the view that the family can change in order to solve the problem. At this stage the worker primarily is listening and thinking. Only limit- ed efforts are directed at expanding expressions of feelings or changing feelings or problem definition. The important objective at this time is to hear from everyone.

Family members will not always sit patiently to hear what other members have to say. They experience difficulty in remaining in a lis- tener status. There are likely to be interruptions and, if the first speaker does not stop, simultaneous talking. In this event the worker does need to become active to avoid repetition in the session of what the family or- dinarily experiences at home. The stage is set for problem solving by disallowing interruptions. At the same time each participant is assured that his or her point of view will be heard. Strenuous efforts by the worker may be needed along these lines in some families. Minuchin, Montalvo, Guerney, Rosman, and Schumer (1967) found it necessary in their experience with severely disorganized families to remove some family members to a position behind a one-way glass when persistent interruptions revealed their inability to listen to others. Even at this beginning stage, the worker's efforts to regulate the conversation may afford the family an experience that they have not had before, and this may enable them to feel that the worker and treatment have something to offer them.

There may also be a reaction to the interviewing situation that is quite the opposite of interruptions and simultaneous talking. Some family members may be extremely reticent to say anything, much less express an opinion, point of view, or difference. The worker will be aware of halting speech, looking down, and looking to other family members for cues, or avoiding involvement. Such reticence can be as much of an obstacle to problem solving as overactivity. The worker may attempt to draw the individual out during this initial phase of the interview by asking for elaboration or may comment on how the situation makes for difficulty in talking, thereby offering encouragement. It may be useful to ask whether other family members can enable the reticent person to speak. These efforts to gain the reticent member's participation become particularly important in the case of the family member whose contributions have not been valued by others. In response to the worker's attitude, other family members may begin to respond differently to the reticent member. The reticent behavior gives diagnostic information about patterns of power, deference, and decision making in the family.

While a prime purpose in this initial contact is achievement of diagnostic understanding, the efforts to elicit information from all members represent a change for family members. For many families this is a requirement that they respond differently to each other. Insofar as they can respond to and benefit from this requirement, treatment has begun for them.

Having said that at this stage the worker's effort is focused on developing understanding of each family member's definition of the problem, we must step back a bit to expand our concept of the worker's role. We intend for the worker's activity to be even more complex than we have just portrayed it. The purpose of this more complex behavior is to gain further understanding of how the family system works in relation to the presenting problem. To this end the worker will ask questions of family members to develop information that will tell whether his or her hunches are right about what is wrong in the family. These hunches may be based on conceptions of constructive communication processes, as was evident to some degree in the preceding discussion. Or they may be based on conceptions of needed family structure, of appropriate modes of handling affect and feeling, of likely casual sequences or circular causality.

We have noted thus far that each member brings to the worker his or her definition of the problem. We have also noted that each family member adapts not only to the problem, but to every other member's adaptation to the problem. Thus, the worker engages in an approach to questioning that is directed by hypotheses about why the family is working the way it is and which assumes and reveals the circular responsiveness of family members to each other. Mother may just have given a description of Henry's behavior. Father may be asked for interpretation of the same behavior and a report of what Mother did in response to it. Judy or Mother may be asked what Father did when Mother responded the way she did. And Mother and/or Henry may be asked what Judy was doing in the meantime. Henry may be asked what prompted him to engage in the behavior in the first place. Consequently it may be revealed that Henry smashed his toys on the floor when Mother was criticizing Father, thereby interrupting the criticism, and that when Mother scolded Henry for being rough with his toys, Father moved to protect him from the scolding. Judy may tell that Father usually gets more angry at Henry when Mother is not around, and Henry reveals that Judy tattles on him to Mother. Questions about context may reveal that Mother's strictness and scolding of Henry has increased in recent weeks and that this is temporally associated with both the death of Mother's sister and Father's taking on a part-time job to bolster family income.

Such new information confirms or disconfirms the worker's hunches about what is wrong and forms a basis for decision about what lines of questioning may still be needed. Even so, both the questions and the answers may produce confusion for a family which brought the view that Henry's behavior was simply obstinacy or an attention-seeking device, undermining their original definition of the problem and providing a new basis for thinking about it.

Our central point at this stage is neither to criticize the family nor to produce change, but to develop a broad understanding on which treatment planning can be based. However, both teaching by the worker and implicit learning by the family occur through this mode of questioning, providing new information and new image which offer some beginning basis for change.

Up to this point in the initial contact procedure, the role we have defined for the worker requires an exploratory, investigative stance. It minimizes commentary on family operations but does require the worker to regulate relations between the worker and family members and among family members as they participate in the interview. The worker values each member's contribution and is thereby supportive of each, but he or she also sets expectations for participation. The pairing of support and participation becomes particularly evident in the next stage of the session, in which there is an effort to define the family problem.

Stage 3: Working Toward Problem Consensus

Social workers often see the problem differently from the way the family does, but they still need to start with the family's definition of the problem. The worker sees the problem presented by the family as evidence of failure of problem-solving processes and thus as a symptom of the problem, while the family sees it as the problem. In the procedure we have outlined, the worker's efforts are directed both to solving the problem and to increasing family problem-solving capacity. The following example will illustrate what we mean.

The problem is presented by parents who are concerned with altering the behavior of a child. In such a case the worker can operate on the premise, likely to be shared by the parents, that the parents have both the prerogative and the responsibility to regulate the behavior of the child. The worker wants to support them in this and to help them with it. A dual purpose is suggested: The first need is to correct the child's behavior, and the second need is to build the parents' capacity to correct the presenting problem and others that may occur. The family's problem-solving mechanisms have not been working successfully in relation to the presenting problem. Since the family is not asking for help with their problem-solving routines, but only for help in correcting this problem, the effort to change problem-solving routines must be focused on these routines as they apply to the presenting problem.

This should lead the worker to inquire what kinds of efforts have been made by the parents to correct the problem, in order to understand what has not worked and the reasons for the lack of success. Throughout the discussion the parents can be credited for their continuing involvement with their child as a manifestation of their concern for the child's welfare. They can also be credited for not giving up on their child and for their wish to be successful as parents in enabling their child to perform well and to succeed in life. The worker's accreditation of the parent's concern and caring may be something the child has not heard before through all the parents' commands, controls, accusations, blame, and punishment. Such new awareness may make it possible for the child to manifest a wish to have a good relationship with the parents, even if there is not always a wish to please them. Both the parents' and the child's feelings about what has been happening may be aired.

Along with this accreditation of good intentions and recognition of continuing involvement and concern, it becomes obvious that the techniques and strategies used by the parents have not been successful in regulating behavior, as evidenced in the discussion of what has been tried. Having supported the parents' wish to succeed with their child, the worker may now be in a position to suggest that new strategies are needed. If the parents can accept this, a basis for work with the parents has been established.

Of course, the effort of the worker to establish an alliance with the parents may produce a negative reaction in the child. A positive relationship with all family members must apply to the child as well as the parents. The worker will relate both to the child's feelings about being present and to her or his definition of the problem. While feelings of anger and blame are likely to be expressed, the worker may also hear the child's wish for approval and understanding from the parents and the desire for a positive relationship with them. If, by the worker's focus on the positive wish instead of the blame, the parents are able to hear something new from their child, a change in family feeling may be begun. At a minimum, the child may experience enough of the worker's support and concern to enable him to consent to the helping relationship.

In this situation the parents and the identified problem child may be the central actors, but, using the circular questioning method detailed for Stage 2, the worker also solicits views and reactions from others. The worker conveys an interest in what each has to say as a member of the family, valuing their presence and their contributions. Their responses may emphasize support for or blame of parents or their sibling. The worker attempts to understand how they have related themselves to the problem or how they have been affected by it—by becoming involved in trying to solve it or by withdrawal—and how they see themselves and other family members relating to it now.

Acceptance of the problem focus defined by the family at the outset appears necessary to the family's willingness to participate in treatment. At the same time, the requirement that the family participate emphasizes the family role in finding a solution to the problem. Without the latter requirement we would expect no change in family organization and a continuation of the problem or problematic behavior. Oxley (1977) noted that during the treatment of some nonvoluntary families, members other than the identified patient began to focus on their own problems as their comfort in treatment and their self-esteem increased. We see this as a healthy shift from the initial problem focus, an increase in the sense of individuality and separateness of the members, which is necessary to a positive sense of togetherness and solidarity.

In the procedure we have described, the worker is supportive of all family members, even those in apparent opposition to each other. The means the worker uses to provide the support are based on recognition of the need of family members for positive relationships. Communications that drive them apart are relabeled as caring, concern for the well-being of others, and a wish for connectedness. We do not see this relabeling as deception or trickery. It is an effort to identify positive aspects of family relationships. The family members' continuing engagement with one another is seen as an expression of their meaning and importance to one another, however negatively such feelings have been verbalized. Expressions of hostility and blame are common in many families and seem easier than expressions of caring and concern, which paradoxically seem more threatening. They entail a risk of rejection which negative feelings do not. Satir (1983) suggests that low self-esteem lies behind the hesitance to risk the expression of positive feeling. Worker efforts to relabel and thereby promote a positive relationship with the worker and among family members may not have an immediately successful effect. They bear repetition, however; along with other efforts, they will have a cumulative, positive effect.

Stage 4: Focus on Interactional Mechanisms

The fourth stage in the social worker's efforts to engage the family furthers the worker's diagnostic effort. The worker will have gained in understanding how the family works to cope with its problems from the previous stages. The effort at this stage is more specifically directed at understanding the family's ways of dealing with the presenting problem. This stage can be approached in several ways.

Members' Response to Worker's Questions

One approach is for the worker to inquire of family members how they have responded to the problem, how it has affected them, and what they have tried to do about it. Some members will have been more affected, others less so. Less affected members may have remained uninvolved and may show little feeling or reaction. Others, who are more involved, may have attempted to remain aloof but now are willing to manifest their reactions and suggestions. Still others may blame, depreciate, or get angry or aggressive. Some may have attempted to talk it over without productive results. Patterns of involvement and withdrawal, of support and opposition are evident in these differing responses. The worker may comment on the responses to emphasize that each family member does have some connection to the problem, even if he or she has tried to ignore it. This base of connectedness to the problem is the primary incentive for participation in problem solution.

The worker-imposed requirement that each family member hear what the others have to say allows for new information—other members' ideas about a solution—to be shared for the benefit to all. Members who may have already heard other members' ideas for solution can become more conscious of differing ideas about what to do and the reactions of others to their own ideas. They can consider what seems to have helped or hindered solutions and recognize the need for negotiation of these differences. The worker specifically draws such reactions and differences to their attention and asks who in the family does what in the face of differences about how to cope and how each responds to the other's response. Awareness of the difficulty in dealing with differences may ultimately be the basis of agreement to participate in treatment. The wish to do something about how they get along with each other may serve as a common problem definition, a rallying point.

In such a talking approach to problem solving, the worker elicits a response from all present family members, requiring others to listen while one member talks and assuring that each one's turn to talk will come. In some families this regulation of communication may require considerable effort on the part of the worker.

Family Discussion

An alternative approach is to ask the family members to talk with one another about how to solve the problem, while the worker observes what happens when they do. Though the worker may assume that there will be a replay of family operations similar to their usual ones at home, this assumption should be validated. Frequently family members will confirm that this is the usual routine and express dissatisfaction with the process. Often they will report restraint in their behavior due to the presence of the worker, thus confirming the systems theory assumption that the entry of a new member alters the operation of the system. That may be a positive sign about the treatability of the family, but it is not to be assumed that the restraint will necessarily continue in subsequent sessions.

Whether or not family members have been restrained in this procedure, the worker will have acquired some knowledge of the family's mechanisms for problem solving and an awareness of operations that frustrate its problem-solving work. The most observable difficulties are in communications. Communications may be unclear; topics may be changed before issues are resolved, statements interrupted, blame affixed, support offered. Statements may be addressed to nobody in particular, and some individuals may attempt to speak for others. Third parties may enter disputes as peacemakers or allies of one or another member. Various aspects of family relationships, such as levels of respect and caring for others, become evident in this flow of communications. Family solidarity and cohesiveness may be manifest or demonstrably lacking. Each family member also gains a sense, from how others respond to him, of whether he is affirmed, supported, and accepted, and by his own response he conveys to others whether he is affirming and accepting of them, or rejecting and critical.

Communications represent strategies for negotiation and problem solving that have in the past been learned and reaffirmed, and now are apparently in continual use. It is possible that what the worker observes at this point is the simple result of faulty negotiation procedures such as failure to listen intently or respond relevantly, and what is needed is for the family to learn new negotiation procedures. The family can begin to learn from the worker's efforts, beginning with the initial interview, to regulate the conversation.

It may be evident to the worker that family members do not feel very good about each other at this point; negative feelings may be intense with manifestation of undiminished hostility. Struggles for power or control may be revealed, with no one yielding in that struggle, or with one family member accepting a completely one-down position without a struggle. Triads may be tightly locked into position. Verbal and nonverbal communications are evidence that those conditions exist. Changing communication modes or routes may be impossible or may not help. Traces of goodwill and the ability to recall positive feelings are important in the willingness of family members to continue both in treatment and in relationships with one another.

Two-Party Discussing

A third alternative approach for Stage 4 is also diagnostic in effect but has a clearer treatment component. The worker may select a specific issue which has been referred to in the discussion and ask an involved pair of family members to work on it. They are asked to talk to each other to try to solve the problem. Other family members are asked to observe. The worker is in a position to observe that happens between the two parties involved and what the behavior of other family members is.

Both participants usually direct their efforts at getting the other person to see their own point of view. They may both become wider ranging in their arguments, increasingly insistent and intense, or one of them may become insistent and the other withdraw. Both may turn to the worker or to the other members of the family for support when their frustration at gaining the understanding of the other reaches a certain level. The worker may respond to this sense of frustration and hopelessness at being unable to work out their difficulties by helping each participant to become more aware of her or his own feelings of anger and despair and those of others. Noting the strategy that each participant has used in relating to the other and the other's response, the worker may inquire whether they see this description of their interaction as accurate and ask for their estimate of the effectiveness of their actions. In the midst of this awareness of anger and despair, the worker needs to know whether there is also a wish and a hope for change. Some clients may find the possibility of change so inconceivable that they dare not hope for it. The worker's attentiveness to these feelings and accurate description of the participant's interaction conveys understanding and can give rise to hope. Further, the worker's expressions of hopefulness, if warranted, may be useful.

The worker may suggest a brief attempt to continue negotiations between the two participants, with guidance from the worker. Such efforts at guided communication are demonstrations of the treatment procedures and may help the family see that alternate ways of coping hold some hope of correcting the problem it is experiencing. The worker regulates the conversation by requiring (1) that the two participants not interrupt each other; (2) that the other person respond relevantly rather than with a topic change to another issue or a different experience; and (3) that the speakers talk about their own feelings and needs, rather than talking about the other person and what the speaker thinks the other one should be doing.

The emphasis is on the immediate experience in the interview rather than on past events, though past events may be the starting point of the discussion. Thus, A might be talking about feeling understood, or hurt, or lonely, or unsupported by B, not only in relation to an earlier event but in the present discussion of the event. B might respond empathetically or in anger, but focus on the present moment's responses makes the issues more alive and less subject to recall's distortions. The intent is to make it possible for family members to feel that their views and feelings have been heard, an experience they have often not had in their own efforts at problem solving.

Whether the effort succeeds at this point or not, it serves as a demonstration of the kind of work that would take place during treatment. If it does not fully succeed, the worker is clearer about the amount and kinds of effort needed to help. Behind the ineffective negotiation procedures lie the varied needs of the individuals and the reasons that each has for not being able to accept the other's view. They may reflect an effort to maintain integrity and individuality or a struggle for control and power. Such difficult relationship issues will need to be addressed in the treatment.

While the worker is observing how two family members work on a specific family issue, simultaneous observation of the behaviors of other family members is possible. Other family members may not be able to remain in the observer role; they may become distractors, allies, or peacemakers or otherwise inject themselves into the negotiations. The reasons for such behavior are many and varied. Children may feel threatened by a too tense exchange between parents and act to draw attention away from the argument and onto themselves. A sibling may identify with the feeling of another child generated in the interaction with a parent. A parent may feel strongly about the behavior of the other parent in relation to a child.

However well intended, these behaviors have negative side effects. They inject another relationship into an issue that could, and frequently should have been, resolved by two persons. In effect, the issue is left unresolved rather than resolved. The original disputants are more divided than they were before. The third person becomes occupied in the intervening role and is not free to pursue his or her usual separate activities.

The worker may respond in several ways. The worker may choose to ignore these behaviors at this time, being alert to whether their occurrence is a regular pattern of behavior. The worker may move to block the activity of the third party, indicating that others' observations will be asked for later. Or the worker may comment on the sequence of behaviors among the three family members, inviting discussion of the sequence (not of the problem) by all three. Feelings and reactions of each of the participants to the immediate events then become the focus of the discussion. The worker ascertains whether the family members are aware of the sequence and whether they see it as helpful or not.

Use of any of these three procedures at this stage in the initial contact is likely to be brief, since the social worker is seeking primarily to understand how the family is working and to test quickly whether they can respond to worker intervention. At the same time however, it will be seen that these interventions are useful not only in initial contacts but also in ongoing treatment. Ongoing treatment often proceeds in similar fashion.

Stage 5: Reaching a Treatment Contract

The final stage of the social worker's efforts to engage the family in treatment is achievement of an understanding with the family members about what they want to have changed and what they want from treatment and from the worker. The emphasis shifts from what is wrong to how the family wants things to be, and how the worker can help them get there. The focus is on the effort to define goals and establish a working contract between the social worker and the family about their ongoing work together. Again, the process is similar to but more complex than that required in individual treatment.

The prior stages of the engagement effort have been preparation for the family to approach this one, but considerable work remains to be done. The discrepancies in problem statement now must be resolved into a problem definition to which family members can subscribe as one that they are willing to work on. The shift from what is wrong to how they want things to be moves away from complaining to positive, goal-oriented activity. It is not an easy shift to make. The definition of the kind of help needed from the worker is difficult to achieve, since the family has only the present experience with the worker to go by and consequently knows little about what the worker and agency have to offer. Agreement on the problem definition and how the worker will help are both needed.

In resolving the many issues that arise in contracting with a family about the problems and the goals of treatment, another type of worker activity is required. While previous stages have been worker-directed and structured, they have minimized analytical comment and feedback to the family about the way the worker sees the family working (or not working) together. Worker activity has focused on the process of the family session. In this stage the worker participates with his or her own observations and restatements and focuses on key aspects of the problem.

The worker's effort is directed at achieving a problem definition that is in harmony with the family's needs and wishes. The worker may see a variety of family problems that the family members themselves do not see. He may be aware, for example, that a marital problem exists and that it interferes with the solution of the problem that the family has presented. The worker may make the connection, but the family may not be able to see this as the problem to be solved. If the presenting problem was a child's behavior, the focus at this stage is not on how the parents can get their marriage together, but on how they *together* can cope with the child's problem. The parents may be able to accept the need to join together to help the child, but they may not see the need to work on the marriage in general. While they may subsequently come to see that work on the marriage is needed in order to help their child, the starting point in treatment is with the problem they see and are willing to try to solve.

The worker's emphasis on what the family would like to accomplish in treatment requires the worker to seek responses from family members about what each wants and is willing to do about the problem. A number of difficulties will be encountered in these responses. One is that goals will be stated in terms of the need for someone else to stop doing something or to be different. Unfortunately, such statements make the definition of the family goal difficult if not impossible. They are statements about expectations of others rather than expectations of self. They concern behavior to be eliminated but not behavior that is to replace what is now occurring. They do not convey an image of what desirable family life would be like. All family members are not likely to find such definitions acceptable. The work of the previous stages of the initial contact should have helped to take the edge off some of these tendencies to blame or scapegoat, but it will not have eliminated them. More work is needed to arrive at acceptable definitions.

Another difficulty is that responses from family members may be in global terms. Either the specifics of change do not become clear, or the proposed changes in the family seem so extensive as to appear unattainable. Demands on others and global expectations reflect the continuing difficulty family members have in defining problems or in communicating their needs in a way that others in the family can accept and agree to. If they had other ways of addressing the tasks that the worker now puts to them, they probably would not need treatment. Specific help is needed.

One means the worker has of helping with these difficulties is the ability to restate or reformulate the problem. The worker may use knowledge of the members and of the group acquired earlier in the session. Knowledge about how members see themselves connected to the problem and about their wish to continue as a group may be used to convert negative statements into positive ones, global statements into more specific objectives. "I want him to stop arguing" or "We are always fighting" may be reformulated to "I wish that we could talk things over." General unhappiness and dissatisfaction may be converted to a wish for family members to "show more appreciation" or to "get along better." In rare instances members may comment about specific things they themselves can do to improve and may show signs of willingness to do them. The worker may offer formulations that express expectations and goals for the family rather than for individuals, or re-formulate statements about problems to make them specific rather than global. The general adjustment problem of a family member may be specified in terms such as "planning how things will be when Sally returns home from the hospital" or "what we can do so grandmother won't be so unhappy." Agreement from members to work to solve these problems and achieve these goals is then sought.

Along with the effort to restate goals, the worker draws attention away from individual behavior to focus on the interactive process between members. For example, she or he may offer observations about family interactions which help to clarify for the family the nature of their difficulties. The worker may comment that when members disagree, they become more forceful in their arguments, and the resistance of each stiffens. Nothing changes, and they may therefore wish to consider other means of resolving disagreement. This would be followed by a question about what they wish to do about it. Or the worker may note that when the parents, or any pair of family members, were working on a disagreement, they were distracted by a third member of the family, leaving their disagreement unresolved. This may be proposed as something that could be changed. This attention to the interactive process and the effort to define the problem as one of interpersonal relationships rather than as a problem of the individual serves to reduce defensive behavior and minimize guilt. It should help to free members from resistance to participation in family problem solving.

The worker at this stage also needs to learn what kind of help the family had expected and to define what kind of help he or she has to offer. The worker's means of helping will, in part, have been demonstrated by his behavior in the interview prior to this point, but these means may be very different from what the family wants. There may be a range of expectations of the worker, from removing a member from the home for placement elsewhere, to "straightening out" a member; to getting a member to go to school, or to work, or to a doctor; to refereeing the family arguments; to helping the family find a way to get along or to talk things over. The worker may judge the requests as desirable or undesirable directions in which to move as needed or unneeded, as possible or impossible to fulfill, given the range of his skills or the availability of services in his own or other agencies. A request for placement may be accepted and recommended, or it may be countered with a recommendation of family counseling and an offer of worker involvement in that way. However the family and the service requests are evaluated, the worker's thinking and judgment about both must be conveyed to the family for discussion and decision. The worker needs also to convey his own and his agency's capacity to respond to the requests.

The family's response to the worker's evaluations, suggestions, and offers of help provide further data on which to base judgments about family potential for change and responsiveness to helping efforts. The new information and direction serve to upset the family's usual interchanges. The new inputs may be resisted, in order to maintain the usual balance, or they may be assimilated, in order to promote change.

Whether the family can begin to change or even accept the possibility of change depends on a number of factors, some of which have already been noted. The family's value of family togetherness is one such factor. Even though disaffection and discouragement about the family's situation may be great, there may still be hope that things could be different. Some members, however, may have already lost hope completely, and they cannot be interested in participation in the family. A second factor has to do with the willingness of members to risk. A member's willingness to respond positively to a worker reformulation that says, in effect, "I want you, care about you, wish to be with you," implies a willingness to risk the possibility that other members may not share those desires. Behind this willingness must lie a strong need and perhaps some confidence that other members do care and share the same wishes. Worker sensitivity can sometimes enable a member to claim ownership of such sentiments when this might not under other circumstances be possible.

Another factor affecting members' consent to participate and willingness to change is the fear that the individual will be lost in pursuing the goals of the group, that he or she will be unhappily bound to the family and never be free to leave or to grow as an individual. All the procedures described are intended to convey the worker's support for both individuality and connectedness, and not just for a connectedness that keeps the individual inappropriately bound to the family. If, as a consequence of worker activity, the family indicates a willingness to continue in treatment, it is a sign of their capacity to accept outside contributions to their problem solving, and perhaps also of the worker's skill in conveying helpfulness and trustworthiness.

We have described in some detail a procedure for assessment and engagement of the family at the time of initial contact. The process need not always be lengthy, however. With some families it will be simple and short; with others it may take several hours. If a clear family and worker agreement does not result, the work may have to be carried over into second sessions. Workers may eliminate some stages and still achieve clarity, begin work on a problem, or arrive at a contract with greater efficiency.

A FAMILY LIFE CHRONOLOGY

Taken in the context of our earlier emphasis on the here-and-now and the lack of emphasis on history, our inclusion of Satir (1983) at this point and the taking of a family life chronology may seem misplaced. Though the effort represents a different approach to treatment, the information obtained can become useful in the ongoing phases of our problem-solving orientation.

The interview begins with learning to know who each person is and what they see as their reason for being present. Questioning about the circumstances that prompted their being here provides the basis for wanting to know basic facts about who is who in the family—names, dates of birth, death, marriage—and who else is in the family. At this point such questions of fact are relatively unthreatening, seem appropriate to the family, and serve as a means to put the family at ease. The process is more than a collection of answers to questions.

The development of the chronology elicits information about relationships between family members, the parents in particular, how they developed, how others in the family, particularly their parents, felt about them and what else was occurring in their families at the time. The chronology helps to develop images of self and of each other as separate persons, beyond their usual role relationships. Children may, for example, see their parents as persons, not only as harsh rule-makers. Parents can see themselves in the context of the larger family, how they were influenced by parent and sibling behavior and how this is determining present behavior. Questions relating to births, illnesses, deaths, marriages, and other important family events—and about how different family members responded or coped with such events—may begin to reveal patterns of coping and possible repetition from generation to generation. The therapist is alert and responsive to the reactions and behavior of other family members to the information being given.

Familiarization with the past may prompt a desire not to repeat patterns. If both parents are in the home, getting the chronology from both may reveal the origins of current differences between them regarding roles or ways of doing things. In the questioning, the therapist serves as a model of communication. The facts are important, but the means of questioning serve to convey respect and to value the contributions of each family member. Questions about, and the presence of, members of several generations enable family members to see themselves in a larger context. As differences and differentness are revealed, the therapist reminds the family that opinions and ways of doing things do not necessarily imply that one is right and the other wrong—they are just different, and they now have a new opportunity to choose how they want things to go.

It should be evident that such an approach does not seek history solely for the sake of facts, but is intended to free family members to grow, to be different in their family behavior, and to contribute in a different way to family problem solving. Though Satir put the chronology effort at the beginning of work with the family, it suggests, and is the essence of, a very different approach to treatment. Seen in the context of our approach, additions to the chronology may be sought when new issues arise such as illness, loss of job or income, or a child leaving home. Family information may help when problem solving around such an issue gets stuck in disagreement or lack of ideas for how to cope or move.

Therapists in the Bowen (1978) approach to family treatment develop a family genogram, a diagram that records much of the same information as does Satir's chronology (McGoldrick and Gerson, 1985). The diagram uses separate symbols for males and females, represents them by generation, giving dates of birth, death, and marriage, and represents whether individuals had a close, intense, or distant relationship. The genogram serves similarly as a record of family membership, history, and events over at least three generations. Here its purpose is slightly different than either ours or Satir's: It is less focused on the presenting problem. Obtaining the data and learning about the family are accompanied by teaching the patients about what to look for and how families work. The genogram offers a cognitive grasp of the family's behavior and enables the individual to be more detached, less emotional about family connections, and a separate person, not simply an extension of other members' wishes and intentions. The interest in family history facilitates personal growth and separateness. As we have noted before, change in one member necessitates change elsewhere in the family and may be both welcome and/or threatening.

One other means of recording information about a family and its problems that is needed for assessment and treatment planning is an eco-map. The map may initially show members of the current, immediate family, as well as of the extended family with whom they interact and who might be or become relevant to presenting problem solution. It is less focused on developing a full genogram or chronology. It includes not only family members, but other individuals, services, agencies, or resources and shows whether they are connected in a problematic or helpful way.

SUMMARY

Our concern in this chapter has been to further the understanding of the nature of treatment and the social worker's role in it. Treatment that promotes change in any family member or any set of interactions may be considered family treatment, since it will upset family balance. Conjoint family interviews may be used in treatment but are not synonymous with treatment. A variety of modes of involving family members is possible. Criteria for worker decisions about whom to involve and how to involve them have been suggested.

The worker's task in the initial stages of contact with family members is twofold. The first task is to come to an understanding of the nature of the problem presented by the family and of the nature of the family's difficulty in solving the problem. This assessment effort is concurrent with the worker's second task of engaging family members in the treatment effort. Engagement is complex because different family members may disagree about both definition of the problem and solutions to it, and they may also differ in their willingness to participate in working at solutions. The section on engaging the family had delineated worker activity pertinent to both of these tasks.

While the section on beginning treatment has focused on procedures, we have also considered some of the ways in which the worker's knowledge about family systems is used in assessment and in the worker's contract with the family for further treatment. In our family treatment approach, the worker conceptualizes the presenting problem as a problem of the family system, as one that the family needs to come to terms with rather than a problem of an individual within the family. In this frame of reference, the worker proceeds in a way to help the family think of the problem that way, too. The worker's intent is not to fault the family for the existence of the problem but to indicate that the existence of the problem requires the family to respond and to cope in some way. The worker conveys a willingness to help and to use her or his skills in finding ways of coping, offering hope that constructive solutions can be found which may motivate the family's problem-solving efforts.

Our inclusion in this chapter of efforts to obtain a family life chronology and a family genogram may seem to emphasize history taking and to minimize our focus in earlier sections on here-and-now relationships. We have sought to convey that the chronology and the genogram are developed not in isolation as background but rather to facilitate understanding of current roles of self and others and of patterns of interaction. Obtaining such information and understanding is not limited to the beginning of treatment. New areas of exploration become relevant as new issues arise in the treatment process. We include these efforts as integral to our treatment approach, not to suggest a different approach to treatment.

REFERENCES

Bowen, M. 1978. *Family Therapy in Clinical Practice*. New York: Jason Aronson.

Cirillo, Stefano, and DiBlasio, Paola. 1992. *Families That Abuse*. New York: W.W. Norton & Co.

Gordon, T. 1970. *Parent Effectiveness Training*. New York: Peter H. Wyden, Publisher.

Haley, Jay. 1978. *Problem Solving Therapy*. San Francisco: Jossey-Bass.

Kempler, Walter. 1981. *Experiential Psychotherapy Within Families*. New York: Brunner/Mazel Publishers.

McGoldrick, Monica, and Gerson, Randy. 1985. *Genograms in Family Assessment*. New York: W.W. Norton & Co.

Minuchin, S., Montalvo, B., Guerney, B., Rosman, B., and Schumer, F. 1967. *Families of the Slums*. New York: Basic Books.

Oxley, G. 1977. "Involuntary Clients' Responses to a Treatment Experience." *Social Casework* 58:607–14.

Satir, V. 1983. *Conjoint Family Therapy*. Palo Alto, CA: Science and Behavior Books.

Solomon, M.A. 1977. "The Staging of Family Therapy: An Approach to Developing the Therapeutic Alliance." *Journal of Marriage and Family Counseling* 3:59–66.

Strean, H. 1974. "Role Theory." In *Social Work Treatment*, ed. F. J. Turner. New York: Free Press.

Part II

Intervention Strategies

Part II consists of 11 chapters focused on intervening with families in order to change dysfunctional patterns of interaction. In this part the theory and concepts presented in Part I are operationalized in work with specific populations. However, the populations we have chosen to discuss by no means form a definitive group, and their inclusion does not imply preference with regard to other populations seen in family treatment. They simply represent a sampling of the kinds of families and family problems that social workers encounter in contemporary practice. The choices resulted from our own practice experiences, discussions with practitioners in social work agencies, and information provided by students in field work placements.

Chapter 6 addresses the problems of single-parent families and the techniques used in treating this population. The stages through which the family passes in transition from two-parent to a one-parent family are discussed, together with specific strategies for intervention during the transition period.

Chapter 7 discusses cultural diversity in family treatment. A selected group of families from different cultures are presented, with emphasis on family organization and family relationships. Effective techniques are also discussed, and practitioners are advised to be aware of the traditional values of the family undergoing treatment.

Chapter 8 focuses on the shifting roles of adult children and their aging parents, as well as the difficulties encountered when adult children must take a major role in decision making relative to the welfare of their parents. We look at existing attitudes toward the older members of society and the process of aging as conceptualized in theory. The significance of earlier parent-child relationships and lifestyles of the parents is discussed, and problems encountered in engaging the family that is composed of adult children and their parents are explored. The impact of role reversal, spouse-parent relationships, and adult sibling relationships and how to deal with them are also examined.

Chapter 9 presented a contemporary view of societal attitudes toward homosexuality, as exemplified in gay and lesbian relationships and activities. Attention is focused on both the difficulty experienced by this group in finding a comfortable place in society and the responsibility of professionals in working with gay and lesbian couples and families. Effective intervention strategies under different circumstances are also discussed.

Chapter 10 addresses the problems of poverty families and the techniques for treating this population in contemporary society. The impact of external systems in shaping the structure and functioning of these families' needs is emphasized. The uniqueness of this type of family in relation to communication, rules, and expectations is highlighted. Procedures for intervening with the problem poverty family are discussed, with emphasis on the value of home visits, working with extended family members, and maintaining a suitable climate for effective intervention.

Chapter 11 discusses mental illness in the family and the experiences of family members in coping with this problem. The use of a psychoeducational approach in treating family and patient is introduced and the role of the social worker as the therapist is explained.

Chapter 12 focuses on AIDS and other terminal illnesses. Different classes of chronic illness are identified, but AIDS and its sources of infection are highlighted. The phases of treatment of the family with a member who has AIDS are explained and the necessary preparation by the therapist is described.

Chapter 13 is concerned with the treatment of families involved in cases of child abuse and other family violence. We develop an understanding of the abusing parent and of the necessity of addressing the unmet needs of the parents who abuse their children. We note the importance of establishing a relationship between worker and parents that attends less to placing blame for the abuse than on assisting change, as well as involving the abused child in treatment. Attention is drawn to violence that may be occurring among other members of the family, especially the parents, and the importance of attending to that as well.

Chapter 14 describes treatment of families with alcohol- and other substance-abusing members. Much attention is focused on the alcoholism of the adult male. Treatment procedures for alcoholic women and substance-abusing children are also introduced.

Chapter 15 is focused on the family as it struggles through the process of dissolution, culminating in divorce. The phases of family dissolution and the impact of social forces on the breakup of the family are discussed. A variety of issues that must be addressed by both family members and social workers engaged by them in effecting change are also presented.

Chapter 16 is concerned with remarriage after divorce or widowhood and the adjustment of the reconstituted family that is created by this union. The reconstituted family is viewed from a systems perspective, and various family patterns are discussed. The problems that reconstituted families are likely to encounter, the adjustments necessary for satisfactory functioning, and some suggestions for treatment are included in this chapter.

CHAPTER 6

Therapy with Single-Parent Families

For more than two decades, the number of families headed by one parent, usually referred to as single-parent families, has increased dramatically. Many reasons have been given for the increase in this form of family organization, including the changing view toward marriage and divorce. For example, cohabitation of male and female partners without a legally sanctioned marriage and the bearing of children by single women no longer draw the condemnation of society that was once all but assured. Similarly, divorce is sought and received by legally married couples at an unprecedented rate—and without the disapproval such action would have drawn in the not too distant past. And the bearing of children by unmarried women and adolescent girls, who are faced with the necessity of functioning as single parents, is a fairly common occurrence. Whether we accept these actions as causative factors or reject them as too simplistic, the family headed by one adult or adolescent female is frequently encountered by professionals who provide services to families.

Because the status of single-parent family is acquired in a variety of ways, it may present different sets of problems. A family headed by one parent may be the result of a divorce; the death of one parent; desertion or disappearance of a parent; or the birth of a child to an unmarried adult or adolescent. The head of the family in each of these situations is usually a female; however, this is not always the case. Included in the one-parent family organization is a relatively new component, the single-parent father. The number of fathers raising children alone has increased in recent years. Some of the increase is believed to be due to the women's movement, which has enabled many women to achieve social and economic benefits commensurate with those available to men. This provides women with ways to define themselves in roles outside the home, unrelated to raising children (Greif, 1986). These advances sometimes place mothers in a more favorable position than fathers to provide economic support for the children at the time of divorce. It is possible, in some cases, that this might impact the courts' decisions in favor of fathers who petition for custody of children. Of course, this is not the only reason fathers receive custody. It is awarded for other reasons, including mutual consent of both parents.

In spite of the growing number of one-parent families, the literature does not reflect the same therapeutic attention to this group as that given to the two-parent family. This chapter will present some of the characteristics of single-parent families, a way of assessing the problems they present, and some strategies for intervention.

FAMILIES IN TRANSITION

Divorce

The breaking up of a family brings many different reactions from those involved. When a one-parent family is created by divorce, one of the spouses may not be willing to give up the relationship and for this reason may engage the other in a long and bitter struggle. In other cases, parents may agree to divorce but battle long and seriously over custody of children and the division of property (Morawetz and Walker, 1984). Such behavior on the part of parents usually impacts heavily on the children and frequently results in feelings of blame for the parents' divorce. While the granting of divorce through the court legally terminates the marital relationship, this may not be an accomplished fact. Symptomatic behavior of a child may be indicative of the parents' desire to continue the relationship. This is present in the situation in which divorced parents seem always to find a reason to remain involved around some aspect of a child's behavior or about what a child needs from the noncustodial parent. For example, a mother may express her inability to cope with her son's behavior and ask her divorced husband to visit and discipline the boy, which continues a relationship between the parents. Such behavior usually results from an underlying inability to achieve emotional separation due to feelings of guilt and a need to atone for past mistakes.

Death of a Spouse

Single-parent status that results from the death of a spouse often brings forth a different reaction than in the case of a couple who obtains a divorce. The surviving spouse may need to immortalize the deceased spouse, especially when a happy marriage is terminated by death. This may be realized through a child who is seen as the embodiment of the deceased parent. A child is usually chosen for this role because of his or her similarities to the deceased parent—such as physical appearance, patterns of speech, or mannerisms (Morawetz and Walker, 1984). If the surviving parent is able to accept the child's own unique qualities and characteristics as different from the deceased parent's, this role can be a positive one for the child. However, a negative influence can occur if the parent is more concerned with maintaining the memory of the departed spouse than supporting the growth and development of the child. Professionals working with single-parent families caused by the death of a spouse should be alert for any inappropriate use of children in perpetuating the memory of the deceased. When this is discovered; immediate action should be taken to help the surviving spouse work through feelings of loss in ways other than through the child.

Economic Hardship

Economic hardship is frequently experienced by the single-parent family. This is especially so with female-headed families in the early stages of transition. In an increasing number of cases, the financial well-being of the family is tied to the earnings of both parents. And when one parent leaves the home, family income can be seriously diminished. A lack of financial resources can cause a ripple effect with regard to meeting the needs of family members. For example, a custodial parent's inability to provide a child with the necessary resources to continue participating in activities with peers or to purchase clothing in the manner previously experienced can seriously impact the child's feeling of self-esteem. This loss of self-esteem may be reflected in withdrawal behavior, diminished school performance, or disruptive behavior at school and in the home.

Involvement of Grandparents

A lack of sufficient financial resources can also force a single parent, most of whom are women, to return to her family of origin. Although well intentioned, this can lead to additional problems if the grandparents see the mother's return with her children as a sign of weakness and relate to the mother as incapable of carrying adult responsibility. A more wide-ranging problem is also likely if the grandmother assumes control over the mother and her children by giving advice as to how the children should be raised and insisting they obey her rules rather than those established by the children's mother. If the mother has failed to achieve a sufficient level of separateness from the grandmother, she will be unable to contradict her wishes and may choose indirect ways of dealing with this problem. One way the mother might choose to deal with the problem is by joining with the children against the grandmother. While this may sabotage the grandmother's effort to exert control, the children will likely realize the existing conflict between mother and grandmother and become confused as to whom they should obey. In such cases, children may act out in inappropriate ways, which further complicates the problem.

Children as a Burden

In other situations, the dissolution of a marriage may force a mother who has functioned primarily as a homemaker to enter the workplace in order to provide for the family. If she is unable to let go of self-pity and anger over the circumstances of her life, the children's presence may be experienced as a burden. In this case, any effort on the part of children to make the mother's life more bearable may be perceived as an intrusion, and any request from them is likely to be resented (Morawetz and Walker, 1984). When a child's request is met with parental resentment, the results are usually negative. The child may turn to some form of maladaptive behavior, such as running away from home or joining a gang, as a way of expressing his or her discomfort.

Positive and Negative Roles for Children

It should be noted not all single parents are consumed by self-pity and anger over the loss of a spouse—in which case children may be viewed in a more positive light. For example, when children are not perceived as a burden, their effort to assist the custodial parent is likely to be accepted and in some cases rewarded. Consider the case of an older child who is able to help care for younger siblings. The reward for this activity may be elevation to an adult role in the single-parent family system, which in some ways replaces the noncustodial parent. While a new division of labor is necessary in moving from a two-parent to a one-parent family, fulfilling the role of the absent parent must be handled with care. For example, if a child is given added responsibility to compensate for the absence of a parent as a temporary measure and is removed from this position and allowed to return to childhood activities commensurate with his or her age, it is unlikely that the experience will be seriously damaging. However, if such added responsibility becomes permanent and the child perceives the custodial parent as more needy than himself or herself and moves beyond the caretaker role within the home to confront and respond to problems experienced by the parent from the outside world, the role becomes that of a "parental child." In this case, we see a child who has abandoned his or her youth to become prematurely sophisticated, and overly responsible; who lacks interest in participating in age-appropriate activities and is alienated from peers by this lack of participation. The power of a parental child may also be seen in excessive efforts to control the behavior of siblings and, in some cases, the behavior of the parent with regard to social activities, such as going out with friends and dating (Morawetz and Walker, 1984). Helping professionals will find it very difficult for the parental child to give up the status and power of this position. However, immediate attention should be directed toward decreasing the responsibility of the parental child by returning the parent to the appropriate role of authority and the child to normal association with peers.

Unresolved Mourning

The problem of unresolved mourning in a single-parent families is reported by Fulmer (1983). While this is experienced by many families in transition from a two-parent family to a one-parent family, he found this to be especially noticeable in the low-income family. Negative pressures such as unemployment, crime, and accidents within the environment of the low-income single-parent family are experienced with such frequency and intensity that the occasions to mourn are far greater than in other families. The frequency of this occurrence tends to deplete the capacity to mourn losses, and this unresolved mourning can lead to depression (Fulmer, 1987).

Adolescent Single Parents

The adolescent single parent presents a somewhat different picture than the adult single parent. She is almost always still living with her parents and is not faced with problems of divorce or the need to mourn the loss of a husband. Most of her problems are family related, as reflected in the interaction she has with her family en route to a single parenthood. A state of crisis is precipitated by the adolescent's pregnancy. Intense emotion and conflict will usually surface around this experience, and several solutions to the problems brought on by the pregnancy are likely to be considered, including the possibility of abortion. As the state of crisis gradually subsides and the family becomes more accepting of the pending birth of the child, a more positive attitude will follow. Living arrangements, care for the baby, financial support, and continuing the adolescent's education become the primary focus of attention (Jemail and Nathanson, 1987). As a result of this positive attitude, the adolescent becomes closer to the family and spends more time at home and less time with peers. This change of behavior is rewarded by the family, who sees her as more mature, affectionate, and understanding.

Following the birth of the child, conflict around issues of child care are likely to resurface as efforts are undertaken to determine who is responsible for what care. The role of the adolescent single parent is also further clarified. If the family is functioning well, nurturance of the child becomes their primary concern. However, if the family is not functioning well, sometimes family members may detour negative feelings through their interaction with the child (Jemail and Nathanson, 1987). In this case, professional help is usually required to return the family to an acceptable level of functioning.

When working with adolescent single parents and their families, Weltner (1986) suggests that professionals will be well advised to use interventions that match the families' particular level of functioning. For example, sometimes a family has difficulty in managing resources, in which case it is unlikely that the basic needs (food, shelter, medical care, etc.) of the adolescent mother and the nurturance needs of her child will be met. The helping professional must then determine who in the existing social network has resources and can assume the executive role in meeting these needs. If no one in the client's social network can meet this requirement, it may be necessary in some situations to seek shelter in a public-supported facility until assistance can be mobilized.

In another situation, the family may be able to meet basic needs, but unable to provide structure and the necessary limits. Enabling efforts in this case should focus on clarifying expectations. This might include assigning specific tasks to each family member and assessing the adolescent's developmental level as it relates to her need for structure, limits, and safety. The family should be organized around these needs, which will allow the adolescent single parent to continue her education and contacts with friends.

When the family provides most of what is required to nurture and protect the adolescent single parent and her child but differences and dissatisfactions still exist, professionals should examine the boundary structure within the family. If boundaries are blurred, are too rigid, or show signs of boundary violations, interventions should focus on defending individual and subsystem boundaries and developing generational boundaries where indicated (Weltner, 1982).

PHASES OF ADJUSTMENT

The single-parent family will usually pass through a number of pre-dictable phases on the way to readjusting to its new status. Morawetz and Walker (1984) and Korittko (1991) have recognized these phases, and their work provides the basis for our discussion of the single-parent family's adjustment after the departure of one parent. While all families may not experience the phases of adjustment in sequential order as we will discuss them, an awareness of the process through which the single-parent family passes in regaining its equilibrium will serve as a useful framework through which to view it in preparation for intervention.

Reaction to Change Phase

This phase is characterized by ambivalence, confusion, anxiety, and sometimes a sense of rage and a feeling of being unable to cope with the experiences brought on by the change in family status. The way the family reacts depends on many things, including the organization of the family system and the circumstances under which the change in family status takes place. In some families, divorce comes after a long period of estrangement, and both parents are in agreement that ending the marital relationship is preferable to continuing an unsatisfactory existence. In this case, they are likely to be more able to help their children cope with the anxiety associated with the breakup of the family than parents who reach divorce with one partner feeling he or she is being unfairly rejected or abandoned. Morawetz and Walker (1984) suggest that children whose parents divorce under this circumstance may feel intense anxiety about the parents' welfare and torn by the demand of one parent that the child share his or her anger at the other parent. The sudden death of a parent may also leave children without assurance that their lives contain the necessary order and stability to make them feel secure.

When help is sought during the reaction to change phase, the presenting problem is usually a child who is difficult to control and likely to be engaged in antisocial or delinquent behavior. The parent who owns the problem and seeks help is most likely overwhelmed by the responsibilities inherited as the result of single parenthood and is experiencing feelings of despair and an inability to cope with the demands of daily life. It is not unusual for parents to hope for a magical solution and enter therapy expecting specific concrete advice that will resolve their problems and restore a sense of well-being to their lives. Some may even hope for a return of the departed spouse or expect the therapist to rescue them from their unbearable pain. Professional helpers must be careful not to be triangled into the family as a permanent stabilizer. While the role of stabilizer may bring temporary relief and meet the parent's expectation for the moment, it will succeed only in stabilizing the system without changing it. This is not to say the therapist should never join the family as a temporary stabilizing measure. Such action is sometimes necessary as a bridge to the ultimate goal of changing the family system. However, once the family has achieved a more functional alignment, the therapist should relinquish the role of temporary stabilizer.

Therapeutic intervention in the reaction to change phase of the single-parent family should focus on helping the family put the issues that led to the change in family status into proper perspective. This might require the therapist to help the family reach a better understanding of a troubled marital relationship, which sometimes includes extended family involvement and many separations before divorce. In this phase the single parent is also likely to experience feelings of uncertainty about managing the family without the ex-spouse. The therapist should focus on reducing feelings of incompetence in the custodial parent as he or she attempts to cope with the responsibilities of the single-parent role.

Mourning the losses resulting from divorce or death of a parent is usually incomplete at this point, and help with the process of mourning should be provided to various family members. This includes helping them express different feelings. For example, children may be helped to express their feelings about the loss of the absent parent. In the case of a parent's death, where issues around the illness and death have been suppressed, the therapist may have to help all family members express their repressed emotions before a functional readjustment of the family system can be realized.

Reordering of Priorities Phase

The second phase of adjustment of the single-parent family reflects the realignments that occur as family members try to accept and adjust to a number of changes brought on by the absence of a parent. Change in the family's economic status, which often occurs, may have wide implications for reordering priorities. For example, the family may be forced to move to less expensive living quarters, which will usually be in a new neighborhood. This requires adjustment to a different environment, and school-age children must adjust to a new school situation. At the same time, the social life of the custodial parent is likely to change. In many cases, relationships that are enjoyed by married couples are no

longer available after divorce or death of a spouse. The loss of these relationships can happen for different reasons. Sometimes when there are
no longer both spouses to relate to, socializing can become somewhat
awkward for both other married couples and the single parent. Some
friends may feel uncomfortable about continuing the relationship after
a divorce for fear it would give the impression of taking the side of one
partner and being against the other. Sometimes the single parent may
also be perceived by married couples as a threat to their marital relationship, which is not conducive to continuing social contacts. When
single-parent status results from the death of a spouse, the remaining
spouse may withdraw from previously established social contacts—a
way of letting go of the past and making a new beginning. Associating
with new friends is usually less likely to remind the single parent of the
loss of his or her spouse which, in turn, may help with the adjustment to
the new status of the family system.

Children may experience a decrease in physical and emotional access to their parents after divorce. Physical access is likely to be limited
to weekends with the noncustodial parent. In the case of the custodial
parent, usually the mother, full-time employment may leave her with
less than sufficient time to meet the emotional needs of her children.
Sometimes this situation can be alleviated by a change in the management of time. This change may require the parent to give up some of
his/her tasks within the home and assign them to children who are capable of performing the task involved. It might also be necessary to advise the care-giving/wage-earning parent who is concerned about the
needs of the children that it is all right to give some responsibility to
them while making himself or herself more available for emotional and
informational support.

The reordering of priorities phase is a very demanding period during
which the family is faced with the need to accept the permanent nature
of a reality that is often painful and unwanted. The problems that
emerge often reflect anger and violence expressed in delinquent acts by
children. It is not unusual for the family to deny the connection between
the new single-parent family status and the acting out behavior of children. Although such a connection may be obvious to the professional
helper, it is usually most productive at this stage of family adjustment to
focus on the problem as explained by the family instead of attempting to
address their resistance in a direct manner (Morawetz and Walker, 1984).

Korittko (1991) also found that dysfunctional triads within the family tend to surface more clearly at this time, and he believes these triads
should be dealt with in the therapeutic encounter. For example, he

suggests that people who are assisting the family such as grandparents, friends, and other relatives be brought into the therapy sessions. Here the relationships between the custodial parent, the children, and the third person involved in the dysfunctional triad should become the focus of intervention.

The Settling Down Phase

During this phase, many things are involved. If the custodial parent has been holding on to the possibility that reconciliation might be possible, this is given up. This way of thinking is replaced by acceptance of the fact that the single parent must learn ways to interact with the ex-spouse in the best interest of the children. Reaching an agreement to continue sharing responsibility for the children is usually of primary concern. If the ex-spouse is unwilling to continue in the role of a responsible parent, the custodial parent must decide to carry most of the responsibility or turn to others for help.

This is also the time at which children learn to live without the absent parent or accustom themselves to dealing with two parents in separate households. The family is ready to move toward establishing a new social life. The single parent may begin to seek social situations that will provide the opportunity to meet and interact with members of the opposite sex, which includes dating and in some cases contemplation of remarriage. However, the resumption of such activity by the parent may come into conflict with the children. The younger child may see the parent's dating as reducing his or her availability at a time when it is most needed or as an act of disloyalty to the noncustodial parent (Morawetz and Walker, 1984). The child's sense of responsibility for protecting the parent from further hurt is also likely to surface. It may take the form of trying to become an uninvited chaperon or behaving in other ways that will interfere with the development of the relationship.

The single-parent family does not emerge from this phase as a problem-free system. Yet it is a time at which family members strive to achieve a balance in relating and sufficient feeling of security to move in and out of the family system without creating unmanageable problems (Korittko, 1991). The problems that surface in this phase of adjustment are likely to reflect the family's fears resulting from threats to this delicate balance. Intervention should be concerned with supporting the balance in the family system and providing for differentiation among its members (Korittko, 1991).

Separation and Gaining Independence Phase

The separation and gaining independence phase usually signals the successful separation of children from parents and parents from children. The child establishes his or her own life and faces the possibility of a different relationship with the single parent who must let go of the parent-child relationship that previously existed. While emergence from this phase usually indicates a more adequately functioning single-parent family, separation is not always a smooth process. The process itself unbalances the family system, and a new balance must be found. A positive outcome will reflect the maturity of the child and the confidence of the parent in managing a life of new relationships. Nevertheless, some children may find it difficult to separate from a single parent and, as a result, will engage in behavior that will delay the separation and demand active involvement between parent and child. Such behavior as teenage pregnancy and alcohol and drug abuse may surface during this phase of single-parent family adjustment. Intervention should focus on the intense feeling that exists between parent and child as well as the confusion and ambivalence shared by both (Korittko, 1991).

The preceding framework can be useful in viewing single-parent families who are seeking adjustment to their new status. However, therapists should never overlook the importance of the individual makeup of each family, its history, and its prevailing symptoms.

BEGINNING WITH THE FAMILY

The single-parent family seeks help in the same manner and for many of the same reasons as the two-parent family. Contact with the therapist is usually initiated by the parent as a result of some type of disruption in the way the family wishes to present itself to the outside world, or because someone in the outside world expects a different presentation than that which is given by the family. The initial contact may come because (1) the mother no longer feels able to manage a child's inappropriate behavior, (2) the school pressures the mother to seek help because the child's adjustment within the school is unsatisfactory, or (3) the child's behavior may have brought him or her into contact with law enforcement agents and the parent must get help if the child is to remain in the home. The parent may also initiate contact with the therapist to get help for herself or himself. However, this is far less frequent than seeking help around difficulties created by a child.

In most cases, the first therapeutic encounter is likely to be by telephone, at which time the therapist should obtain certain factual information. Depending upon the therapist's decision, this information may be minimal or rather extensive. If only limited information is sought, the following should be included: a brief statement of the problem as seen by the caller, address, telephone number, composition of the family, information regarding eligibility (if relevant), time and place of first appointment, and who is to be present for the first interview. In case more extensive information is desired, the family problem should be explored in more depth, including its duration and the factors leading up to it; what the caller sees as causing the problem; and the number of family members living in the home and significant members who live elsewhere. Information about the ex-spouse's involvement with the family is also important. If there is active involvement, has he or she been informed of the decision to seek help and is he or she in agreement with this decision?

Most family therapists like to see all family members who live together for the initial interview. However, exceptions are not uncommon and may be made in cases where the therapist determines mitigating circumstances that warrant seeing only a part of the family, and is of the opinion that a meaningful beginning can be made by seeing only these members. Such a case arises for the therapist when planning the first interview with a one-parent family that reached this status by separation or divorce. Here, it is useful to have the parent seeking treatment comment on whether or not the absent parent should come to the first interview. If this (custodial) parent is opposed to having the ex-spouse attend, and it appears that his or her presence will make for a difficult beginning, exclusion from the first interview is appropriate. The noncustodial parent might be seen alone or with the children in a later interview (Morawitz and Walker, 1984).

The first interview with a single-parent family is not unlike the first interview with a two-parent family. In both interviews, the social worker concentrates on the comfort of the family and the involvement of each member in discussing family problem. Careful attention is given to what is reported, how it is reported, and who makes the report. It is also important to look for emotional closeness and distance among family members as well as communication patterns, especially how children respond in the interview and how the parent reacts to their participation. The first interview usually proceeds along the lines of specific stages. During each stage, the social worker focuses on developing information in sequence to be used later in formulating tentative hypotheses and a working plan for involving the single-parent family in a therapeutic relationship. (For details of the stages of the first interview, see Chapter 5.)

As the social worker or other professional engages the family in a continuing relationship, new information will develop. This information may result in the need to involve the extended family and/or the noncustodial parent. In some cases, meeting with individual family members may also be appropriately undertaken. However, meeting separately with individual family members must always be undertaken with a great deal of care in order to maintain the proper balance in the therapeutic relationship.

THERAPEUTIC INTERVENTION

After the first interview with the single-parent family, the way in which the therapist proceeds is determined by the existing problems. Also, new problems are likely to surface as interviews continue, and new goals must be established and new interventions undertaken (Haley, 1976). The following are some problem areas that may surface in work with single-parent families, as well as some ways to help family members move to a more effective level of functioning.

Unresolved Mourning

One of the problems frequently seen in work with single-parent families is unresolved mourning. In this area, Fulmer (1987) suggests the necessity of connecting the family's symptoms to the unresolved mourning in a specific way. When the parent seeking help is a mother who has not mourned the loss of her deceased husband, the therapist may engage her in discussing memories of her husband and looking at pictures of him. The mother may also be given an assignment to talk with someone who knew her husband or bring relatives who knew him into a therapy session (p. 34).

If children have not mourned their losses, once the mother has overcome her resistance to mourning she will be in a better position to help them. The therapist may then help her become more sensitive to the children's needs and encourage her to talk with them about their feelings of loss and share with them memories of the deceased husband/father (Fulmer, 1987, p. 35). Nevertheless, mourning alone is usually not enough to bring complete relief of family symptoms. In addition to unresolved mourning, these symptoms have other contributing causes that must be considered. For example, if depression is experienced, medication is likely to be required; delinquent behavior might be helped by strengthening the executive functioning of the parent as head of the family; and if drug abuse is involved, a period of detoxification and group treatment will be needed. These and other measures may be required to restore the troubled single-parent family to effective functioning.

Boundary Problems

Within the family system there is a set of rules that define who participates in family transactions and how they will participate (Minuchin, 1974). These rules form a boundary around each family subsystem that protects subsystem integrity and maintains differentiation between the systems. One of the problems frequently encountered with families in transition is some type of boundary disruption. This is especially noticeable in the single-parent family where one parent is absent and the formation of a new family structure is required. Consider the boundary disruption that might occur when the custodial parent, usually the mother, is forced to return to her family of origin because of insufficient financial resources. It is not unusual for the grandmother to violate the boundary of the single-parent family by becoming overinvolved with the functioning of both her daughter and grandchildren. If the mother-grandmother relationship is satisfactory, this may happen because of the grandmother's desire to be helpful to her struggling daughter. When the relationship is less than satisfactory, the grandmother may see her daughter's return as her inability to handle her own problems and may use this opportunity to point up the daughter's inadequacy as a mother and relate to her as someone who needs guidance in performing adult roles. This is likely to cause disagreement between mother and daughter regarding the children's behavior and the daughter's child-rearing capabilities. This may very well result in a generational boundary violation, with the single parent joining with her children against the grandmother. The goal of therapy in this situation is to establish appropriate boundaries between generations and individuals. Since the children will experience confusion regarding who is in charge of the family and whose wishes they should obey, it is usually a good idea to see the single parent and the children together in order to reestablish the appropriate parental hierarchy. The grandparent(s) may be seen in separate interviews while this is being accomplished to help them accept the daughter's ability to be a parent to the children.

A different kind of boundary problem will occur when the single parent lacks validation from other adults and turns completely to a child for this validation and support. In this case, the boundary between parent and child is likely to become enmeshed. An enmeshed (diffuse) boundary is conducive to excessive closeness between parent and child and at the extreme will no longer differentiate separate functioning. With the parent seeking support from the child regarding the ability to function as a parent, the child will perceive the parent's search for help and most likely move into an adult role in relation to the family's executive functioning.

Therapeutic intervention in this situation will require the development of appropriate roles and tasks for the child who has assumed adult responsibility. This may include having other children take on some of the responsibilities this child has previously assumed while he or she engages more in age-appropriate behaviors (Weltner, 1982). These interventive measures will help move the child from the diffuse boundary shared with the parent and pave the way for restoration of the hierarchial structure of the family. A support group for the parent will also be useful in strengthening his or her feeling of competence in carrying out the executive functions of the family.

The necessity of maintaining appropriate boundaries is also emphasized by Greif (1986, 1987), who researched the experiences of custodial fathers. He found that in accepting this new role single-parent fathers sometimes cease to be parents and focus more on becoming a friend to the children. He suggested this might reflect the father's feeling of insecurity about how to react in the single-parent role. As a result, he may become more lenient and the boundary between father and children may become too permeable, in which case he is unable to provide a balanced family structure. In other situations the single-parent father may establish a rigid boundary between himself and the children by setting rules and expectations that severely limit a child's ability to express himself or herself. A reconstruction of appropriate boundaries is the obvious goal of intervention of these cases. However, this must be done with care in order to prevent increasing the father's feelings of insecurity in his role as custodial parent. Intervention with the father should be undertaken with a complementary approach to the children. For example, children may be asked to accept the new status of single-parent family by agreeing to do age-appropriate chores around the house, while, at the same time, the father is being helped to establish a clear boundary between himself and the children (Greif, 1987). Maintaining appropriate boundaries is also important when the father begins to date. The presence of a permeable boundary can control excessive interference into the father's dating by the children, but it allows them to discuss this and other social issues.

TECHNIQUES

There are many intervention techniques that can be used in helping single-parent families cope with families brought on by a change in family status, as demonstrated by the following examples.

Reversals

"A reversal is an intervention in which the therapist directs someone in the family to reverse (his) her attitude or behavior around a crucial issue in the hope that it will elicit a paradoxical response from another family member" (Minuchin and Fishman, 1981, p. 248). This technique is recommended when one family member is willing to cooperate and follow direct advice while another member is not. When reversals are given, the person who is the object of change should not be present, as success depends on the element of surprise, which causes a spontaneous reaction to an unexpected change of attitude (p. 248). Reversals can be used effectively in helping single-parent families handle a number of problems. For example, a 14-year-old girl complained that her mother never let her make any decisions. The mother established the rules her daughter was to follow and watched over her so closely that she rebelled and withdrew from her mother. The mother also complained that her daughter wanted to behave like an adult but was much too young for this and needed the control she provided. She was firmly convinced that the control she exercised over her daughter was appropriate and resisted all efforts to change even the smallest detail of the way she related to her daughter. The therapist told the daughter she should not withdraw from her mother but rather should turn to her for more advice. She agreed and did nothing without asking her mother for advice. The daughter's many requests soon overwhelmed her mother, who gradually retreated from her previous position.

Minuchin and Fishman (1981) report their work using reversal with a 13-year-old boy who was failing his school work as a reaction to constant pressure from his parents. The parents were instructed to tell the boy they were not really so concerned about his grades anymore. If he failed and had to stay home and attend summer school, that would be all right because they would then be able to watch over him all summer and would at least know he was safe (p. 248). The unexpected reversal of the parent's attitude produced a spontaneous reaction from the boy. His grades improved and the parents were pleased with the results.

The successful use of reversals is dependent upon the willingness of one segment of the family to reverse a position that will affect another segment of the family, as indicated by the 14-year-old girl and the parents of the 13-year-old boy.

Reframing or Relabeling

When the therapist uses reframing or relabeling, he or she is attempting to change the way the family conceptualizes the situation they are experiencing. If this is successful, the meaning attributed to the situation is changed and so are its consequences (Horne and Passmore, 1991). When a family enters treatment, it brings its own explanation of the problem it hopes to eliminate.

When a single-parent mother with her son and daughter were seen together for the first interview, she explained that the difficulty they faced was caused by the boy's rebellious behavior and his unwillingness to attend school. She felt she was also losing control of her daughter, whom she thought was influenced by her son's behavior. The boy thought his mother was too demanding and he could never please her regardless of how hard he tried. After much discussion, the therapist stated that he saw a somewhat different picture emerging. The mother made all the rules that governed the family, and when the children tried to participate they were dismissed by the mother as too young to understand what was best for themselves and the family. In other words, everything had to be done her way. The behavior the mother defined as being out of control was the only way the children knew to bring the mother's attention to their needs. Instead of acting to defy their mother, they were trying to communicate with her in a way that she could not understand. The therapist then suggested that it might be helpful if family members could listen to each other and try to understand what each one wanted from the other. This transformed the problem from a mother struggling to deal with two adolescent children whose only purpose was to defy her, to a problem of a family with dysfunctional rules and boundary difficulties affecting the behavior of all family subsystems.

There are many other problems encountered and many other interventions that can be used effectively in working with single-parent families. All interventions are undertaken with the hope of changing the behavioral sequences that support the presenting problem. When this occurs, the protective function performed by the problem is no longer necessary for the family system, as its members learn new ways of relating to each other.

SUMMARY

The single-parent family, except in the case of the unmarried mother, must give up a parent who was once an integral part of the family and adjust to a new life without this family member. The family therapist should have knowledge of the transitional stages through which the single-parent family passes and the behavior its members are likely to display. It should also be remembered when interacting with this family that there is a member who is no longer functioning in the normal capacity of parent but may be having a significant impact on the current functioning of the family. Extrafamilial support, including extended family, is important in the early life cycle of the single-parent family. The losses experienced and the changes that occur in restructuring the family often result in scapegoating or overreliance on a child who may abandon normal childhood activities and assume the role of an adult. These and other issues will confront the therapist who intervenes with the single-parent family. A family system approach that includes establishing appropriate boundaries around individuals and subsystems will be beneficial in solving family problems.

REFERENCES

Fulmer, Richard H. 1983. "A Structural Approach to Unresolved Mourning in Single-Parent Family Systems." *Journal of Marital and Family Therapy* 9(3): 259–68.

_____. 1987. "Special Problems of Mourning in Low-Income Single-Parent Families." *Family Therapy Collection* 23:19–37.

Greif, Geoffrey L. 1986. "Clinical Work With The Single-Father Family: A Structural Approach." *International Journal of Family Psychiatry* 7(3):261–75.

_____. 1987. "A Longitudinal Examination of Single Custodial Fathers: Implications for Treatment." *American Journal of Family Therapy* 15:253–60.

Haley, Jay. 1976. *Problem Solving Therapy*. San Francisco: Jossey-Bass.

Horne, Arthur M., and Passmore, J. Lawrence. 1991. *Family Counseling and Therapy*, 2nd ed. Itasca, IL: F.E. Peacock Publishers.

Jemail, J.A., and Nathanson, M. 1987. "Adolescent Single-Parent Families." *Family Therapy Collection* 23:61–72.

Kissman, Kris. 1992. "Single Parenting: Interventions in the Transitional Stage." *Contemporary Family Therapy* 14(4):323–33.

Korittko, Alexander. 1991. "Family Therapy with One-Parent Families." *Contemporary Family Therapy* 13(6):625–40.

Minuchin, Salvador. 1974. *Families and Family Therapy*. Cambridge, MA: Harvard University Press.

Minuchin, Salvador, and Fishman, H. Charles. 1981. *Family Therapy Techniques*. Cambridge, MA: Harvard University Press.

Morawetz, Anita, and Walker, Gillian. 1984. *Brief Therapy with Single-Parent Families*. New York: Brunner/Mazel Publishers.

Weltner, J.S. 1982. "A Structural Approach to the Single-Parent Family." *Family Process* 21:203–10.

———. 1986. "A Matchmaker's Guide to Family Therapy." *Family Networker* 51–55.

Wescot, Mary E., and Dries, Robert. 1990. "Has Family Therapy Adapted to the Single-Parent Family?" *The American Journal of Family Therapy* 18(4):363–72.

CHAPTER **7**

Cultural Diversity in Family Treatment

Families who seek help from social workers and other professionals hold diverse group memberships. They bring unique cultural traits that contribute to individual and group identity. Knowledge of how each family communicates between its members and to the outside world, its belief system, and its values will provide clues about how family problems originate and also suggest pathways to possible resolution. The assessment of any family must include gathering sufficient information about these three areas, which shape family interactional patterns, to enable the therapist to put the problem into proper perspective and help the family begin to view it in a different way. The primary objective of the therapeutic encounter with families is to alter existing interactional patterns in such a way as to improve family functioning.

If the goal of changing families is to be realized, the therapist must know something of the family's value orientation—which is necessary in understanding the meaning of the family's behavior. This is important because family members from different backgrounds may manifest the same behavior for very different reasons. Consider the family member who is reluctant to express himself or herself freely when interacting with the therapist. For the Asian client, it might be the result of a traditional reticence in sharing feelings with someone outside of the family. The African American family member who displays the same behavior will most likely not be adhering to cultural values at all, but will be reacting to a lack of trust in the therapist, who represents the majority controlled institutional structure of contemporary society. American helping professionals are likely to have a negative perception of a lack of eye contact on the part of the client. This could be a serious misreading of behavior if the client is a Puerto Rican female who has probably been taught to lower her eyes and avoid eye contact with others. Jewish clients often inquire about the therapist's qualifications, which satisfies their need for reassurance but will likely be perceived by some therapists as an affront to their knowledge as a professional. Physical punishment is also commonly used by many families from different cultural environments in disciplining their children. When this is encountered by the American therapist, it may be seen as child abuse. There are many other similar examples where the same behavior has an entirely different meaning to different families. As a result, the therapist will be well advised to carefully consider the family's cultural background when interpreting behaviors encountered in treatment (McGoldrick et al., 1982).

In this chapter we will pay special attention to three family groups, the African American family, the Asian family, and the Hispanic/Latino family. We realize that, by concentrating on these three groups, we are omitting a large segment of the families seen in therapy. However, much of what we will discuss is applicable to a wide range of families. Additional families and their problems are presented in other chapters throughout this book.

THE AFRICAN AMERICAN FAMILY

The contemporary African American family is viewed as a social system that interacts with a number of other systems. It adheres to a class structure in the same manner as other racial and ethnic groups. Family structure is affected by conditions existing in the wider social environment and is influenced by the efforts of family members to meet their needs and the demands of society.

The African American family may be viewed as occupying three classes across the socioeconomic spectrum and exemplifying behavior in keeping with the class occupied. For example, the middle-class African American family is positioned between a small upper class and a larger low-income group. Unlike the middle- and low-income groups, the upper-class African American family is not likely to seek help from a social work agency. The social work agency is the medium through which social workers usually provide services to families and is the focus of our discussion. The needs and the helping process regarding low-income families, including African Americans, are addressed in another chapter in this book. In other words, the upper class is not likely to use the services we will discuss, and the low-income group's use of services is described elsewhere in our discussions. Therefore, we have chosen here to focus our discussion primarily on the middle-class African American family, which is likely to seek relief from family problems through the use of a social work agency.

Family Structure and Functioning

When using a social systems approach to provide an appropriate framework within which to assess family functioning, it is necessary to consider the totality of interactions and interdependencies that influence the family's behavior. In keeping with this approach, this chapter views the middle-class African American family as a system composed of subsystems. The family itself is seen as a subsystem within the broader network of the African American community and wider society.

The typical middle-class African American family of today consists of two parents and two or three children sharing the same household. The husband-father carries the primary provider role for the family, although it is likely that the wife-mother also is employed. The father is very much involved in the rearing of children, and the household usually does not include extended-family members.

As a social system, the African American family interacts with and is influenced by both the African American community and the wider society. These two systems have different expectations, and different behaviors are required in order to succeed and earn status. The reference group in the wider society is the conjugal white family, usually of middle- to upper-middle-class status, and this status is determined by employment, education, and income. In the African American community, status is based more on consumption patterns and other visible achievements than on employment, education, and income. As a result, different lifestyles emerge in each situation. This difference in lifestyle between the African American community, in which these families are rooted psychologically, regardless of where they reside physically, and the wider society, in which they must also participate, places an extremely heavy demand on the family in its effort to adapt to both systems. The situation also has tremendous impact on the socialization of African American children, whose parents must try to prepare them to deal successfully with both experiences. It is necessary for the African American family to incorporate the values of two different reference groups, with two distinct lifestyles, if its members are to participate successfully in the American dream and compete for the rewards available through this process. White families need not engage in this type of socialization process to prepare their children to function in society.

In the attempts of African American families to meet the requirements of the wider society while satisfying the needs of family members,
an interchange of customary roles is not uncommon. The widely accepted rule that the husband-father performs the instrumental functions
while the wife-mother carries out the expressive functions is not a sufficient conceptualization of the African American family to examine the
perceptions it holds and the manner in which it functions. It is well established that the wife-mother frequently plays a major role in the exe-
cution of instrumental functions, but it is not so well known that the
husband-father performs many expressive functions.

This pattern of functioning within the African American family is
tied to a history in which the African American female had greater access to the economic opportunity structure of society than the male.
Both partners generally accept this way of contributing to the well-being
of the family. We are not suggesting that instrumental and expressive
functions are necessarily mutually exclusive in any case, but the husband-father is likely to be much more involved in performing expressive
functions and the wife-mother in performing instrumental functions
than their white counterparts.

This departure from the widely accepted norm of family functioning
should not be interpreted as deviant behavior or an automatic source of
conflict in family relationships. However, social workers should take
into account the lifestyles that have emerged from the experience of this
group in America. Attempts to assess African American family functioning by using only the norms of the white family may result in something less than accurate measurement.

Couple Relationship

One of the keys to understanding family interactional patterns is knowledge of existing family relationships, such as those experienced between
couples. Catherall (1992) suggests that a holding function for one another's feelings is provided by all people in intimate relationships. This
includes being able to identify with another's feelings and understand
them but to refrain from acting on them. Emerging patterns and coping
styles in a couple's relationship should be given careful attention by
professionals, and this information can be helpful when reflected back to
the couple in a coherent way (Laveman and Borck, 1993).

Scanzoni (1971) believes that the relationship between husband and
wife can be thought of in terms of a reciprocal exchange of rule duties
and rights. The more fully the husband fulfills his chief role obligations
as provider, the more fully the wife is motivated to fulfill her chief

obligations as "expressive agent" or "socio-emotional hub" of the conjugal family (pp. 199–200).

This suggests that the relationship between a couple is significantly influenced by the rewards provided by the husband. Occupational status, education, and income are primary factors in the husband's ability to provide these rewards. Scanzoni also found that, among white families, the greater the husband's claim on these three status symbols, the more rewards he provided to his wife, and the more positively both husband and wife considered their primary relations. However, this was not the case with African American couples. An increase in these indicators of social position and the provision of greater rewards to the African American wife did not bring a corresponding increase in her positive perception of her relationship with her husband.

Scanzoni contends that the concept of relative deprivation may be responsible for this difference between the two groups. This concept is based on the fact that even though the African American family now has greater access to the opportunity structure and claims more rewards from it than ever before, the rewards are not equal to those received by white families of similar educational levels. At the same time that African American family rewards are increasing, the expectations of the family are increasingly based on the opportunity structure's standards of rewards to their white counterpart. As a result, there is an inevitable comparison between the lesser rewards they receive and the greater rewards received by whites, which produces a feeling of deprivation on the part of African Americans.

In connection with the idea of relative deprivation, we suggest the African American wife's failure to show an increase in positive feeling for her husband as a result of his earning of increased rewards is in no way an attempt on her part to punish him. Neither does it reflect a lack of appreciation for the increased rewards. Instead, the African American wife's expression is a reflection of her dissatisfaction with the opportunity structure's double standard of distributing rewards. In addition, there is an awareness on her part that the opportunity structure is controlled by whites, which is a strong reminder that the African American family is not in complete control of its middle-class status. Therefore, a certain tentativeness is associated with the increased rewards the husband provides, and the wife with a history filled with uncertainties does not allow herself to experience fully the rewards that can also be denied by powers beyond her control.

The African American wife is also supportive of her husband and ascribes to him the role of primary provider for the family. Her failure to increase or decrease expressive responses in direct proportion to the provision of status rewards is likely to be reassuring to her husband, who does not completely control the rewards he is able to provide. This also frees the husband from fluctuation in his wife's affections toward him. It follows, then, that the quality of the African American husband-wife relationship is not dependent upon the amount of status rewards he can provide. Therefore, social workers might find it useful in the intervention process to gain knowledge of the extent of mutuality in the perception of roles between the African American husband and wife, as well as the extent of satisfaction experienced in relation to their role performances.

With the entry of more and more women into the workplace, society now accepts this as a normal occurrence. However, it should be noted that most African American husbands have always accepted their wives' employment as normal and, in many cases, necessary. This acceptance is most likely a result of the long history of African American women having greater access than African American men to the existing economic opportunity structure. Nevertheless, it is customary for the African American wife to keep a low profile in relation to her working and performing instrumental functions within the family. It is probably fair to assume that both the wife's history of participation in the labor market and her de-emphasis of the role of her employment in family functioning are largely responsible for the absence of threat to the husband's provider role. Hence, her employment is likely to offer little threat to their relationship. While the possibility of conflict arising from the wife's employment should not be ignored in working with the family, it is not likely to be the primary source of disruption.

We also support the position of Hines and Boyd-Franklin (1982) and Pinderhughes (1986), who advise caution in assessing the wife's attitude toward the shortcomings of her husband. For example, the wife's vacillation with regard to her husband's exercising responsible behavior is not usually a reflection of her inability to be realistic and objective in matters pertaining to his performance. Instead, this failure to hold him strictly accountable most often indicates her identification with her husband's frustrations with society's denial of opportunities and rewards accorded his white counterpart. As a result, the wife may not always be firm in holding him to what might be viewed by the larger society as responsible behavior.

The distribution of power between the African American husband and wife is another key to understanding their relationship. The social worker intervening with the African American family can no longer approach the task with the traditional view of the family as a matriarchy.

Neither can the popular conceptualizations relative to the distribution of power and authority that exist within the white family be applied to the African American family. Contrary to the perception of the white wife relative to the rewards provided by her husband, the African American wife does not attribute more power and authority to her husband out of deference for his provision of increased reward. It should also be remembered that the African American family operates from an equalitarian power structure, which is to say that power and decision making tend to be shared by husband and wife (Mullings, 1985).

It is important that the relationship between African American couples be viewed within the context of their experiences as African Americans. Social workers and other professionals working with this family group should have some knowledge of this heritage. We also suggest that caution be exercised in drawing conclusions about couple relationships. This should not be based solely on variables known to influence the relationship of white couples. An exploration and differential evaluation of the specific attitudes of each African American couple toward their individual roles will enhance understanding of their conflict.

Socialization of Children

One of the primary functions of any family is the socialization of its children. Usually we think of this process as teaching the child values and expectations in keeping with the dominant society. While this is true for African American children, Spurlock (1983) suggests it is common for many African American parents to prepare their children for the possibility of rejection. And most African American children will at some time experience rejection based on their race.

African American parents also seem to be aware of the particular vicissitudes that may arise in their children's transactions across family boundaries, as a result of their being nonwhite and relatively disadvantaged. Consequently, parents try to communicate to children the values and specific role obligations that will enable them to cope with the greater stresses that inevitably face the members of African American families (Scanzoni, 1971, p. 82).

McAdoo (1974), who seems in general agreement with Scanzoni, suggests that the socialization of African American children requires them to become a part of the dominant culture while also internalizing the values of the African American community. This socialization process, which prepares the child to function successfully in two different social systems, places a heavy burden on the child, and its impact should be taken into consideration by social workers and others seeking to understand the child's behavior.

African American parents also expect their children to earn greater rewards from the opportunity structure than they themselves were able to achieve. This requires, among other things, holding on to middle-class status and taking advantage of opportunities to move up the socioeconomic ladder. One of the proven ways of socioeconomic advancement is education, which makes access to the opportunity structure less difficult. Parents, therefore, emphasize the need for their children to obtain education that prepares them for participation in the dominant culture with middle-class status. In many cases, these parents select the best schools for their children, sometimes at great personal sacrifice, in the hope of enhancing their opportunities for success. Scanzoni also found that many African American middle-class parents warned their children of the consequences of associating with people who might interfere with their social and economic advancement. This kind of intensity of purpose may result in parent-child conflict in some situations, with the child struggling to differentiate from a family that is seen as far too controlling. In this case, the social worker needs to examine family boundaries and other systemic aspects of family functioning. As in the case of any other family, adjustments to allow for greater individuation among family members must be considered.

There is a likelihood, however, that a congruence exists between the perceptions of the African American parent and child with regard to these socialization activities. There may be a mutual understanding and acceptance of roles and behaviors. This can be a result of the parents' communicating to the child her or his difference as it relates to the majority population and teaching the child how to cope with the consequences of being different. When this understanding is present, it minimizes the likelihood of confrontation and conflict centered around socialization activities. Cooke (1974) offers support for this conclusion in her reference to the socialization of the African American male, in particular. She suggests the lesson usually learned by the male child is that "the often ambivalent role of polarities projected by his parents, especially his mother, when rearing him is preparation for his later subordinate role in a white society" (p. 81).

Therefore, behavior that in a different set of circumstances might be perceived as a likely conflict-producing situation, involving an overactive parent and a rebellious child, should not always be viewed as such in African American parent-child interactions. Social workers should proceed cautiously in reaching a decision relative to the implications of this behavior. It will be useful to determine the extent to which a congruence of perceptions exists in the parent-child relationship before planning specific intervention strategies.

Support Systems

In the American population as a whole, demographic factors of age, occupation, and education account for much of the difference in mobility among individuals. As African Americans continue to make progress in closing the gap between themselves and whites in terms of education and occupation, it is likely they will have greater geographical mobility. Such mobility often places individuals and families in unfamiliar surroundings, which results in a disruption of opportunities for feedback about themselves and validations of their expectations of others (Caplan, 1974). In other words, geographical mobility often severs the family's connection with its support systems. Gary (1983) points up the importance of social networks in providing support for families in the African American community. He suggests that these networks influence decision making and contribute to individual and family adjustment. In other words, these supportive networks provide African Americans with a source of support upon which they can depend.

While this is applicable to any family, African American families are likely to find the loss of social support systems more disruptive than white families do. These families use the white family as a reference group in relation to the achievement of rewards from the dominant society, but it also has expectations that are framed in terms of the African American community and the family's own previous experiences. This means that the family requires feedback and validation from the community as well as from the wider society. White families are not faced with this duality, since, as a rule, they seek validation only from sources within the dominant culture. Therefore, they experience less difficulty in moving from one location to another and maintaining or establishing the pattern of ties necessary for preserving their psychological and physical integrity.

Cassel (1973) also suggests that there are differences among the reactions of people to incomprehensible feedback (support disruption). The risk involved is not shared equally by all who experience breakdown in feedback regarding expectations and evaluations of behavior that serve to support and guide actions. For example, Cassel posits the existence of a dominant-subordinate factor in which a position of dominance tends to minimize the effect of experiencing loss of support, while a subordinate position tends to increase the effect. When we consider that the African American family occupies a subordinate position to that of the white family in the dominant society, we believe it agrees with Cassel's finding to assume that this nonwhite family will experience greater difficulty when their support systems are disrupted.

The role of African American culture as a source of support for the African American family must not be overlooked. Chestang (1976) states that the function of this culture is to deal with environmental threats in such a way as to guarantee the survival, security, and self-esteem of its people (pp. 99–100). We agree and suggest further that African American culture is tied to the institutions of the African American community that serve as a resource for the survival and security of the family. It is within the context of this culture that African American people get a sense of what can be described as we-ness, or peoplehood.

When feedback through familiar cultural channels is limited or disrupted for any reason, the African American family's perception of itself as a viable unit is likely to suffer. For example, a breakdown in the supportive network of the family may occur when it moves from one geographical location to another, leaving behind friends, relatives, familiar institutions, and accustomed ways of relating. The effect of the breakdown is most likely to surface when the family experiences a threat to its integrity. Such a threat may be brought on by conflict among family members, or it may result from transactions with systems outside of the family's boundaries that necessitate the use of resources beyond those customarily used by the family for support and assistance in performing tasks. In the absence of familiar sources upon which to draw for help, the family may find itself, as Caplan suggests, unfamiliar with the communication signals that enable it to perceive the expectations, friendliness, or hostility in the immediate surroundings. As a result, family members, unable to feel safe and valued, are more likely to become susceptible to a crisis in functioning.

The African American family has traditionally maintained an extensive extended-family network of blood-related and nonrelated individuals upon whom it depends for various kinds of assistance. Most social workers can readily envision the structure of an extended family that is connected by biological ties and the likelihood that role-sharing might occur under certain conditions. However, an extended family that includes nonrelatives may be somewhat more difficult to visualize. Yet, this type of extended family is not unusual among African American families, especially those from less affluent backgrounds. The inclusion of nonrelatives in this way is sometimes born of necessity, and a very close relationship is likely to develop that includes the sharing of responsibilities, in the same manner as would be experienced in an extended family network based on biological ties. When nonrelatives are involved in the extended family network, social workers should view this as an integral part of family support and bring them into treatment as a part of the family when necessary.

Theoretical Perspective

From a theoretical point of view, a systems perspective is necessary in work with African American families, as it is with all families. We find symbolic interaction theory especially useful in viewing the functioning of the African American family. This frame of reference addresses not only the concepts of status (or position) and role but also questions of socialization and personality. While status and role are important considerations in work with families, socialization and personality are essential in understanding their behavior. In our view, socialization refers to "the process by which the human organism acquires the characteristic ways of behaving, the values, norms, and attitudes of the social units of which he is a part," and personality is "the development of persistent behavior patterns" (Stryker, 1964, p. 133). These patterns of behavior are the result of experiences over time and should be viewed in this context when working with African American families.

In the final analysis, Blumer (1969, p. 2) suggests that symbolic interactionism rests on three basic premises:

1. Human beings act toward things on the basis of the meanings that the things have for them.
2. Meanings are derived from, or arise out of, the social interactions that one has with one's fellows.
3. These meanings are handled in, and modified through, an interpretive process used by the persons in dealing with the things he [or she] encounters.

In applying these guiding principles of symbolic interactionism to work with African American families, we favor a sociological-psychological approach to the explanation of meanings attached to experiences. We do not overlook the importance of the meaning of things toward which the members of these families act. However, we suggest that the meanings they attach to these things are influenced by a history of experiences common to African American people. For this reason, the meaning given to an experience in the context of social interaction not only is an expression of what family members derive from the experience itself, it also reflects the disappointments, successes, happiness, and fears of earlier times. For example, when the mother expresses dissatisfaction with her child's poor grades in school, the meaning she attaches to this experience comes from her own observation of the difficulty she and her people have had in earning rewards from the opportunity structure of the wider society. She also realizes that education is at least one way of making access to this structure less difficult, and that poor grades mean a greater struggle for success.

Consider also the African American husband who adapts to his wife's working by accepting increased responsibility for child care and housekeeping chores, and who shows little concern over the equal distribution of power that exists between himself and his wife. The meaning this has for him is shaped by his awareness of the difficulty long associated with the male's access to employment and the greater opportunity for African American females. Therefore he reacts not only to what is encountered physically—that is, his wife's working—but also to this experience as modified through an interpretative process that is influenced by his previous experiences. The husband responds to a symbolic environment created in part by his own internal processes.

A symbolic-interactionist conceptualization of human behavior lends itself to exploration and understanding of the uniqueness of the African American family experience. It suggests the likelihood and significance of individual reactions to a symbolic environment that is derived from the meaning the person attaches to what is experienced. We suggest that the experience of these people in American society shapes the meaning they give to what they encounter in various transactions with their environment. And their response to other persons and situations, based on this meaning, will influence the way others respond to them. We believe that viewing African American family interactions within a systems-interactionist framework allows for the most complete understanding of the family's transactions, member with member, and members with the world outside of family boundaries.

Specific Treatment Considerations

The primary objective of family treatment is to alter dysfunctional interactional patterns between family members. Many family therapists believe this can be accomplished while obtaining only a minimum of history information about the family. We agree with this approach for the most part, but we believe an exception is necessary when working with African American families. Among the reasons for this shift in emphasis is the cultural heritage of African American people in general, which is distinctly different from that of other racial or ethnic groups.

The circumstances surrounding the development and maintenance of the African American family in America have also resulted in a variation of lifestyles among these families. Therefore, in order to make a differential assessment of family functioning and to plan for effective intervention, the social worker needs to examine selected aspects of the family's history, depending on the difficulty experienced.

Not only is information regarding history important in understanding the functioning of African American families, but certain kinds of this information are essential. Our concern is for experiential information rather than strictly chronological developmental data. The experiences of the parents as children growing up in their families of origin; their coming together as a couple; their ideas about raising their own family; and the impact social, economic, and political forces have had on their lives are all important experiences that usually prove to be profitable areas for exploration. However, social workers must keep in mind the specific problem being presented by the family and develop the necessary information around this difficulty, instead of routinely developing generalized information about the family.

For example, if the problem is presented as the parents' frustration over the child's apparent lack of interest in school, it would hardly be necessary or profitable to explore in detail how the parents became interested in each other and what each wanted from the marriage. Instead, it would likely be most productive to examine what they want for their child and how they arrived at these expectations. A better understanding of the situation might also be realized by obtaining some idea of what their own parents had expected of them as children and their vision of possible obstacles to the child's future participation in the economic opportunity structure. It is likely that the parents' frustration in such cases is rooted in a desire to see the child prepared for a better life than they have experienced, and failure to take advantage of educational opportunities is for them a painful disappointment.

When the parent-child relationship is the target of intervention, it will be helpful to explore socialization patterns, including the parents' own experiences with the socialization process in their families of origin. While this information is useful in work with nonminority families as well, it has special significance in intervening with African American families. The African American child undergoes a unique and demanding socialization process that incorporates the values and expectations of two different cultures, as we have noted. Socioeconomic success is also an important family value that is imparted to the child as he or she is taught to participate successfully in the economic opportunity structure of the wider society. Although the socialization experience of African

American children does not automatically produce a pathological situation, it does have the potential for problem development and should be fully explored when parents and children are experiencing difficulty in communicating and relating to each other.

When the African American wife becomes overburdened by the demands of her role, which includes family nurturer and supporter and system balancer within the wider society, helping professionals should consider the weight of these demands when providing relief. Pinderhughes (1986) suggests the African American wife must demonstrate, among other things, strength, persistence, flexibility, and caution. However, under stress these behaviors can easily slip into abuse of power, stubbornness, inconsistency, and immobility. We agree with Pinderhughes' belief that change efforts should focus not on eliminating these behaviors, but on moderating them. Much might be accomplished by relabeling these negative behaviors as an indication of the wife's steadfastness in carrying out her very complex and difficult role. Support might also be offered in helping her to delegate responsibility that could be appropriately carried by other family members.

With many families, especially those who come for help after a recent change in geographical location, we suggest an examination of the family's support systems. Hansell (1976) has suggested a number of attachments to various resources as instrumental in helping people cope with the kind of distress that is usually experienced in the loss of social supports. Although he was concerned primarily with the individual, some of his ideas are also applicable to families and can provide direction for social workers intervening with African American families, especially where a breakdown in sources of support has been established. The following points are extrapolated from Hansell's suggestions (p. 33):

1. The family must be attached to appropriate sources of information. The family in unfamiliar surroundings may not have sufficient access to sources of information; in this case the worker can connect the family with individuals, groups, or organizations with which they can communicate and from which they can receive necessary information.
2. There should be attachment to resources that will enable the family to realize its identity as a functioning unit. If the family has lost its connection with familiar resources that have customarily fed back to them information about what is expected and how well they are meeting these expectations, the worker must provide for new sources

of validation. This can often be realized by helping the family establish interdependent connections with other families, or with other persons outside its boundaries, with whom members can share mutual interests and activities and can develop trust. This attachment will allow the exchange of suitable information and increase feedback to the family about its operations.
3. It is essential that the family be attached to groups of people who regard it as belonging. These might include religious groups, political groups, and so on that have the capability of assisting the family with various tasks.

When support systems are disrupted, the worker should examine the family's attachment to these resources and plan to effect connections where indicated. The primary objective is to connect the family with others who will be able to "speak their language" and with whom family members can feel comfortable, build trust, and gain a sense of self and a feeling of security.

In the case of the less affluent African American family there is usually a reluctance to seek help for family problems from organizations that provide mental health services. In the first place, there is a tendency to think of those who receive these services as being of unsound mind. Furthermore, help with problems is usually sought from more familiar sources such as the extended family, clergy, and trusted friends. Turning to a social service or mental health agency is often a last resort and usually comes as a result of referral from agencies such as the schools or courts. In such cases, the social worker should expect and be ready to deal with resistance to taking help and should realize that long-term treatment is not likely to succeed. Therefore, therapeutic efforts should be focused on helping the family experience some desired change as soon as possible, regardless of how small it might be.

When the African American middle-class family is viewed as a social system, the similarities between it and the white middle-class family are far greater than the differences. However, if we are to understand the African American family, we must examine its functioning within a framework that allows us to view what is different and determine what, if any, impact this difference has on family transactions.

It is well to remember that self-determination is very important to African American families. This determination is likely to be reflected in the family's transactions with other systems. We suggest that social workers also take into consideration the local and national sociopolitical climate at the time of the therapeutic encounter, as the struggles of the middle-class family may be related to these phenomena.

THE ASIAN FAMILY

Asian Americans with long exposure to Western ways of life behave in a different manner than more recent arrivals, especially those who arrived as refugees. This reflects a greater degree of assimilation on the part of early arrivers, most of whom immigrated as a matter of choice in contrast to refugees who are usually fleeing political or economic oppression. Nevertheless, there are many common characteristics shared by all Asian American families. We will discuss some of these characteristics and focus on those that are peculiar to specific groups.

East Asians come from a cultural background very different from that of the West. This includes philosophical approaches to life that do not stress individual independence and autonomy. Instead, the individual is superseded by the family, which adheres to specific hierarchical roles for all family members. For example, men occupy the higher positions within the hierarchy, and relationships between husband, wife, and in-laws are strictly prescribed. The same applies to relationships between parents and children (Takeshi and Lau, 1992).

In East Asian cultures, issues of obligation and shame are paramount and control much of the life of those who share these cultures. Obligation comes in a traditional sense, with roles and status ascribed to individuals. For example, the status ascribed to men as leaders of the family carries with it the obligation to provide adequately for the material needs of the family. If this obligation is not met, shame and loss of face will follow as the actions of the leader are exposed to public view. In addition, the withdrawal of community confidence and support in the family leader's ability to fulfill his obligation increases the shame he will experience. Such action by the community also causes him to wonder if he can find support anywhere, and, if not, he must consider facing life alone. Shame and the fear of losing face is a devastating experience in Asian culture that can serve to motivate conformance to community and family expectations (Shon and Ja, 1982).

Contrary to the value western society places on free and open speech, limits are placed on communication in most East Asian cultures. They believe communicating should depend upon specific characteristics of the persons involved. Such things as education, occupation, age, sex, and social status come into play in determining how communication will take place. For example, who will initiate the conversation, who will change the subject of the conversation, who will be most accommodating, and who looks away first when eyes meet depend on these status qualifications (Shon and Ja, 1982). A high value is placed on harmonious interpersonal relationships, and whenever possible direct confrontation is avoided. As a result, the communication system of most Asians is characterized by indirectness. As might be imagined, the preferred Asian style of communication could present some problems for the American-trained therapist, which will be addressed later in this chapter.

Family Structure

The Asian family is characterized by a strong emphasis on specific roles for family members. Unlike the American position, which emphasizes the time-limited nuclear family, the traditional East Asian family is not limited in time or to only the nuclear family. Instead, it is extended to include all generations of the family from the beginning of time, and the individual is seen as a product of these generations. As a result, the individual's behavior impacts all generations of the family, and this burden of responsibility takes precedence over any concern the individual might have.

Arranged marriages, once prominent in the traditional East Asian family, are gradually disappearing. However, the family still has considerable influence on mate selection, and usually marriage does not occur without the family's blessing. As might be expected in the patriarchal system that exists in Asian families, the wife has very low status—below that of her husband, her husband's parents, and her husband's older siblings (Shon and Ja, 1982).

The roles of the parents are fairly clearly defined. The father is the family leader who makes all of the decisions, exercises unquestioned authority, and carries responsibility for the welfare of the family. The enforcement of family rules and the disciplining of family members is also the father's responsibility. As a result of his authority, the success or failure of the family is attributed to his leadership or the lack thereof.

The mother's role in the Asian family is one of nurturing and taking care of her husband and the children. This kind of emotional caretaker has traditionally been seen as the mother's primary role. Until recently, she was not allowed to engage in work outside of the home, which is still frowned upon in the traditional family. However, with the increasing number of East Asian refugees coming to America, finding employment and providing for the family has become more difficult for the father. In many cases, the women are able to find jobs and fit into the workplace with little difficulty and, out of necessity, are doing so in large numbers. This threatens the traditional authority of the father, who, in the eyes of the Asian community, is less than a successful provider when his wife must help with the support of the family. The mother's earning capacity and larger contribution to the welfare of the family elevates her status in the eyes of the children. Needless to say, this change in the mother's role may cause problems in the family, especially in the relationship between the parents.

With regard to roles of children in Asian culture, as might be expected, sons are more highly valued than are the daughters. The oldest son is the most important child and often receives better treatment and is given more respect than his siblings. Along with this preferential treatment, he is also given more responsibility. He serves as a role model for younger children, who are expected to accept and follow his guidance. This role responsibility is in preparation for succeeding his father. When the father dies, the oldest son becomes the leader of the family. If, for any reason, he is unable to carry out the responsibilities of the leadership role, the next oldest son usually fulfills the position (Shon and Ja, 1982).

An additional twist in the leadership of the family sometimes occurs when the son takes the reins after the father's death. Because of the strong emotional attachment that has developed between mother and son over the years as the mother performed the role of emotional leader of the family, the son will respect her wishes. In this way, although the son is the reputed leader, the mother's wishes control the son's actions and, in a very real sense, she rules the family.

Therapeutic Considerations

Most Asian Americans experience difficulty entering into therapy. Several factors seem to be involved: They are usually unfamiliar with Western concepts of mental health; their problem-solving approach is to seek help from within their own cultural groups; and seeking help from outside their groups carries a social stigma and it is undertaken only as a last resort. The process of becoming more familiar with western mental health concepts is indeed slow, as many of the terms used have no equivalent translation into the traditional language of Asian Americans. Perhaps the strongest barrier to this group's entry into treatment is the importance given to the status of the family in the eyes of the community. It is the belief in Asian culture that one seeks help from outsiders only if he or she is "crazy." And the cause of being crazy is placed at the door of the family. For the Asian family, this problem may be seen as punishment for past family misbehavior; as a hereditary trait that runs in the family; or as an indication of poor guidance and discipline by the family leader (Shon and Ja, 1982, p. 222). With the importance placed on the family in Asian culture, it is easy to see why Asian Americans are reluctant to become involved in using services that are likely to expose the family in the community in a negative manner.

When the Asian family does come for treatment it tests the knowledge and skills of the therapist, who must handle the family's concerns with care and understanding. Confrontation and directness are considered to be rude and impolite, and practitioners should not ask direct and confrontational questions in the initial contact (Agbayani-Siewert, 1994).

To begin with, the therapist is likely to be put in charge by parents who perceive him or her as a knowledgeable expert who will guide the family's behavior in the proper direction. At the same time, the family expects the therapist—as an authority figure—not to be passive, but to direct and to fulfill most of their expectations. This will not be done if the therapist waits for the process of the session, especially in the first interview, to flow from the family in order to better observe family interactions. This is likely to be seen by the family as a passive approach to their problem and reflective of a lack of knowledge and skill on the part of the therapist. And once this judgment is made, it is unlikely that the family will return to therapy.

In order to hold the family's interest, the therapist should take a directive stance in the initial session. This does not mean that he or she should tell family members how to live their lives, as this would be another turnoff. Instead, the therapist should direct the flow of the discussion by determining when each family member should speak and what the focus of the discussion should be. Although the thinking of many Asian Americans has been modified through the process of assimilation and acculturation, most of them still honor some of the traditional family values. Therefore, proper respect should be shown for the roles of family members. For example, the father, who is the leader of the family, has risked his reputation by seeking outside help and most likely feels ashamed and defeated. If he feels he is being criticized or his role diminished in any way, he may not return. It is important in the initial session to reinforce the father's role within the family by addressing him first with initial inquiries and requests. This is expected in East Asian culture and will be helpful in establishing a good therapeutic relationship.

The importance of the mother's role should not be overlooked, especially as it relates to the children who are primarily her responsibility as the nurturing leader of the family. A very close emotional bond exists between mother and children, which should not be viewed in a negative way. However, the therapist who is not familiar with the traditional family dynamics of Asian families may erroneously interpret this close-ness as a symbiotic relationship. In such relationships, separation be-tween mother and child, with the development of more outside interest for the child, is usually recommended. Such an attempt to weaken the bond between mother and child will promote resistance, and, in many cases, the family will discontinue treatment.

It is essential that the therapist be aware of the communication style of Asian families. The Asian family may never feel as comfortable as would an American family in giving information and expressing feel-ings, especially to an outsider. However, the communication process in treatment can be greatly enhanced if the therapist shows patience and understanding. For example, the Asian family will try to learn some-thing about the therapist before revealing family problems, and the ther-apist must be willing to reveal something of himself or herself before seeking information about the family. However, this does not mean that the therapist must reveal the intimate details of his or her life. When the family has reached the point of beginning to talk about their prob-lems, it will most likely be done in an indirect manner, with the impact of the problem being minimized. Here the therapist must not become impatient and adopt an aggressive style of inquiry. Any effort by the therapist to become more aggressive and speed up the information-gathering process will be seen by the family as harsh and insensitive. If, however, the therapist is patient and can pick up the meaning buried in the downplayed issues and indirect messages, the Asian family will gradually respond over time.

The possibility that the Asian family will express disagreement with the therapist is highly unlikely, although such feelings may be present. To express anger or criticism toward someone to whom they have given high status and who has been helpful to them would be considered dis-respectful. Therefore, the therapist must pay close attention to nonverbal communication such as body language, facial expressions, voice changes, and changes in the pace of speech in order to identify and deal with the issues that give rise to feelings of disagreement. Throughout this process, the therapist should not push the family too hard or too fast toward treatment objectives, keeping in mind that many Asian fam-ilies never feel comfortable deviating from their cultural style of ex-pression (Shon and Ja, 1982, p. 227).

THE HISPANIC/LATINO FAMILY

The Hispanic family (sometimes referred to as Latino) is a compara-tively new and rapidly increasing group, which was formally defined by the United States government (Castex, 1994). As set forth by the Office of Management and Budget (1978), a Hispanic is defined as "A person of Mexican, Puerto Rican, Cuban, Central or South American or other Spanish culture or origin, regardless of race" (p. 19269). According to this definition, Hispanics come from 26 nations, which means they are an extremely diverse group with differences in language, economic resources, and customs. The popular assumption that all Hispanics are fluent and literate in Spanish is untrue and should be kept in mind when interacting with this group. Although it is highly unlikely that most professional practitioners will encounter clients from more than a few of the identified nations, they should be intellectually, emotionally, and clinically prepared. The following brief profiles are provided as an introduction to work with Hispanic/Latino families.

The Puerto Rican Family

This family shares many cultural characteristics with the Asian family, including turning to family members for help in times of stress and seeking help outside only as a last resort. Like most Hispanics, Puerto Ricans are committed to family life, which they see as a strength. They adhere to a patriarchal system with the father exercising unquestioned authority (Longres, 1995). Stress in the Puerto Rican family is usually revealed through somatic complaints and attributed to external factors.

As in the Asian family the father also has unquestioned authority as head of the family and can make family decisions without conferring with his wife. Failure to show respect to the Puerto Rican male assaults his manliness and the integrity of his family and brings into question his self-esteem as a human being (Puerto Rican Congress of New Jersey, 1976). Along with his authority as head of the family the husband is expected to protect and provide for family members. However, this does not preclude the use of outside resources that contribute to the well-being of the family (Vidal, 1988; and DeLaRosa, 1988).

The woman's responsibility is to care for the home and keep the family together. This includes performing all of the household chores and raising the children. She also has the major responsibility for providing discipline for the children; however, the father has the final say. Sometimes the mother serves as mediator between father and children, which can be the source of difficulty if the mother forms an alliance with the children that tends to isolate the father from family affairs (Garcia-Preto, 1982). Gender differences are also pronounced and again men are the privileged ones. For example, the wife must remain faithful to her husband while he is allowed to engage in extramarital affairs.

Children are expected to care for younger siblings and older parents. Spankings are acceptable as discipline for children in the Puerto Rican culture. They are often criticized by parents but seldom praised or rewarded for good behavior for fear that they will lose the respect they are required to show. This could be very disappointing and might lead to negative behavior by the adolescent who is well acclimated to the American way of life, where rewards for good behavior are expected and usually given.

The Therapeutic Process

The Puerto Rican family is likely to respond best to a warm and understanding relationship with the therapist. In many cases language is a major issue as well as a barrier in therapy. Frequently parents are unable to speak English and the interview must be conducted in Spanish. If the therapist is not fluent in Spanish an interpreter must be used. While children are often able to serve as interpreters this is not advised. Parents view children serving as interpreters as speaking for them (parents), which violates the cultural norm that requires children to be quiet in the presence of adults, especially strangers. It would also shift the structure of the family by placing children in a superior position (Garcia-Preto, 1982, p. 177). In keeping with cultural expectations, the husband should be addressed first, followed by the wife, and the children last, in descending order according to age. The family is likely to discuss emotional problems more readily with a female therapist, since women traditionally handle emotional concerns in Puerto Rican culture. Taking directives may be easier when they are given by men, which is also in keeping with the position of authority occupied by males. Keeping scheduled appointments may not be easy for the Puerto Rican family because of the informality of their culture. In some cases, in order to reach the family and maintain a therapeutic relationship, home visits may be necessary (Mizio, 1979).

The Mexican Family

The proximity of the United States and Mexico has facilitated the immigration of Mexicans at an ever increasing rate. Most Mexican Americans live in the cities and, like most other minority groups, experience discrimination in jobs, housing, and education. In spite of less than an egalitarian environment awaiting them, they continue to migrate in the hope of improving the economic conditions of the family. Further, not all Mexicans enter the United States legally. And since the 1960s, U.S. legal alien status has not been granted to most Mexican immigrants (Falicov, 1982). As a result, these undocumented immigrants experience social alienation and, out of fear of detection, are reluctant to seek medical treatment or psychological counseling. When they are seen by professionals, they usually present a wall of resistance that is shown by reluctance to share information that they believe might lead to discovery of their undocumented status. Therefore, family therapists must be prepared to engage these families, and this preparation includes not only awareness of the fear of detection, but also knowledge of the cultural factors that influence the development and organization of the Mexican American family.

Family Organization

The Mexican family is organized along hierarchical lines with roles clearly defined. The husband is the provider and protector of the family, and the wife assumes the role of homemaker. Loyalty to the family is demanded, and respect for parental authority is expected throughout the lifetime of the children. Honesty and dignity are fundamental values, but autonomy and individual achievement are not emphasized. The Mexican family is also characterized by an extended family network. In addition to the nuclear family, this network includes all members of the family of origin, the children's godparents, and kinship ties up to fourth cousins. Intergenerational interdependence characterizes the extended family supportive network, including the sharing of many family functions such as caring for and providing discipline for children and giving emotional and financial support when needed (Falicov, 1982). Family rules are organized around age and sex, with older males having the greater authority. Individuals usually live in families of origin, families of procreation, or the extended family through all development stages, and all life cycle events are celebrated by the family (p. 138).

The prevailing norm for the marital subsystem is that the husband provides for and protects the family, with the wife assuming the role of homemaker. Concerning children, the father disciplines and controls, with nurturance and support being given by the mother. Throughout the adolescent years, children are not encouraged to work outside of the home. They are punished for acts of disobedience and poor manners. Belittling and threatening children are common child-rearing practices. In the father's absence, the mother may allow the children to disobey his wishes, and she frequently mediates for the children with the father, which increases her influence with them. Many parental functions are also performed by grandparents and other members of the extended family network.

Strong ties are encouraged within the sibling subsystem. As a result, Mexican children usually look to each other for friendship and have few friends outside of sibling relationships. In adulthood, both closeness and distance are seen among siblings. For example, emotional support and other forms of help are common among this group, but they also experience disagreements and resentments toward each other. Both behaviors are related to earlier life experiences where support and cooperation are emphasized and, at the same time, older children are given authority over younger children. Support for each other in later years is a positive carryover from childhood. However, attempts by older adult siblings to exercise authority over younger siblings usually brings resentment. Nevertheless, disruption in relationships are seldom permanent, and crisis situations will most likely bring them together again.

The Therapeutic Process

In gathering information from the Mexican American family, it will be helpful to know if they were born in America or immigrated from Mexico. If they are an immigrant family, some information should be developed about the length of residence in the United States and the difficulties experienced by family members in the assimilation and acculturation process. This must be done with care and understanding. Evasiveness on the part of the family may be due to the illegal status that they do not wish to divulge. They also prefer a casual attitude by the therapist toward appointment times and they expect the therapist to take the initiative in treatment and advise the family of ways to solve their problems. Most Mexican American families believe family conflicts and financial difficulties are the source of their emotional problems (Moll et al., 1976). While they may appear guarded, they do want help with their problems and are more responsive to a subtle approach to exploring feelings. Therapists will find indirect approaches to changing the Mexican American family most effective, including the use of paradoxical interventions and positive reframing, especially with the resistive family.

To promote the formation of a therapeutic relationship, the therapist should keep in mind the culture-specific expectations of the family. For example, initial contacts among Mexicans tend to be formal, polite, and reserved. Therefore, the therapist should address the family accordingly, using last names during the introductory process with adults. And given the cultural importance of parent-child interactions over marital interactions, it is more acceptable to the family in the initial stages of contact with the therapist to focus on parent-child interactions rather than marital issues. It will be useful, in this connection, to keep in mind that "only the highly acculturated or middle-class couples contemplating separation or divorce are likely to request marital treatment" (Falicov, 1982, p. 150). In any case, if it appears necessary to address marital issues, it should not be undertaken until after a strong therapeutic relationship has been established. An overall strategy designed by the therapist to avoid both direct confrontation and demand for greater disclosure is preferable to the Mexican American family throughout the treatment process. If the therapist is fluent in the use of the family's native language, it will usually be helpful to use it. (For details of conducting the initial interview, see Chapter 5).

CULTURAL PRINCIPLES

While this chapter presents information on family operations in specific cultures, it is impossible in one chapter to provide all the information needed on all the different cultures engaging social work attention. Therefore, in ending the chapter, we present some general principles for social workers in attempting to be culturally understanding, competent, and relevant.

Montalvo and Gutierrez (1983), writing out of their experience with Puerto Rican families in Philadelphia, note that there is no guarantee that knowledge of the culture permits the therapist to become necessarily more effective in dealing with families. In addition, "it helps if therapists orient themselves beyond the elements making this family a member of a particular ethnic group, searching for what is basic to families rather than what are idiosyncratic cultural dimensions that tend to make the family alien to the therapist" (p. 17). Culture becomes troublesome in family therapy when therapists question whether they are attributing psychopathology to a person who is really behaving normally in that person's particular culture.

Social workers and other professionals must be aware that cultural information can also be used by families as a defense against change. This is pointed up by Montalvo and Gutierrez (1983) in their reference to the family who wishes to justify its intrusive behavior, reflected in remaining with their daughter who is seeing her boyfriend, by telling the therapist that this is their customary way of always being together. They also indicate that in their culture women do not keep company with men alone until they are much older than their daughter and are able to find their own housing. By employing these tactics, the family can take the therapist away from reality, thereby causing him or her to deal with a cultural image of the ethnic group instead of the reality of a family problem. Montalvo and Gutierrez suggest that therapists should focus on the broader processes that connect the minority culture to its immediate surroundings in order to prevent themselves from being distracted.

These authors also draw attention to the need of family therapists to be attentive to the way the processes and sequences of family life are working themselves out. To a large extent, things such as hierarchical versus nonhierarchical relationships, patterns of relationship, organization, stability, conflict, and collaboration, which are familiar to therapists, are present in all ethnic variations. Therapists searching for them will see similarities or differences and can then direct inquiry to determine what of this is particular to a culture or peculiar to this family. They can effectively organize themselves around their ignorance of the family culture by searching for the family's ways of thinking and by having the family teach them the ways of the culture, and by asking about the meaning attached to words or events, including such things as what are insults or words of praise or appreciation.

Thus, for example, in our emphasis on the usefulness of varieties of communication in solving family problems, we have noted earlier in this chapter that Asian families hesitate over certain kinds of communications. When the therapist observes such an absence or hesitation, the present point of view would affirm cultural sensitivity and prompt him or her to ascertain whether this is a cultural or family pattern before promoting such communication.

Montalvo and Gutierrrez note further that some family behaviors may be tied not to the ethnic culture but to the surrounding social institutions such as the world of the school or of work, and to the family's economic status. Family boundaries and processes may be more wired to the labor market than with intrafamily relations. The therapist will do well to be concerned with understanding the nature of the family's use of institutions in breaking away from cultural patterns which may or may not be helpful. By way of example Montalvo and Gutierrez refer to dropout youngsters looking for employment, noting that, contrary to expectations, more youngsters in the group come not from single-parent families, but from two-parent families where the father has no job or steady employment. In this case, the approach to father and son cannot be strictly in terms of their function in the intricate triangle with the mother, but on how those relationships are affected by the interaction with and the transition to the job market.

Finally, the overwhelming fact of exchange—the interaction between the family of the subculture with the institutions of the host culture—has to be central to any understanding of the cultural dimension in family therapy. To make the cultural dimension more central than the family's interactions with the surrounding institutions is to invite excess (Montalvo and Gutierrez, p. 31).

SUMMARY

In this chapter, we have discussed the impact of culture on the behavior of three family groups, as well as on professionals who work with these families toward appropriate change in family functioning. Differences in family structure have been emphasized, and the need to consider these differences in exploring the problems families experience and the development of intervention strategies are examined. Specific therapeutic considerations based on cultural diversity are presented. A systems perspective is suggested as the appropriate approach for working with all families regardless of cultural background or ethnic identity. Some general principles were set forth in order for social workers to enhance their understanding of the role of culture in the life of various ethnic groups, and how it is used by families to maintain the status quo as well as to promote positive change. Family therapists are also alerted to the necessity of both searching for the family's ways of thinking and learning more about their culture by asking about the meaning attached to words and events, including such things as what are insults and what are considered to be words of praise or appreciation. Finally, we have pointed up to all helping professionals who are working with families that the interaction between the family of the subculture with the institutions of the host culture is central to understanding the cultural dimension in family therapy.

REFERENCES

Acosta, Frank X., Yamamoto, Joe, and Evans, Leonard A. 1982. *Effective Psychotherapy for Low-Income and Minority Clients*. New York: Plenum Press.

Agbayani-Siewert, P. 1994. "Filipino American Culture and Family: Guidelines for Practitioners." *Families in Society* 75:429–38.

Blumer, H. 1969. *Symbolic Interactionism: Perspective and Method*. Englewood Cliffs, NJ: Prentice-Hall.

Caplan, G. 1974. *Support Systems and Community Mental Health*. New York: Behavioral Publications.

Cassel, J.C. 1973. "Psychiatric Epidemiology." In *American Handbook of Psychiatry*, vol. 2, ed. G. Caplan. New York: Basic Books.

Castex, G.M. 1994. "Providing Services to Hispanic Latino Population: Profiles in Diversity." *Social Work* 39:288–96.

Catherall, D. 1992. "Working With Projective Identification in Couples." *Family Process* 31:355–67.

Chestang, L. 1976. "The Black Family and Black Culture: A Study of Coping." In *Cross Cultural Perspectives in Social Work Practice and Education*, ed. M. Sotomayor. Houston: University of Houston, Graduate School of Social Work.

Cooke, G. 1974. "Socialization of the Black Male: Research Implications." In *Social Research and the Black Community: Selected Issues and Priorities*, ed. L. Gary. Washington, DC: Institute for Urban Affairs and Research, Howard University.

DeLaRosa, M. 1988. "Natural Support Systems of Puerto Ricans: A Key Dimension for Well Being." *Health and Social Work* 13:181–90.

Falicov, C. 1982. "Mexican Families." In *Ethnicity and Family Therapy*, eds. M. McGoldrick, J. Pearce, and J. Giordano. New York: Guilford.

Garcia-Preto, N. 1982. "Puerto Rican Families." In *Ethnicity and Family Therapy*, eds. M. McGoldrick, J. Pearce, and J. Giordano. New York: Guilford.

Gary, L.E. 1983. "Utilization of Network Systems in the Black Community." In *The Black Experience*, ed. Audreye E. Johnson. Davis, CA: International Dialogue Press.

Hansell, N. 1976. *The Person in Distress*. New York: Human Sciences Press.

Hawkes, G., and Taylor, M. 1975. "Power Structure in Mexican and Mexican American Farm Labor Families." *Journal of Marriage and the Family* 31:807–11.

Hines, P.M., and Boyd-Franklin, N. 1982. "Black Families." In *Ethnicity and Family Therapy*, eds. M. McGoldrick, J. Pearce, and J. Giordano. New York: Guilford.

Kronus, S. 1971. *The Black Middle Class*. Columbus, OH: Charles E. Merrill Publishing Co.

Laveman, L., and Borck, J. 1993. "Relationships Conflict Resolution Model: A Short Term Approach to Couple Counselling." *Family Therapy* 20:141–64.

Longres, J. 1995. "Hispanic Overview." *Encyclopedia of Social Work*, 19th ed. Washington, DC: NASW Press.

McAdoo, H.P. 1974. "The Socialization of Black Children: Priorities for Research." In *Social Research and the Black Community: Selected Issues and Priorities*, ed. L. Gary. Washington, DC: Institute for Urban Affairs and Research, Howard University.

McGoldrick, M., Pearce, J.K., and Giordano, J., eds. 1982. *Ethnicity and Family Therapy*. New York: Guilford.

Mizio, E. 1979. *Puerto Rican Task Report—Project on Ethnicity*. New York: Family Service Association.

Moll, L.C., Rueda, R.S., Rega, R., Herrera, J., and Vasquez, L.P. 1976. "Mental Health Services in East Los Angeles: An Urban Community Case Study." In *Psychotherapy with the Spanish Speaking: Issues in Research and Service Delivery* (Monograph No. 3), ed. M.R. Miranda. Los Angeles: University of California, Spanish Speaking Mental Health Research Center.

Montalvo, Braulio, and Gutierrez, Manuel. 1983. "A Perspective for the Use of the Cultural Dimension in Family Therapy." In *Cultural Perspectives in Family Therapy*, ed. C. Falicov. Rockville, MD: Aspen Systems Corp.

Mullings, L. 1985. "Anthropological Perspectives on Afro-American Family." In *The Black Family: Mental Health Perspectives Proceedings of Second Annual Black Task Force*, ed. M. Thompson-Fullilove. San Francisco: San Francisco General Hospital.

Pinderhughes, E.B. 1986. "Minority Women: A Nodal Position in the Functioning of the Social System." In *Women and Family Therapy*, ed. Marianne Ault-Riche. Rockville, MD: Aspen Systems Corp.

Puerto Rican Congress of New Jersey. 1976. *Folk Medicine in a Homogeneous Puerto Rican Community*. Trenton, NJ: Author.

Scanzoni, J.H. 1971. *The Black Family in Modern Society*. Boston: Allyn and Bacon.

Shon, S., and Ja, D. 1982. "Asian Families." In *Ethnicity and Family Therapy*, eds. M. McGoldrick, J. Pearce, and J. Giordano. New York: Guilford.

Spurlock, J. 1983. "Black Child Development and Socialization." In *The Black Experience*, ed. Audreye E. Johnson. Davis, CA: International Dialogue Press.

Stryker, S. 1964. "The Interactional and Situational Approaches." In *Handbook on Marriage and the Family*, ed. H.T. Christensen. Chicago: Rand McNally.

Takeshi, T., and Lau, A. 1992. "Connectedness Versus Separateness: Applicability of Family Therapy to Japanese Families." *Family Process* 31:319–40.

Vidal, C. 1988. "Godparenting Among Hispanic Americans." *Child Welfare* 67:453–59.

CHAPTER **8**

Helping Adult Children and Their Elderly Parents

When we think of the physical structure of a family, the configuration most often visualized is that of parents and children living in the same household. In this family, the parents are the adult members and occupy the hierarchical position that carries with it the executive authority for family operations. However, this is not the only family composition that social workers encounter in professional practice. As covered in Chapter 6, some families are headed by only one parent; others include relatives outside the nuclear family, friends of long standing, and so on—all of whom interact with each other in ways that form a functioning unit.

One family makeup with which social workers are familiar consists of elderly parents and their adult children. The members of this family do not usually live in the same household, and executive responsibility for the family system is not necessarily carried by the parents. In fact, the reverse is most often the case. When adult children are involved in planning and providing for their parents' needs, it is usually because the parents are unable to carry this responsibility for themselves. Subsequently, the children, in most cases, occupy the position of final responsibility. This is not to say that the aging parents have no part in the decision-making process, but the adult children assume a major role in assuring a viable existence for their parents.

ATTITUDES TOWARD THE AGED

An awareness of the increasing number of older citizens and their need to participate in society in meaningful ways is well established. Yet, underlying attitudes seem to grow out of our well-established belief in individuality, self-reliance, and productivity as symbols of a preferred lifestyle. This lends support to the value placed on youth and leaves little room to reward the accomplishments of the elderly.

A number of stereotypes exist about older persons in our society. Among these stereotypes is the belief by some that they are economically burdensome, are socially undesirable, lack intelligence necessary for learning new skills, are nonproductive and susceptible to illness, and so on. Yet, research has found most negative stereotypes about the elderly to be untrue. Most of this population are engaged with their families, have frequent contacts with them, and are able to perform in their major activity roles. Thus, social workers and other professionals intervening in situations involving the elderly should be careful not to fall prey to negative attitudes. Instead, they should view the aged differentially as individuals, the same as other clients, and proceed to meet their needs in the manner most appropriate for each situation.

THE AGING PROCESS

In order to work effectively with the family that includes adult children and their elderly parents, it is essential to have an understanding of the aging process and how it affects both parents and children. Although growing old is a normal phase in the individual life cycle, it is often the most difficult to accept by the older person who experiences it, as well as by the person's children who witness it. In various ways, aging represents an ending process frequently associated with loneliness and dependency for the elderly. It is also a constant reminder of one's own mortality to younger persons who observe the aging of their elders.

The desire to understand the aging process and its impact upon individuals and society continues to gain attention. Several theories have been suggested as a basis for understanding the process of growing old and the behavior shown by older people. We are in agreement with those who believe that older people display behavior indicating that they tend to disengage to some extent from the interactional processes of society. The extent of disengagement and what causes it to occur continues to generate discussion. However, there are two well-established theories we will discuss as a basis for helping social workers and other professionals better understand older people and the problems they experience: the theory of activity and the theory of disengagement.

Activity Theory

It is widely assumed that aged persons become increasingly less active and withdraw from some of the roles they have customarily fulfilled, or have these roles withdrawn from them. Many researchers have looked to activity among the aged for answers to the problems of adjustment in later life. Early researchers, Havinghurst and Albrecht (1953) and Burgess (1954), reported the existence of a positive relationship between social activity and life satisfaction among older people. However, it should be noted that not all interpersonal and noninterpersonal activities contribute to life satisfactions (Lemon et al., 1972). For example, solitary activities such as watching television, reading a book, and social participation in formal organizations have no significant influence on feelings of satisfaction. Older people tend to gain satisfaction through informal activity with friends that contributes to the development of mutual trust and the establishment of confidants. If one has a confidant, he or she can decrease social activities and continue to experience a satisfactory adjustment. This supports the belief that the presence of an intimate relationship can help overcome the loss of role or a reduction of social interaction. Therefore, it seems safe to conclude that older people may benefit more from having someone in whom they can confide than engaging in activity per se. And the people involved, the nature of the activity engaged in, and the degree of confidence shared among participants are important in promoting feelings of well-being among the elderly.

Disengagement Theory

In studying the aging process, Cummings and Henry (1961) presented findings that indicated that the existence of older people was characterized by withdrawal from participation in the interactional processes of society. They defined this withdrawal as disengagement on the part of the aged, supported by the decreasing number of people with whom the aging individuals were involved and the amount of interaction they experienced with these associates. Underlying this decrease in involvement with others was a change in the personality of the elderly person, which resulted in increased preoccupation with the self. This formal presentation by Cummings and Henry set forth the early framework of disengagement theory.

Over the years, since these findings were reported, a number of researchers and writers have focused their attention on this theory. Bell

(1976) was among those concerned with the theory of disengagement, which he explains as follows:

> By and large, the theory posits a functional relationship between the individual and society. The fact that individuals age and die and that society needs a continual replacement of "parts" is a fundamental tenet of the theory. In this view, both the person and society comprehend the necessity of the situation. As a consequence, the individual who can no longer produce effectively is expected to withdraw (i.e., disengage) from the ongoing social life about him...The disengagement processes which eventuate in a self-oriented personality are held to contribute to the maintenance of psychological well-being in late life. (pp. 31–32)

Thus, disengagement theory suggests that disengagement from active society by aging people is a natural phenomenon from which both the individual and society benefit. Society gets a "new part" that enables it to continue at an optimal level of functioning, and the disengaged individual finds satisfaction in a new self-centered role. It is further implied that social and psychological withdrawal by older people from active participation in the social life around them may be a necessary part of a successful aging process.

The suggestion that the elderly person wishes to withdraw from social life as a normal consequence of growing old has been challenged by other researchers, including Tallmer and Kutner (1969). They suggest that certain concomitant life stresses associated with aging could produce the withdrawal reported by Cummings and Henry. In replicating the Cummings and Henry study, they studied the relationship of three independent variables—ill health, widowhood, and retirement—to the disengagement process. Their data provided substantial evidence that disengagement is not caused by aging but is the result of the impact of stresses, physical and social, and these stresses may be expected to increase with advancing years.

Other contemporary researchers and writers have disagreed with disengagement theory posited by early researchers as the willful withdrawal of older people from the social life around them. They suggest that not all older people are disengaged from social activities and that most of those who are disengaged have done so for reasons other than a wish to retreat to a life of isolation. Among those who support this position are Fineman (1994), Fry (1992), and Glenwick and Whitbourne (1977).

We also agree with the view that disengagement is a differential experience of older people that has a strong relationship to the conditions of life as experienced by the individual.

LOSSES EXPERIENCED BY THE AGED

Underlying the disengagement process of the aged is the experience of loss in several areas of functioning. Schwartz and Mensh (1974) speak of natural losses that occur over time in a more or less gradual manner. This includes functional deterioration with regard to vision, hearing, central nervous system functioning, use of body muscles, and so on. They also mention "culturally determined and circumstantial losses such as the breaking up of one's social network, economic loss, loss of assigned roles, and loss of options and/or privacy" (p. 8). In order to understand older people in their situations, social workers must be familiar with these losses and their potential effect on the life circumstances of this group.

Physiological Aging

Physiological aging is an area of medical expertise involving biological processes of the body, and we will deal with it only briefly and in relation to a few physical changes that can be readily observed. This is a significant part of the life cycle and perhaps the most noticeable process of change among older people. Signs of physiological change may vary to some extent among individuals and are most noticeable as the body begins to be somewhat less efficient in the performance of its customary life-sustaining functions. Among these changes is a gradual dehydration of muscles and other deteriorations that affect the normal functioning of body organs. This is usually accompanied by a loss of physical dexterity and feelings of tiredness. Some increase in blood pressure may also be experienced. Recovery from injuries and the healing of wounds are relatively slower among the elderly. Visual and hearing impairment, together with central nervous system changes that can result in forgetfulness and some decline in mental alertness, may occur.

While these physiological changes are recognized as part of the aging process, they do not indicate an automatic onset of illness or the need to curtail older persons' performance of major activity roles. To the contrary, most people are able to continue their major activities in spite of physiological aging.

The elderly themselves are painfully aware of these changes, which come at a time when they are usually involved with fewer people and less frequently than in earlier life. It is well for the social worker to be aware that older people may mourn the loss of physiological functioning in the same manner they experience the loss of a relative, a position, or a status in life. For the elderly, activity is at least one means through which they can maintain contact with the world around them, and good health may be the key to sustained activity.

Psychological Aging

The process of aging psychologically is not completely separate from the biophysical process of aging. Indeed, it is very closely related in many ways. Biophysical influences are recognized, for example, in the tendency of older people to show a decrease in memory for more recent events, while at the same time demonstrating vivid recall of events and experiences that occurred many years before. This shift in memory to past events usually reflects on a period in the life cycle of aging individuals when they perceived themselves as more successful. Since a number of changes occur in later years that tend to threaten the self-image of the older person, perhaps this is one way of connecting with the experience of usefulness.

Among the losses experienced by older people, the most inevitable is the breakup of their social network. Schwartz and Mensh (1974) suggest that one of the prices for surviving into the later years of life is the likelihood that most friends and associates, and sometimes many family members, are eventually eliminated, for various reasons, from the network with which the elderly interact. Included in this process are the disruptions usually brought on by retirement. The social network of the retiree as it relates to economics, status, and roles represents perhaps the most significant disruption. In terms of economic loss, many older people, upon termination of gainful employment, are faced with a change in the standard of living to which they were accustomed. For those who were able to maintain a barely adequate standard of living while fully employed, the loss of income by retirement frequently plunges them into poverty—with all of the psychological implications of this status. For example, the elderly couple who manages to live independently, by careful management of the husband's income, might find themselves needing to depend more upon their children for financial assistance after his retirement. This is likely to interfere with feelings of independence and contribute to a sense of growing insecurity for the older people.

Certain social losses also accompany disengagement from gainful employment. The reality of retirement usually means the end of a number of social and collegial activities such as lunches, attending conferences, union meetings, picnics, and so on. The older person does not easily replace these associations and in many cases may well drift toward a life of increased loneliness.

The emphasis of society on a youth culture imposes some limitation on the coping ability of the aged population. Physical attractiveness, strength, and success in competition are important attributes of a youth-oriented culture. However, these attributes diminish with age, and the elderly can no longer compete successfully for rewards that demand these attributes. Skin wrinkles, loss or greying of hair, and other physical indications of aging may also contribute to inferior feelings. If there is a decrease in sexual capacity or less enjoyment from the sexual experience, this, too, can contribute to feelings of depression in aging individuals (Panser et al., 1995). However, there is considerable disagreement among researchers and writers with regard to change in the sexual capacity of older people.

Intelligence and learning receive a good deal of attention from those who study and work with the elderly. It is generally accepted that a close relationship exists between these attributes, but some studies of intelligence show a decline with age, some show no change, and still others show an increase in intelligence among older people. The reason for the disparity may be the measuring processes used. The aged do not share common experiences with the younger group on whom most tests are standardized. Therefore, they cannot be expected to respond in the same way to material drawn from the experiences of young people (Carp, 1973, p. 119). As a result, an accurate measure of intelligence among the elderly is not likely to be obtained by the use of such instruments.

Carp also found a general lack of interest among the elderly in taking intelligence tests. Most of them think these tests have very little intrinsic value, and this usually results in low motivation for taking such a test, which is likely to have a negative influence on the outcome.

Thus we conclude that a true determination of change in intelligence among older persons has not yet been achieved. In regard to learning, there is little evidence of change in learning itself among the aged. Nevertheless, learning in older people may be affected by interest and motivation in relation to what is to be learned. In other words, the degree of learning may be reduced if the new knowledge or experience is not in keeping with individual interest. Learning scores are also reduced by a slower rate of responses, which might be caused by disease or other biological dysfunctions common to the aging process. In summary, there is no support to indicate universal intellectual decline with increasing age (Warner Schaie, Willis, and O'Hanlon, 1994).

According to Botwinick (1973), role relationships between men and women change during later years, as evidenced by women demonstrating more assertiveness and men showing more of their submissive impulses (p. 66). It is well to keep in mind that such changes can be problematic, especially when they involve a marital relationship. Consider the case of a husband who retires from his employment after many years of working and providing for his family. His retirement income is much less than his previous earnings, so his wife accepts a part-time job as a nursing aide and becomes involved in her work and the collegial atmosphere of the hospital. In addition to elevating her status to that of employee and breadwinner, she is the beneficiary of social gains no longer shared by her retired husband. By reason of his own change in role and status, the husband may experience serious damage to his self-esteem, and this can find expression in a deterioration of the marital relationship. Often, the deteriorating marital relationships of aging couples somehow manage to involve one or more of the adult children. The struggle that is likely to follow can soon escalate to a point where the family can no longer cope with the conflict, and help is sought from outside the family group.

WORKING WITH THE FAMILY

The focus of this section is on family transactions as experienced by adult children and their aging parents and the underlying dynamics of the functioning of families of this composition. The interactions between adult children and their parents must be understood before intervention into dysfunctional processes that may occur as a result of these interactions can be undertaken.

We cannot overemphasize that the elderly are members of families, and their problems can best be viewed in the context of family interactions. Contrary to popular belief, ties between parents and their adult children are not always severed. Instead, contacts between them are quite frequent in most cases. Therefore, family therapy involving adult children and their parents is not only appropriate but necessary in many situations where the aged members are experiencing difficulty.

Adult children generally behave in a responsible manner toward their parents. When they do not, the situation is often complicated by a constellation of personal, social, and economic forces. Therefore, in order to work effectively with adult children and their parents, the social worker must make a careful assessment of the existing situational and emotional factors as they relate to the transactions occurring between the two generations. Within the broad guidelines of this assumption, we will consider some of the forces operating in extended family relations.

Defining the Problem

The assessment begins with some notion of how the presenting problem might be viewed. Savitsky and Sharkey (1972) report that there is little difference in the way a family presents itself to the social worker when it comes for help, whether the problem is aged parents or a rebellious adolescent. In either case the problem presented is frequently not in itself the problem with which help is most urgently needed. This is not to say the worker should ignore the problem as initially defined by the family. It is obvious that what the family presents is what they have singled out as their present concern, and this must be addressed in a way that is acceptable to them. We are suggesting, however, that when the problem presented concerns the aged parents, the worker should not overlook other possible aspects of the problem. For example, aging parents can create a great deal of anxiety for their children as a result of their inability to function independently or to accept altered roles in relation to the children. Adult children may also be experiencing guilt over their own inability to effectively meet the needs of their elderly parents.

When such underlying concerns are interfering with the problem-solving process, it may be necessary to focus on these concerns as a way of helping the children find the true source of their discomfort, en route to a more appropriate view of the parents' situation. The following case demonstrates what a family may bring to the social worker and what often lies beneath their expressed concerns.

> The daughter requested and was granted some time for herself and her husband with the social worker at the nursing home where the 76-year-old mother was recently admitted. They had been seen during the admission process, at which time both expressed satisfaction with the care the nursing home purported to provide. Nevertheless, the daughter was now complaining vigorously, with support from her husband, about the care her mother was receiving. She described her mother as a very neat person who was accustomed to clean surroundings and having her food prepared as she liked it. The daughter reported that on her last visit she had found her mother wearing clothes that were not clean, and she did not finish her meal. She was sure the food had not been properly prepared. Finally, the daughter wondered if it had not been a mistake to place her mother in the nursing home. When questioned about this she was able to reveal a great deal of fear and concern about her mother's poor health; the demands her presence in their home had made on both her and her

husband; and how much they had tried to provide the care she needed but had failed in these efforts. Nevertheless, the daughter still felt responsible for her mother's care and was not sure they could entrust this responsibility to the nursing home.

There was no objective reason for the complaints offered by the daughter about her mother's care. Further exploration revealed that the primary problem was not the mother's care in the nursing home, but the anxiety her disability had created for the daughter and the guilt generated around the family's inability to care for her. A part of the work to be done here was to help the daughter and her husband cope with their feelings about themselves in relation to the health and physical needs of the wife's aged mother.

Relationships

Knowledge of the relationship that exists between adult children and their parents is crucial in work with the extended family. This is so, regardless of the problem presented. The social worker will find it useful to obtain some sense of the kind of parent-child relationships experienced during the developmental stages of the adult children, and how this relationship developed over the years.

If the adult son or daughter shared a relationship with his or her parents during the early years that provided for growth and was experienced as satisfactory, the current relationship is likely to be sufficiently strong to make constructive problem solving a successful undertaking. On the other hand, if the earlier relationship was characterized by conflict and this conflict was not resolved, efforts to work with parent and child at a later time are likely to be very difficult. This past unresolved conflict may return and interfere with the adult child's ability to help the parents and the parents' ability to accept help from the child.

Bringing the adult child and parent together in a therapeutic situation when earlier conflicts have not been resolved can produce undesirable consequences. For example, the child may see it as a chance to get revenge for what were perceived as earlier injustices from the parent. And the parent might view the coming together as an opportunity to renew the struggle to control the behavior of a disrespectful child. Sometimes guilt is encountered over past failures on the part of both parent and child. In any case, when the aging parent cannot function independently and needs the assistance of the adult child, the worker must act to resolve the conflict, if at all possible, and provide the help needed by the elderly family member.

It is usually helpful in these situations to assist the family members involved to talk about past and present experiences in order to deal with the guilt and anger that have characterized their relationship, and to reach a level of understanding that will allow the necessary planning to take place. Care should be taken to prevent the encounter from becoming only an opportunity for each to blame themselves or place blame on the other. We have found it helpful in such cases to encourage self-responsibility for all by focusing on the way each individual is experiencing the other and what each can do to help change the way they are relating to each other.

It is well to recognize that the prospect is not always good for resolving long-standing conflicts in relationships between parents and adult children. A major problem experienced by social workers in cases of enduring parent-child conflict is getting the children involved with the parent and the problem situation. This apparent lack of interest is a primary factor in maintaining the conflict. The following case example demonstrates resistance to involvement with a parent when conflict remains.

Mrs. O, formerly a very successful buyer for a large department store, had for many years spent much of her time away from her family. Her misunderstandings with her two daughters apparently began during early childhood when the demands of her job prevented their spending time together. To compensate for this Mrs. O frequently bought them expensive gifts. When the daughters started to demand more of her time in pursuit of a closer relationship, she interpreted this as unreasonable and showed her irritation by threatening to discontinue the expensive gifts. At other times she would picture herself as a "poor misunderstood mother" and threaten to harm herself if her daughters "did not love her." Her husband also got his share of the blame from Mrs. O for the daughters wanting to spend more time with her. She considered Mr. O inadequate as a husband and father whose income as a clothing store salesman was considerably less than hers. They seemed to live in constant disagreement, and their verbal battles were well known throughout the neighborhood. When the daughters graduated from high school, both chose universities outside of the state, much to the mother's dismay, as she perceived this as "running away" from her. And she never permitted them to forget this "ungrateful act."

Soon after retirement, Mrs. O began experiencing serious health problems. Mr. O, who suffered from asthma and arthritis, had retired earlier and was experiencing a great deal of difficulty himself. However, they were able to manage for a few years, but finally sought help when Mrs. O's physician recommended specialized care, and preferably a warmer climate. Both daughters were now married and lived in an ideal climate for their mother's condition. When contacted to see if they could be of assistance in planning for her, one daughter stated her mother still blamed her for "leaving home" and "ruining her health." The daughter left no doubt that she did not want her mother to move to the area where she was currently living. She expressed the belief that whatever she tried to do would be misinterpreted by her mother, and she was not willing to undergo the emotional strain of further involvement. The other daughter thought any closer involvement with her mother would destroy her marriage, as Mrs. O thought she had married "beneath herself." She said her husband and her mother "hated each other," and she saw no way of improving her own relationship with her mother. The daughters were not willing to be involved beyond making limited financial contributions, if this was needed, in providing care for their mother.

This represents a seriously damaged relationship between adult children and parent. Only minimal participation in planning can be expected from the children in such cases.

We agree with those who maintain that when the conflict is unresolved, aged parents and their children will not be able to live comfortably together. When living arrangements for a parent are involved, it would be ill-advised to consider having the parents move into the home of a child with whom there is long-standing unresolved conflict. This is not to say that all hope of improving the relationship should be abandoned. If any evidence of positive aspects of a relationship remains, the worker should try to revive and build on what is left. However, until some improvement is realized in such cases, living arrangements should be separate.

Role Reversal

In working with aging parents and their adult children, it is important to understand the role shifts that occur between them. This shift in roles between the two generations may be considered role reversal. In other words, the elder who has carried the accustomed role of protector and provider for the child at an earlier point in time now gives up this role to the adult child and becomes the receiver of these benefits.

It is necessary to point up the disagreement that exists with regard to the concept of role reversal involving adult children and their elderly parents. The literature reflects the views of some authors who do not accept role reversal as an appropriate definition of what takes place when the adult child assists, protects, and provides for the parent who is unable to plan appropriately and provide for her or his own needs. For example, Brody (1990) believes that role reversal is a destructive concept and suggests that its use be discontinued. Gurland (1990) thinks role reversal has probably outlived its usefulness, but is reluctant to discard it until something better is found. Jarvik (1990) agrees with Gurland that use of role reversal should not be abandoned by professionals until something else that reflects the purpose and utilization currently supported by role reversal is found.

The aged parent does not make a complete psychological transition from the adult role to that of a child, nor does the adult child completely transfer from the role of child to that of a parent. The fact that both have long experience and emotional investment in their previous roles makes a complete psychological transition of roles unlikely. Yet the adult child is frequently required to assume responsibility in relation to the aged parent that is normally associated with the parental role, and to this extent parent and child are operating in a role-reversal position, which can result in conflict for both participants. Consider the situation in which the adult child is required to make decisions that will affect the way the parent is to live for the remaining years of life. The child, especially one who has experienced a good relationship with the parent, is likely to perceive such action as causing the parent pain and will have a great deal of difficulty accepting the responsibility for making such decisions. In this context the concept of role reversal denotes a shift in role responsibility within the aged parent–adult child relationship.

In our experience, role reversal frequently takes place amid a great deal of resentment on the part of parents, and much guilt is often evidenced by children. The parents are likely to view the takeover by children as another loss, which is met with a struggle to maintain as much control as possible over their own lives. On the other hand, children often perceive their actions in assuming decision-making power over their parents as degrading the persons for whom they have the greatest respect. Most children feel strongly that it is their duty to honor their parents with respect, rather than promoting within them feelings of helplessness by taking over control of their lives. The fact that this shift in roles comes at a time in the life cycle of the parents when they are less able to regain the decision-making function in their lives, and thereby may remain dependent upon the adult children, is likely to increase the burden of guilt for these children.

The child's ability to take an adult role in relation to the parent depends largely upon the degree to which separateness or individuality was established in the family at an earlier stage. When this has been realized, family members possess a differentiated self, and neither parent nor child needs to view the other as an extension of the self. As a result, the adult child will be more likely to maintain objectivity in relation to the needs of the elderly parent.

Problems can occur for adult children in spite of their intellectual awareness of the parents' needs. Although children may realize that their parents are unable to function independently and a shift in roles may be necessary, they frequently need help in accepting the change on an emotional level. Parents may also need help in handling their feelings in relation to depending upon the children.

The giving up and taking on of responsibilities as inherent in the role reversal process is not limited to the two generations directly involved. The systemic properties of family functioning come into play, and family interactions at various levels are involved. Field (1972) says: "The assumption of increased responsibility for their parents' welfare may create for the children a serious dilemma, as they find themselves conflicted as to whether their responsibility to their parents interferes with the adequate discharge of their responsibility to their own children" (p. 131).

At the time added responsibility is brought on by the needs of aging parents, many adult children are still very much involved with their own nuclear families. For example, some may still have children in school or just beginning their careers who look to them for help at the same time as the elderly parents. It is also likely that many of these second-generation adults will be deeply involved in their own careers, and this, too, will claim a good deal of their attention. Role shifts involving aged parents under these conditions present the adult children (second generation) with quite a dilemma. In some cases they may need direct help in sorting out and establishing priorities that will allow them to continue functioning in their various roles. When there are also problems in relationships between these extended family members, the social worker must understand the nature of the conflict and determine where changes are needed and can be realized.

Loss and Grief

It is important for social workers to consider grief and mourning over losses when working with aging persons and their families. Older people experience increasing difficulty in replacing losses due to diminishing inner and outer resources and may grieve over a loss that seems rather insignificant to young observers. There is little doubt that society fails to appreciate fully the dynamics of loss and, as a result, does not deal with it appropriately in many cases, especially where the aged are concerned. This is reflected in the reported perceptions children have about the experiences of their aged parents. Simos (1973) found that adult children recognized parental mourning most often when the loss involved significant others, such as spouses or children. Yet old people also may "grieve over the death of a pet, the loss of a job, a social role, self-esteem, independence, a lifetime home, or right to drive an auto-mobile, or the failure of bodily functions or sensory activity" (p. 80).

As further evidence of children's misunderstanding of loss experienced by their aged parents, Simos (1973) reports:

> Isolation and denial as defenses against the pain of loss were seen by children as lack of feeling on the part of the parents. Feelings of helplessness and despair, normal reactions to loss, were experienced as burdensome parental traits. A desperate attempt to hold on to remaining possessions or life styles was seen as stubbornness. (p. 80)

Social workers involved in work with adult children and their aged parents need to be especially alert to the possibility of loss among older members. The likelihood that children may misunderstand the impact of such losses must also be kept in mind. When this is indicated, intervention should include helping younger members to relate realistically to the losses of the older members.

Lifestyle

Knowledge of the lifestyle of old people is also useful in gaining an understanding of their social adjustment. The aging individual who has spent a lifetime actively involved in various activities may find it difficult to accept the inactivity to which older people are often relegated in later years. Those whose primary activities during their most productive years were centered around work and family may be faced with loneliness and isolation when these supports are no longer available. Simos (1973) found that many elderly persons with such lifestyles had developed such a narrow range of interests, coupled with poor social skills, that they were unable to engage in social activities. Others were able to respond socially only when the opportunity was provided by the initiative of other people.

Another problem frequently encountered in work with this type of extended family unit is the conflict resulting from the extreme dependency of the aging parent on the adult child. This usually develops when a parent who has enjoyed a very close and dependent marital relationship attempts to transfer dependency needs to a child in the absence of the spouse. In such cases, the smoothness of the symbiotic interactions between the parents is likely to have hidden the existence of the prevailing dependency, and the children will have been presented with a picture of independent functioning. This false perception on the part of the children can contribute to a misunderstanding of the parents' behavior with regard to fulfilling dependency needs through relationships with them during the later years. In this case, conflict is likely to develop between parent and child, necessitating help outside of the family to clarify the situation and provide both parent and child with a realistic basis for relating.

Social workers will find it helpful in alleviating conflict about the dependency of the aging parent on the adult child to gain some understanding of the relationship that previously existed between the parents. Awareness of the former lifestyle of older people is also useful in assessing their adjustment and intervening on their behalf.

Conflicts and Disagreements

Disagreements between children may be encountered in work with the multigenerational family. These disagreements may arise from misunderstanding, lack of information, rivalry between children, and so on. When failure to agree is centered around information deficits, often the situation can be corrected through improved processing and sharing of information among family members.

When rivalry between the children is involved, however, the problem is much more difficult. Not only are the principals in the rivalry situation adults, but many are also parents of adult children to whom the rivalry is likely to have been passed. When this is the case, the third generation may be involved in the problem. A tremendous amount of energy has usually been invested by the second-generation adults in various forms of competition and differences over the years. As a result, their responses are influenced by a lifetime of thoughts, feelings, and experiences based on these unresolved rivalries. When these adults are seen in relation to problems involving aged parents, they are likely to have relatively fixed positions. Each child is interested primarily in working his or her own will successfully. The struggle between these adult children can easily reach the level where the parents' needs become secondary to the children's need to prevail.

In such situations, each side may seek additional support and gain momentum as the struggle continues. Spouses and children frequently become involved in the conflict, and sometimes other relatives and friends lend their support to one of the sides. The following case summary reflects the difficulty that can be encountered when disagreement about planning for an elderly parent is based on rivalry between adult children.

The patient, a frail man of 75 years, was brought to the Adult Consultation Clinic by his daughter, who explained her difficulty in continuing to maintain him in her home. As a result, she was seeking help in planning for a new living situation for her father. The father did not take kindly to the possibility of residing in a special-care facility and wanted to contact a son with whom he thought he could live. The daughter was obviously distressed at the mention of her brother's involvement but gave in to her father's wishes. Soon after the father's contact with his son, the son called the clinic to arrange an appointment and requested that all consideration of his father's entering a residential facility be discontinued.

In the following weeks, several members of this extended family were involved. The "tug of war" between the son and daughter was readily seen. Charges and countercharges relative to respective efforts to gain control of the patient's finances and other properties were heard from both. Each pulled in other relatives who were sympathetic to their respective views, and these relatives were as firmly fixed in their opinions as the children. Although the son could not arrange for his father to live with him and presented no alternative plan, he could see his sister "getting her way" and "maintaining an advantage with their father." He suggested the possibility of court action to protect what he perceived as his own interests, and his sister was also willing to battle with him through court proceedings. It was obvious that the aged father's needs were being ignored as the struggle intensified between the children, and the extended family's energies were now also being spent in the contest.

The social worker must keep in mind the needs of the aged parents and refrain from becoming completely consumed in the struggle between the children. This kind of struggle usually neutralizes efforts to plan for the parents, and significant change in the rivalries between the children is likely to require long-term intervention. Therefore, in the interest of the parent, it may be necessary to make clear to the children the way the social worker is experiencing their struggle, which will not be dealt with specifically until an acceptable outcome has been realized on behalf of the parent. In this case, the focus of intervention is removed from the children's struggle with one another to the needs of the parent and what can be done in this regard.

Conflicts and disagreements may also develop between adult children and their parents as they interact on behalf of the parents. Consider the following situation where parents insisted on compensating the efforts of children by doing something for them in return. When this was discouraged, the parents became even more determined to repay them in some way. They insisted on helping with housekeeping chores, paying for groceries at the market, and so on. Finally, having become thoroughly annoyed with the parents' behavior and realizing no improvement in their efforts to curtail it, the children sought professional help. When the adult couple was seen by the social worker, it was decided that further use of direct confrontation with the parents was not likely to improve the situation. It was therefore suggested that they should try something different. The new strategy was not only to allow the parents to help with chores, but to find something for them to do. And when they insisted on paying for groceries, they were to be allowed to do so. After repeated experiences with this new attitude on the part of the children, the parents felt they were being unfairly used and refused to perform chores or go to the market with the children. As a result, the adult children regained control over what they considered their responsibility, and the parents gave up the need to repay the children for their willingness to help them.

Role of the Spouse

It is also important to understand the role of the spouses of adult children when aging parents are included in the family group—both relationships between this adult pair and relations between the spouse and the parent. If the adult child and spouse enjoy a satisfactory relationship, work involving the aged parent will most likely proceed without representing a serious threat to the relationship of this subsystem. However, when the spouse relationship is characterized by disagreement and tension, the strain of involvement with the aging parent is likely to escalate the conflict. The resulting struggle between the spouses will interfere with the social worker's efforts to intervene on behalf of the elderly parents. If, in addition to a good relationship between the adult child and spouse, relations between the spouse and the parent-in-law are also good, the intervention process usually proceeds without major conflicts or disruptions, and outcomes are likely to be acceptable to all concerned.

When there is conflict between the spouse and the elderly parent, the work to be done will be difficult. This conflict creates the likelihood of disruption in other family relationships, especially between adult child and spouse and sometimes between the adult child and the parent, as the reciprocal aspects of relating within the family system take over. In most situations, these types of relationships are readily identified, and the strategies commonly used by social workers in dealing with relationship problems are usually sufficient. Nevertheless, the fact that problems can develop out of what appears to be satisfactory relations between adult children and spouses should not be overlooked. This outcome is not uncommon, especially in cases where one of the principals in the relationship has adapted to a deficit in the functioning of the other, and this adaptation is taxed by closer involvement with an extended family member such as an aging parent. For example, consider the spouse who over the years has adapted to the necessity of meeting the dependency needs of the husband or wife and gives the appearance of enjoying a satisfactory relationship. When the parent is brought into the picture, the role of this spouse may be required to expand to the point of meeting the needs of not one but two dependent people. This is especially so if the aged member needs assistance with routine maintenance or in the area of decision making. The dependent spouse will usually have trouble carrying executive responsibility relative to these needs of the parent, as indicated by the following case summary:

> Mr. and Mrs. J had been married for 15 years without children when Mr. J's father came to live with them. Mrs. J was the strong member of this marital pair, and her authority and overall assertiveness in relation to family matters were accepted by Mr. J, who preferred to remain in the background. It soon developed that the aging father required a great deal of supervision with regard to his behavior and personal hygiene but was resistive to any effort to control his activities. The burden of responsibility increased considerably for the wife, as she found her husband unable to provide any direction for his father. In various ways he deferred decision making and care for the aging parent to his wife. When they were unable to work this out, Mrs. J asked for help. Although she was very fond of her father-in-law and had not objected to his moving in with them, she had not anticipated the problems he brought into their lives, especially her husband's reactions to his father's needs. In retrospect, Mrs. J could see that she had, in some ways, been a "mother" to Mr. J but was unwilling to "add a new baby" at this stage of her life.

This situation represented a real threat to the marital relationship, and this relationship was crucial in meeting the needs of the aging father. The social worker chose to focus on the interactions between the marital pair as it related to roles, expectations, and so on. While alternative plans for Mr. J's father were discussed, neither wished to have him placed outside of their home, and Mr. J was gradually able to take on some of the responsibility for his father.

Encounters of this type clearly indicate the importance of the role assumed by the adult child's spouse and the necessity of understanding the spouse's relationship within the family unit. Social workers will find it very useful, in working with families in which elderly parents are members, to pay special attention to the spouse without kinship ties to the parents. If this individual experiences conflict in existing family relationships or is unwilling to accommodate the intervention process, the realization of desired outcomes from such activity will be difficult.

SUMMARY

With the steady increase in the elderly population in the United States, many adult children are seeking help in planning for their aging parents. We have presented in this chapter some guidelines for understanding the aging process and how it affects older people, as well as those who are involved with them. Some of the problems encountered in working with adult children and elderly parents have been examined, and suggestions for intervention have also been discussed.

The guidelines given for understanding and working with this family group are based on the culture and traditional values existing in the United States. While some of the strategies and techniques are applicable to work with immigrant populations, practitioners who engage in work with such groups should consider the cultural values to which they adhere and the unique position the elderly may hold as a result of their age. Awareness by practitioners of their own attitudes toward older people will reduce the possibility of inappropriate input and enhance the likelihood of successful therapeutic outcome.

REFERENCES

Bell, B.D. 1976. *Contemporary Social Gerontology*. Springfield, IL: Charles C. Thomas, Publisher.

Botwinick, J. 1973. *Aging and Behavior*. New York: Springer Publishing Co.

Brody, E. 1990. "Role Reversal: An Inaccurate and Destructive Concept." *Journal of Gerontological Social Work* 15:15–22.

Burgess, E.W. 1954. "Social Relations, Activities, and Personal Adjustment." *American Journal of Sociology* 59:352–60.

Carp, F.M. 1973. "The Psychology of Aging." In *Foundations of Practical Gerontology*, 2nd ed., eds. R.R. Boyd and C.G. Oaks. Columbia: University of South Carolina Press.

Cummings, E., and Henry, W.E., eds. 1961. *Growing Old*. New York: Basic Books.

Field, M. 1972. *The Aged, the Family, and the Community*. New York: Columbia University Press.

Fineman, N. 1994. "Health Care Providers' Subjective Understandings of Old Age: Implications for Threatened Status in Late Life." *Journal of Aging Studies* 8:255–70.

Fry, P.S. 1992. "Major Social Theories of Aging and Their Implications for Counseling Concepts and Practice: A Critical Review." *Counseling Psychologist* 20:246–329.

Glenwick, D., and Whitbourne, S. 1977. "Beyond Despair and Disengagement: A Transactional Model of Personality Development in Later Life." *International Journal of Aging and Human Development* 8:261–67.

Gurland, B. 1990. "Symposium on Role Reversal: A Discussant Responds." 15:35–38.

Havinghurst, R.J., and Albrecht, R. 1953. *Older People*. New York: Longmans Green.

Jarvik, L. 1990. "Role Reversal: Implications for Therapeutic Intervention." *Journal of Gerontological Social Work* 15:23–34.

Lemon, B.W., Bengston, V.L., and Peterson, J.A. 1972. "An Exploration of Activity Theory of Aging: Activity Types and Life Satisfaction Among In-Movers to a Retirement Community." *Journal of Gerontology* 27:511–23.

Panser, L., Rhodes, T., Girman, C., Guess, H., Chute, C., Oesterling, J., Lieber, M., and Jacobsen, S. 1995. "Sexual Function of Men 40 to 79 Years: The Olmsted County Study of Urinary Symptoms and Health Among Men." *Journal of American Geriatrics Society* 43:1107–11.

Peterson, J.A. 1974. "Therapeutic Intervention in Marital and Family Problems of Aging Persons." In *Professional Obligations and Approaches to the Aged*, eds. A. Schwartz and I. Mensh. Springfield, IL: Charles C. Thomas, Publisher.

Savitsky, E., and Sharkey, H. 1972. "The Geriatric Patient and His Family: A Study of Family Interaction in the Aged." *Journal of Geriatric Psychiatry* 5:3–19.

Schwartz, A.N., and Mensh, I., eds. 1974. *Professional Obligations and Approaches to the Aged*. Springfield, IL: Charles C. Thomas, Publisher.

Simos, B.G. 1973. "Adult Children and Their Aging Parents." *Social Work* 18:78–85.

Tallmer, M., and Kutner, B. 1969. "Disengagement and Stresses of Aging." *Journal of Gerontology* 24:70–75.

Warner Schaie, K., Willis, S., and O'Hanlon, A. 1994. "Perceived Intellectual Performance Change Over Seven Years." *Journal of Gerontology* 49:108–18.

Wolk, R.L., and Wolk, R.B. 1971. "Professional Workers' Attitudes toward the Aged." *Journal of the American Geriatrics Society* 19:624–39.

CHAPTER 9

Gay and Lesbian Couples and Families

Providing professional services to those who openly follow the gay/lesbian lifestyle is relatively new. As a result, many misconceptions exist with regard to who they are, how they should react in open society, and how the non-gay/lesbian community should react to them. However, it is becoming increasingly important that professional care givers, especially social workers, understand the life processes of this group, as homosexuals are no longer content, nor should they be, to live unfulfilled lives of secrecy or denial. Therefore, we hope to provide some information that might serve as a basis for a beginning appreciation of homosexuality as a legitimate and acceptable lifestyle as is heterosexuality, with both being susceptible to problems created by interaction with other individuals and institutions in contemporary society.

The size of the homosexual population is unknown. Estimates given by researchers usually carry a wide range, which is indicative of the uncertainty of actual numbers. For example, in discussing families headed by lesbian couples in the United States the estimated number of lesbian mothers ranged from 1.5 million to 5 million (Hoeffer, 1981; Falk, 1989; Gottman, 1990). Given the negative attitude of society toward the homosexual lifestyle—which causes untold numbers of lesbian mothers and others to deny their sexual orientation—it is fair to assume that these estimates are far from accurate (Hare, 1994). It seems sufficient to say that homosexuality as a lifestyle is prevalent in today's society and these individuals, couples, and families will experience a myriad of life adjustment problems that will require professional help. If social workers and other professionals are to provide this help successfully, they must subject themselves to a self-examination that explores their own knowledge, thoughts, feelings, and attitudes in relation to homosexuality. This process will include, for most professionals, further knowledge of the prevailing circumstances and experiences surrounding gay men and lesbians and how this impacts their lives as well as the lives of those who offer help.

It is generally accepted that homosexual men are referred to as gay and women as lesbian. In our discussion, we will follow this reference pattern for the most part. However, for reasons of facilitation, when making statements that apply to both groups we will use only the term gay.

SOCIETAL ATTITUDES

While there has been some progress in recent years, many Americans still have extremely negative attitudes toward homosexuals. These attitudes, based largely on myths that are supported by misinformation, result in what is widely known as homophobia, a term that depicts an existing fear of and/or dislike for homosexuals and homosexuality. Among the myths held by many in American society are beliefs that (1) homosexuals are more easily compromised than heterosexuals and should not be trusted with positions of influence and authority; (2) homosexuals will involve children sexually if they are unable to find an adult sexual partner; (3) homosexual parents will raise homosexual children; (4) homosexuality is a social corruption that threatens current civilization; (5) homosexuality is a mental illness; and (6) gay men choose to be gay (Levitt and Klassen, 1974; Berger and Kelly, 1995). There are no data to substantiate any of these conclusions. In the case of the belief that homosexual parents produce homosexual children, studies have shown that most homosexuals are raised by heterosexual parents.

Gay and lesbian individuals are found in all socioeconomic levels of society and in all ethnic, racial, and religious groups. White North American gays and lesbians are usually thought of as representing the dominant culture, while gays and lesbians of color represent the minority culture, and are often grouped as black, Hispanic, Native American, Latino, Asian, and others. Although they share many common problems with gays and lesbians from the dominant culture, those from the minority culture face an additional barrier, which is the scrutiny of their own culture, where there is usually less acceptance of homosexuality (Falco, 1991). In speaking of lesbians of color, Falco points up the dilemma faced by this group in being pitted against both cultures and having to decide which to embrace. If they choose to identify more closely with their own culture, they are likely to experience more difficulty in coming out due to the existing level of cultural acceptance. Should they choose to identify with the dominant culture, which is more accepting, they will lose contact with their own culture. Obviously neither choice is satisfactory, and the homosexual of color (minority) must learn to negotiate an unfriendly set of circumstances created by the negative attitudes of two cultures and may be expected to seek help in finding a comfortable place in society.

Professional helpers should consider each family system individually, including strengths, weaknesses, and patterns of functioning in crisis situations. The effect of any loss of connection with the client's minority culture must be examined, and help should be provided to the client in coping with family pressures and the level of acceptance within the dominant and minority cultures (Falco, 1991).

In spite of negative attitudes toward homosexuals, the legal rights of gay people are undergoing positive change. For example, 24 states had decriminalized homosexual acts between consenting adults by 1993. Some type of nondiscriminatory laws affecting homosexuals have also been passed by a number of municipalities, and benefits for partners of gay and lesbian employees have been made available by some major companies and universities (Tully, 1995). With a continuation of this trend, equal treatment under the law is possible in the future. However, this is far from reality at this time, and discrimination continues in many areas of gay life. The emotional burden gay people must carry is tremendous and gives rise to many life problems.

PROBLEM AREAS

Coming Out

Reaching self-identification involves a process in which gay and lesbian individuals make known to others their sexual preferences. This process is defined as "coming out," sometimes referred to as "coming out of the closet." This stage in the gay lifestyle has been discussed by various authors, including Woodman and Lenna (1980), Kus (1990), and Moses and Hawkins (1982). This is a difficult experience for most homosexuals. As a result, many may be seen by social workers and other helping professionals. Although triggered by the coming out process, the call for help is usually to address other problems, such as inability to sleep, anxiousness, and feeling uncomfortable with other people.

Kus describes four stages through which gay and lesbian individuals pass in the coming out process: the identification stage, the stage of cognitive changes, the acceptance stage, and the action stage.

The identification stage is usually reached during the teenage years. This does not parallel the determination of one's sexual orientation, which occurs during the early years of life, if not before birth (Money and Ehrhardt, 1972). Gays and lesbians reach the point of identifying their homosexuality in various ways. This may include experiencing unsatisfactory sexual relations with an opposite-sex partner; falling in love with someone of the same sex; exploring the meaning of homophobic expressions such as queens, dykes, gays, and so forth. Having been socialized to believe that only a heterosexual orientation leads to happiness and that homosexuality is unacceptable, gays and lesbians experience a very uncomfortable time in the identification of their own sexual orientation. In this stage of the coming out process the individual is usually beset with feelings of loneliness, fear, shame, an inability to focus on meaningful life tasks, and, in some cases, depression, suicidal ideation, and the beginning of alcoholism.

The stage of cognitive changes follows the identity changes of the previous stage and is characterized by the change from a negative perception of homosexuality to a more positive notion about gays and lesbians as well as their place in society. "However, this stage does not entail fully accepting being gay or lesbian as a positive state of being" (Kus, 1990, p. 35). For example, some fear of rejection and possible violence is still present during this stage and it is not unusual for gays and lesbians to engage in passing as heterosexuals. This often takes the form of dating the opposite sex and, in some cases, even gay bashing. Further indication of the tentativeness of the emerging positive perception of the gay lifestyle can be seen in the migration of homosexuals to distant cities where they can explore gay and lesbian communities without revealing their homosexuality to family and friends. For some, there is also an almost paralyzing fear of being discovered that permeates all aspects of life. In spite of some continuing uncertainty about coming out to others in the stage of cognitive changes, most gays and lesbians begin to give some clues to their identity—such as objecting to gay and lesbian jokes and no longer pretending to be dating the opposite sex.

In the acceptance stage of coming out, the individual becomes more comfortable with his or her sexual orientation. There is less stress than in stages one and two, and increased ability to relax. Feelings of guilt and symptoms of depression disappear, and an overall good feeling about oneself emerges.

The fourth and final stage begins with the internalization of the good feeling of self-acceptance experienced in the acceptance stage. Stage four is characterized by action. For example, the individual may intentionally disclose his or her sexual orientation, increase open association with other gays and lesbians, and become politically involved in issues that promote their causes. While individuals in this stage may be rejected by employers, family, and others after disclosing their identity, they are able to turn to other gays and lesbians for support.

Adolescents

Informing others of one's being gay or lesbian is more difficult for adolescents than it is for adults, which is probably due to the fact that adolescents are still subject to the authority of their parents, who often react negatively to the coming out of their adolescent children. Jay and Young (1979) report 58 percent of the mothers who learned of their children's homosexuality reacted in a negative manner. The common response by an adult who learns a child is gay or lesbian is punishment, or an attempt to have the child seen by a therapist in the hope that he or she can be "cured" of this problem. Coming out to heterosexual peers is also risky, as it is almost sure to result in ostracism of the gay or lesbian adolescent. Children who experience difficulty establishing their homosexual identity are not likely to seek help with this problem on their own. However, they may come to the attention of professional helpers through efforts of parents, as previously mentioned. In some cases, these children may turn to social workers and other professionals for help with difficulties they are experiencing—such as, relationships with parents or peers, difficulty in school adjustment, and the like—which are related to their gay identity problems. If in the process of exploring the problem presented by the adolescent, homosexuality is revealed as the underlying issue, the helping professional's strategy should be guided by the stage the adolescent is experiencing in relation to his or her sexual preference.

If an adolescent client wishes to refrain from coming out to others, the helping professional may assist the client in functioning as well as possible while presenting himself or herself as heterosexual. However, if the client has already been identified as homosexual or wishes to be identified as such, the professional helper may act as advocate for the client, including interacting with parents on the client's behalf when this is indicated. Advocacy in this situation might include providing the parents with accurate information about homosexuality and encouraging a positive, open relationship between the adolescent and his or her parents (Moses and Hawkins, 1982).

Adults

Gay and lesbian adults usually find coming out to others less difficult than do adolescents, due in part to the increased freedom they enjoy in directing their own lives. Adults most often first identify themselves to other gay people through a sexual encounter or by going to places frequented by other gays and lesbians and displaying appropriate behavior, which is showing unmistakable interest in the same gender (Moses and Hawkins, 1982). This connection with the gay community provides the adult with an outlet for self-expression in a supportive atmosphere, a situation that is almost never available to gay adolescents. While coming out is usually easier for adults, it is not always without problems. Some adult homosexuals may find themselves uncomfortable with some of the behaviors practiced in the gay community with which they are beginning to associate. With the help of a social worker or other professional, these individuals can be helped to fit better into the existing structure of the gay community, as well as finding alternative support systems. Having the opportunity to be in contact with other gay people provides strong support for the individual who is beginning to establish a gay or lesbian identity.

Informing Parents

At the beginning of the self-identification process, many homosexuals are very uncomfortable. Among their greatest concerns is reaction outside of the gay community, especially the possibility of negative reaction from their parents. This concern is justified, as some parents have such strong negative feelings when learning their child is gay that the relationship between them is seriously damaged and, in some cases, ended. Given the fact that revealing a gay or lesbian identity to parents can be costly, some gay people still feel they should tell their parents either because of the guilt they experience by withholding this information or out of hope that telling them will strengthen their relationship. When helping these clients resolve problems in coming out to their parents, social workers and other professionals should explore the existing relationship between parents and children and help the client determine what would be gained if parents were informed of his or her sexual preference. When the primary motivation is guilt, some time should be spent helping the client cope with these feelings before revealing their sexual identity to parents as well as determining how best to inform them.

If the primary motivation for coming out to parents is to improve family relationships, the social worker should help the gay client assess his or her existing communication skills as well as those of their parents. When good communication and relationship skills are not in existence, or if other family problems are present, the revelation of a homosexual client's sexual preferences is not likely to enhance family relationships (Moses and Hawkins, 1982). However, we agree with Moses and Hawkins that adult gay people who want to tell their parents about their sexual preference should be supported. At the same time, they need to be made aware of the probable consequences of this action and to understand their reasons for wanting to share this information with their parents. When parents are going to be told, it is usually helpful for clients to discuss with the social worker or other professional counselor how parents will be informed. Here is where role-playing with the client what and how he or she will communicate, as well as what the parent might say in return, can be useful. It not only provides support for the client but furnishes a glimpse of how the parent will most likely respond.

It is not unusual following the shock of learning that a son or daughter will follow a gay lifestyle for parents to seek help in understanding homosexuality and in learning how to cope with the reality of this lifestyle. They will most likely be confronted with questions from friends and relatives that will include the many myths and misunderstanding usually associated with gay and lesbian individuals. When these parents are seen, they will likely have many questions—some of which may seem quite impertinent. However, these clients should not be made to feel their questions are irrelevant; instead they should be listened to very carefully and given forthright and informative responses. Parents can also be helped by receiving accurate information, including available resources to further their knowledge of homosexuality. For example, social workers should focus on clarifying myths and other areas of misconception. Selected reading material about homosexuality will also be helpful and might be suggested to parents who are struggling to understand the new lifestyle in which their son or daughter is engaged. And any ideas the parents may have about therapy for their homosexual son or daughter in order to change him or her to heterosexual should be discouraged. They should be given a realistic appraisal of the positive and negative consequences of the gay lifestyle, including what they can expect and what their son or daughter can expect. They should also be encouraged to establish contact with parents of other gays or lesbians as a source of support.

Informing Heterosexual Friends

It is usually easier for homosexuals to tell close, nongay friends about their gayness than it is to tell parents and other relatives. However, their heterosexual friends do not always respond in a positive manner. Coming out to friends, as in coming out to parents, should be given careful thought before following through, and clients should be aware of why they want to tell friends and what the anticipated consequences might be. For example, if the friend is known in an employment situation, it would be advisable to consider the impact this information could have with regard to job security and career advancement if the heterosexual friend should react negatively (Moses and Hawkins, 1982).

In the event of substantial negative reaction to coming out to parents or friends, helping professionals may need to teach clients some ways of coping with this situation. The use of supportive techniques designed to counter feelings of guilt and self-doubt about being gay will be helpful. Problems may also surface when gay people do not trust positive or neutral responses to coming out. Here, the client's lack of trust might be explored as it relates to the behavior of the individuals involved. This type of reality testing can be useful in determining the source of the problem. If the positive responses are accompanied by supportive behaviors, the client's negative perception of these behaviors can be challenged. The focus should then shift to the client's possible underlying feelings of guilt about being gay and the doubt he or she might have about sincere acceptance by nongay people. The goal of this type of intervention is to introduce the gay client to ways of assessing the reactions of other people based on their actual behavior and also gaining some insight into his or her feelings about being gay.

Gay clients may also react to negative responses to their gayness with anger and resentment. While this is preferable to self-doubt, when anger is shown, efforts should be directed toward helping the client differentiate between personal anger over being hurt and anger at society for its attitude toward gay people. If the anger is personal and the perpetrator is someone with whom the client wishes to continue a relationship, it will be helpful for the client to consider not only his or her hurt, but also the hurt the other person feels and why he or she feels this way. If the relationship is to be maintained, help should be offered in assisting the client to find ways to deal with the risk involved while continuing to reach out to the person whose reactions are hurtful. In many cases, people who behave this way toward their gay friends actually feel they are the one who has been hurt and sometimes have difficulty taking a conciliatory view of the situation. This is due to the heterosexual's belief that he or she has been betrayed and is actually the victim in this relationship. Therefore, the gay person deserves and should accept the negative reactions. Under these circumstances, if the client feels he or she can no longer bear the pain caused by these negative reactions, it may be advisable to end the relationship.

Other problems are likely to surface for homosexuals as they struggle to find a comfortable existence in a homophobic society. Alcoholism is a major problem in the gay and lesbian communities: Alcohol is the drug of choice used to deal with bad feelings generated by homophobia. Suicide is another problem area for gays and lesbians, some of whom believe self-destruction is the only way to rid themselves of internalized homophobic thoughts (Lapierre, 1990). Helping professionals should explore the underlying causes of these problems and focus on changing the forces that make these destructive efforts necessary.

INTERVENTION WITH GAY COUPLES

Therapy with couples, whether gay or nongay, is concerned with discovering and making known to the couples the options that exist in their relationship and helping them make choices from these options. The choice may not always be to remain together, and helping professionals should not focus on trying to keep couples together if their choice is to separate. Instead, when a couple has considered the options available and chooses to end their relationship, therapeutic efforts should be focused on helping them adjust their lives around the choice they have made.

Another factor to consider in working with gay couples is the difference between gay and heterosexual love relationships. One of these differences is reflected in the length of the relationship. It is generally recognized that same-sex couples do not remain together as long as married nongay couples do (Weinberg, Williams, and Pryor, 1994). This must be taken into consideration in counseling gay couples, and the idea that the typical couple is monogamous and remains in a lifelong relationship should be abandoned. Same-sex couples simply do not fit into the heterosexual marriage model, and helping professionals will be well advised to assist gay couples in developing relationship styles that are personally satisfying. Moses and Hawkins suggest that this may sometimes involve abandoning the total sharing concept usually applied to heterosexual couples and helping gay couples develop a more independent relationship style in which each partner maintains separate bank accounts, bedrooms, and in some cases living arrangements.

While this approach is consistent with the realities of the gay lifestyle, it does not mean that couples who prefer a more traditional relationship should be discouraged from attempting to develop it.

Gay couples may seek help for a number of reasons, many of which are similar to those of heterosexual couples. For example, a gay couple might experience strain in their relationship when their families of origin have difficulty relating to the reality of the gay lifestyle. Concerns about the security of employment and housing, if knowledge of their union is revealed to employers and housing authorities in case of rental housing, can interfere with their functioning as a couple. Infidelity, perhaps the most sensitive of all problems in the gay relationship, is a primary source of disruption and the method of its resolution is crucial to continuation of the relationship. It is not unusual for the partner who has remained faithful to make an unconditional demand that the unfaithful one change his behavior. Such a demand will most likely be rejected as unreasonable and may be sufficient reason to end the relationship (Carl, 1990). Infidelity also increases the threat that AIDS will become a factor in gay relationships. Although the presence of AIDS does not automatically end the relationship when the illness is discovered, medical services and psychological counseling are usually needed and will be sought by the couple.

Social workers and other helping professionals must have a good understanding of gay male cultural and clinical issues and be willing to intervene in the nontraditional family system created by gay men (Shernoff, 1995). Whatever problem is presented must be explored by helping professionals just as in the case of heterosexual couples. We generally agree with Carl and others that issues of hierarchy, boundary location, and triangles are lucrative areas for exploration in beginning work with couples and families regardless of clients' sexual orientation. The impact of outside influences and subcultural differences should also be evaluated, together with information about the families of origin—including family patterns and roles that might be handed down through generations. The professional helper should seek a clear understanding of communication patterns during problem assessment and consider ways of improving communication when indicated. For example, when the problem is poor communication between parents and the gay couple, it is likely to be due to a lack of knowledge and acceptance of the gay lifestyle. In this case, the communication barrier may be broken by providing the parents with good written information about homosexuality. They should be instructed to read it by themselves and then discuss it with their son and his lover (Silverstein, 1990). The social worker as professional helper might also choose to meet with the gay couple and their parents for a full discussion of guilt, fears, and resentments, which interfere with good communication.

There are many other problems experienced by gay couples that will require professional intervention. However, we agree with Patten (1988), who suggests that homosexual and heterosexual relationships share many more similarities than differences. And, in the final analysis, both are looking for understanding, tenderness, and love. Therefore, generally speaking, professionals working with same-sex couples will realize success using the same techniques used with heterosexual relationships.

INTERVENTION WITH LESBIAN COUPLES

Like all other couples, work with lesbian couples requires an understanding of how individuals relate to each other. In lesbian relationships, the overall communication pattern is one of equality. The decision to seek help from professionals is difficult for most lesbians due to a lack of trust of professionals. However, when contact is made, a show of knowledge and genuine concern can make disclosure in the therapeutic situation less difficult for clients. Their skepticism of professional intervention can also be overcome if the professional shows respect for their status and existence. This can be accomplished by an open and nonjudgmental approach reflected in the use of such words as partner, instead of boyfriend, or husband and significant relationship, instead of marriage, when talking about social support systems (Hall and Stevens, 1990).

In beginning with lesbian couples, Hall and Stevens suggest that the helping professional should first look to the external environment in which the couple lives for sources of stress in their relationship. In keeping with this approach, it will be helpful to know how the couple experiences the local community. Are resources for support available and is the couple able to access them? What does the family of origin of each partner think about the union of the couple and how do they relate to them? Do racial, ethnic, or class differences exist between the women? What are the resources of each partner? Does the couple have sufficient time and privacy for relating? Whenever problems exist as a result of these outside stresses, effort should be made to decrease the impact of these stressors on the couples' relationship before internal problems are assessed. For example, if a problem exists because of a difference in class, an open and honest discussion of earlier life experiences and how they might relate to current likes and dislikes could be helpful. If the couple cannot find sufficient time for relating, work schedules and other commitments might be discussed and compromises sought that could lead to sharing more private time together.

Internal stress for lesbian couples is almost a given. Living in a hostile society can severely limit access to many resources. If support is not received from family and friends, the couple may be forced to rely almost completely on each other to meet their needs for affection and acceptance. The emotional bond created by this situation often leads to a state of interdependence in which both partners experience a diminution of self that can lead to a state of fusion (enmeshment) in which the two become one (Krestan and Bepko, 1980). When faced with this problem, the helping professional should provide support by encouraging each partner to develop separate friends and activities, which will help restore clear boundaries between the couple and contribute to an improved sense of self.

If the state of interdependence or fusion persists to the extent that a clear sense of self is lost, the professional counselor should conduct further exploration. If, for example, substance abuse by one partner is found and the other is so completely focused on the addictive behavior that she develops a co-dependent relationship, this should be given immediate attention. Appropriate action might include specialized counseling and referral to Alcoholics Anonymous or some other self-help group.

INTERVENTION WITH GAY PARENTS

Families may be headed by gay men or lesbians. However, it seems fair to assume that the latter is more prevalent, as lesbian couples are bringing children into the family through adoption, heterosexual intercourse, and artificial insemination (Lott-Whitehead and Tully, 1993). Gay parents with children may also be a reconstituted family as children of one or both partners are brought into a gay or lesbian union. The same is accomplished when a gay or lesbian single parent joins with a lover and establishes a family consisting of two adults and children. When a gay family is formed in this manner, it requires a period of adjustment the same as in a heterosexual reconstituted family. It is natural in either case for children to see the new parent as an intruder who will compete for the natural parent's time and attention, which is likely to be met with extreme jealousy and resentment. The gay couple should be helped to realize that these negative reactions are also experienced by nongay couples who incorporate children in a reconstituted family. This should help to remove any feeling they might have that their gayness is responsible for this behavior. Strain may also be experienced by the adults in this situation. If there has been no discussion of possible difficulties and no agreement reached on the responsibilities of each partner before the lover moves in, the natural parent is likely to be somewhat protective of the children. When this occurs, the lover is likely to feel rejected as an outsider and resentful of the closeness between the children and their parent. Helping professionals should help lovers to be very deliberate in exerting any kind of authority in relation to the children or in demanding more time with the natural parent. In this way, he or she is less threatening to the children, and the likelihood of gaining their respect and becoming an integral part of the reconstituted family will increase over time. Open communication and acceptance of the children's feelings and concerns is always important in resolving these difficulties.

An increasing number of lesbian couples create their own nuclear family through alternative insemination. Regardless of whether the family is created in this manner or by incorporating children from a previous marriage, gay parents experience the same issues relative to parenting that nongay parents experience. However, the gay parent faces additional issues that are not experienced by heterosexual parents, including the many prejudices and misconceptions directed toward same-sex parents. While there is no evidence to substantiate the belief that gay and lesbian parents will have a detrimental impact on the lives of children, many have doubts about themselves as parents when they are constantly subjected to criticism. Professionals can be helpful in such cases by putting these parents in touch with other gay or lesbian parents in their area. However, support groups are not always available, and clients can also be helped by learning ways to counteract negative comments by others. This can be accomplished by helping clients learn the facts about gay and lesbian parenting and making this a firm part of their belief system. This will enable them to respond more convincingly to others who make inaccurate remarks. For example, the gay parent who does not find a more assertive approach too threatening may counter false statements with accurate information and request that the offensive party refrain from making such remarks. Obviously, choosing such a tactic will depend on whether or not the parent is openly gay (Moses and Hawkins, 1982).

Many gay parents are concerned about revealing their sexual orientation for fear of disruptions in their lives—including problems with child custody. Another concern of the gay parent is that the children's peers will learn of the parent's homosexuality, causing them to react negatively toward the children, who will suffer from this experience. As a result, it is not unusual for the gay parent to spend more time with heterosexuals and more time passing as a nongay parent than does the gay person without children (Moses and Hawkins, 1982). We agree with the thinking of Moses and Hawkins that lesbian mothers, and presumably gay fathers, should reveal their sexual orientation to children as soon as possible. Many of these parents may need help in coming out to their children, and the way in which this is done and the content of the process depends upon the age of the child. The younger child is less likely to understand the implications of being gay or lesbian, and at the same time will be less concerned about the social aspects of having a gay parent than the older child. While older children may be concerned about how their peers might react to the knowledge that their parents are gay, this usually subsides after a short period of time (Moses and Hawkins, 1982).

Parents should plan the coming out process to children in the same manner as they would in coming out to adults. When necessary, this includes rehearsing or role playing with the social worker, or other professional counselor, how the parent's sexual orientation will be revealed to the child and how the parent might respond to the child's reaction to learning that his or her parent is gay. It is important to help the client present his or her gayness to the child in a positive light. Moses and Hawkins suggest that the parent's sexual orientation be shared with children in a reasonably matter-of-fact manner, communicating their satisfaction with being gay and that this does not change the love they have for the children. While the response is likely to be positive, some children may be concerned about their parents' sexual preference. If the child reacts negatively to this information with a show of anger or name calling directed toward the parent's homosexuality, it will be helpful for the parent to focus on the anger and hurt the child is experiencing rather than criticizing the child for the outburst of anger. The concerns of older children may be successfully dealt with by presenting them with facts and encouraging discussion around their concerns.

Although most professional helpers agree that parents' coming out to children is important, some parents resist sharing knowledge of their sexual preference with their children. These parents are likely to be uncomfortable with their gayness and may be helped by discussing with the professional counselor the reasons he or she is not ready to come out to the children. Fear about how the child will react is often among the parents' reasons for resistance. In this case, it should be pointed out that children will most likely eventually realize that there is something different about their parents. And it is better to deal with this in the open where it can be discussed in a positive manner rather than keeping it hidden, thereby increasing the likelihood that the difference they recognize will come to be seen as something very wrong and degrading.

However, after careful discussion, if a parent is not sufficiently comfortable about his or her gayness to talk about it with assurance and comfort, coming out to children should be delayed until he or she is more at peace with being gay or lesbian.

Sometimes professional helpers may find themselves opposed to parents' telling children about their homosexual lifestyle. When this is the case, the professional should take a good look at himself or herself for any negative thoughts about homosexuality or entrusting children to gay parents. If such thoughts are present and cannot be overcome, the client should be referred to someone more amenable to working with the problems involved. (For additional information on working with reconstituted families, see Chapter 11.)

PROFESSIONAL RESPONSIBILITY

The primary responsibility of social workers and other professionals who work with gay and lesbian clients is the same as it is in work with nongay clients. Their responsibility is to help clients learn ways to deal with life problems that will promote greater satisfaction in individual and family functioning and in relations with others. However, we live in a society that values a heterosexual lifestyle, and professional helpers, whether gay or nongay, are influenced in various ways by this societal norm. For this reason, it is necessary for professionals to evaluate themselves as helpers to determine the extent of their own biases and how these biases might impact their work with clients who practice a homosexual lifestyle. This is especially important for heterosexuals working with gay and lesbian clients. In addition, these professionals should have wide knowledge of the gay lifestyle. This knowledge can be greatly increased by appropriate reading about homosexuality, which will also help counteract the prevalence of homophobic ideas in contemporary society.

Social workers and other professionals should also know about community resources and their function in the gay community. This includes information about gay bars, social clubs, and other support groups to which gay clients might be referred in order to increase their knowledge of the gay lifestyle within the community and help them feel more comfortable in associating with others who share their lifestyle.

Gay professionals who provide services to gay clients will need to consider where they are in relation to their own gayness. This includes whether or not they have come out to others and how comfortable they are with being identified as gay or lesbian. Overidentification with clients could be a problem and should be guarded against. Support in achieving self-fulfillment as a gay person should be the major objective of work with gay and lesbian clients; however, the reality of living a gay lifestyle in a heterosexual society should not be minimized.

Professionals who are unable to respect the right of gay clients to determine their sexual orientation and enjoy life in a manner appropriate to that orientation should not attempt to engage them in a therapeutic relationship. If the client's gayness is revealed during the helping process and the helping professional is unable to maintain a satisfactory comfort level in continuing with the client, he or she would be well advised to make a referral to someone who is able to more appropriately meet the client's needs.

AIDS

It is essential for professionals to be prepared for working with clients who are diagnosed with human immunodeficiency virus (HIV positive), as well as with those who carry a diagnosis of Acquired Immune Deficiency Syndrome (AIDS). Since this subject will be addressed in more detail in Chapter 12, our discussion here will be brief.

It should be noted that the groups most affected with AIDS in the United States are gay and bisexual men (Solomon, 1990), and what we will be discussing here is based on experience with the male population. In spite of new knowledge, AIDS continues to be seen by many people as a gay male disease (Weinberg, Williams, and Pryor, 1994). Individuals and couples who are HIV positive or diagnosed with AIDS may turn to professionals for help for various reasons, including patients referred by physicians who realize they need counseling and emotional support, and couples who seek help on their own for relationship problems exacerbated by the illness. Anger and depression are common among gay couples after learning that one partner (sometimes both) has been diagnosed HIV positive. Usually disagreements are centered around how the infection occurred and from whom it was received (Patten, 1988). Although arguments are focused on issues of fidelity, the underlying concern and the one most readily available to intervention is the fear of losing a partner and being abandoned. Professionals working with these clients should help them realize that this is not the time to give in to panic reactions. Patten suggests the use of reframing techniques such as telling the couple no one is dying at this point and their disagreements are a way of remaining close while expressing their fear of being separated. The purpose here is to set the stage for directing the couple's energy toward more constructive endeavors.

In working with gay individuals and couples with AIDS, the use of standard modes of psychotherapy can be helpful, but the use of any of these modes alone will probably be insufficient. What is needed usually goes beyond what takes place in the office of the professional helper. Support networks are essential, and some family work is often useful. The amount of supportive resources available will vary according to where clients live. The larger metropolitan areas usually offer support groups for people who are HIV positive; people who have AIDS; couple support groups; family support groups; and many other services designed to enhance the lives of people with AIDS and AIDS-related conditions (Carl, 1990). If clients do not have sufficient outside support in place, this should be discussed and efforts made to connect them with the necessary supports. This experience can help many individuals and couples obtain some perspective from others that will help them to deal more effectively with reality of their own lives.

We agree with Carl and others who believe professional helpers should encourage couples to develop joint goals, if they do not already have them, when seen in counseling. These goals should be short to medium range so that results can be experienced without waiting for an extended period of time. Care should be given in presenting the idea of setting goals in order to avoid an aura of finality. Having joint goals that are obtainable within a reasonable period of time will help couples with AIDS or AIDS-related conditions feel they are living and not just waiting for an uncertain future. This can be further reinforced by discussing issues of arrangements for care, finances, wills, beneficiaries of insurances, and similar concerns. Professionals will be well advised not to overlook the issue of such arrangements in the early sessions with clients.

It will also be helpful to know something about the standard medical treatments for clients with AIDS and AIDS-related conditions. Although various techniques commonly used in psychotherapeutic undertakings are useful in work with gay individuals and couples, it remains most important to see that as many supports as possible are in place for everyone involved in the therapeutic process.

DEALING WITH LOSS AND GRIEF

When a gay or lesbian love relationship ends with the death of one partner, the remaining partner may need help in dealing with his or her loss in the same way as the remaining partner of a heterosexual union. When such help is indicated, the helping professional should guide this individual through the experience of grieving by providing a safe and accepting climate in which the gay or lesbian client can allow feelings to emerge. Painful memories and feelings will need to be experienced. They should not be covered over by the use of tranquilizers or sedatives. Instead, professionals should let gay and lesbian clients know that it is acceptable to feel whatever he or she is feeling. When indicated, pictures and other articles may be used to facilitate focusing on specific memories that will help complete the grieving process.

Clients concerned about maintaining control of their feelings may be encouraged to call the social worker or other professionals between scheduled contacts, if they should feel themselves losing control. Other clients may be able to cope with their feelings by learning and using relaxation techniques (Saunders, 1990).

SUMMARY

Following a gay lifestyle in a heterosexual-oriented society is difficult and causes many problems for the gay and lesbian populations. The problems are experienced in many forms, including homophobic reactions from an unaccepting society; rejection by family and friends; child-custody fights; and the struggle to come out to others at various times in their lives. Social workers and other professionals who work with gay and lesbian individuals, couples, and families should have knowledge of the gay lifestyle and how it differs from the lifestyle of heterosexuals. This understanding will better prepare them to undertake a variety of therapeutic tasks concerning problems ranging from adolescent struggles in coming out to helping an adult grieve the death of a partner.

It is essential for all professionals to be aware of their own biases, if any, toward gay people and to overcome them before undertaking work with this group. They will find that many problems experienced by gay and lesbian clients are similar to those experienced by nongay clients, and the same intervention techniques can often be used to help both groups. However, gay clients will usually need something more, and the use of support groups is recommended in most cases. Helping professionals should be familiar with the existence of support groups and able to help clients access them and integrate themselves into the gay community.

REFERENCES

Berger, R.M., and Kelly, J.J. 1995. "Gay Men Overview." *Encyclopedia of Social Work*, 19th ed. Washington, DC: NASW Press.
Carl, D. 1990. *Counseling Same Sex Couples*. New York: W.W. Norton & Company.

Falco, K.L. 1991. *Psychotherapy with Lesbian Clients*. New York: Brunner/Mazel Publishers.

Falk, P. 1989. "Lesbian Mothers: Psychosocial Assumptions in Family Law." *American Psychologist* 44:941–47.

Gottman, J. 1990. "Children of Gay and Lesbian Parents." In *Homosexuality and Family Relations*, eds. F.W. Bozett and M.B. Sussman, pp. 177–96. New York: Harrington Park.

Hall, J., and Stevens, P. 1990. "The Coupled Lesbian." In *Keys to Caring*, ed. R.J. Kus. Boston: Alyson Publications, Inc.

Hare, J. 1994. "Concerns and Issues Faced by Families Headed by a Lesbian Couple." *Families in Society* 75:27–35.

Hoeffer, B. 1981. "Children's Acquisition of Sex Role Behavior in Lesbian Mother Families." *Journal of Orthopsychiatry* 51:536–43.

Jay, K., and Young, A. 1979. *The Gay Report*. New York: Summit Books.

Krestan, J., and Bepko, C. 1980. "The Problem of Fusion in the Lesbian Relationship." *Family Process* 19:277–89.

Kubler-Ross, E. 1969. *On Death and Dying*. New York: Macmillan.

Kus, R.J. 1990. *Keys to Caring*. Boston: Alyson Publications, Inc.

Lapierre, E.D. 1990. Homophobia and Its Consequences for Gay and Lesbian Clients." In *Keys to Caring*, ed. R. J. Kus. Boston: Alyson Publications, Inc.

Levitt, E., and Klassen, A. Jr. 1974. "Public Attitudes Toward Homosexuality." *Journal of Homosexuality* 78:29–43.

Lott-Whitehead, L., and Tully, C.T. 1993. "The Families of Lesbian Mothers." *Smith College Studies in Social Work* 63:265–80.

Money, J., and Ehrhardt, A. 1972. *Man and Women, Boy and Girl: Differentiation and Dimorphism of Gender Identity from Conception to Maturity*. Baltimore: Johns Hopkins University.

Moses, A., and Hawkins, R. Jr. 1982. *Counseling Lesbian Women and Gay Men*. St. Louis: C.V. Mosby.

Patten, J. 1988. "AIDS and The Gay Couple." *The Family Therapy Networker* 12: 33–39 (January/February).

Saunders, J.M. 1990. "Gay and Lesbian Widowhood." In *Keys to Coping*, ed. R.J. Kus. Boston: Alyson Publications, Inc.

Shernoff, M. 1995. "Gay Men: Direct Practice." *Encyclopedia of Social Work*, 19th ed. Washington, DC: NASW Press.

Silverstein, C. 1990. "The Coupled Gay." In *Keys to Caring*, ed. R.J. Kus. Boston: Alyson Publications, Inc.

Solomon, J. 1990. "Aids and Caregivers." In *Keys to Caring*, ed. R.J. Kus. Boston: Alyson Publications, Inc.

Tully, C.T. 1995. "Lesbian Overview." *Encyclopedia of Social Work*, 19th ed. Washington, DC: NASW Press.

Weinberg, M.S., Williams, C.J., and Pryor, D.W. 1994. *Dual Attraction*. New York: Oxford University Press.

Woodman, N., and Lenna, H. 1980. *Counseling With Gay Men and Women*. San Francisco: Jossey-Bass.

CHAPTER **10**

Income Loss, Poverty, and Families with Multiple Problems

Families with multiple problems have long been known to social workers and are a frequent challenge to our skills. Their needs, as we come to understand them, emphasize that success in our efforts to help them requires change in both the internal functioning of the family as a group as well as public policy and the social service delivery systems of which we are a part. Not all families with multiple problems are poor, nor are all poor families beset with the multiplicity of problems that are a frequent consequence of income loss and poverty. But we begin by noting some of the connections between poverty status and the multiplicity of problems.

Our approach to the multi-problem family is consistent with the systems approach outlined in earlier chapters—viewing the family as an organized system of interacting subsystems engaged in varying ways and degrees with external systems. Events in other systems are seen as influences on internal family relationships; conversely, events inside the family system are seen as affecting the nature of transactions with external systems.

The behavior of external systems is viewed as particularly important in the internal operations of multi-problem poor families—to the ways in which family members engage each other in seeking to have their needs met, to gain cooperation, establish order, negotiate differences, or otherwise regulate family activity. Attention is paid to the way that current problems evoke, and current patterns reenforce, unproductive modes of relating and problem solving.

Many multi-problem families have been poor for lengthy periods of time. Studies of families that have been economically self-sufficient and unexpectedly experience income loss provide a beginning understanding of the difficulties that families in longer-term poverty may experience.

Sales' (1995) study of recently unemployed workers points to the kinds of economic resources needed by them and their families. The longer unemployment persists, the greater the percentage of families who have exhausted their unemployment benefits, their savings, earnings, borrowing and private charity resources, and help from family and friends, and who become dependent on government programs. Sales notes, as have others, that economic resources serve to buffer the effects of unemployment on workers and their families. The struggle to connect to resources and learning how to manage with a lower level of support strains both the unemployed worker and the family.

The strains become evident in the correlation of periods of high unemployment in the economy with the general increases in rates of alcoholism, crime, and mental illness. Typically in our society, individuals gain a sense of status and worth from employment even if they do not like the particular work they do. Loss of work and of economic self-sufficiency affects both the worker and the family. "Extreme poverty and homelessness can affect people's feelings about themselves, make some people 'Crazy' and leave many more feeling helpless, powerless and despairing; and can lead to substance abuse as an escape from misery" (Parnell and VanderKloot, 1991, p. 187).

Workers may lose status and authority within the family as well as outside. They react to the loss of employment and economic support with feelings of shame, humiliation, worthlessness, anger, anxiety, depression, and, in some instances, free-floating hostility, increased drinking, paranoid ideas, depression, and thoughts of suicide. Other family members may experience similar feelings (Borrero, 1979). Further, conflicts arise among family members as a result of the lack of financial resources and concerning how the fewer resources should be allocated. Also, roles may change when additional members of the family seek to produce income. The unemployed worker may take on unaccustomed functions within the family. The resulting stress may be accompanied by increased drinking and physical abuse, creating further problems for all members.

Liem and Liem (1988) looked at factors other than money that might buffer the stress of loss of employment. In general, the emotional climate in the home and the wife's positive performance of household, child-rearing, and marital responsibilities eased the stress for the unemployed husband. The family role performance of the newly unemployed workers (in this case, husbands) was an early casualty, preceding negative changes in the wives' performance of family roles. Husbands and wives reported significantly less cohesion and more conflict than did spouses in a comparison group. Norms for performance in family roles did not change, but performance deteriorated with the lengthening of unemployment.

Other family problems—truancy, delinquency, alcohol or other substance abuse, incest, physical abuse, neglect, separation, or divorce—may be present or may be exacerbated by the lack of economic resources. And they may stand in the way of coping effectively with the economic aspects of life.

Clearly, there is a relationship between poverty and the problems of the families we will be discussing, but it is also clear that not all of their problems are attributable to poverty. In defining their goals with the family, social workers need to distinguish which problems are due to situational distress. Family members experience withdrawal, alienation, developmental delays, learning disorders, and frequent emergencies (Williams, 1994). In addition to the usual life cycle stresses, they are likely to experience the disruptions of imprisonment, addictions, mental illness, poor health, frequent loss and or change of employment, and change in family responsibilities and roles due to any of these (Williams, 1994).

Wood, Valdez, Hayashi, and Shen (1990) note that expenditure of a disproportionate share of family income on housing was a factor in families becoming homeless, and that homeless—compared to housed—poor families reported more spouse and child abuse, more drug and mental health problems, and weaker support systems. Neighborhoods are deteriorating, and strong community organization, standards, and values are frequently not available to provide needed supports for the family when help is sought (Aponte, 1991; Jenkins, 1990). Family energy is consumed with the task of dealing with multiple control agencies and their disparate requirements.

"Millions of American families have not been able to absorb the economic shocks of the 1970s and 1980s. Loss of employment, escalating drug abuse and violence, physical and social deterioration of neighborhoods, and reductions in social services and entitlements have virtually paralyzed communities. Without stable communities to support them, many families have become powerless to meet their basic needs" (Williams, 1994, p. 48).

Kantor, Peretz, and Zander (1984) cite the impact of poverty in reducing the chances for the children of these families to attain good health, educational achievement, and economic self-sufficiency. Because their lives are often disrupted by emergencies and other unpredictable events, they frequently suffer from exhaustion and hopelessness, lowered school performance, and reduced social contact. Poverty and limitation of choice often lead to unplanned pregnancy, protracted dependency, and ongoing poverty. Bandler and Grinder (1975) note that the pain and isolation of poverty also create a limitation of perspective, of the representation of the world and what might be possible in it. It is therefore necessary to "connect the client with the world in some way which gives a richer set of choices."

For poor families, external "systems have such a powerful impact because they are dependent on them for survival. In a stable environment it is normally sufficient to address the individual/family unit, assuming a degree of constancy and stability in the larger systems sphere. This is not a realistic assumption in the urban centers of the United States.... We can no longer deny that our institutions are not adequately performing the functions for which they were designed.... Part of the solution to the fiscal crisis has been to target social programs for cuts and to blame the poor for their poverty" (Parnell and VanderKloot, 1989).

All of these difficulties suggest the need of varieties of services and treatment for the family. "Unfortunately, the unemployed population appears to resist traditional counseling services" (Sales, 1995, p. 492). Serving them requires methods that meet their needs for resources as well as help with internal issues.

The problems of family functioning in poverty-level families will not be resolved without some change in the family's poverty status. Income maintenance by itself does not appear to be a sufficient solution, however. Bishop (1980) notes that while unemployment is clearly disruptive to marriages, the provision of income maintenance either in the form of AFDC-U or a negative income tax has also increased the rate of marital dissolution. Thus, though the provision of income is necessary for family functioning, some changes in family functioning must also occur if the family is to be extricated from the perpetuation of individual and family problems, and from poverty status. Further, adequate external system supports, such as the worker orientations and agency commitments described below, are essential to motivate change in poverty families and to forestall the repetition of present patterns in succeeding generations. Extrication from the poverty status rests not only with the family but also with a change in the perspectives of the external systems that affect it. We are concerned with facilitating change at both levels.

EXTERNAL SYSTEM/FAMILY SYSTEM OPERATIONS

Jenkins (1990) notes that "compared to the power of the state, the family is powerless." There is the need to be clear about the system level at which intervention needs to occur. At the societal level, policies and programs that allow each family the needed income for basic necessities should be in place and should be comprehensive and provide service in the many facets of their lives in which need may occur (Schorr, 1991; Conte, 1983; Halpern, 1991).

Further, negative attitudes and sometimes outright hostility toward the poverty family may be manifested by the public, by agencies, and by workers. Middle-class values lead to expectations of certain responses from the family and to disparagement and rejection when the family does not manifest these responses. The feedback to the family depreciates the family's image of itself and of its individual members. When the family is lacking in self-enhancing feedback from the outside world, the esteem of family members for each other suffers. Self-esteem, useful as a source of strength and motivation, is diminished, and the burden of promoting it is left totally to the already overburdened family.

Another negative impact that external systems have on the poverty family is the existence of policies that divide families rather than bring them together. In some states, policies are still in effect that provide support for mother and children when father is not there, but do not support them when he is present but unable to provide financial support. This serves to divide the family and inhibit family strength and growth.

Other agency policies that divide and fragment the family are services to the health or mental health needs of some family members but not of others, or attentiveness only to the physical or mental health of a family member without attention to the family circumstances that affect health.

Agencies that require the family to conform to agency policy operate as though the family is an extension of the agency, subject to its bidding. Instead of providing support to the family's own problem-solving efforts, the policies of agencies and the actions of workers often serve to inhibit the capacity for independent thought and action. In conceptual terms, the family loses its boundaries as a separate system and becomes incorporated as part of the agency system, thus increasing rather than decreasing its dependency. Families known to more than one agency may find themselves faced with contradictory requests, which may result in breakdown of family structure or family boundaries.

Family interaction with other, less official or public systems may operate similarly. The extended family, the siblings or parents of the adult family members, sometimes provides little or no support. In poverty families these persons are often psychologically or materially not in a position to be supportive and are themselves in need of support. When a relationship exists, extended family members often see the members of the poverty family as people to be controlled or directed or drawn upon for their own support. Consequently, the inputs to the family system from the extended family leave it diminished in capacity for independent operation.

Extended family members, however, can be helpful in providing supports, sometimes financially and materially, sometimes in services such as child care or homemaking during illness. Stack (1974) has noted the particular means of helpfulness of kin and kinlike networks. When such relationships are tenuous, family members can sometimes be helped to strengthen them, to their own gain.

Often problem poverty families simply lack connection with the outside world. Friendships are meager or nonexistent. Encounters with institutions such as churches, schools, and health services are dreaded and avoided. The potential for connectedness, interest, and self-affirmation is not available.

In these and other ways, external systems can affect the processes operative within the family and leave its members alienated, depreciated, distrustful, and hostile toward the outside world. They are thus more intensively dependent on one another for affirmation and rewards and are subject to heightened interpersonal tension. Fewer exchanges with external systems mean that family members often lack awareness of the standards and expectations of the outside world. There is a lack of knowledge of what may be available to them or how to make use of what is available. Agencies sometimes even operate to make such information inaccessible to family members. Therefore, problem poverty families often lack the repertoire of appropriate knowledge and behaviors available to them. The family system has in effect been closed off to inputs from the outside world that could be potentially helpful in solving the family's problems. Because of deficits of information and skills, contacts with social institutions often end in failure and disappointment.

Thus, a negative interaction occurs between the poverty family and external systems. Over time, relationships deteriorate unless processes are set in motion that alter the behaviors of either the family or external systems, or both. The failure to achieve the desired positive connections must be attributed to the stance of the outside world *and* to the family's limitations. New behaviors initiated by the family or by the external systems affect the interaction between them and offer hope of improvement in the family and in its relationship with the outside world. If new information and resources are made available, the family has to be able to respond to make effective use of them. It may need assistance in learning to respond to the altered situation, since its responses have been tailored for the external systems as they had been behaving. Treatment, therefore, must contain a substantial element of advocacy to change external systems. In other instances, the limitations in the family's knowledge and coping skills should be the focus of treatment.

Learning how and where to find and acquire better housing, employment, day care, educational and health services, and competence in relating to the people they have to meet in the process are among the knowledge and skills areas needed (Ziefert and Braun, 1991). The benefits of these services and the acquisition of skills in relating to the people involved will alter transactions with the outside world. The emphasis on here and now and what is to be done, which is reflective of family treatment in general, is a particularly useful orientation with this stressed group of families.

INTERNAL FAMILY SYSTEM OPERATIONS

The nature of the problem poverty family's boundaries, rules, communications, and identity follows from the nature of the family's relationships to external systems. The negative nature of the relationships with external systems for these families has been defined; there is little in them to offer either adult or child a sense of positive meaning or affirmation. As breadwinners or as clients of an income maintenance program, adults feel depreciated and find no status; children receive minimal affirmation or recognition for their efforts in school. Consequently, for gratification of personal needs, each member turns to other family members. The need to seek all gratifications within the family places undue stress on internal family operations. Unsatisfactory patterns develop and persist as long as the family's position in the community persists.

Boundaries

Family boundaries define the various subsystems in the family structure (see Chapter 2). The marital pair first forms a marital subsystem, which may become a parental subsystem. Family operations and strength depend in large measure on the ability of the adults to form a strong bond with each other. Satisfaction in their own relationship derives from that bond, as does the ability to support each other in child rearing. In problem poverty families, however, the relationships between the adults are characterized by distance, conflict, and transiency. They interact with each other primarily as parents, minimally as spouses.

Some evidence of the difficulty in parental bonding is the fact that up to 60 percent of poor families are headed by female single parents. For a variety of reasons, the adult pair are not available to each other or their children as a parental pair. In these instances, the maintenance of a separate household has fallen on the mother. Her income is less and the demands on her are greater.

While communicational and interactional problems (which we will describe shortly) are primary sources of the inability to form a strong marital bond, the structural outcomes must also be considered. When relationships do not work, partners may withdraw from them, psychologically or physically or both, and the withdrawal may be temporary or permanent. Or they may engage in overt conflict, verbal or physical or both. In families with children, a parent may withdraw from the parenting function as well as from the spouse role. Withdrawal from the parenting function represents the relinquishment of parental leadership. The role of the withdrawing spouse/parent may thus become more that of a child than of a parent. The usual generational lines are crossed.

When the failure of marital bonding results in conflict that cannot be contained within the bounds of marriage, a second form of generational boundary violation may occur. A parent may seek a member of the child generation as an ally, sometimes to gain support for self, sometimes as a means of attack against the spouse. If both parents have remained in the home or are significant for the child, the child is placed in an untenable position between them.

The parental child, as we have labeled this usually older child in Chapter 2, who responds to this boundary breakdown by moving to comfort or support one of the parents increases his or her isolation from the other parent. Thus he deprives himself of the support of the other parent and may thereby accentuate the conflict between the parents. He may seek to reconcile parental differences, a function that places him more in the parent generation, or he may actually take on parental functions. Or he may develop other emotional, physical, or behavioral symptoms because of this uncomfortable positioning. Cues from the parents will suggest to the child the ways in which he is needed.

The breakdown in parental leadership is manifest also in those instances in which children move into parenting roles with other children. Such movement may be prompted by the parent, and it gains parental approval. While it often results from parental conflicts or default, it may in other instances often be necessary for a child to perform in the role of a parent, as for example when work, illness, or errands leave both parents unavailable. (This becomes even more likely in single-parent families.) An older child may take on a child-caring role with younger siblings during after-school hours, before the parents return home from work. Or a child may be asked to undertake extra household tasks during an illness of one of the adults. Troubles may arise when parents have not provided sufficient direction.

> An older girl was left in charge of several siblings who began fighting with each other. Having no instructions from the parents about what to do about this behavior, she separated them and did not allow them to play together until the parents returned home. The younger sibs complained to the parents who, in turn, chided the girl for her actions. No instructions were offered about what to do if the behavior recurred. The girl was left with negative feelings toward her siblings for causing her trouble and toward her parents for not supporting or directing her. The younger siblings were likewise left with angry feelings and a reduced need to be cooperative.

In these circumstances, the parents failed to provide a clear, unambiguous structure within which the parenting child and the other children could relate, leaving cause for disagreement and fighting. Where parental leadership is clear, all children will know their limits and responsibilities during a parent's absence.

The likelihood of a child's becoming a parental child seems greater in problem poverty families than in other families. The parents' poor position in the outside world, as we have suggested, leaves the parents with reduced need satisfaction, self-esteem, and status within the family. These factors combine to reduce parental assertiveness and leadership. Seeking affirmation and status, they may more readily seek a child as an ally or yield to the wishes of a child, especially when these needs are not met by a spouse who may have similar needs and may be unable to meet the other's needs. Furthermore, in single-parent families, which many of these families are, the tendency to rely on parental children increases.

Rules

Closely related to a lack of structure evidenced in generational boundaries and parental leadership is a lack of clear and consistent norms and rules for behavior. In problem poverty families, parental responsibilities in setting limits to behavior often are not fulfilled. What is a limit today may not be a limit tomorrow, or even ten minutes from now. A limit defined by one parent may not be held to by the other parent.

Behavior is regulated by injunctions on a particular piece of behavior but with no further explanation about why it should be stopped, about circumstances under which it is permitted, or about what desirable behavior should be substituted. Children consequently have no consistent guides for behavior that they can internalize and thereby become self-regulating, either in the parent's presence or away from them. Parents are constantly required to regulate the activity of the children, leaving them totally enmeshed and absorbed in child care and less free to meet their own needs. They feel overburdened and overwhelmed.

The parents' abdication from regulation or their total withdrawal from the family, either temporary or permanent, leaves relationships disrupted and reenforces the sense of inconsistency and instability. Parental behavior in this area is also attributable, at least in part, to the parents' limited status outside the family and their own and family members' reactions to that status. Where the parents have themselves been raised in similar families, these behaviors are learned in their families of origin.

Such interaction of course interferes with the growth and development of the children and the parents. The process does not allow for individuation and separation of family members but instead keeps them dependent upon and bound to one another. It is a kind of being "stuck" together that is very different from being able to see oneself as an individual; it is an individual who takes satisfaction and enhances her or his identity out of belonging to the family. The "stuck togetherness" is similar to the situation of "enmeshment" described by Minuchin and Montalvo (1967) and to the "undifferentiated" family situation described by Bowen (1978).

Similar, but less often described, is the lack of clear expectations and rules about marital behavior. Dissatisfaction with marital relations may result. Adults may think of themselves primarily as parents and devote little attention and effort to their roles as spouses. Frequently spouses are unsure of themselves as males or females. They become aware of their spouse's expectations primarily when they fail to meet them, not through transactions that result in explicit definitions of what is expected and desired. Complaints are frequent; the freedom to say what "I want, need, or would like" is lacking, as is the means for expression. As in parent-child relationships, it is easier for spouses to learn what is not wanted than to learn what is wanted. Role performance cannot be achieved with confidence. Since role expectations are not clearly defined, the interpersonal process leaves spouses feeling insecure and lacking in self-affirmation.

Communications

When clear and consistent rules for behavior are lacking, communications are likely to be dysfunctional to family stability and problem solving. Communication is characterized by interruptions, simultaneous talking, topic changes, and unclear meanings. Members do not really listen to each other and frequently do not really expect to be heard. When others respond, it is often to make a counter point of their own, rather than to respond to what has been said. Voices escalate in volume in an effort to be heard, and in the noise, affect rather than content is communicated. The verbal message is lost and is not responded to. Interaction reveals affect and feelings rather than information and ideas, and the interpersonal aspect of the message predominates over the content aspect. In some instances, limitations of language ability affect the ability to achieve understanding and solution of a problem. The families are thereby impoverished in their attempts to generate information and solutions to problems. On the other hand, positive, clear communications in low-income Spanish-speaking families, for example, have been shown to enable reduced difficulty on the part of asthmatic children in managing their asthma attacks (Clark and associates, 1990).

These characteristics of communication in poverty families, as contrasted to other problem families, differ in intensity, not in kind. Intense need and seeking on the part of family members are implied. In such families, consequently, efforts at problem solving by means of verbal communication are unproductive. Nothing in the family changes as long as communications operate in this manner. Furthermore, the members' frustration with one another and their sense of isolation are increased. They get no sense of being listened to and really heard. They do not obtain understanding, self-affirmation, or nurture from the unresponsiveness or arguments of others.

The communications thus reflect family relationship and structure. The isolation or lack of support within the structure that one or more members may feel becomes evident through the lack of supportive communications and the volume of negative messages directed at them. Members feel isolated from other family members or fear that others are allied against them. For example, when a child communicates as though he or she were a parent, one of the parents may feel as if the other parent and the child are allied against him or her. Or parent communication may seem to derogate a spouse in favor of a child.

Thus the communicative effort at both the content and the relationship levels serves to perpetuate the unsatisfying relationship rather than to change them. A homeostasis is reached, and problem solving does not occur. Family structure is maintained in its disabling form. The family system is stable (morphostatic) but in a form that gradually leads to less rather than more effective functioning.

Identity, Integration, and Solidarity

A number of writers have attested to the importance of a sense of family identity in family coping and problem solving. In our view, this is both consequence and cause of the problems of family functioning. The image that members hold of the family as a group has meaning for the individual and is important for individual growth and role-taking within the family. The image may take various forms, such as "the people I live with"—an image that suggests a feeling of disconnectedness and of not belonging or being valued by others. Or the image may be "the family that I belong to"—an image that suggests a sense of cohesion and belonging, really a valued part of the group. Rabinowitz (1969) observes that it is this sense of being a group that is lacking in poor, multi-problem families:

> Researchers participating in the Wiltwyck study were struck by how little these families seem to be recognized by their members as groups of people who belong together. Parents seem to disassociate themselves from each other and from their children. They seldom have conversations with each other or with a child.... Both enjoyment of family life and any positive valuing of family relationships are notably absent.... Although they maintain a family form they do not develop a family consciousness. (p. 180)

Having a sense of the family and of belonging to it is as important to individual functioning as is the sense of separateness of self. But it is difficult to develop a positive image of the family in the midst of the structural and communication deficits found in poverty families. The modes of coping with problems and of handling relationships have served to drive members apart rather than to promote a sense of unity and harmony. The family's material status also has its effect. It becomes easy, when material necessities and the means for acquiring them are lacking, to doubt, argue, and blame, and over time to come to feel alienated and apart from the group. The group, in turn, holds insufficient meaning or value for the individual, since it is not a source of nourishment or support. Members are not likely to be committed to preserving it or making an effort to improve it.

We have observed the opposite effects in certain cases, however. In some families the children are able to become upwardly mobile. Such families seem to be characterized by a family theme, defined by the parents, or other parenting figures, which conveys that though the external world is hostile, the family can succeed if everyone joins together. Goals of survival and achievement are emphasized. Parental leadership is strong, and rules are explicit and clearly enforced. Long-term family survival is given priority over immediate individual goals. Staying together and working together are essential to survival. Under these circumstances, individuals can achieve and advance despite poverty. The individual is enhanced through the *esprit de corps* of the family group. In some instances, however, the individual may experience a sense of rigidity and overcontrol and have difficulty achieving individuality or separateness from the group.

TREATMENT APPROACH TO FAMILY PROBLEMS AND PROBLEM SOLVING

All too often, social workers and other helpers have concluded that reality problems such as income, housing, and health care must be solved before obvious problems of individual and family coping can be addressed. Our approach addresses both aspects concurrently, not sequentially. It is necessary to focus simultaneously on the problems and realities posed by life and external systems for the family and on the way in which the family manages its relationship with those realities. Solutions to the very real problems of employment, housing, health care, and job and school performance are achieved by the way in which the family works at the solutions. Interactions between family members that encourage or discourage, help or hinder, and speed or slow progress are a concurrent focus of family work.

This orientation to families is consistent with an emphasis that has long existed in some places in social work. Perlman (1957) writes that the social worker has the dual task of achieving solution to a problem and increasing the problem-solving capacity of the persons being served. She delineates how this is accomplished in work with individuals. We will emphasize the means for developing the problem-solving capacity of the family group.

AGENCY ORIENTATION AND METHOD

As the "hard to reach" label often applied to this group of families attests, the traditional approaches in family agencies, mental health services, and public social services have not been successful in meeting their needs or gaining participation in treatment efforts. First of all, it is necessary to conceptualize the problems as those of the family—for the staff to "think family" in looking at the presenting problem. The approach we are putting forth envisions work with all members of the family, frequently in conjoint sessions, and often in the home though sometimes in the office. Success in engaging the family requires that workers relate to family-defined needs and concerns including material ones, rather than those of the worker or referral source. And, given unpredicted occurrence of new or unanticipated problems, the traditional once-a-week, by-appointment approach must yield to telephone or in-person availability as needed.

While these strategies have been used with a variety of families, their use with poverty families is especially necessary for successful engagement. In these aspects of beginning the treatment and continuing throughout the treatment effort, the worker acts to meet real needs, both material and psychological, while also working to develop trust, to teach and educate by instruction and demonstration, and to alter structure and interrupt dysfunctional interactive processes between family members. Such activity implies not only special efforts, orientation, and attitudes on the part of workers but also a special commitment of agency purpose and resources that is not always required in treatment of other families.

WORKER AND TIME INVESTMENT

Different combinations of workers and allocations of time have been utilized in engaging multiple-problem families. So often their needs are immediate, or problems occur simultaneously with several family members, or agencies to which one or another member is known have conflicting expectations. They feel themselves to be in crisis. With all that is happening, one person cannot be responsive to all aspects of their lives.

In some instances, attempts to work with the family begin as endeavors to coordinate the efforts of agencies that have been working with different members of the family, with each agency having expectations for family participation, some of which may be confusing. A meeting of representatives of all agencies with the family leads to a designation of a therapy team, clarifies for the family what is known about them, and serves to define the goals of the family. This has been found to be particularly useful in enjoining participation in treatment in cases of child abuse and neglect in which the parents do not acknowledge the violence (Cirillo and DiBlasio, 1992).

This may be followed, in some instances, by a "multiple impact" approach. A team of professionals schedules a full day or more for its

initial meeting with the family, generally at an office. The several therapists meet together with the entire family. As they become clearer about
the problems, who is affected by them, and the roles of various family
members, different members of the team meet separately with subsets of
family members, such as parents or children, for further assessment and
work on specific aspects of the problem or on particular relationships. At
some point, the team meets separately to clarify their understanding
and to formulate a plan and/or make recommendations.

In other instances, contact begins by the family's bringing a problematic family member to the agency or clinic with the request to treat or
change that individual. Sufficient time is spent with the patient and the
family to understand the circumstances that prompted the family action and how the individual's behavior affects and is affected by other
family members, and to develop an initial plan for treatment that relates to the problems and offers help for all affected members.

In another variation of worker time investment, the worker is moved
into a heavier time commitment in the home. The therapist is responsible only for three or four cases and spends a day or more weekly in contact with the family, assisting in location of resources, medical care, and
housing, as well as promoting joint activities and helping to resolve conflicts inside the family and relationships outside of it. That much time
with the family offers a good opportunity to observe family operations
and to promote constructive methods specific to the situations that arise.

Therapist Attitudes

Social workers need a substantial degree of self-awareness and self-
examination about their similarity to and difference from the poverty
family with regard to their own family experience, social class, and ethnic and cultural background (Aponte, 1991). The tendency of workers to
judge the family solely on the basis of their own life experience needs to
be replaced by efforts to see the family in its social context. An attitude
of positive regard for the family is essential, one that assumes that they
are doing the best they know how, given their situation, but need help in
finding more useful ways (Parnell and VanderKloot, 1991). Similarly,
workers need to be aware of the family's consciousness of their difference from the worker and the ways in which this is a barrier to the worker's attempt to join with the family.

Problem poverty families often exhibit behaviors that test the worker's attitudes, interest, and concern. Previous experience with workers
may enhance the family's doubts about the worker's interest, reliability,
and concern. Families often report experiences of not being responded

to, being rejected, and being controlled by workers and agencies. Repeated and consistent responsiveness is needed to overcome the family's wariness and lack of trust. During the initial phase, families distance themselves in various ways, such as absence at the time of scheduled appointments. Workers have responded by seeking clients at other locations if they were not home at the unexpected time. When they are home, families often leave the radio or television on at loud volume or have friends, neighbors, or relatives present. Such behavior may continue over many months, though it decreases over time as workers persevere and family members become convinced of the worker's interest and dependability.

BEGINNING TREATMENT

A first principle of work with multi-problem families is the familiar "start where the client is." In finding "where they are," it is particularly important to identify the needs and goals of family members since they often don't see the need for treatment or change. Family members need to be able to see what is in it for them, especially in those instances in which the referral was because of the actions of only one of them.

Second and third principles follow closely upon the first: Work with the family as a group, and work at home or at least be available for work at home. A significant corollary is that, even though, as we have noted above, these families do not see themselves as in need of counseling or therapy, therapeutic change efforts do not have to wait until the family's material or service needs have been met. The following sections show the ways of working with these principles.

In the worker's efforts during beginning stages to join the family and establish a good working relationship, it is important to remain aware of the harsh realities confronted by poor families. Workers' willingness to help families deal with these realities by seeking to understand their living conditions, cultural patterns, value systems, and goals needs to be conveyed. Gwyn and Kilpatrick (1981) emphasize this as being of particular value in working with poor black families. Sherman (1983) also stresses the effort of the worker and family to identify, clarify, and achieve goals that are important to the family in dealing with both material and interpersonal problems. Developing tasks related to these roles and building skills needed to complete the tasks are important aspects of the worker's and family's agenda. These activities serve both to solve problems and increase family problem-solving ability. Worker bridging and advocacy with school systems, for example, conveys willingness to help with practical issues while also developing the family's ability to handle them (Aponte, 1976). Respecting family autonomy in setting goals and in seeking their active participation gradually decreases the likelihood of the unresponsiveness described above. Rabin, Rosenberg, and Sens (1982) found that efforts to create an atmosphere of familiarity were particularly helpful in establishing a working relationship with the family. Workers attempted to become known as family members through informality and the sharing of personal experiences and feelings, including anger. They also made extensive efforts to know the resources, practices, and values of the community and to become known in it. These efforts enabled families to be in more positive contact with the world beyond themselves and to reduce their sense of isolation.

Treatment at Home—Talk and Activity

Treatment time spent in the home has the advantage of adding to the worker's understanding the family's problems, both internal and external, and its ways of dealing with them. Workers can engage family members on the spot in a process of evaluating what happened and whether some alternate response would have achieved better results. Also, work in the home lends itself more readily to approaches not so specifically suggestive of treatment but which allow the worker to be seen as friend and member of the family. It also enables the participation of more members of the family than would referrals to separate services for the individual problems of family members.

Talk

In initial contacts with the family, the worker seeks to understand how the family sees its situation and defines its problems. Out of concern that material needs are met, the worker moves toward solution, offering help and direction sometimes without explicit labeling of the problem (Montalvo and Gutierrez, 1983). Needs are great and demands sometimes seem unsatiable, but they are real and not just a manifestation of psychological dependency. Meeting needs is essential to the functioning of the family on the material level. It is also important psychologically in conveying a sense of being valued and cared about.

As the contact progresses, more explicit efforts are made to identify problems and set goals for the worker's and family's work together. Family members have difficulty in acknowledging problems. The worker emphasizes the wish to help rather than requesting that the family change. In some instances, it is useful to caution against talking or telling too much (Kagan and Schlossberg, 1989). The introduction of a caution against changing too much or too quickly conveys the worker's respect for the family and paradoxically—either in defiance of the worker or from the family's own need to change—has resulted in new behavior.

Activity

Schorr (1991) sees helping with household tasks, such as cleaning, as leading in natural ways to talking and development of a working relationship. Repairing or making clothing, fixing toys and furniture, and setting hair have all been reported. Family members may learn from such demonstration of the worker's skills.

Other activities such as art, crafts, and games serve to promote a sense of connectedness but also quickly reveal the nature of family interaction. For example, in playing games, parents have been known to have difficulty in providing consistent rules and structure. In this context, the worker can undertake to enforce game rules, modeling these activities for the parents and encouraging them to take over.

Some problems and concerns are revealed in the family's telling of them to the worker. Others are revealed in the interactions between members observed in the worker's participation with the family members in various activities. There are problems for the family to solve and problems in the problem-solving process to be corrected. Worker activity is directed to both.

Minuchin (1965) demonstrates one way in which work proceeds on both levels. In the early part of each session, specific concerns that have arisen are defined. Involved family members are asked to work on that concern while other members observe. The worker directs the interaction between family members in the problem-solving process. Within the overall definition of problems in family relationships, different problems may be addressed in each meeting with the family. These moves gradually make the definition of the problem to be solved more explicit. The problem to be solved becomes the problem in the family's problem-solving process. An example from our practice serves to illustrate what we mean:

> A sequence began with the father's expressed concern about the inability of the high school graduate daughter to mobilize herself to find employment. Father was pushing mother to get the girl to "move." Her compliance would help with material needs and would serve as self-affirmation for him. Mother was defending the girl's inactivity, experiencing father's demands as an attack on her. Father became angry and discussion ended.
>
> The worker focused attention on the parents' communication about the problem. Both agree that the sequence was typical, and both were dis-

satisfied with the outcome. The worker agreed that the daughter's unemployment was a valid concern but promoted discussion between the parents so they could, as a parental subsystem, join together in helping their daughter. Both parents valued the opportunity for further discussion, particularly for the further expression of their respective points of view. Each of them felt the other had heard them in a new way. Mother could sense father's feelings of helplessness in helping the daughter. Father became aware that mother, beyond her defensiveness, shared his concern for the daughter's immobility. The interaction could now shift from "attack-defend" to "what can we do?"

In summary, initial contacts are characterized by the worker's efforts to become part of the family and thereby gain the trust of family members and their willingness to work on problems confronting them. Worker participation involves being available when needed, arranging to meet the family at home, encouraging the participation of as many members as possible, and being responsive to needs, problems, and process as they occur. The worker may participate through discussion or activity, or both. Activity covers a wide range, from games to tasks in the home to accompanying family members on visits to an agency, a clinic, or a school.

This emphasis on participation in the family is highly congruent with the activity orientation and the here-and-now emphasis of the family therapy field. The worker is placed in a position from which it is possible to alter the actions of family members by introducing information and behavior which the family itself does not generate, in order to achieve more favorable outcomes. Less emphasis is placed on insight and awareness than on trying new behavior and ways of relating. Worker participation makes support, information, suggestions, and other interventions possible when assessment indicates that they will be most meaningful. Proposing change in the midst of process offers opportunity for immediate tryout. The worker's intention is to provide nurturance and to demonstrate new coping skills which the parents may emulate and adopt as their own, activities called "parenting the parents."

INTERVENTIONS IN FAMILY COMMUNICATIONS

The interventions described in this section are directed to the family's problem-solving operations that have resulted in ineffective responses to internal or external problems. Some of them have been introduced in the discussion of initial engagement of the family, when they are indeed useful and often needed.

When family communication patterns are faulty, they do not result in decisions to change or undertake new action. Things are left hanging when attention is diverted, or there is overt disagreement and no way to resolve it. As the family persists in its unproductive ways, positive feelings shared among members dissipate. The worker's role in regulating the family's communications must therefore be an active one.

Satir (1983) suggests communication procedures that apply in treatment of problem poverty families, and Minuchin (1965) offers rules for the regulation of communication in treatment sessions. The worker's activity regarding communications in poverty families is not notably different in kind from that used in other families. The need to persist in regulation due to the family's intense persistence in familiar modes is increased, however.

The worker may attempt to state rules of communication at the outset, though this is not generally effective, or may simply attempt to regulate communications according to the rules. The particular topic or problem under discussion may be money, schoolwork, employment, going out, housekeeping, caring, or obedience. Any topic or presented problem serves the purpose. The worker's attention is directed to the way in which the family works on the problem.

The first rule for such communication disallows interruptions. The worker conveys an interest in what each member has to say, making clear that other members will have their changes to be heard. The worker may block interruptions in various ways. A verbal intervention may be used: "I want to hear what mother is saying. Then I will hear from you." Sometimes a hand motion directed to the interrupter and a body inclination toward the speaker will serve the same purpose. In other instances the worker may need to move himself between the speaker and interrupter to block the interruptions. Though the noninterruptions rule is useful when there is much simultaneous talking and interrupting, it is not absolute. Interruptions for purposes of seeking information or clarification have been found to be useful (Alexander and Parsons, 1973), and worker directives may permit or encourage such interruptions.

There are other forms of interruption. Two members discussing an issue may be interrupted by a third. The third person may be diverting attention to his own needs or may, in the midst of intense disagreement, take sides or assume a peacemaker role. While this is interruption of process rather than of speech, it leaves the situation unclear and lacking in resolution. The worker who becomes aware of the pattern therefore may draw attention to the process or block its reoccurrence. The worker may give recognition to the interrupter's anxiety and the reasons for it or may return to the original speakers to encourage them to work on the issues at hand.

The worker also seeks to have family members be specific about the person to whom a communication is addressed, and what it is that the person is being told. Thus, if a parent is complaining about the children that "they never" or "they always," the worker may determine which child is of particular concern and ask the parent to address that child about a specific behavior. Similarly, in response to a generalized complaint about a spouse, the worker might suggest talking to the spouse about a specific incident. One intent in this procedure is also to help family members talk to each other rather than to the worker. Talking to the worker rather than to the family members carries a message about the inability of family members to talk usefully with one another, and thus it represents an impasse in their communication. A second intent of this procedure is to begin the process of separating persons out as individuals. It makes clear that persons have separate identities and are not simply a part of the family mass.

The language deficit in problem poverty families may mean that members have difficulty putting into words what they feel or want. Workers can usefully put things into words for family members, being careful to verify that this expresses what the individual wishes to convey to others. Rephrasings are often necessary to capture the meaning intended and to enable the person being addressed to understand. Failure in comprehending may be neither lack of clarity of expression nor lack of understanding, however. Rather, the hearer does not like what is being said. Once it is certain that the hearer is clear about what is being said, his or her disagreement or agreement with it may be pursued.

Many communications reflect a continuing tendency to express blame, anger, or hostility. Behind angry communications lies an unexpressed wish for relatedness and self-affirmation. Angry expression defeats the fulfillment of the wish and does not gain the end desired. For example: "You never take me anywhere" sounds like an accusation, which arouses defensiveness. The wish for companionship and relatedness is not revealed. If it were revealed, it might serve to bring the sender and the receiver of the message together in a new way. Similarly, a parent's command to a child may be perceived as hostile or controlling, but it may be due to concern about what may happen to a child in the present or the future. The child hears only the command and resists, but if the caring or concern can be identified and labeled, a new, more responsive relationship might develop. The worker may relabel or rephrase such negative communications to draw attention to the wish imbedded in them and to the self-defeating aspects of their continued use. This activity alters communication processes as well as the relationships among family members.

The injunction to address remarks to someone specific implies an expectation that the person addressed will respond relevantly. If the communication has been clear, relevant responses are easier, and irrelevant ones are easier to detect. Topic changes are the most frequent form of irrelevant response. These often come in the form of countercomplaints or the raising of another issue that takes precedence in the eyes of the respondent. Though it may be a defensive maneuver, it has the overt effect of substituting a new issue for one already stated, which is then left unresolved. The worker may regulate the irrelevant responses in several ways. He may comment that the response did not seem to connect with the original comment. He may ask the speaker whether the response was what he wanted the other to comment on. Or he may ask the respondent to reply to a specific aspect of the previous remark.

These directives require family members to convey clear, explicit messages, and to listen. Since verbal expression and active listening are frequently not part of the family's repertoire, compliance with the worker's directives will not be easy, automatic, or prompt. The intense and immediate need of family members to be heard and recognized will promote the persistence of established patterns. However, if the need to be heard and recognized is to be gratified, it is important that the old patterns be interrupted. There may be extreme difficulty in interrupting them. Minuchin (1965) has removed some family members to another room behind one-way glass, with another worker, to make certain that their listening status is enforced. Most interviewing situations, either at home or in an office, do not allow for such separation unless there are coworkers for the family. In that case separate discussion may be possible, though separate listening or observation is not. Even then, space limitations may prevent the separation. In the most difficult situations, workers may have to schedule separate interviews for different family subsystems.

The worker's efforts to enable the exchange of information that is useful to problem solving also have the effect of reducing the negative affective component of the communications and enhancing positive messages. Over time, as issues are dealt with and members feel heard, the noise level is reduced, and the aggressive, hostile overtones become minimized. The atmosphere becomes more conducive to positive feeling about other members and about the family group.

In problem poverty families there is frequently a need to reduce the negative affective component of communication in relation to the informational or content aspect. In this regard they appear to contrast greatly with other families, in which the communication of feeling and information has been inhibited. However, feeling may also be inhibited in some members and some problem poverty families. In that event, worker activity seeks to draw out the member who is silent or who avoids expression of feeling in what she or he says. This effort enables that member to produce missing information or to express feeling for family reaction and processing.

The worker's regulation of the family process through these rules of communication blocks or alters existing processes within the family. The underlying assumption is that effective use of language to convey information and meaning is essential to problem solving. When meanings and exchange about the problems become clear, effective problem solving can take place.

The worker's regulation of the communication process during the interview also provides family members with a different experience with one another. New information can alter the images they have of one another and provide them with new understanding. The experience of being listened to and understood provides affirmation of self and a greater readiness to listen to and appreciate others. The communication process the worker requires in the interview can be modeled by family members for use in day-to-day exchanges when the worker is not there. In addition to correction of the family problem-solving process, specific family problems such as school attendance, finances, health, or employment are also being solved.

INTERVENTIONS IN FAMILY STRUCTURE

Interventions in structure are designed to do several things. They serve to support the adults as parents who can provide the direction and structure needed by the children for adequate socialization and emotional growth. In this there is an implication that there will consequently be less need for the children to function as parents or for generational boundaries to become unclear and diffuse. Interventions in this area also seek to strengthen the marital relationship, if there is one, or to provide the single parent with some source of satisfaction of the need for growth and emotional support outside of the relationship to the children.

The first aspect of worker intervention in structure relates to family rules. Engagement with the family in activities or in interviews ensures the worker's presence during parent-child interactions, which reveal the inconsistencies about rules and expected behaviors. A worker engaged with a child in a game or activity can make his or her expectations of the child's behavior in the game clear and consistent. Parents may observe and use the worker as a model, or the worker may be able to discuss with parents what has happened, what the parents might have done if the worker had not been there, and whether the parents see the intervention as useful. Discussions can elicit what behaviors parents want from their children and can clarify whether the means the parents use are successful in obtaining those desired responses. Their wish to be good parents and to have children who know how to behave, to be responsible, and to succeed is identified and openly supported. Parental directives to a child, even when they sound hostile or attacking, may be redefined, for both parent and child, as an expression of parental concern. Parents may be more readily able to acknowledge such wishes and concerns as they feel the interest and support of the worker. If a parent, for example, responds with an angry "no," the worker may label this as the parent's concern to provide guidance for the child. This relabeling provides the child with new information about the parent's behavior and also increases parental awareness of the caring component of his or her own behavior.

The worker may also clarify whether the parental directive is just for the present situation or for other similar occasions also. If it is also for other occasions, the parent may be encouraged to provide explanation or further instruction. Rewards for compliance and consequences of noncompliance are discussed in advance. If the parent does delegate household or parenting tasks, the parent may be helped to be explicit about the exact duties, how much authority the child has over the other children, and what they are to do when other children do not cooperate. Such discussions assume that parents are operating out of a deficiency of knowledge and skills about parenting and can gain by awareness and specific direction. They also, by implication, leave the parents in control of the structure provided for the child. The child can be gratified by parental attention. As his behavior becomes more consistent and tests the parent less and less, he can also be gratified at the fewer occasions for hostile outbursts. Parents can be relieved that the child has become clear about the rules for behavior and welcome the reduced need to regulate it.

Another aspect of worker intervention in structure relates to the role of the parental child. The delegation of responsibility to a parental child has served to provide the parent some needed support. It also puts the child in a special position with the parent. Both parent and child may therefore have difficulty in relinquishing the special relationship. The parental child needs to feel that other activities and relationships can be rewarding. The worker therefore acts to move the child back to a child's role and to connect him with his peers, as well as to connect the parent more explicitly to the adult generation.

In the sense that parents compete with their children for recognition and attention, they operate more as members of the child generation and less as an adult subsystem. The worker's attention, therefore, needs to be directed to enabling both parents to move back into the parent generation. They need to feel that becoming more active as parents can produce results and be gratifying. If needs for self-affirmation and affection have been met by the child, the worker moves to connect the parents with other sources of adult support.

Where both parents are present in the home, this means work on strengthening the marital relationship, in addition to strengthening parental functioning. Work on the relationship between the parents, similar to any such effort in marital counseling, can be productive. Work on communication processes, on clarification of roles and expectations, and on finding ways of gratifying and supporting each other is useful, as it is for any other couple. Achievement of some success as parents may also reduce the stress on the marriage. Successful involvements outside the home, such as a satisfying work situation, can also be useful in relieving the burden on the marriage for satisfaction of emotional needs, putting the partners in a better position to be responsive and giving to each other.

Where only one parent remains in the family, the worker similarly seeks to reduce the parent's dependence on the children for support, gratification, and self-affirmation. Relationships with other adults are encouraged, and if none exist, the worker may provide a bridge to new associations with peers or peer groups. Single-parent associations, therapy groups, or family life education programs may provide both support and guidance. Encouragement of the parent's participation with peers in recreational, educational, or community-directed activity has specific value of its own, but it also emphasizes to the parent his or her worthwhileness and provides needed separateness from the children.

WORK WITH THE EXTENDED FAMILY

The client family may have at some point turned to extended family for help with material needs or other problems, with the result that extended family capacity to help may be exhausted or never have been available. The reverse is often the case, with extended family problems adding to those of the client family. Problems of mental illness, substance abuse, and marital relationships of siblings or their parent generation require involvement, investment of time, and often side-taking.

Getting these extended family persons connected to sources of help becomes necessary to relieve the client family. The finding that extended family is not always a resource is supported by Lindblad-Goldberg and Dukes (1985) in a study of single-parent black families known to a community clinic and a comparable group of nonclinic families. "In terms of reciprocity of emotional support, clinic mothers felt they provided significantly more emotional support than they received from all network members, especially family members." The same was true of instrumental needs.

In other instances, the problem is more one of conflicted relationships. The parent or parents have not separated and are overconnected to families of origin. They are still struggling with issues of control or being cared about and find themselves unable to maintain their separateness from parents or siblings. Material dependence may inhibit individuation and achievement of psychological independence.

The situation of Mrs. B is illustrative. She was separated from her husband, who was extremely controlling. She had no special job skills and had never had outside employment. She was referred by the school because of her second son's loud talking and foul language in school and at home, where she found him hard to control. At first contact, she and her three children were living with and dependent upon her parents. Her mother had always been overprotective of her as demonstrated by Mrs. B's report that her mother had accompanied her to the school bus stop until she was in high school. She continued to operate in this controlling manner with Mrs. B and was directive with the children as well. Mrs. B had never become fully independent of her mother, and grandmother was competing for the role of mother, the role of grandmother being nonexistent in this instance. The children reported that they felt like Ping-Pong balls between their mother, who was trying to handle parental responsibilities, and grandmother. Treatment for the family included helping Mrs. B to find ways to enter the job market, to find separate housing once she got work, to provide structure for the three children, and to be firm with her mother that she was responsible for the children's care and discipline, and that she (grandmother) would not have this responsibility but would be called upon for counsel and advice.

REDUCING FAMILY ISOLATION

Reconnection to extended family may also serve to reduce isolation. Where family networks are small, other networks in the community may serve as connections and support. Delgado and Humm-Delgado

(1982) identify natural support systems in the Hispanic community in addition to the extended family—the religious institutions, social clubs, and folk healers. Piazza and delValle (1992) emphasize the importance of the therapist's becoming aware of the resources of the cultural and ethnic community by attending their meetings and learning to know individuals in them and what they are doing. Members of client families can respond to members of their cultural community. They need to hear "the complexity of the family's story within the context of society's stories in a way that simplifies the story for ordinary, daily family life" (McGill, 1993). Learning the cultural story helps in showing how others have dealt with similar problems and connects them to persons in their own group who might be helpful.

In addition to connectedness to community in the ways just discussed, facilitating connectedness to community institutions and services is a core element in assisting these families. The bridging effort often requires the worker to accompany one or more family members to new locations to establish contacts with the workers providing those services or with members of other families who are participating. Since some family members may be more ready than others to participate, the worker must direct attention to the way some members undermine the efforts of others to relate to new services or individuals.

The family's increasing openness to these new relationships may be attributed to the trust they acquire in the worker. It is also, in part, a function of the restructuring of the relationships and communication processes. The family's use of these resources offers more natural support for the family and may reduce over time the amount of worker investment required.

REORIENTING EXTERNAL SYSTEMS

In the systems frame of reference only part of the family's isolation and lack of positive relations in the community may be attributed to the family itself. We have suggested that the operations of external systems often work to the direct disadvantage of the family, through policies that divide the family or restrict the resources available to it. In addition, agencies sometimes work at cross-purposes, further undermining the performance of individual members and the integrity of the family group.

Family members may learn, when they don't know how, to relate to external systems in ways that produce advantages for them. But direct worker intervention is often needed to help loosen interpretations of restrictive policies or to coordinate when policies of different agencies are at cross-purposes. The worker's interpretation to agencies of the functioning and needs of the family is one direct way of intervening. Case conferences with several agencies are often needed. Joint conferences between the family members and workers from several agencies may also be helpful. These are particularly significant when a given agency is acquainted with only part of the family and is unaware of or does not understand significant aspects of the family situation. The effort of the family worker is to orient all personnel involved to the family as a whole.

Worker brokerage on behalf of the family brings full circle the range of interventions with poverty problem families. Though we have directed our attention primarily to work with the family itself and to the need to participate with the family in engaging agencies, we do not thereby minimize the importance of the worker's role of broker and advocate for the family.

NOTES ABOUT COWORKERS AND AGENCIES

The work with problem poverty families suggests a number of reasons for the involvement of more than one worker with a family. The first has to do with the need for the ready availability of workers. The family's sense of urgency as well as the immediateness of some needs often require quick responses, when a specific worker may not be available. A second worker involved with the family may be able to meet these needs or to help them cope with the issue.

A second reason for the involvement of more than one worker is for simultaneous work on family issues by subsets of family members. Subsets of family members may be separated to work simultaneously on the same issue, or to continue work on a separate issue by one subset of persons. Parents and children may be separated into subsets for work on a particular issue, or a parent and a child may become a subset, while other children are withdrawn to observe or work on different problems. These arrangements are more feasible if more than one worker is engaged with the family.

A third reason for using coworkers is that simultaneous work on the involvements and concerns of more than one member of the family as they affect the family may be necessary. The extent of worker activity required would sometimes exhaust the time, if not the energy, of a single worker. The multiple problems of problem poverty families require that some problems be given priority over others, but long delays in the work on any of them may not be possible. The involvement of a second worker may avoid the necessity of leaving work on a particular problem incomplete while another crisis is addressed.

Coworkers of different sexes are suggested, to offer models of the ways males and females can work together as well as the ways two adults can work together. While their joint work can generally be expected to be harmonious, it may also demonstrate conflicts. Family awareness of these conflicts is not destructive if the workers can also demonstrate means for the resolution of disagreement.

The presence of a second worker can provide support for a family member when, in the midst of all that is going on, the other worker may not be aware of the need. A male's support of the wife's position may offer something new to the husband. A female worker's support of the husband can have similar effects. Disagreements with persons of the same or opposite sex and efforts to resolve them may also provide a new experience for family members. Besides being advantageous for the family, a coworker's presence may be an advantage to a worker who has become overidentified with a member of the family and has thereby lost the ability to be effective with the group. A coworker can sometimes spot such pitfalls and help extricate the therapeutic effort from them.

The involvement of more than one worker with the family requires substantial agency—and thereby community—commitment to the family. Intervention with problem poverty families also requires agency commitments to change in attitudinal orientation, information supply needs, scheduling arrangements, and adequate provision of services and resources to help these families. Such commitment of personnel and services on behalf of the poor is largely lacking. Unless increased commitments are made, it will be difficult to know how much of the despair and conflict in individuals and families can thereby be lifted and how much more direct work on the family's organization and process will be needed.

PREVENTING FAMILY BREAKDOWN

Our presentation has focused on a rehabilitative approach to families with already severe problems. It is encouraging to note the increasing numbers of family support programs that serve families in an educational mode designed to assist families before functioning becomes so problematic. Much in the manner of settlement houses of an earlier era, programs have been initiated to relate to childhood education and health concerns. They are, however, focused on the entire family and strive to "enhance family stability, develop parental competencies, and promote the healthy development of children. Interdependent services address concrete survival needs and the personal adjustment and development of the parents" (Lightburn and Kemp, 1994, p. 16).

Family support programs tend to be neighborhood oriented in order to provide easy access. They assume that members have strengths that can be developed and do not focus on deficits of the families. Educational groups for fathers, mothers, children, or combinations of family members offer learning, times of celebration, and times to work together. Activities serve to foster family cohesion, as well as understanding of family roles and role performance, and to make new acquaintances and thus mitigate social isolation.

TREATMENT PROGRAM EFFECTIVENESS

The techniques and strategies described here have been tried and found useful in a variety of settings with problem poverty families. They have been shown to work where other types of efforts with similar families have produced minimal or no change. However, our experience, and that of others we have referred to, does not suggest that this approach and these techniques always produce change. It only suggests that the conceptual orientation and techniques may in some instances be more effective than other strategies.

There is no systematic research on the application of these techniques to problem poverty families. Such research would require before-and-after measures of family performance and would match the change against change in families that had not experienced treatment.

Generally positive results are reported based on the clinical experience with the families. Empirical data are less available. Numerous family preservation or family restoration programs designed to avoid removal of a child from the home or to restore a child to the family operate with similar intensity. Seitz, Rosenbaum, and Apfel (1985) report findings of a ten-year follow-up of poverty families who had received family support that showed improvement in family functioning—they were self-supporting, showed a slow, steady rise in becoming self-sufficient, delaying subsequent childbearing for a median of nine years, and showed improved socialization and school performance for male children as well as improved mother-child relationships. (See also Whittaker, Kinney, Tracy, and Booth, 1990.)

One statewide empirical study of family preservation programs (Schuerman, Rzepnicki, and Littel, 1994) found little difference in outcomes for referred families as compared to families served in standard programs. However, the families in the treatment groups were found to have been better functioning before referral so that little change would be noted from their time in the program. The researchers point to the need for better tools to assess family functioning.

SUMMARY

The many facets to treatment of this group of families point to the need for intensive involvement of treatment programs. Increasing numbers of intensive family service units, employing many of the treatment ideas presented here, are organized to provide intensive contact, especially at the beginning of contact, sometimes limited to a 90-day period. They include the multiple-impact efforts, multiple-worker assignment, treatment in the home features which we have cited. Programs designed to deal with all aspects of family functioning are likely to be more effective.

REFERENCES

Alexander, J.F., and Parsons, B. 1973. "Short Term Behavioral Intervention with Delinquent Families." *Journal of Abnormal Psychology* 81:219–25.

Aponte, Harry. 1976. "Underorganization in the Poor Family." In *Family Therapy: Theory and Practice*, ed. P. Guerin, pp. 432–88. New York: Gardner Press.

———. 1991. "Training on the Person of the Therapist for Work with the Poor and Minorities." *Journal of Independent Social Work* 5(3–4):23–39.

Bandler, R., and Grinder, J. 1975. *The Structure of Magic*, Vol. I. Palo Alto, CA: Science and Behavior Books.

Bishop, J.H. 1980. "Jobs, Cash, and Marital Instability: Review and Synthesis of Evidence." *Journal of Human Resources* 15(3):301–34.

Borrero, Michael. 1979. "Psychological and Emotional Impact of Unemployment." *Journal of Sociology and Social Welfare* 7:916–34.

Bowen, Murray. 1978. *Family Therapy in Clinical Practice*. New York: Jason Aronson.

Cirillo, Stefano, and DiBlasio, Paola. 1992. *Families That Abuse*. New York: W.W. Norton & Co.

Clark, Noreen, Levison, Moshe, Evans, David, Wasilewski, Yvonne, Feldman, Charles, and Mellins, Robert. 1990. "Communication Within Low Income Families and the Management of Asthma." *Patient Education and Counseling* 15:191–210.

Conte, J. 1983. "Service Provision to Enhance Family Functioning." In *Child Welfare: Current Dilemmas, Future Directions*, eds. B.G. McGowan and W. Meezan. Itasca, IL: F.E. Peacock Publishers.

Delgado, M., and Humm-Delgado, D. 1982. "Natural Support Systems: Source of Strength in Hispanic Communities." *Social Work* 27(1):83–89.

Gwyn, F., and Kilpatrick, A. 1981. "Family Therapy with Low Income Blacks: Tool or Turnoff." *Social Casework* 62(5):259–66.

Halpern, Robert. 1991. "Supportive Services for Families in Poverty: Dilemmas of Reform." *Social Service Review* 65:343–63.

Jenkins, Hugh. 1990. "Poverty, State and the Family: A Challenge for Family Therapy." *Contemporary Family Therapy* 12(4):311–25.

Kagan, Richard, and Shlossberg, Shirley. 1989. *Families in Perpetual Crisis*. New York: W.W. Norton & Co.

Kantor, David, Peretz, Anne, and Zander, Rosamund. 1984. "The Cycle of Poverty—Where to Begin." In *Family Therapy with School Problems*, ed. Barbara Okun. Rockville, MD: Aspen Systems Corp.

Liem, Ramsay, and Liem, Joan. 1988. "Psychological Effects of Unemployment on Workers and Their Families." *Journal of Social Issues* 44(4):87–105.

Lightburn, Anita, and Kemp, Susan. 1994. "Family Support Programs: Opportunities for Community-Based Practice." *Families in Society* 75(1):16–26.

Lindblad-Goldberg, Marian, and Dukes, Joyce. 1985. "Social Support in Black, Low-Income Single-Parent Families—Normative and Dysfunctional Patterns." *American Journal of Orthopsychiatry* 55(1):42–58.

McGill, David. 1992. "The Cultural Story in Multi Cultural Family Therapy." *Families in Society* 73:339–49.

Minuchin, S. 1965. "Conflict Resolution Family Therapy." *Psychiatry* 28:278–86.

Minuchin, S., and Montalvo, B. 1967. "Techniques for Working with Disorganized Low Socio-Economic Families." *American Journal of Orthopsychiatry* 37:880–87.

Minuchin, S., Guerney, B., Rosman, B., and Schumer, F. 1967. *Families of the Slums.* New York: Basic Books.

Montalvo, Braulio, and Gutierrez, M. 1983. "A Perspective for the Use of the Cultural Dimension in Family Therapy." In *Cultural Perspectives in Family Therapy*, ed. Celia Falicov. Rockville, MD: Aspen Systems Corp.

Parnell, Myrtle, and VanderKloot, J. 1991. "Mental Health Services—2001: Serving New America." *Journal of Independent Social Work* 11(2):183–203.

Perlman, Helen. 1957. *Social Casework.* Chicago: University of Chicago Press.

Piazza, Jane, and delValle, Carmen. 1992. "Community-Based Family Therapy Training: An Example of Work With Poor and Minority Families." *Journal of Strategic and Systemic Therapies* 11(2):53–69.

Rabin, C., Rosenberg, H., and Sens, M. 1982. "Home Based Marital Therapy for Multi-Problem Families." *Journal of Marital and Family Therapy* 8(4):451–62.

Rabinowitz, C. 1969. "Therapy for Underprivileged Delinquent Families." In *Family Dynamics and Female Sexual Delinquency*, eds. O. Pollack and A. Friedman. Palo Alto, CA: Science and Behavior Books.

Sales, Esther. 1995. "Surviving Unemployment: Economic Resources and Job Loss Duration in Blue Collar Households." *Social Work* 40(4):483–94.

Satir, Virginia. 1983. *Conjoint Family Therapy*, 3rd ed. Palo Alto, CA: Science and Behavior Books.

Schorr, Lisbeth. 1991. "Children, Families and the Cycle of Disadvantage." *Canadian Journal of Psychiatry* 36:437–41.

Schuerman, John, Rzepnicki, Tina, and Littel, Julia. 1994. *Putting Families First.* New York: Aldyne-deGruyter.

Seitz, V., Rosenbaum, L.K., and Apfel, N.H. 1985. "Effects of Family Support Intervention: A Ten Year Followup." *Child Development* 56:376–91.

Sherman, R. 1983. "Counseling the Urban Economically Disadvantaged Family." *American Journal of Orthospsychiatry* 40:413–25.

Stack, C. 1974. *All Our Kin.* New York: Harper & Row.

Whittaker, James, Kinney, Jill, Tracy, Elizabeth, and Booth, Charlotte. 1990. *Reaching High Risk Families.* Chapter 3, "The Homebuilders Model." New York: Aldyne-deGruyter.

Williams, Betty. 1994. "Reflections on Family Poverty." *Families in Society* 75:47–50.

Wood, D., Valdez, R.B., Hayashi, T., and Shen, A. 1990. "Homeless and Housed Families in Los Angeles: A Study Comparing Demographic Economic and Family Function Characteristics." *American Journal of Public Health* 80(9):1049–52.

Ziefert, Marjorie, and Braun, Kaaren. 1991. "Skill Building for Effective Intervention with Homeless Families." *Families in Society* 72(4):212–19.

CHAPTER **11**

Family Treatment for Mental Illness

Social work involvement with the problems of mental illness has been both varied and broad, including direct service to the mentally ill individual and work with the families of the person with the mental illness. Work with the patient and work with the family were in a sense seen as separate spheres. In some settings, social work efforts were primarily with the family, while therapy with the patient was prescribed and conducted only by a physician. Contact with family members was necessary because members were often upset by the patient's behavior or were seen as upsetting to the patient and impeding his or her progress in treatment. Attempts were sometimes made to bar them from contact with the patient during hospitalization. Families were seen as needing treatment for themselves and for their part in the patient's problem.

The observation that patients sometimes seemed to recover in the hospital but relapse upon return home provided additional impetus for such a stance. Alternatives to releasing the patient to the family when the patient was thought to be ready to leave the hospital—release to places such as half-way houses or foster families—came to be preferred. More recently, such directedness in separating the patient from family gave way to the recognition that families and patients do continue involvement with each other, that families do want and do try to help and be a resource, and that helping their relationship to work is desirable.

Social workers did direct work with patients, in addition to the family contact, when the primary therapist was a physician or psychologist. The social work focus was on the patients' social adjustment—developing comfort and skills in relation to school or employment and other areas of engagement with the outside world. Though this work was considered to be therapeutic, it was not focused on the illness itself. In other places, social workers also provided psychotherapy with the patients, sometimes closely supervised by a psychiatrist, or at least in close collaboration with one who could prescribe medication or administer other physical forms of treatment. In the recent past, social workers have operated more independently in direct treatment of patients.

In a number of research projects of families, including members diagnosed as schizophrenic, the family was seen not only as interfering with treatment but as causative of the illness. These projects identified facets of family structure, role relationships, and communication processes that were problematical and confusing to all family members. In this view, schizophrenia was seen as an illness of the family system, not only of the individual.

From this latter position, the resulting recommended treatment goal was change of the family organization, and secondarily reduction of the individual's symptoms and behavior. The sought goal of change in patterns of family interaction was established on the assumption that family change would result in the elimination of the identified patient's symptomatic thinking and behavior. In one project, whole families— not only individuals—were hospitalized. The practice of producing change in family relationships became widespread as a mode of treatment. A feeling of blame was thereby added to families already feeling overwhelmed, confused, guilty, and helpless as a result of the difficult behavior of one of their members.

Many families have not felt helped by this approach. They have reacted with denial, ridicule of therapist interpretations, blaming the treatment institution, or other protest, and in search for help for themselves in coping with their schizophrenic member they have formed their own alliance for the mentally ill, often forgoing or totally rejecting the help of professionals. Terkelson (1983) states that such a therapeutic misalliance calls not only for omitting blaming statements to the family, but also for explicit absolution from blame for it, plus a full explanation of the illness.

In the current view, the problems of the family and the problems of the patient are seen as interactive with each other, since research has not supported the concept that the family is the sole cause of schizophrenic illness. The problems of relationship and communication identified in the research, while often present in the family, are not unique to families of persons with schizophrenic illness and have often been noted in families of patients with other diagnoses or presenting problems. Also, while it seems likely that the set of family behaviors and relationships are of long standing, research has not established that they predate the onset of illness.

Thus, these family behaviors are now seen as the family's response to the illness, admittedly often not helpful to the patient and often adversely affecting the patient's adjustment or recovery. With offers of help in coping with the patient's communications and behavior, family members can acknowledge that their responses to the patient have solved neither the patient's difficulties nor their own. Thus, the family needs and can accept help in understanding the illness and in learning how to cope with the difficult behavior they encounter.

How social workers can understand and be helpful to families with members with a diagnosis of schizophrenic is the focus of this chapter. Family work in relation to other psychiatric disorders, while encompassing many of the same understandings and approaches to treatment, requires different information bases and will be referred to by only passing reference.

NATURE OF THE ILLNESS

The patients we have in mind have an illness that is both severe and likely to be long term. They and their families face periods of crisis brought on in active phases of the illness by the onset or return of symptoms—crises that raise questions about hospitalization and how the family should respond. Times when symptoms seem to be in remission leave their own uncertainties about how much of patient behavior is part of the illness and how the family can respond in the most constructive way.

The *Diagnostic and Statistical Manual* (DSM-IV) identifies the symptom characteristics and behaviors of a general type of schizophrenic illness as well as several subcategories in which certain characteristics of the general type are predominant. Delusions, hallucinations, incoherent thinking, catatonia, and flat affect are basic characteristics. Thus, their ideas about reality are very different than those of other persons. Delusions that someone is able to read their thoughts, grandiose notions about who they are, or hallucinations of having seen, heard, or otherwise sensed something that others did not may be very difficult for family members to accept or tolerate. In some instances, such misconceptions or reality may lead to extreme suspiciousness or withdrawal on the one hand, or belligerent, assaultive, or bizarre behavior on the other.

Accompanying such disorder thinking is a reduced level of activity, productivity, and functioning at work or school and home, and in level of self-care. Lower level functioning both precedes and follows by months the occurrence of the more bizarre thought disorders and behaviors noted above. These, too, are difficult for family to explain, accept, or tolerate.

The foregoing symptoms are what family members and others can see. Kopeikin, Marshall, and Goldstein (1983) draw attention also to the patients' subjective experience during their illness. They experience distraction—"I jump from one thing to another. If I am talking to someone, they only need to cross their legs or scratch their heads and I am distracted and forget what I was saying."

They also experience overload—"It's like being a transmitter. The sounds are coming through to me but I feel my mind cannot cope with everything. It's difficult to concentrate on any one sound. It's like trying to do two or three different things at one time."

Sensitivity is another aspect of their illness experience—"I have noticed that noises all seemed to be louder to me than they were before. It"s as if someone had turned up the volume...I notice it most with background noises, you know what I mean, noises that are always around but you don't notice them."

For others, misperceptions become frightening, fill patients with fear or dread—"Everything is in bits...if you move, it's frightening...a jumbled mess...soon the houses lift off buildings on both sides of the road, as if it's flat and you could see right over it like a mad horse or something." Torrey (1982) and Anderson, Reiss, and Hogarty (1986) similarly refer to the patient's heightened sensitivity, the flooding of memories and emotions, the difficulty in processing of stimuli, and the altered sense of self as experienced in he/she experiences.

As we have implied above, understanding of the etiology and causes of such illness have been unclear and much debated. An organic base or, at least, a predisposition has been assumed to exist, but has not been successfully or specifically identified. Taylor (1987, p. 115) says "how the abnormalities occur remains largely a mystery" and goes on to cite accumulating evidence from electronic imaging of the brain that there are grounds for confirming an organic base. Johnson (1987) also notes that framing schizophrenia as a family illness overlooks the possible biological vulnerability and is therefore an insufficient base by itself for treatment. These positions concur with that of Falloon, Boyd, and McGill (1984) who in their more extensive review of the literature state that "there is no adequate research to support the theory that schizophrenia is caused by disturbed relationships in the absence of any other predisposing factor" (p. 30).

FAMILY INTERACTION: PROBLEMS IN COPING

Given the problems of thought and perception, severe withdrawal from contact, and the bizarre, assaultive, and most generally inexplicable behaviors of the patient just described, problems of adaptation and coping in families with a schizophrenic member seem an understandable and inevitable reaction. Family members describe their stress, not knowing what to do to stop or control the behavior. Feelings of helplessness and hopelessness descend upon them. They express sadness at the "blighted" life of a formerly promising child. Their grief at this loss of their child may justify and benefit from special attention (MacGregor, 1994). They report feelings of shame and guilt, efforts to shield the patient and themselves from public view, and the resulting isolation from family, friends, and the larger community and its institutions. Other family members report feeling tied down and not able to live their own lives. They experience a financial drain, which is no small part of the situation (Willis, 1982).

Family members use a variety of means to cope with their stressful situation (Fox, 1992). They deny, explain away, hide, control, or attribute patient behavior to calculated deviousness or to contrariness. They readily recognize that their efforts to deal with patient behaviors have been unsuccessful in controlling the behavior, with no possibility of eliminating it. In some instances, family members' responses seem to exacerbate the unwelcome behavior, with the circular interaction resulting in regression, even to the point of hospitalization.

Such circularity of family-patient interaction has been noted in families without schizophrenic members. It will now be useful to draw attention in more detail to its occurrence in these families.

Theories in Family Interaction

We make use of the observations from several theories about the family's relationship to schizophrenia. They are helpful in understanding the family's interaction, and are not efforts to blame the family for the disease or say that such patterns of relationship are causative. We see as important four general interrelated areas of family interaction touched upon with differing emphasis by different theorists: separation-individuation, family structure and roles, family communication, and expressed emotion.

Separation-Individuation

A lack of differentiation of self from other members of the family has often been observed in these families (Bowen, 1978; Lidz et al., 1965). Family members are not and do not see themselves as separate persons. Family members, in particular the patient, are seen as extensions of the self. They tend to respond identically to events and behaviors, and they frequently speak for each other, making decisions for another without recognizing that the other might have a different reaction or opinion. An example may illustrate.

> A 35-year-old single male was referred for outpatient care after hospitalization. He had never lived away from the home of his parents except for his time in the hospital. He was accompanied on his first visit to the clinic by his mother, who in a joint interview said that she was going to get his hair cut since it was now warmer spring weather. The patient did not object. Other discussion furthered the impression that this reflected a larger and repeated pattern, and that the patient would have great difficulty making decisions if his mother did not make them for him.

It is not possible to discern how such a pattern of interaction began—whether with the patient's passivity or withdrawal or with the mother's directive controlling efforts. Either could have been, and now likely is, a response to the other. More important than searching for its origin is finding a way to interrupt the cycle if the patient is eventually to become capable of self-care and eventually independent.

Wynne, Rykoff, Day, and Hirsch (1958) used the terminology "pseudo-mutuality and pseudo-hostility" for such a lack of boundaries—a kind of relationship of mutuality that came at the expense of one's individuality. The patient had developed neither a sense of separateness from others nor an identity of his own.

Stierlin, Levi, and Savard (1973) talk of the need in these families for the development of *related individuation*—the ability and willingness of the members to establish individual boundaries while remaining related. Family members can then articulate their own positions while remaining able to concur in the positions of others, and/or to resolve conflicts with them.

Family Structure and Roles

The lack of separateness of overcloseness just described was at times thought of as due to emotional disturbance or to the needs of the parent or sometimes the spouse. Later thinking, however, saw the overcloseness within the larger family context. Lidz and associates (1965) noted the problems of the parents with each other, a marital schism, and the resulting attempt of the parent to become closer to the patient. Schism could arise out of disagreement over how to respond to the schizophrenic patient's behavior—with perhaps one of them seeing it as something normal that would be outgrown and the other seeing it as deviant, one siding with the patient and the other opposing. Bowen (1978) saw this as family triangulation. Difficulty in closeness between the parental pair led to distancing between them and the attempt by one or both to increase the closeness with the patient.

In the observation of Lidz and associates and Bowen, and also expressed by Haley (1967), was the inherent blurring of generational boundaries, with the child being both parental companion or peer as well as child without needed role models or direction for behavior. The overcloseness with one parent left the patient distanced from the other, in the middle of the parental conflict. In instances in which one of the parents is the patient, a child can become a "parental child," taking over the ill parent's role and adding confusion to the family hierarchy and to the patient's difficulty in defining self and a role for self.

Communication

Wynne and Singer (1963) noted that communications in the families they studied were often blurred, fragmented, and disconnected, leaving members unclear about what they were being told or what was being asked of them. The result of such ambiguity was a great deal of confusion and emotionality, as well as erratic and at times inappropriate distance or closeness.

Both verbal and nonverbal aspects of communication serve to define relationships or avoid defining them, leaving family members unsure of their role or position. Incongruence between verbal and nonverbal, or between verbal, messages can put an individual in a bind—unable to ascertain whether to respond to one or the other. Words can be well meaning and positive but spoken in an angry tone of voice that conveys a more powerful negative message.

An example would be a mother's complaint to an adolescent child whom she is visiting during hospitalization that he should greet her more warmly; but when he moves to give her a hug her body stiffens, leaving him to feel that the gesture is unwelcome. The son is confused and in a bind, not knowing what the parent really wants. The patient is placed in a double bind if he attempts to clarify what the other person really wants and is met with "You know what I mean, I don't have to explain."

In some instances, family members are impervious to what is being said by others, placing their own interpretation on the words, convinced that their understanding is accurate, but leaving the patient confused and misunderstood. Explanations are offered for the patient's behavior without checking for the patient's own views or explanations. These problems are further elaborated in the following paragraphs on expressed emotion.

These paragraphs support the idea that an increased ability each family member to be clear about what they are saying and to whom they are saying it, and the opportunity to express difference and disagreement, is important in these families as it is in all other families. Other aspects of communication are evident in the handling of feelings and emotion.

Expressed Emotion

While family therapists have often encouraged open and direct communication of both positive and negative feelings and expectations to other family members, more recent thinking and practice has cast doubt upon such an approach to treatment. The patient's inability to process information, described above, suggests that both the nature and amount of communication and expressed emotion by family members need regulation in order to be helpful.

Expressed emotion (EE) is defined as having two components: expression of criticism and hostility and emotional overinvolvement. Ratings of criticism and hostility have been made with a variety of instruments, including direct observation of family interaction. Some have taken into account not only the content of what has been said but also tone of voice and speed of talking.

Attempts to overprotect the patient include self-sacrifice and emotional upset on the part of the family member. Overprotection is intrusive, such as treatment of the patient as a child or as incompetent. The earlier concepts of the lack of separation and differentiation on the part of family members are relevant here, as is the idea that intrusive family members overfunction when the patient underfunctions.

Both the emotional expression and the overprotection are seen as the family members' responses to patient behavior. They arise out of the anxiety and stress family members experience as well as the insufficient social support that is available (Fosler, 1993). Fox (1992) reminds that instead of attributing blame to the family for such expressions, workers should direct attention to the feelings that arise out of the patient's behavior and its stress on the family. Even though the expressions may be attributed to family concern or caring, negative consequences seem to follow.

Kuipers and Bebbington (1988), in their review of research on expressed emotion, report a number of studies that show high EE as a factor in the patient's relapse. Other studies have indicated that family intervention as a part of the overall treatment program reduces the relapse rate. Questions remain about whether one of the two components of EE is more significant than the other, in what ways it is related to the family's coping resources, and whether it is high primarily during acute episodes of the illness or was an ongoing part of family life either before or after hospitalization. (See also Miklowitz, Goldstein, Doane, Nuechterlein, Strachan, Snyder, and Magana-Amato, 1989.)

Leff and Vaughn (1980) sought to sort out the effects of life events and expressed emotion in the family in terms of their impact as precipitants of relapse in schizophrenic and depressed patients. They concluded that, in two sets of families studied, an increase of independently occurring life events (such as changes in employment, health, residence, or household membership) resulted in an increased level of expressed emotion in the family and were a factor in relapse and rehospitalization. However, no significant differences were noted between the families of depressive and schizophrenic patients.

Need for Family Services

With the increased emphasis on community care instead of long-term inpatient care, families are extensively involved in care provision. Given the extremely difficult patient behaviors and the levels of anxiety, burden, confusion, and lack of knowledge and ability to cope effectively, the need on the part of family members for professional assistance is great. Unfortunately, family members report disappointment in their contacts with mental health professionals. Holden and Lewine (1982) report that mental health professionals were seen as the primary resource for 53 percent of the respondents in their study, but that 33 percent felt their contacts with mental health care professionals were not helpful. Also, 38 percent of respondents felt frustrated after their contacts. Hatfield (1983) reports similar frustration and anger in her studies. She outlines the characteristics of both the helper and the kinds of help that family members said they wanted and needed.

Needs that Hatfield's respondents identified were for the understanding of symptoms, suggestions for coping with patient behavior, contacts with people who are having similar experiences, substitute or respite care, alternate living arrangements for the patient, understanding from friends and relatives, relief from financial distress, and, finally, therapy for themselves.

DeChillo (1993) also sees collaboration with the family as important. Similar to Hatfield's studies of nurses' responses to families, DeChillo identifies a list of worker characteristics desired by family members. They want helpers who listen attentively, conveying a caring attitude, who can educate the family with clear, reliable information, appreciate family expertise and see them as a resource, give practical advice, and include them in goal setting. On all these aspects, DeChillo's families scored social workers lower than social workers scored themselves.

At this point their disappointment and complaints about clinics, hospitals, and professional staff—including social workers—seem entirely relevant. East (1992) draws attention to the ever present concern on the part of many professionals to provide treatment for the patient by "protecting" him or her from the family. Training in a family orientation that sees the family as a resource rather than as stressor and family members as a means of support is basic to achieving family collaboration in the treatment process.

TREATMENT FOR FAMILY AND PATIENT— A PSYCHO-EDUCATION APPROACH

A comprehensive program envisages family participation from the beginning of hospital admission through discharge, and continuing thereafter on an outpatient basis. The primary goal is to avoid relapse and rehospitalization. Helping the family to achieve that goal is both an intermediate objective and a partial means to that end. Given the forgoing description of patients and families, these goals include efforts to reduce the family's sense of guilt and shame (Iodice and Wodarski, 1987) as well as the overinvolvement and emotionality to the extent they occur. Goals also include promoting positive communication and problem solving, and fostering the patient's separateness and individuality are closely related.

Family treatment does not by itself ensure positive outcomes. The patient's continuance of medication has repeatedly been shown to be necessary (Falloon, 1983). The family's role in encouraging the patient to continue the medication is important. Educating the family about the illness, developing helpful ways of responding to crises and everyday contacts, and putting them in contact with other families in similar situations are all essential parts of the program.

Initial Engagement

Social workers are frequently the first professionals to have contact with the family, for inpatient as well as outpatient admissions. (More specific reference to avoidance of an inpatient admission through crisis intervention programs is developed below.) Objectives of the first contacts include information gathering and engaging the family in the treatment process, both of which are important in planning and instrumenting treatment. They are similarly important as a beginning of the discharge plan, for which the social worker has key responsibility (Tuzman and Cohen, 1992). Treatment focus is on the patient (Atwood, 1990). Family and its members are seen not as in need of treatment but as collaborators in need of support and direction in coping with the patient. The help needed is in redefining how to structure the way they relate to the patient, a sense of what is their responsibility and what is or can be the patient's responsibility.

Eliciting the Family's Experience

In addition to information the family can give about the patient's symptoms, history of the illness, and prior treatment, the social worker elicits information about the stress they have experienced and their efforts to cope with the illness. Listening closely to each member's experience conveys the worker's understanding and interest in the family as well as in the patient. Their observations about patient behavior and their ideas about the kind of care needed are sought. Combinations of stressors that the family or individual members may have experienced are identified. The family's past involvement with the patient is accredited as caring and interest, even where it may have been negative and produced undesired results. Such accreditation is particularly important in obtaining their consent to participate in a treatment plan, when their past experience with the patient and professionals may have left them angry, discouraged, and resistant to further involvement. From such inquiry the worker learns where things may have gone wrong in previous contacts.

Introduction of Treatment Method

The manner of operation of the present treatment program and team is described, and the social worker offers self as a bridge and facilitator to the treatment team.

Early in the contact it is important to provide information about the nature of the illness, its various manifestations, and what is known and not known about causes (Anderson, Reiss, and Hogarty, 1986). Family members can gain some cognitive grasp of what the patient is experiencing and a more objective picture of what it is they have to relate to. This educational focus emphasizes that they did not cause the illness and that they cannot cure it, and it helps to relieve them of blame for the illness, though family members carry both guilt and shame for it. Time is well spent in this educational aspect in responding also to their feelings. Families are typically seen in groups with other families in this process, giving them the opportunity to feel less alone with their situation and to learn how other families have come to cope. Patients are not usually a part of these family groups. These psycho-educational approaches may very slightly in the number of sessions devoted to information provision and ventilation of feelings about patient symptoms and behavior.

Negotiating Family Participation

Family willingness to participate, as well as the value of participation to them, may vary according to the number of previous crises they have experienced with the patients. It may be important to recognize negative experiences with prior services and to emphasize the differences in the present approach. In the beginning of treatment modulation of overoptimism or overpessimism on the part of either patient or family are important considerations. Kotcher and Smith (1993) note this also in the introduction of new medication.

Patient willingness to have the family participate may also need to be developed. The level of anger at the family may be high. Patients who have had difficulty separating from the family may deny any need for them and assert their independence.

Other Emphases

Another facet of the work at this stage focuses on problem solving and skill development (Falloon et al., 1985). This phase develops with the family an understanding of what level of activity and responsibility they can reasonably expect of the patient, and how to communicate their expectations clearly with a minimum of emotion and intrusiveness. Family members might rehearse possible communications in the family groups. By this point in the treatment program, some patients and family members may meet together with the worker regulating the communication to discuss patient and family expectations. Patients have a similar need to learn new ways of communication. Though enhancement of patient-family communication is desirable, the new experience may be difficult, as in the following instance:

> A catatonic outpatient had been verbally uncommunicative except with reference to names of various operas to which he often listened (e.g., *La Forza del Destino*). With the worker's encouragement to be more specific about what he wanted or his response to the issue at hand, his mother, with whom he lived, experienced his verbalizations as demanding and threatening and pressed for his return to the hospital.

Among the essentials of needed communication are clarity about what each person intends to convey and also to whom in the family the message is addressed, and checking that the receiver of the message has correctly understood and has an opportunity to give response. The focus on the "how" of communication may be done in relation to specific problems, such as what the discharge plan will be. Marley (1992) calls these aspects elucidating, naming, differentiating, and consensual validation. He also identifies disagreement among therapists about how to relate to psychotic communications, as in the incident above, but points to the value to both patient and family at some point in the process of attempting to understand their meaning.

Family problems other than those engendered by the patient's illness are likely to become evident over time in these problem-solving sessions. Splits between family members, particularly marital disagreements and the side-taking of one parent with the patient against the other, are revealed. Siblings of the patient or parents may also participate on one side or the other. It is initially necessary to focus on and resolve disagreements as the affect the patient, either postponing or shifting to separate sessions a direct focus on problems in the marriage or other issues.

Nevertheless, the resolution of problems of others in the family may be significant for the patient as well as for the others. Our discussion thus far has had in mind primarily the situation in which the patient is an adolescent or young adult. Boyd-Franklin and Shenouda (1990) refer to the situation in which the patient is a parent with young children. They outline the necessity of work with all the family subsystems in order to provide an understanding and stable environment for the patient. This includes work on the children's school and behavior problems, on marital problems, and with the extended family system.

Continuing Treatment

Prevention of relapse or rehospitalization is a primary determinant in the length of the family involvement in the process we are describing. Different programs devote a varying number of sessions to the educational, problem-solving, or skills-training emphases, or the handling of crises. Issues about the termination of contact or developing additional goals eventually come to the foreground. Some families may opt for continuing work on more general family problems or reduced frequency of contact (Anderson, Reiss, and Hogarty, 1986). Ferris and Marshall (1987) report efforts made by their family groups to develop resources to enhance the lifestyles of the patients by working to develop opportunities for further education, suitable employment, alternative housing, and networks with other families of the mentally ill.

Groups at this stage serve both patient and family in expanding community connectedness and by educating themselves and the community. The social worker or other professionals may become less central and be shifted to a more consultative role. However, if family or patient choose to terminate contact they are invited to return whenever concerns or problems reemerge.

Case Management

The efforts of the families described in the previous paragraphs imply the existence of a variety of needs on the part of these chronic patients and the demand for a variety of services to meet them if patients are to remain in the community. In early contacts, it falls to the social worker to inform the family of available services and of their particular usefulness, and to facilitate connection to them. Over time, the family may be helped to take on some of the effort of coordinating and connecting the needed services in order to work out the best plan of care.

Unfortunately, many of the services are expensive, and questions have been raised about cost effectiveness. Community and family care has been considered better for patient adjustment but has not reduced costs as much as had been hoped for. The result has been a shift in emphasis, from producing a care plan of maximum benefit to containment of costs (Belcher, 1993) by reducing eligibility for services or limiting the extent of care provided.

Recent changes in the length of stay for inpatient care may place profound limits on the extent of assistance social workers can provide to families and patients during the hospitalization phase. The 3 to 12 months, thought of as long-term care as recently as 1989, has been reduced to 7 to 45 days. Short-term care, formerly 4 weeks or less, is frequently only 1 to 14 days (Farley, 1994). Shortened time limits restrict both the time a worker has to engage the family in a treatment plan and the extent of the family's involvement in it. Primary attention is of necessity directed to planning for discharge and what happens after that.

In these circumstances, the availability of a network of other services to meet patient and family needs becomes crucial. While short-term hospitalization can serve as crisis intervention, continuing service is needed to enable family and patient to handle ongoing understandings and decisions about medications, activity level, work, and interpersonal and social contact. Community care requires support services such as day hospitals, sheltered workshops, and alternatives to family housing; however, development of these resources has not kept pace with the emphasis on deinstitutionalization. Social work's concern for patient and family extends to these aspects of care as well.

Lourie and Katz-Leavy (1991) describe the extensive need for a variety of services and agencies to work together on the mental health needs of children and their families. An extensive Child and Adolescent Service System Program (CASSP) has been developed. In this program, as in the approach we have described, families were included as equal and participating partners in the interdisciplinary treatment team for their particular family member. They were recruited also in the efforts to assess, involve, coordinate, and expand existing services.

Medication

The use of medication is crucial in the treatment of schizophrenia during both hospitalization and outpatient after care. Investigations that have tested whether family work of the type described here is sufficient by itself to avoid relapse and rehospitalization have shown that it is not (Falloon et al., 1985). Similarly, medication by itself without family involvement during in- or outpatient status is less effective in the long run.

While social workers cannot prescribe medication, their knowledge of its importance and effects is vital. They can facilitate family and patient awareness in this area and help them to devise means of ensuring that schedules will be kept. Social workers may see the patient and/or the family more frequently than the prescribing physician, especially during the patient's stay in the community. They need, therefore, to acquire knowledge of and ability to observe effects and side-effects, as well as patient symptoms and behavior, that may be indications of patient need for change in kind or amount of medication. This role for the social worker may be even more crucial in less populated areas where physicians are available only part time or on call (Hiratsuka, 1994).

Ready Availability of Help

The onset of the illness and the possibility of relapse are critical times for patient and family. The ready availability of professional help at such times, to evaluate the ongoing situation and the impact of new stressors or developments, can have a profound impact on what happens next, and on the long run. Langsley and Kaplan (1968) report a project in which schizophrenic patients for whom a first hospital admission was sought were randomly assigned for family treatment or hospital admission. Available members of the treatment team spent hours with patient and family at this initial contact, developing understanding of patient and situation and seeking to engage and meet the needs of the family, much as we have described here. They made a home visit the following day, and were available frequently in person for several weeks and by telephone between inperson contacts until the immediate crisis that had led to the request for help was resolved. Appropriate referrals for treatment of ongoing family problems were made. Though some of the family treatment patients needed days of hospitalization during the following year, the number of days and overall costs were significantly less than for those admitted at initial contact.

In-Home Treatment

Meeting the family at home visits was at the core of a treatment project for a variety of families, including those with adolescents who were violent or suicidal (Seelig, Goldman-Hall, and Jerrell, 1992). A team of professionals met the family at home for a beginning 8- to 12-hour multiple-impact session at the beginning of contact. Representatives of referring agencies and significant extended family and other nonfamily members were included. Twelve-month follow-up of this 90-day treatment program showed that three-fourths of the adolescents were still living at home. In some centers, mobile teams can be available for emergency home visits without prior plan for contact.

Patients with Other Diagnoses

Whether the approach to schizophrenic families that we have outlined is suitable for families of patients with other diagnoses has not been extensively reported. Of special concern would be the kind of program needed for patients with a dual diagnosis of schizophrenia and substance abuse. Anderson, Griffin, Rossi, Pagonis, Holder, and Treiber (1986) report that multi-family groups with a psycho-educational component for various psychiatric and behavioral disorders have been found to be useful. Their own investigation of work with groups of families of patients with affective disorders compared groups having a psycho-educational focus to those with a process focus. Families of the affective disorder patients benefitted from both orientations, but the ones in the psycho-educational focus groups were more satisfied with the experience. Holden and Anderson (1990) report positive experience with a psycho-educational approach with depressive patients and their families. Schwartz and Schwartz (1993) confirm its usefulness with this group of families. Brennan (1995) reports positive reactions to a psycho-educational approach by bipolar patients and their families, but outcome data and comparison to other forms of treatment were not available.

While it is evident that some of the same issues reside in families with patients of other diagnoses, such as the borderline disorder (Berry and Roath, 1982; Levin and Williams, 1982), and that family treatment has been helpful, psycho-education has not been a specific part of the approach, though other aspects of family work have been found to be useful.

SUMMARY

In this chapter, we have set out elements of an approach for working with patients diagnosed as schizophrenic and their families. The illness is severe and chronic. Nothing we have described suggests the possibility of cure, but the approach centers rather on the hope that recurrence of the most severe symptoms and disturbing behaviors can be averted, and that rehospitalization may be avoided, so that patients can remain in the community. Associated with this primary goal is the hope that they and their families acquire methods of coping with the stresses they experience and methods of relating and problem solving that contribute to their overall sense of well-being and health.

Though there are many elements of similarity in the treatment programs to which we have referred, there are also variations between them. Programs differently emphasize crisis intervention, the number of educational sessions with the family, the time devoted to education or ventilation about the illness, the point at which educational and problem-solving work with the family and patient together supercede the multiple family groups, and the overall duration of contact. Thus it seems impossible to point to any one element as primary, but at the same time it is possible to note that various projects report lower relapse and rehospitalization rates when family work is part of the treatment protocol (Atwood, 1990; Falloon et al., 1985; McFarlane, 1983; East, 1992). Efforts to reduce EE have been shown to reduce the risk for release (Kuipers and Bebbington, 1988; Miklowitz, Goldstein, Doane, Nuechterlein, Strachan, Snyder, and Magana-Amato, 1989). These efforts also enable families to feel better about the service they get for themselves and the patient, being more knowledgeable about the illness (Posner, Wilson, Kral, Lander, and McIlwraith, 1992).

Social Worker as Therapist

Social workers clearly can undertake a substantial portion of the therapy with families of schizophrenic patients. Becoming well informed about the nature of the illness and the available medical treatment, they can undertake the education of the family about the illness (Walsh, 1988). They do need to see the family as interested, as a resource, and as collaborators in helping—definitely not as culprits in causing the illness. Most social workers do not need to be convinced of the importance of family treatment, and some individual work with the patient may still be indicated. Social workers need to be in possession of skills in working with the family, including skills for handling family communication in a new way that promotes separateness, reduces overinvolvement/intrusiveness, lowers the level of affect, and promotes problem solving. Also in the repertoire of needed skills is the ability to work with groups of families and other members of the treatment team. The ability to help family and patient establish and maintain contact with other agency support systems and other social networks is also of considerable importance. Work with these families is long term, but the marks of success in maintaining them in the community and in their family relationships can be rewarding.

REFERENCES

Anderson, Carol M., Griffin, Suzanne, Rossi, Albert, Pagonis, Irene, Holder, Diane P., and Treiber, Renate. 1986. "A Comparative Study of the Impact of Education Versus Process Groups for Families of Patients with Affective Disorders." *Family Process* 25:185–205.

Anderson, Carol M., Reiss, Douglas J., and Hogarty, Gerard D. 1986. *Schizophrenia and the Family*. New York: Guilford.

Anthony, J.D., Jr. 1992. "A Retrospective Evaluation of Factors Influencing Successful Outcomes on an Inpatient Psychiatric Ward." *Research in Social Work Practice* 2(1):56–64.

Atwood, N. 1990. Integrating Individual and Family Treatment for Outpatients Vulnerable to Psychosis." *American Journal of Psychotherapy* 44(2):247–55.

Belcher, John R. 1993. "The Tradeoffs of Developing a Case Management Model for Chronically Mentally Ill People." *Health and Social Work* 18(1):20–31.

Berry, S.L., and Roath, M. 1982. "Family Treatment of a Borderline Personality." *Clinical Social Work Journal* (10):3–14.

Bowen, Murray. 1978. *Family Therapy in Clinical Practice*. New York: Jason Aronson.

Boyd-Franklin, N., and Shenouda, N.T. 1990. "A Multi-Systems Approach to the Black Inner-City Family with a Schizophrenic Mother." *American Journal of Orthopsychiatry* 60(2):186–95.

Brennan, Joseph. 1995. "A Short Term Psychoeducational Multiple Family Group for Bipolar Patients and Their Families." *Social Work* 40(6):737–45.

DeChillo, N. 1993. "Collaboration Between Social Workers and Families of Patients with Mental Illness." *Families in Society* 74(2):104–15.

Diagnostic and Statistical Manual-IV. 1994. Washington, DC: American Psychiatric Association.

East, E. 1992. "Family as Resource: Maintaining Chronically Mentally Ill Members in the Community." *Health and Social Work* 17(2):93–97.

Falloon, Ian. 1983. "Behavioral Family Interventions in the Management of Chronic Schizophrenia." In *Family Therapy in Schizophrenia*, ed. William McFarlane. New York: Guilford.

Falloon, Ian, Boyd, Jeffrey, and McGill, Christine. 1984. *Family Care of Schizophrenia*. New York: Guilford.

Falloon, Ian, Boyd, Jeffrey, McGill, Christine, Williamson, Malcolm, Razani, Javad, Moss, Howard, Gilderman, Alexander, and Simpson, George. 1985. "Family Management in Prevention of Morbidity of Schizophrenia." *Archives of General Psychiatry* 42:888–96.

Farley, Joan. 1994. "Transitions in Psychiatric Inpatient Clinical Social Work." *Social Work* 39(2):207–12.

Ferris, P., and Marshall, C.A. 1987. "'A Model Project for Families of the Mentally Ill." *Social Work* 32(2):110–14.

Fosler, Mary. 1993. *The Relationship between Selected Family Factors and Schizophrenia*. Unpublished Doctoral Dissertation, University of Maryland at Baltimore.

Fox, P. 1992. "Implications for Expressed Emotion Within a Family Therapy Context." *Health and Social Work* 17(3):207–13.

Haley, J. 1967. "Toward a Theory of Pathological Systems." In *Family Therapy and Disturbed Families*, eds. I. Boszormenyi-Nagy and G. Zuk. Palo Alto, CA: Science and Behavior Books.

Hatfield, Agnes. 1983. "What Families Want of Family Therapists." In *Family Therapy in Schizophrenia*, ed. William McFarlane. New York: Guilford.

Hibbs, E.D., Hamburger, S.D., Kruesi, M.J., and Lenane, M. 1993. "Factors Affecting Expressed Emotion in Parents of Ill and Normal Children." *American Journal of Orthopsychiatry* 63(1):103–12.

Hiratsuka, Jon. 1994. "Working with Medicine on the Brain." *NASW NEWS* (February).

_____. 1994. "Mental Health Upgrade Urged in Reformed Bill." *NASW NEWS* (February).

Holden, D., and Anderson, C.M. 1990. "Psychoeducational Family Intervention for Depressed Patients and Their Families." In *Depression and Families: Impact and Treatment*, ed. G.I. Keitner, pp. 57–184. Washington, DC: American Psychiatric Press.

Holden, Deborah F., and Lewine, Richard R. 1982. "How Families Evaluate Mental Health Professionals, Resources, and Effects of Illness." *Schizophrenia Bulletin* 8(4):626–33.

Iodice, J., and Wodarski, J., 1987. "Aftercare Treatment for Schizophrenics Living at Home." *Social Work* 32(2):122–28.

Johnson, Harriette. 1987. "Biologically Based Deficit in the Identified Patient: Indications for Psycho-Educational Strategies." *Journal of Marital and Family Therapy* 13(4):337–48.

Kopeikin, Hal, Marshall, Valerie, and Goldstein, Michael. 1983. "The Psychoeducational Approaches." In *Family Therapy in Schizophrenia*, ed. William McFarlane. New York: Guilford.

Kotcher, Marilyn, and Smith, Thomas. 1993. "Three Phases of Clozapine Treatment and Phase-Specific Issues for Patients and Families." *Hospital and Community Psychiatry* 44(8):744–48.

Kuipers, Liz, and Bebbington, Paul. 1988. "Expressed Emotion Research in Schizophrenia." *Psychological Medicine* 18:893–909.

Langsley, Donald, and Kaplan, David. 1968. *The Treatment of Families in Crisis*. New York: Grune and Stratton.

Langsley, Donald, Pittman, Frank, Machotka, Pavel, and Flomenhaft, Kalman. 1968. "Family Crisis Therapy—Results and Implications." *Family Process* 7(2):145–58.

Leff, Julian, Kuipers, Liz, and Berkowitz, Ruth. 1983. "Intervention in Families of Schizophrenics and Its Effects on Relapse Rate. In *Family Therapy in Schizophrenia*, ed. William McFarlane. New York: Guilford.

Leff, Julian, and Vaughn, Christine. 1980. "Interaction of Life Events and Relatives' Expressed Emotion in Schizophrenia and Depressive Neurosis." *British Journal of Psychiatry* 136:146–53.

Levin, Elliot, and Williams, R.J. 1982. "Family Therapy for the Borderline Patient." *International Journal of Family Therapy* 4(4):220–33.

Lidz, T., Fleck, S., and Cornelison, A.R. 1965. *Schizophrenia and the Family*. New York: International Universities Press.

Lourie, Ira, and Katz-Leavy, Judith. 1991. "New Directions for Mental Health Services for Families and Children." *Families in Society* 72(3):277–85.

MacGregor, Peggy. 1994. "Grief: The Unrecognized Parental Response to Mental Illness in a Child." *Social Work* 39(2):160–66.

Marley, J.A. 1992. "Content and Context: Working with Mentally Ill People in Family Therapy." *Social Work* 37(5):412–17.

McFarlane, William. 1983. "Multiple Family Therapy in Schizophrenia." In *Family Therapy in Schizophrenia*, ed. William McFarlane. New York: Guilford.

Miklowitz, David, Goldstein, Michael, Doane, Jeri, Nuechterlein, Keity, Strachan, Angus, Snyder, Karen, and Magana-Amato, Ana. 1989. "'Is Expressed Emotion an Index of a Transactional Process? Parents' Affective Style." *Family Process* 28:153–67.

Mishler, Elliot, and Waxler, Nancy. 1967. "Family Interaction Processes and Schizophrenia—A Review of Current Theories." In *The Psychosocial Interior of the Family*, ed. Gerald Handel. Chicago: Aldine Publishing Co.

Posner, C.M., Wilson, K.G., Kral, M.J., Lander, S., and McIlwraith, R.D. 1992. "Family Psychoeducational Support Groups in Schizophrenia." *American Journal of Orthopsychiatry* 62(2):206–18.

Ryglewicz, Hilary. 1991. "Psychoeducation for Clients and Families: A Way in, Out, and Through in Working with People with Dual Disorders." *Psycho-Social Rehabilitation Journal* 15(2):79–89.

Schwartz, Arthur, and Schwartz, Ruth. 1993. *Depression: Theories and Treatments*. New York: Columbia University Press.

Seelig, William R., Goldman-Hall, Barry J., and Jerrell, Jeanette, M. 1992. "In-Home Treatment of Families with Seriously Disturbed Adolescents in Crisis." *Family Process* 312:2135–49.

Stierlin, H., Levi, I.D., and Savard, R. 1973. "Centrifugal Versus Centripetal Separation in Adolescence." In *Adolescent Psychiatry*, eds. S. Feinstein and P. Giovacchini. New York: Basic Books.

Sullivan, M.A. 1991. A Family System-Oriented Approach to the Treatment of the Homeless, Mentally Ill Older Woman. City University of New York, Ph.D. Dissertation.

Taylor, E.H. 1987. "The Biological Basis of Schizophrenia." *Social Work* 32(2):105–21.

Terkelson, Kenneth. 1983. "Schizophrenia and the Family: II, Adverse Effects of Family Therapy." *Family Process* 22:191–200.

Torrey, E. Fuller. 1982. *Surviving Schizophrenia: A Family Manual*. New York: Harper & Row.

Tuzman, L., and Cohen, A. 1992. "Clinical Decision Making for Discharge Planning in a Changing Psychiatric Environment." *Health and Social Work* 17(4):299–307.

Vaughn, C.E., and Leff, J.P. 1976. "The Influence of Family and Social Factors on the Course of Psychiatric Illness: A Comparison of Schizophrenic and Depressed Neurotic Patients." *British Journal of Psychiatry* 129:125–37.

Walsh, Joseph. 1988. "Social Workers as Family Educators about Schizophrenia." *Social Work* 33:138–41.

Webster, J. 1992. "Split in Two: Experiences of the Children of Schizophrenic Mothers." *British Journal of Social Work* 22(3):309–29.

Willis, Mary. 1982. "The Impact of Schizophrenia on Families: One Mother's Point of View." *Schizophrenia Bulletin* 8(4):617–19.

Wynne, L.C., and Singer, M.T. 1963. "Thought Disorder and Family Relations of Schizophrenics." *Archives of General Psychiatry* 9:199–206.

Wynne, Lyman, Rykoff, L., Day, J., and Hirsch, S. 1958. "Pseudo-Mutuality in the Family Relations of Schizophrenics." *Psychiatry* 21:205–22.

Ziter, M.L. 1987. "Culturally Sensitive Treatment of Black Alcoholic Families." *Social Work* 32(2):130–35.

CHAPTER 12

Treatment for Families with Chronically and Terminally Ill

Members *(With Special Reference to Persons with AIDS)*

Family togetherness and family adaptability are both severely tested at times of illness of a family member. Even brief illnesses or periods of incapacity due to accidents make explicit or implicit demands to shift responsibility, allocate time differently, temper wants in favor of other's needs, and adjust the image of other family members as persons and role-takers, if only for a short period of time. Short-term adjustments may or may not be easily made, and they are dependent not only on the way the family has been organized but also on the stage of the family life cycle at which the illness occurs, on the ways in which illness has been handled in the past, and on the kind and causes of the present illness and its meaning to the family.

Long-term illnesses make all the same demands for adaptability. In addition, they require accommodation to the changes that might be taking place due to the advance of the family life cycle or those due to changing stages or phases of the illness. The need to cope with the long term may not only exacerbate the stress of the illness itself; it may also result in reenforcing family patterns that were dysfunctional for family members or make for difficulty in moving to new patterns that allow for members' growth and life enhancement.

Families with differing membership composition—traditional nuclear, single parent, extended, remarried, gay or lesbian—will all have adaptability tasks specific to their membership. So will a network of relationships with people who may not be blood relatives but who may be considered family in specific instances. Each type of family group will have different needs for services and resources as well as changing, ongoing relationships with the health care team. Further, the role and position of the stricken member is a significant variable in the family's response.

Families with members who have Acquired Immune Deficiency Syndrome (AIDS) will be our central focus. We intend, thereby, to provide the reader a general framework for thinking about family functioning and ways of helping in a variety of chronic illness situations.

KINDS OF CHRONIC ILLNESS

Rolland (1987) offers a classification of types of chronic illnesses. They can be grouped according to three dimensions—by nature of onset, by difference in course, or by degree of progression and ultimate outcome. Some illnesses are sudden in onset, with ready recognition that something is different and that drastic, immediate, and long-term adaptation on the part of the patient and the family will be necessary. Accidents with handicapping results may have similar impact. The family may experience this as a crisis, having had no opportunity to prepare for change, nor prior experience with similar circumstances. In other instances, the onset is gradual, giving patient and family time to integrate the significance of the illness and to plan.

The course of illness is not the same in all instances. In some cases the course may not be constant, with periods of remission or relapse. In other instances signs of illness are constant. They may proceed to a fixed level of disability or worsen progressively. They may ultimately be fatal, or life shortening, or primarily incapacitating and limiting. According to these categories, the onset of AIDS is gradual, but its course is progressive and ultimately fatal.

The time span from initial infection with the Human Immunodeficiency Virus (HIV) to the appearance of the first manifestations of AIDS may be as long as ten years. But, as will be shown later, although the time span from first symptoms to death is relatively short in most AIDS cases, some patients are living beyond the anticipated time—a circumstance that creates its own issues for patient and family. Awareness of such change in timing and progression may come first to the patient and vary among family members, suggesting yet another complication in family adaptation.

Sources of Infection

One of the first questions asked by both patient and family about illness, chronic or not, is what caused it? How did you get it? Can I get it?

Years of uncertainty and misinformation about causes of AIDS fostered intense anxiety and were a genuine basis for fear. Eventually, the accumulation of data about who became infected with the Human Immunodeficiency Virus (HIV) and subsequently became ill permitted an understanding of how it was spread. A recent report of the Centers for Disease Control (1994) shows that, for adolescent and adult males of all races/ethnic groups, the chief source of exposure is through sexual activity with other men. The next highest number of cases comes through sharing of needles in injecting drug use. Substantially smaller percentages of males are infected through heterosexual contact with injecting drug users or are hemophiliacs who have been recipients of contaminated blood transfusions.

For adolescent/adult women, the chief source of infection is injecting drug use, or through heterosexual contact with an infected injecting drug user or with a bisexual male. This is true for most racial/ethnic groupings except for Asian/Pacific Islanders and American Indian/Alaskan natives, where heterosexual contact is a more frequent source of infection than injecting drug use. Also, small numbers of cases are hemophiliac or others who have had transfusions of contaminated blood.

For children, male and female, under age 13 the main source of exposure is a mother with (or at risk for) HIV infection, with small numbers being hemophiliac and transfused with contaminated blood.

For both patient and family, the means of acquisition of AIDS pose problems in coping with this chronic illness that are not present, at least to the same degree, in most other chronic/terminal illnesses. Other patients and families may not be eager to disclose the presence of chronic illness; they may question whether something they had been doing could account for the illness; but generally they do not have to deal with factors that are considered to be stigmatizing and that put them at risk of rejection and ostracism, as do homosexuality and intravenous drug use.

PHASES OF ILLNESS

One similarity in the effects and demands on families for all chronic illnesses, is that they have specific time phases to which family members have to adapt. While the phases may not be identical, the importance of recognizing phase-specific issues and adapting to them is.

Crisis—Diagnosis

The person with AIDS (PWA)—no matter who in the family the person is—and the rest of the family have similar problems after the diagnosis of the illness is established. Prediagnosis time is filled with uncertainty, speculation, and anxiety. One may have expected the worst; another possibly refused to think about it. At diagnosis, some uncertainty may be lifted, but the future is altered, and it appears bleak.

Disclosure: Why? Why Not and to Whom?

But now, at this transition, with whom can the information be shared? If the PWA is gay and has handled that with parents, their response to news of this illness is still an unknown. If parents don't know of the homosexuality (or suspect only drug use), is it worth the hassle of telling them? Even more critical, how will the partner react? If the PWA is a parent, should the children be told? What will be the spouse's response if the PWA is infected through extramarital sex or drug needle sharing? And when the family knows, whom can they tell or talk to? With whom can they share the burden and pain?

In many situations of chronic, disabling, or terminal illness the family has been told or knows the diagnosis before the patient. Among medical personnel, excepting those who sometimes doubt the virtue of informing the patient, there is general consensus that both patient and family should be aware, so that they can be open and free in sharing feelings and making plans. And in the case of AIDS, the patient generally knows first.

Many factors enter into the decision about when and to whom to disclose. They include the patient's own feelings and the anticipation of family members' reactions. Feelings of denial, shame, guilt, and anger, as well as fear of stigma, rejection, and of the burden and pain ahead are experienced by both patient and family. Kaplan (1988) notes that many patients have bought into the cultural view that the disease is a retribution for deviance; this is certainly true for many families. Anger on the part of the patients may be prompted by loss of the ability to perform a job and loss of other resources and may be directed at those through whom the infection was acquired and at self for failing to protect himself or herself. Arguing and fighting may be prompted by the patient's feeling of guilt for having exposed a partner and perhaps an effort to get the partner to leave before the partner becomes infected.

Stuhlberg and Buckingham (1988) note anger reactions from parents, from partners—both hetero- and homosexual—toward the implied unfaithfulness in acquiring the disease. Anger can be at both the illness and its consequences, as well as at the patient's drug abuse or homosexuality.

Whether the PWA talks, and to whom in the family will depend on the degree to which family communications have been open, and on family coalitions of which he or she has or has not been a part. Some therapists believe that if the patient has not been able to communicate with and be a part of family prior to diagnosis, the likelihood of establishing a positive connection at this stage is very slim or doomed to turmoil or further disappointment. The disadvantages of secrecy may outweigh the advantages of disclosure (Mohr, 1988). Others argue that, because AIDS is so debilitating, demanding, and disheartening for the patient and caregivers, it is too much of a burden to be carried alone and that family should know. Active attempts should be made to involve them.

The importance for both family and patient of being informed and able to talk about the situation can hardly be overemphasized. Otherwise, they will be in the position of playing games with each other and be denied the needed mutual support that can come from open and honest communication. The definition of family should, therefore, be broad and include the couple—whether gay or heterosexual—the family of origin, friendship networks, and the family of caregivers.

On the side of openness is the fact that many families are already connected. Frequently they are ready to provide care, even though they may still be unaccepting of the gay or substance-abusing lifestyle. Unreadiness in acknowledging the patient's gay relationships sometimes may lead to efforts by the family of origin to exclude gay partners from the caring team, an effort that would deprive the patient of a close, important relationship. Such a situation calls for therapeutic help in resolving the conflict. Tiblier, Walker, and Rolland (1989) report an instance of bringing together, in therapy, a gay male son and his uncommunicative Irish family at the time of disclosure. In the encounter, the son was able to relieve his mother of a sense of guilt over his gayness and illness and allow her to express her sadness over the years of distance in their relationship.

Family Role in the Decision About Disclosure

Finally, it is the patient's choice to disclose or not to disclose. Help in making the choice and in anticipating the difficult times ahead may be needed. Rolland (1987) advocates inquiry into the family's experience and history with illness and the ways each family member has responded. Using the framework of a genogram (McGoldrick and Gerson, 1985), it becomes possible to see not only the kinds of illness situations with which the family has had to cope, but also each member's feeling about it, their ability to take on added responsibility, and shifts in relationships.

A genogram might reveal, for example, a past experience of parents' initial ability to properly shift their focus of caring to a child during a lengthy illness. They may, at the same time, have had appropriate expectations and not done for the child what the child could do for self. An alternate outcome could also be possible. A closeness may have developed between mother, as primary caretaker, and son in the caretaking relationship that continued beyond the illness and resulted in the father's feeling not only left to the side but also somewhat hostile to the son. This represents a failure to return to the normal family life cycle at termination of an illness. Mother's genogram might reveal that she had an overly responsible caretaking role in her family of origin. Father's genogram could reveal that males did not, for whatever reason, alter their family roles in time of illness. Such information may provide the patient who now has AIDS with a basis for understanding what reception in the family the disclosure of AIDS might encounter. At a later stage, it might help to understand a certain amount of unhappiness generated in the care of the patient.

Family Readiness for Caregiving

Assessment of the family's ability, willingness and readiness to help is important (McDonell, Abell, and Miller, 1991) and requires discussion between them and the patient. Discussion will reveal who is closest to the patient, who cannot or does not want to be involved, and what time, energy, and resources are available. Therapists also need to help the family be clear about what resources and services may be needed, what they will need to do for the patient, and what the patient can do for self. Family members' perceptions of the situation should also enter in— their fear of stigma and isolation, their assessment of their own and the patient's ability to cope. Their ties to religious and other outside groups and the way they view mutual ties also enter in to the assessment of the family's caretaking capacity.

While family contact and investment is desirable, families may overinvolve themselves. Some families feel that they must devote themselves entirely to the patient, that to do otherwise would be selfish and uncaring (Schwartz and Schwartz, 1977). Such family behavior may be the result of feelings of guilt or the manifestation of a chronic family enmeshment. The family may tend also to take charge and make decisions for the patient rather than together with the patient, unless the staff, as we have suggested, makes an active effort to include both family and patient in developing a care plan. Brown and Furstenberg (1992) draw attention to the need in this instance to empower the patient by restoring him or her to a more active role in decision making.

Angry feelings expressed by both patients and families are common. These may be directed at each other or at the medical staff, accompanied by demands that they do or not do something. Particularly in cases in which AIDS is transfusion acquired, the anger toward medical staff is understandable (Gallo-Silver, 1993). In other instances, the anger is displaced onto persons from patient's frustration and need to blame—out of their feelings of helplessness and hopelessness, and as a result of their life situation. Alternately, the anger may be a reflection of unresolved relationship issues in the family.

Chronic Phase

How to lead a semblance of a "normal" life along with the anticipation of death is an ongoing concern, whether facing an enduring disability or an earlier end to life. Return to prediagnosis "normalcy" will not be possible, perhaps not even desirable. Even with months or years left before the time of death, it is easy to succumb to the feeling that life is over, that there is no more living to be done. "How to get through life feeling alive" becomes the issue. Repeated hospitalizations increase the sense of burden and despair. On the other hand, return home may serve to evoke hope and/or the reality that it is not over yet. The emotional "roller coaster" contributes greatly to everyone's stress. The need to pull together may become unduly binding and stifling (Penn, 1983) or come at a time in the family life cycle when a loosening of family connectedness would otherwise be occurring (Rolland, 1987) and when members increasingly seek more of a life of their own.

In the orientation of a gay mental health center, the focus on death is combatted with displays of love, affection, compassion, and humor—such experiences as one might still be able to have (Walker, 1988). In a later report (1991), she emphasizes the creation of a supportive atmosphere for staff as well as patient and family by shifting focus from "dying patient" to "living family." Patients and families may set goals about the kind of experiences they would still like to have, as well as the kind of living they would like to do and that is within their capacity to have.

Jue (1994) reports that in 1988 15 to 20 percent of AIDS patients lived for three years after diagnosis. Such patients took responsibility for making things happen and did not just wait for things to happen to them. They had short-term goals such as doing volunteer work, going places they had always wanted to see, and developing relationships with others with whom they could share experiences and really be themselves. In all illnesses, treatment programs that involve patient and family in decision making "empower" them (see Brown and Furstenberg, 1992) to advocate for themselves and reduce the feeling that things are beyond their control.

With patients who are living longer, there is the necessity of setting of new short-term goals. Other patients become jealous, and the longer-life patient may experience some guilt at surviving. Some of these longer-living patients, feeling good about their longevity, also feel pressure not to draw attention to their longevity, so as not to undermine the continuing need to find new means of treatment.

Drug-abusing patients who continue to abuse create special problems for their family. In their continuing battle with their habit, they have, in many instances, been in recurrent contact with family. At times parents withdraw, feeling they have done enough. Some parents feel responsible and tend to blame themselves for the drug habit and the illness acquired through needle sharing. The patient may continue to use drugs and to deny or avoid facing the AIDS aspect of his situation, and, in a worst-case scenario, may view continued usage as a means to hasten the end. Alcohol abuse, a problem widely encountered in the gay community, may similarly complicate relationships and the family's ability to continue to care for the patient.

The provision of information and the efforts to connect the ill person and family just discussed are inherent parts of an ecosystemic view. Beyond these family ties and those with the medical care staff, widening the connections to sources of support are also important. Family groups may make connections to sources of support and have been found to be useful. Mayers and Spiegel (1992) report that, in a pediatric AIDS treatment unit, family groups were helpful when the patient and family needs for service and direction began to overwhelm staff as well as the families themselves. Groups helped to deal with denial and social isolation of the families to allow for expression of feelings and in general to provide support.

Jiminez and Jiminez (1992) report that while Latino families are accustomed to caring for chronically ill members, including patients with AIDS, special factors make for difficulty in doing so. Latinos account for over 15 percent of AIDS cases, but they are only 8.5 percent of the U.S. population. However, many Latinos have no health insurance so they do not get medical care early and are more likely to suffer complications. Moreover, families are often already caring for elderly members and lack the resources for home-based care. These authors advocate income supports for care-providing families as well as a community organization effort to develop resources and help the families cope with their isolation due to attitudes about AIDS.

Black families also see care provision for sick and elderly family members as a family responsibility (Bonuck, 1993). The definition of family is broad and includes extended kin network, as in the network definition previously advocated for the AIDS network. Black families are less inclined than white families, generally, to seek substitute care for persons with chronic illness (Dungee-Anderson and Beckett, 1992). At the same time, feelings of anger or shame that are evident in the general community response to AIDS create stress for black family caretaking, as does the disapproval of gay sexuality.

Terminal Phase and Mourning

Family and patient may not be at the same place in their readiness to deal with approaching death. The patient may have arrived at acceptance that all has been done that could be done, but family members may feel that the patient is giving up too easily and may urge the patient to submit to yet another form of treatment. A review with family and patient of what is possible and definable as appropriate may help in achieving a sense of resolution.

Patients at this stage of readiness to die may or may not desire constant company. Being alone is not the same as being lonely; patients may know that family is with them even if they are alone. Some may simply wish to withdraw; others may even prefer being alone, because they lack the energy or don't want to be seen in their debilitated condition.

The dying AIDS patient is typically a younger member of the family, rather than older, as in the case of many chronic and terminal illnesses. Parents are left to review their role as parents. They may feel a sense of guilt, a need to rescue (as has often been true of the parent of the drug-addicted patient), or a need to be with the patient constantly. Alternately, their strenuous efforts in caregiving may leave them in need of support and assistance in letting go. Partners of gay patients may have similar experiences.

Grieving on the part of survivors is also different in the AIDS death. Gay partners may or may not be able to find support from their family of origin. And parents and siblings may not have a community to mourn with them, especially if they have maintained secrecy about AIDS or any aspect of it in their contracts at work or other social networks.

THERAPIST HOMEWORK

Family therapists at every stage of work with chronically ill are challenged in their reaction to patient and family behavior. They know the patient's pain and experience stress from it. They are confronted with their inability to restore the patient to health. In many instances there has been a long-term relationship, and, at the time of death, workers experience a sense of loss much as with members of their own family. Sometimes a patient has been cast in the role of a family member with whom there is unfinished business. In such an event, inappropriate expectations or anger may be directed at a patient for failure to follow medical regimen or for behavior that exacerbates illness, such as continued drug use on the part of the AIDS patient. Or a relative may be resented for being either not caring enough or for doing too much or being overdemanding of staff or overcontrolling of the patient. Neither are therapists immune to a tendency to blame the patient for their illness.

In the case of AIDS, therapists are confronted with the important issue of sexual behavior in its various forms. They need to be comfortable talking about sex and sexual behavior. Their fears about contagion need to be calmed. Attitudes about substance abuse and toward gay and lesbian sexuality will certainly surface, and negative therapist attitudes are likely to interfere with the patient's freedom to raise issues as well as with the family's ability to move toward a responsive relationship with the patient. Negative reactions may arise toward female patients who are also parents, aware of the certainty that a pregnant woman will infect her unborn child. Countertransference reactions may occur in female therapists in their capability for mothering with this group of patients.

Large numbers of chronically ill persons are poor, are representative of minority groups, and may have been denied early access to needed care. In service to the chronically ill, and especially with the AIDS families, sexist and racist attitudes in the individual therapist and in the service provision network need to be surfaced and combatted.

SUMMARY

We have placed discussion of work with the AIDS patient and family in a framework useful for service to patients and families with a variety of chronic illnesses. We have drawn attention to concerns specific to AIDS sufferers at various stages of illness, along with the issues that their families and lovers need to confront at each stage. Acknowledgment of the presence of chronic illness is difficult for a variety of diagnoses; the stigma attached to AIDS due to the means of its acquisition makes the initial stages especially difficult for both patient and family. Conflicts between patients, biological family, and the patient's lover and other significant others complicate the situation, defining an important area of work with all of them. Long-term relationships of therapists with these families require therapists to evaluate their own attitudes about the disease and the set of relationships and to deal with the ending of the relationship when the patient dies.

REFERENCES

Berger, R.M. 1990. "Men Together: Understanding the Gay Couple." *Journal of Homosexuality* 19:31–49.

Bonuck, K.A. 1993. "AIDS and Families; Cultural, Psychosocial and Functional Impacts." *Social Work in Health Care* 18(2):75–89.

Boykin, F.F. 1991. "The AIDS Crisis and Gay Male Survivor Guilt." *Smith College Studies in Social Work* 61(3):147–259.

Brown, James, and Furstenberg, Anne-Linda. 1992. "Restoring Control: Empowering Older Patients and Their Families During Health Crisis." *Social Work in Health Care* 17(4):81–101.

Buckingham, Stephen, and Van Gorp, Wilfred. 1994. "HIV-Associated Dementia: A Clinician's Guide to Early Detection, Diagnosis, and Intervention." *Families in Society* 75(6):333–45.

Caldwell, S. 1991. "Twice Removed: The Stigma Suffered by Gay Men with AIDS." *Smith College Studies in Social Work* 61(3):234–46.

Cates, Jim, Graham, Linda, Boeglin, Donna, and Tielker, Steven. 1990. "The Effect of AIDS on the Family System." *Families in Society* 71:195–201.

Centers for Disease Control. 1994. *HIV/AIDS Surveillance Report* 5(4):8–11.

Dane, Barbara, and Simon, Barbara. 1991. "Resident Guests: Social Workers in Host Settings." *Social Work* 36(3):208–12.

Dicks, Barbara. 1994. "African American Women and a Public Health/Social Work Challenge." *Health and Social Work* 19(3/4):123–41.

Dungee-Anderson, Delores, and Beckett, Joyce. 1992. "Alzheimer's Disease in African American and White Families: A Clinical Analysis." *Smith College Studies in Social Work* 62(2):154–68.

Gallo-Silver, L., Raveis, V.H., and Moynihan, R.T. 1993. "Psychosocial Issues in Adults with Transfusion Related HIV Infection and Their Families." *Social Work in Health Care* (18)2:63–74.

Goshros, H.L. 1992. "The Sexuality of Gay Men With HIV Infection." *Social Work* 37(2): 105–09.

Griffith, James, and Griffith, Melissa. 1987. "Structural Family Therapy in Chronic Illness." *Psychosomatics* 28(4):202–05.

Hare, Jan. 1994. "Concerns and Issues Faced by Families Headed by a Lesbian Couple." *Families in Society* 75:27–35.

Icard, L.D., Schilling, R.F., El-Bassell, N., and Young, D. 1992. "Preventing AIDS Among Black Gay Men and Black Gay and Heterosexual Male Intravenous Drug Users." *Social Work* 37(5):440–45.

Jiminez, Mary, and Jiminez, Daniel. 1992. "Latinos and HIV Disease: Issues, Practice and Policy Implications." *Social Work in Health Care* 17(2):41–51.

Jue, Sally. 1994. "Psychosocial Issues of Long Term AIDS Survivors." *Families in Society* 75(6):324–32.

Kaplan, Lauren. 1988. "AIDS and Guilt." *Family Therapy Networker* (January/February):40–41, 80 ff.

Keller, David, and Rosen, Hugh. 1988. "Treating the Gay Couple Within the Context of Their Families of Origin." *Family Therapy Collections* 25:105–19.

Macklin, Eleanor. 1988. "AIDS: Implications for Families." *Family Relations* 37:141–49.

Macks, Judy. 1988. "Women and AIDS: Counter-Transference Issues." *Social Casework* 69:340–47.

Mayers, F., and Spiegel, L.A. 1992. "A Parental Support Group in a Pediatric AIDS Clinic: Its Usefulness and Limitations." *Social Work in Health Care* 17(3):183–91.

McDonell, James, Abell, Neil, and Miller, Jane. 1991. "Family Members' Willingness to Care for People with AIDS: A Psychosocial Assessment Model." *Social Work* 36(1):43–53.

McGoldrick, M., and Gerson, R. 1985. *Genograms in Family Assessment.* New York: W.W. Norton & Co.

Mohr, Ruth. 1988. "Deciding What's Do-Able." *Family Therapy Networker* (January/February):34–36.

Morales, Edward. 1989. "Ethnic Minority Families and Minority Gays and Lesbians." *Marriage and Family Review* 14(3–4):217–39.

Penn, Peggy. 1983. "Coalitions and Binding Interactions in Families with Chronic Illness." *Family Systems Medicine* 1(2):16–25.

Polikoff, Nancy. 1986. "Lesbian Mothers, Lesbian Families: Legal Obstacles, Legal Challenges." *Review of Law and Social Change* 14(4):907–14.

Robinson, Bryan, Walters, Linda, and Skeen, Patsy. 1989. "Response of Parents to Learning That Their Child Is Homosexual." *Journal of Homosexuality* 18(1–2): 59–80.

Rolland, John. 1987. "Chronic Illness and the Life Cycle: A Conceptual Framework." *Family Process* 26:203–21.

Rotheram-Borus, M.J., and Koopman, C. 1991. "Sexual Risk Behavior, AIDS Knowledge, and Beliefs About AIDS Among Predominantly Minority Gay and Bisexual Male Adolescents." *AIDS* 3(4):305–12.

Schwartz, Ruth, and Schwartz, Arthur. 1977. *Visiting the Hospitalized Cancer Patient.* Chicago: University of Chicago Medical Center.

Serovich, J.M., and Greene, K. 1993. "Perceptions of Family Boundaries: The Case for Disclosure of HIV Testing Information." *Family Relations* 42(2): 193–97.

Sheinberg, Marcia. 1983. "The Family and Chronic Illness: A Treatment Diary." *Family Systems Medicine* 1(2):26–36.

Stuhlberg, Ian, and Buckingham, Stephen. 1988. "Parallel Issues for AIDS Patients, Families and Others." *Social Casework* 69:355–65.

Taylor-Brown, S. 1992. "Women Don't Get AIDS: They Just Die From It." *Affilia* 7(4):96–98.

Tiblier, Kay, Walker, Gillian, and Rolland, John. 1989. "Therapeutic Issues When Working with Families of Persons with AIDS." In *AIDS and Families*, ed. Eleanor Macklin. New York: Haworth Press.

Tolley, Nina. 1994. "Oncology Social Work, Family Systems Theory, and Workplace Consultations." *Health and Social Work* 19(3):227–30.

Walker, Gillian. 1988. "An AIDS Journal." *Family Therapy Networker* (January/February):20–32.

_____. 1991. "Pediatric AIDS: Toward an Ecosystemic Treatment Model." *Family Systems Medicine* 9:211–27.

Woody, Robert. 1993. "Americans with Disabilities Act: Implications for Family Therapy." *American Journal of Family Therapy* 21(1):71–78.

CHAPTER **13**

Child Abuse and Other Family Violence

There is little doubt that we live in a violent society. Nightly newscasts regularly inform us of the assaults upon individuals and the murders that have taken place that day. Children in school yards, customers in eating establishments, and people at their places of work or riding public transportation are gunned down with automatic weapons. Children are assaulted by other children at school, and out of their fear of harm they carry weapons for self-protection. A ready anger lends itself to confrontation and violence.

PERVASIVENESS OF FAMILY VIOLENCE

We would like to think that home and family would provide a haven from such fears and dangers. Unfortunately, there are not always the safe haven we would like them to be. Children are physically and sexually abused by parents and parents are assaulted and sometimes murdered by their children; children are physically and sexually abused by their siblings; adult children abuse aging parents; husbands batter their wives, and sometimes the opposite is true. Levinson (1989) finds evidence of many forms of family violence in cultures around the world, of which wife beating and physical punishment of children are the two most common. Adult women are the family members most likely to be the recipient of violence.

Aside from the widespread resort to violence in society at large, what can account for its occurrence at home? What is it about the family, the persons in it, their ways of interacting, their connection to the outside world that leads to violence in one form or another or directed to one individual or another? If we can come to understand it, can we also do something that will intervene and stop it?

This chapter has a focus on physical violence directed toward children. But we begin by noting violence elsewhere in the family, between other sets of family members, and also the factors that frame our analysis and approach to treatment for violent families generally and abused child families in particular.

Van Soest and Bryant (1995) have concluded from their study that social workers have attended primarily to violence within the family and have not shown wider concern about the broader base of violence at the institutional and structural-cultural level. At the latter level "conventional values and everyday social relations form a collective way of thinking which in the United States is white supremacy and patriarchy that becomes part of both individual and societal psyches" (p. 551), ultimately revealing itself "in an easy acceptance of the use and threat of violence as a form of social control and the solution to problems (p. 552). Such a wider societal view supports rather than retards the occurrence of violence within the family.

Feminist therapists "view all forms of violence, particularly that within the family as an act of power, control, and domination that are products of a patriarchal social order. Violent men are exercising control over their partners and children that they and society historically have defined as legitimate. They do so because they feel entitled to assault and victimize" (Leeder, 1994, p. 2).

We concur, given the widespread occurrence of violence in our society, that there is broad social approval for violence in and outside the family. The sanction may have roots in addition to the feminist position just cited.

Frequently more than one member of the family experiences violence. Stacey and Shupe (1983) indicate that child abuse is 15 times more likely to occur in families where spouse abuse is also occurring. Roy (1988) reported from findings in a national study that 45 percent of assaults on battered women were accompanied by similar assaults on at least one of the children. Stark and Flitcraft (1988) found that almost two thirds of abused children in their study were being parented by battered women. Straus, Gelles, and Steinmetz (1980) show that women who were victims of severe violence were 150 percent more likely to use severe violence with their children than women who were not abused. Such figures cast doubt on the frequent view that women are more often the abusers than men. "There is little doubt that if a man is present, he is many more times as likely to abuse the child than is the mother."

Stanley and Goddard (1993) confirm the idea that more than one family member may be abused at a given time or may experience physical and sexual abuse at the same time. Also, a child may be abused by a sibling as well as a parent. In their study, the abused children themselves demonstrated violence or aggressive behavior toward siblings or other children. The tendency to separate in our thinking and in practice the forms of violence and the persons who experience it from consideration of the whole family "may mean that the current method of intervention in child abusive families is less than efficient, or worse, is incorrect."

Avis (1992, p. 228) draws attention to an array of statistics that "lead us to the unavoidable conclusion that male violence and abuse directed against women and children is extremely common...incest, sexual assault and wife abuse are understood as intrinsic to a system of male supremacy, the most overt and visible forms of control wielded by men as a class over women, implicitly sanctioned by the culture." While not disagreeing that much family violence is attributable to males, Erickson (1992) does caution against attributing violent behavior to all males. Consistent with this view, sexual abuse and rape are seen not solely as sexual acts but more as coercion and the use and abuse of power.

A closer look at some of the linkages suggests that "battered women often give their abusers full-time attention in a futile effort to control the level of violence, or they respond by withdrawing from the family—including the children—in an effort to protect themselves (McKay, 1994, p. 30). Women also try to deflect their partner's rage from their children onto themselves. Sometimes they overdiscipline in the hope that the children will behave in their father's presence and forestall attacks upon them, an explanation that helps to account for some of the abuse of children administered by women. We will speak to this in greater detail later, but note for now that the complexities of interaction make for difficulty at times in predicting who will be victim and who will be perpetrator.

We will also point out that the resort to violence has been attributed to the family's socioeconomic status or immediate situational stress, to the personality or character of the abuser, and to the personality of the victim. Each of these may be seen as cause in combination with the others and may be the basis of an interactive process culminating in violence. For example, a couple stressed by recurring illness find their patience waning. One makes a blaming remark to the other, provoking a cycle of angry accusations and counteraccusations, ending only when one physically attacks the other. This sort of explanation of the occurrence of violence implies a reciprocity of participation, including the victim's contribution to his/her own abuse. While we see that the "victim's" characteristics or behavior may be a factor in violent occurrences, that is not the same as equal responsibility for it.

Also implied is an equality of power on the part of wives and husbands, or more generally of females and males, and sometimes of children vis à vis their parents. A feminist point of view has some relevance here (Bograd, 1990). Feminists have considered family therapy approaches that focus on such circular processes to be biased against women. "Feminist theorists have offered power imbalance as the basis upon which conjugal violence is built" (Dobash and Dobash, 1979). Russell (1984) similarly sees the power imbalance as the basis for sexual abuse. Such an explanation, while it may be useful in understanding male violence—both sexual and physical directed toward women and children—and may offer understanding of women's counterviolence to men, may not by itself be sufficient to explain the violence of women toward their children.

DEFINITION OF ABUSE

Having said that violence in the family goes many directions and is closely connected to violence toward children, we define the child-abusing family as one in which children have been subjected to non-accidental physical injury. Given this brief definition, we are limiting or excluding extended discussion of other forms of violence in the family.

Our discussion of sexual abuse is accordingly limited. While it is clearly damaging to the child victim and may be seen as an expression of the power imbalance in favor of males, as is the sexual abuse of the children's mothers, so many other dynamics enter in and would take our discussion beyond our space limitations.

Another excluded topic is abuse that is not physical but is administered verbally and is psychological in effect. This does not fall within most statutory definitions, however much it may concern helping professionals. Psychological abuse includes a broad range of parent-child interactions and results in a variety of outcomes for children; it may, for example, stunt physical growth to the extent of producing dwarfism (Goodwin, 1978).

Neglect also is not considered child abuse, although the separation of abuse situations from neglect situations is not always easy, since neglect readily appears to abuse the child. The issue is most clearly demonstrated in "failure to thrive" children, who may suffer physical ills due to parental neglect. While some of the family dynamics that lead to neglect may appear similar to those found in families of physically abused children, our attention will be on the physically abused child.

Within the physical abuse category there can be great variation. Physical abuse ranges in severity from surface bruises or injuries, to internal injuries, to death. In frequency it may be confirmed on the basis of a single incident or of repeated incidence over extended periods of time prior to actual reporting. Thus, both "mild," single incidents and severe, repeated incidents are reported and confirmed as physical abuse. The dynamics of specific cases may be described within this range of differences, but the same set of dynamics clearly does not apply to all cases.

Other elements complicate the effort to discuss the dynamics of abuse situations. The abuse of one child involves different conceptualizations of family processes than the abuse of several children in the same family. In some situations abuse is inflicted by a sibling rather than a parent. Parents are also involved in the dynamics of such a situation, but in a different way than when the parent inflicts the injury directly. Other forms of violence may not be unrelated to situations in which the child is abused. Sometimes children inflict bodily injury or death on a parent (Post, 1982; Sargent, 1962). Sometimes spouses abuse each other. Though there may be common family processes in all these forms of family violence, we will not attempt to account for all of them. Our discussion focuses on physical violence directed at children by parents.

A MODEL FOR UNDERSTANDING THE OCCURRENCE OF VIOLENCE TOWARD CHILDREN

A natural reaction to child abuse is to wonder how a parent could behave in such a destructive way toward a child who is helpless or at least relatively powerless in the relationship with the parent. One common theory holds that a parent who injures a child must be emotionally unbalanced or mentally disturbed. In this linear, cause-and-effect relationship, the disturbed parent's behavior is traced to internal psychological conflict due to a deprived and destructive childhood of her or his own. Typically, the abusing parent was an abused child. As we shall see, there is merit to this position, but it does not by itself explain the occurrence of abuse. Why does violence occur at some times and not at others, and why is one child in a family injured when others are not?

The characteristics of the abused child are another element in a model that seeks to account for abuse. Children who are sickly, unresponsive, aggressive, retarded, or otherwise unrewarding to the parent have been more subject to abuse than other children.

In addition to the cultural, economic, and social situation of the family which impinges on family functioning, stresses that are situational and transient may also contribute to the occurrence of abuse. A classification of crises in families was introduced in Chapter 4. Some that have been found to be in evidence in studies of abusive families include unwanted or unexpected pregnancies, large family size, loss of family members through death or desertion, marital stress, illness, role changes, loss of income, and other more immediate stresses such as criticism or disappointment.

MODEL SELECTION

Bolton and Bolton (1987) organize their book-length review of the research and writing on family violence, including wife battering and "granny bashing," around this same three-factor frame: the disturbed parent; sickly, unresponsive children; and family stresses. Belsky (1980) uses the same set of factors to understand child maltreatment, calling it an ecological integration. We concur with this framework, though our discussion of the situational elements will focus mainly on the relationships and interaction between family members. Violence does not occur just because the three elements are present; a further negative cycle of interactions emanates from these beginnings and leads to the resulting physical violence.

The following sections draw on the existing literature to identify data and events that are needed for understanding the various elements and the interactions among them. We offer our conceptualization of the process that occurs and identify treatment methodology that has been developed to disrupt the negative processes and to promote the well-being of the abused child, siblings, and parents.

Characteristics of the Abuser

The catalog of characteristics of the parents who abuse their children is lengthy. Social class is one of these characteristics. While it is a given that child abuse and other kinds of family violence occur in families of all social classes, and the number of cases in upper classes may be underreported, the stresses of lower-class living result in greater frequency of occurrence. Since social class may be viewed as a characteristic of both the parent and the social situation, it may be that social situational stresses rather than personality characteristics are the significant aspect that contributes to the perpetration. Both need to be evaluated. This caution would certainly be appropriate in viewing the higher rates of both spouse and child abuse in the black community reported by Hampton (1991). Hampton comments that higher rates may be due to "changing cultural attitudes about which acts of violence are appropriate for use on children." In any event the social conditions under which black families need to survive must be considered.

Osnes and Stokes (1988) point out that abusive parents have been shown to be socially isolated. They also interact less with their children than other parents do. And they have been seen as relying on their children to gratify their dependency needs, having unresolved interpersonal conflict, lacking in preparation for parenting, having a high need for dominance and control, and lacking in personal and social skills (Bolton and Bolton, 1987). In other studies abusive parents have been seen as anxious, depressed, untrusting, impulsive, and tending to have a distorted view of their children, projecting on them their own negative attributes. Parents who abuse their children have frequently themselves been found to have been deprived, subject to parental violence, and suffering from intense need for love and acceptance.

"Attempts to identify personality characteristics that distinguish maltreating parents have been inconsistent and difficult to translate into practice....The reality, however, is that behavioral differences in maltreating parents are now known to be more a function of complex situationally specific variables than any personality element operating within the individual (Bolton and Bolton, 1987, p. 56).

Cichetti and Rizley (1981) concur in the view presented here that intergenerational transmission of violent behavior may be clinically evident but has not been empirically validated. It is not the inevitable consequence of having been physically abused as a child. The most that can be said is "the practitioner must be alert to the possibility that partial learning has taken place and that violence mediating strategies may not be available to an individual based upon learned or observed patterns in their childhood." And though as practitioners we may feel empathy for the abuser out of knowledge of his or her life experience, the perpetrator is still responsible for the abusive behavior.

"It seems that, for the maltreating parent, it is the child who is the source of comfort for the narcissistic adult. The parent is the needy child, and the roles are reversed to allow the child to nurture....It is more common that their relationship with the child and the world around them is where the pathology rests" (Bolton and Bolton, 1987, p. 57).

Characteristics of the Abused Child

A whole array of characteristics of abused children has been reported. Children of both sexes and all ages are abused. Male and female children are abused in about equal numbers. Some studies report that more younger children than older children are abused, but it is not clear that this is generally true since many investigations have focused on younger children. Thus, sex and age, as characteristics of the child, do not appear to be factors in vulnerability. Birth order or sibling position may be a factor. Only child, oldest child, or youngest child positions have all been identified in various studies as more subject to abuse.

Kadushin and Martin (1981) provided an extensive review of characteristics of abused children. They conclude that certain patterns of child behavior are apt to be at high risk for abuse. The irritable child, the negativistic child, the demanding, overdependent child, the hyperactive child, and the unresponsive child impose greater demands on, and offer fewer satisfactions to, the parent.

Physical illness appears to make children more subject to abuse. Lynch (1975) compared abused children with nonabused siblings and found significant differences in the amount of illness experienced by abused children and their nonabused siblings during the first year of life. This was also true during the prenatal period for both groups of children.

In possessing these characteristics, the child contributes unwittingly to the occurrence of the abuse. It is not clear from any studies, however, that the characteristics were always existent prior to the abuse. The inability to determine which comes first, the child's characteristics or the parents response, implies that parental perceptions and the interactive process may be more important than the characteristics of the child by themselves.

Other characteristics of the abused child appear to be important only because they produce certain images in the minds of the parents. The child may represent to the parent a hated parent, spouse, paramour, or sibling because of certain physical features, sibling position, or circumstances of conception and birth. These characteristics are of the order of those Vogel and Bell (1968) have reported as important in the selection of the family scapegoat and may thus help to account further for the selection of the child to be abused.

We would also note that it should be clear from the brief survey that child characteristics do not by themselves account for the occurrence of abuse and certainly do not in all instances evoke a negative response. We do nevertheless conclude, as does Smith (1984, p. 342), that "most research studies which measure the abusive parents' perception of the abused child indicate that most abused children are seen as more difficult by their parents."

Bolton and Bolton's (1987) comprehensive review of studies regarding the characteristics of physical or sexual abuse victims notes that no one characteristic is identifiable as a common factor in a majority of cases.

Furthermore, it becomes impossible to determine whether a given characteristic such as poor self esteem or defensiveness existed prior to, or appeared after, the abuse. Bolton and Bolton reach a similar conclusion with regard to conjugal violence.

FAMILY INTERACTIONS

Dyadic Interaction

The particular characteristics of parent and child in child abuse situations set up conditions for a relationship that is likely to be unsatisfying to either of them. For example, a small child who is sickly and in need of a great deal of care and attention is likely not only to be unsatisfying to the parents but also to place additional demands on them. Parents who in their own development lacked both needed nurturance and a clear understanding of their needs may find the neediness of the child overwhelming, and this may result in unresponsive neglect or an aggressive response. In either case the child may respond with more of the same crying and parent-requiring behavior, rather than less of it, resulting in more of the same response from the parent. In other instances, the infant may not possess any particular physical or mental characteristics, but the circumstances of birth or some other element that prompts a negative image of the infant in the mind of the parents may prompt the negative parental response.

By reference to the situational aspect, we draw attention to the interaction between the abusive parent and the child, the interaction between parenting figures, whoever they may be, and the way these figure into the abuse. Cirillo and DiBlasio (1992) look beyond these relationships to the entire set of relationships, including past and present relationships with families of origin. They use the term "games," which refers to the roles that the various family members play in a particular set of relationships. Given a particular set, the abuse may be an expression of anger toward the spouse or a particular child and simultaneously a signal given by abuser of a sense of unfitness for parenting. The following paragraphs will provide examples.

Gaensbauer and Sands (1980) report an in-depth study of parental and professional staff reactions to child behaviors such as social and affective withdrawal, lack of pleasure, unpredictability and inconsistency, shallowness of affect, ambivalence, distress, and anger. Staff became aware of their own reactions to the child behavior as similar to that of parents. Both they and the parents countered the child with their own tendencies toward withdrawal, unpredictability, anger, and other responses. Clearly, the child's behavior serves as a stimulus to parental action.

Kadushin and Martin (1981) offer further insight into the parent/child interaction. In an extensive and detailed review they document the bidirectionality of parent/child interaction. Their own research on abuse incidents showed that behavior on the part of the child had precipitated the abusive incident, prior to which the parent had tried to deal with the behavior in other ways. "Parents were described as reacting to crying, disobedience, hostility or some other behavior of the child in nine out of ten of the incidents" (p. 114). In their view, children respond selectively, sometimes positively, sometimes negatively, to parent behavior. Parent behavior is contingent upon child behavior as well as the other way around. "The feedback from each party in the interaction has consequences for each, which, over a period of time, establishes the patterns of behavior which characterize the relationship" (p. 149). This is not to say that the child "causes" the abuse, because this is only one of many factors operative, but it does suggest that new interaction patterns could be helpful in precluding further abuse.

For an infant, the behavior cannot in any sense be thought of as premeditated, but only as an expression of the needs of the child and thus an "unwitting" contribution to the situation. Older children have their own ways of expressing their need for a positive parental response. Both their withdrawn and unresponsive behavior, as well as their aggressive behavior, may be means of seeking such response, but neither is likely to be perceived by the parents as rewarding their own need for a positive response from others. When they respond negatively to the child's behavior and thereby fail to meet the child's needs for positive response, they also do not dispose the child to friendly behavior in return. The negative response of each to the other becomes more extreme, until violence to the child results or something else happens to interrupt this sequence. Such sequences are defined as symmetrical escalations by Watzlawick, Beavin, and Jackson (1967). In older children, violence toward the parent may also in some instances be a consequence.

Family Triads

The dyadic interaction of parent and child does not take place in isolation from other forces and events. A number of factors contribute to its occurrence and perhaps, occasionally, to its interruption. Among the more significant of these situational factors is the relationship between the parents.

The dyadic interaction of a single parent and child could fit the description in the previous section. Although we recognize that the burdens of parenting fall heavily and differently on single parents, the following paragraphs address primarily two-parent families or households. Comments at the end take additional note of the situation of single parents.

The dynamic of the interaction differs from one situation to the next. Marital relationships may be in an unusually turbulent state. Women discharge on children their frustrations with dominating spouses whom they cannot attack directly. Sometimes the attack on the child is a means to make the spouse suffer. In a specific instance, the father tore the baby from his wife's breast saying, "Those breasts are mine." In other instances children become injured when they attempt to defend mother from father, or vice versa.

A parent may be instigated in subtle ways to harm the child, such as a remark by the other parent that the child is spoiled and needs stronger discipline, or with "*You* do something." A nonabusing parent may attempt to compensate with tenderness for an abusive partner's handling of a child, giving rise to further hostility in the abuser. Steele and Pollock (1972) report that the nonabusing parent may become abusive when the previously abusing parent becomes more tender.

In family triads, therefore, three different dynamics are likely. The first is that the child is a scapegoat for the hostilities that the parents do not direct at each other for fear of disrupting their relationship with each other. Second, love and attention given to the child are seen as being subtracted from what one parent has to offer the other, which gives rise to jealousy and a consequent attack on the child. The child is seen as depriving the spouse of desired and needed affection. Finally, the attack on the child is also a means of pleasing the spouse in response to a critical comment. In a stable husband-wife relationship, according to Blumberg (1974), "both parents share the responsibilities of child rearing in one way or another. Frustrations can be communicated and solutions or advice can be forthcoming." This is obviously not the situation in the relationships between an abusive parent and a spouse. Their relationship with each other does not meet their needs for love and affirmation, and is not seen as doing so. They are in no position to be supportive of each other as spouses and thus do not offer a base for effective parenting. Smith and Hanson (1975) found that abusive mothers reacted more negatively to difficulties with their husband than to difficulties with their child, that the behavior toward the child "is based not on a rejection of the child as such, but on a rejection of their unsatisfactory social, marital, and parental roles" (p. 522). According to Newberger (1973), "We are coming to see that the essential element in child abuse is not the intention to destroy the child, but rather the inability of the parent to nurture his offspring, a failing which can stem directly from ascertainable environmental conditions" (p. 327).

The third member of the triad need not necessarily be a legal spouse, nor even a spouse. The dynamics of triads would certainly apply to common-law or live-in situations as well. The third person may also be an extended family member, living in the home or not, most likely a parent, but not necessarily. Anyone who has some significance in the life of the parent might serve as the third member of the triad and could evoke the feelings of criticism, blame, loss, jealousy, and anger that lead to the abusive behavior. Single-parent families are thus not exempt from the possibilities of negative triadic interaction, and workers are well advised to obtain information about the participation of seemingly irrelevant or distant persons.

Siblings

There is amazingly little documentation of the position of siblings of the abused child in the occurrence of violence. In some instances siblings are also abused (Johnson and Morse, 1968), sometimes worse than the child whose abuse was first reported. If the abused child is removed from the home, another child is sometimes scapegoated by being singled out for abuse. In other cases, a sibling may ally himself or herself with the parent in attacking a child or even become the means of the parent's attack on the child, similar to the way a spouse can be provoked to attack a child. And a sibling who is neither victim nor perpetrator may live in fear that what happened to the abused child may also happen to him and may doubt the parents' love. In some instances siblings feel they are somehow responsible for the abuse, and they should have protected the abused child (Beezley, Martin, and Alexander, 1976). Whatever their role, their participation in the family will be affected. Treatment also should attend to these various aspects of the siblings' experience, both to enable their own growth and to improve the functioning of the family group.

OTHER SITUATIONAL ELEMENTS

Illness in the parents, like illness in the abused child, can be a factor in abuse. Parents who are ill are limited in ability to meet the child's need and may be frustrated because they are deprived of meaningful roles, either within the family or outside it. Galdston (1965) notes that illness or disability sometimes deprives parents of a meaningful role outside the home as a breadwinner and thrusts them into a more direct but unaccustomed child-caring role when the spouse goes to work. Their inability to adapt to the illness or disability, plus the thrust into the undesired role, both serve to upset whatever balance in relationships existed prior to the illness. Underlying or together with all of these factors may be the frustrations in some families brought about by poor housing and limited resources.

Losses of relationship also appear to be a significant situational element. Losses may be barely discernible, as when the nonabusing parent leaves the house or is unavailable when needed or desired by the child-caring parent. Other losses may be more obvious. The withdrawal of a boyfriend from a relationship or the separation of a spouse can serve to undermine the parent's ability to respond positively to a child. Baldwin and Oliver (1975) report "frequent changes of adults in charge of the children as spouses, cohabitees and relatives came and went" (p. 212). Family change and instability both appear as situational elements contributing to abuse.

Illness and losses might be manageable if the family had other supports. But Holland (1973) reports that abusive families are isolated, including isolation from social agencies to which they had in the past gone to seek to have their needs met. Bennie and Sclare (1969) found "lack of support of parents and parents in-law was often evident, sometimes because of religious conflict, more frequently because of psychopathic attitudes. The management of the deprived home devolved upon one individual, usually the assailant." There is in such situations little relief from child-caring responsibility, or any support when other stresses such as illness, change of housing, loss of employment, or intrafamily conflicts occur. Smith's (1984) review confirms the impact of current life stress in abuse families.

The combination of limited parental coping capacity, the care-requiring characteristics of the child, the tenuously balanced relationships between pairs of triads of family members, and situational stress appear to set the stage for abuse of the child. In some instances material means may discourage violence by allowing relief through the hire of child-care services or making the parent feel rewarded with treats or purchases. Such relief is not available to the economically deprived family. Newberger (1973) points out that welfare programs offer inadequate help in such stressful circumstances. Nor does such relief always serve to avoid violence, as is evident in more affluent families in which abuse occurs. In other instances a responsive environment in the form of an empathetic circle of friends or a caring extended family might be helpful. But where these are not available or helpful, other means of treatment are necessary.

TREATMENT EFFORTS

Interdisciplinary treatment teams and concrete services are both useful and necessary in work with abusive families. Our discussion of treatment will draw on the model proposed above for understanding the occurrence of violence toward children and the interactions between these elements: characteristics of the child, characteristics of the parents, and the situational effects of the environment in which the interactions take place.

Beginnings

Given the violence that has occurred in the family, initial contacts present problems for both the family and the worker. Some of the family's feelings and behavior may be attributable to the explanations given by the referral source and to the family's prior experiences with workers and agencies. Anxiety and defensiveness are sure to be present, along with some degree of hostility as well as a possible underlying sense of guilt and fear of having children removed from the home. The worker, uncertain of the level of aggressiveness that might be expressed and concerned about the continuing danger to the abused child, may anticipate hostility. Both the worker's horror at the abuse and anger at someone who would harm a child are feelings that, if not resolved, could interfere with seeing the parents as persons with their own needs and developing a working relationship with the whole family.

All of the worker's skills in achieving contact, a working relationship, and a definition of the problem(s) to be solved will be called upon. Either by telephone or in person at the home, the first contact needs to be directed to introducing the worker as a source of help rather than as critic or judge so that the family can function effectively for all its members. Substantial effort should be devoted to listening and reducing defensiveness and helping family members to sense that the worker is there for them.

Police have often been involved early in the case, and the legal system's role is important in determining parents' capacity and rights in relation to their children. In these instances, parents come to treatment involuntarily. Although they prefer voluntary clients, therapists have seen the usefulness of the pressure of the legal system in initial engagement of the family, until the family's own recognition of problems and desire for help comes into play (Cirillo and DiBlasio, 1992). In any event, it is important to acknowledge the involvement of the legal system early in the contact.

It is useful at time of first contact to have the referring person present and tell the family what the worker has been told about their situation so that the family begins to understand that the relationship to the worker will be characterized by openness and forthrightness. The worker emphasizes the goals of helping the family with what they see as their difficulties and to be more the family they would like to be. This usually includes avoiding removal of an endangered child or abusive adult from the home if possible. Kagan and Schlossberg (1989) are explicit in recognizing that the families may have difficulty in trusting the worker and in being open about what has happened. This is what is hoped for, and there may be consequences if such an environment does not occur.

Little things at the time of a home visit, such as waiting to be invited in and asking where the family would like you to sit, serve to convey respect and leave them in charge. Giving each person the opportunity to talk and be heard takes everyone seriously and individualizes each of them. Kinney, Haapala, and Booth (1991) note that it may be necessary to separate family members for parts of the session, take time-outs, or even threaten to call the police if the level of hostility or danger becomes too great. It may also be entirely appropriate for the worker to share his or her fears of what might happen, or the sense of being overwhelmed.

The initial focus is on the crisis that resulted in the present contact. What were the stressful events (see our categories in Chapter 4)? How did the events affect the various members? How did each respond? Since many of the families are crisis prone and have had agency contacts before, it is important to understand what their prior experience has been and with whom, as well as their understanding of the present referral.

Interventions with Parents

Meeting Parents' Needs

The worker with abusive parents needs first of all to convey that he or she is there to understand, care, and help rather than to threaten or criticize. A nonjudgmental attitude is essential.

The worker responds to the parents' strong dependency needs and to their need for a parenting, caring person in their lives. Consistency in this accepting and caring position is important because the parents' own feelings of guilt and their previous life experience may lead them to find such an attitude unbelievable and perhaps even frightening. A wish to flee may result from these feelings. Most workers have found that concern about the parents' own needs and feelings should be emphasized with the parents, rather than concern about the child, and this concern should be for the needs of both parents. By this approach, the worker avoids arousing the same feelings of jealousy and neglect that have characterized the family's internal interactions. The applicable principle from conjoint family treatment is the worker's ability to identify with each member present and to avoid siding with one family member against another.

The worker's ability to identify with both parents not only is critical in conjoint sessions; it is also necessary in separate individual sessions. For some workers this may be particularly difficult, at least initially, in relation to the overt perpetrator of the abuse. Blumberg (1974) notes that some spouses are not able to share the worker and that conjoint sessions should come later in the work with the family. Individual sessions may be necessary, especially early in the case. Separate workers from the interdisciplinary treatment team appear in these instances to be particularly useful.

The giving, nurturant approach is manifest first of all through the workers' attitudinal orientation, but giving comes in more concrete forms also. In residential and daycare programs, parents are given relief from child care and the opportunity to observe how others care for children. Parent aides offer assistance to parents in their own homes, providing support and companionship, in addition to assistance with child care. In still other programs, children may be left for short periods of time with child-care staff so that the parent has relief from this responsibility. Services that meet family needs for income maintenance, housing, employment, and medical care are also provided. Some programs consider nurturance to the parents sufficient in itself, since it meets deep needs of the parents that have in the past been unmet and thereby enables them to be more giving to their children. No program can be effective without this base; other elements of treatment may not begin until parents experience an alliance with the worker. However, meeting the needs of the parents by itself is not sufficient. Specifically, parenting skills must be developed, the parents' denial and guilt need to be dealt with, and the social isolation of the family should be ended.

Teaching Parenting

Many activities fall under this broad rubric. The work just described in meeting the parents' needs for nurturance serves to strengthen them as individuals and puts them in better position to function as members of the parental hierarchy. Their task for the family is to give leadership and structure to the organization. With the nurturance they have been offered, energies are freed for them to individualize each other, to be more assertive in setting expectations, to set rules and develop behavioral guidelines for the children, to communicate verbally more frequently and effectively, and to see and respond to each child as a separate person. The following interventions contribute in one way or another to these ends.

Providing parents with the opportunity to observe how others care for their children offers them the chance to learn new skills in child care and to overcome the deficits in their own parental role models. Seeing how others approach a colicky, unresponsive, stubborn, insistent, or otherwise difficult child enables them to learn other, more useful responses. These can be substituted for their own aggressive responses in order to arouse a positive reaction in the child. These opportunities are provided in residential and daycare programs but also constitute an aspect of parent-aide activity. Opportunities of this nature may also be provided by social workers during parental visits with children who are temporarily separated from the family.

In addition to modeling parenting skills, some programs teach specific aspects of child care and offer parents instruction about what can reasonably be expected of children of a given age. Their own experience and models have not provided this knowledge, which is particularly crucial. Instruction is sometimes given individually to parents, sometimes in classes. It may be given by social workers or by other members of a treatment team.

Skills in behavior modification are developed. Parents are taught to "catch the child being good," to identify the child's positive behaviors, and to provide rewards for good behavior by giving positive attention through verbal communication and spending time. Parents learn about adapting the house to the child and how to develop behavioral contracts with the child. For the parents who have withdrawn from the child out of fear or their own anger, gradual steps in reengagement are rewarded. Spouses can be involved in such training as well as in providing rewards to their partners. By these means, mothers "improved their techniques for controlling the children, using less physical punishment. In addition, by increasing the parents' sense of competence as parents and adults, consistent improvement was shown in other areas of family functioning" (Tracy, Ballard, and Clark, 1975).

We emphasize the importance of conjoint work with the parent or parents and the child in several of the projects cited. While didactic instruction for parents has its uses, the conjoint effort provides immediate opportunity for the parent to try new behaviors suggested by the worker, and for the worker to observe the interactional process and to give further guidance to both parent and child in response to what she sees.

Modeling, teaching parenting skills, and providing knowledge about the expectable behaviors of children are all useful in giving parents models and skills they can use to alter parent-child interaction. The negative cycle can be changed to a cycle of interactions that is more rewarding to both. The effort to alter parents' responses to their children, however, can take place only in the context of a relationship in which the parents can clearly experience concern for themselves as persons, and not only as instruments to meet their children's needs. Thus, their learning occurs in the context of being given to and nurtured. The modeling of care-giving behavior has teaching value because it provides parental relief from child care. Learning can occur when teaching is experienced not as a criticism but as a means of achieving a more rewarding relationship with a child.

Parent skills training serves to develop more realistic and consistent responses of parent to child and a clearer expression of parental expectations. This makes the child more clear about the rules and less likely to deviate from parental expectations, so that less demand is placed on the parent for direction and supervision. It also makes the child feel more comfortable, positive, and responsive to the parent. A changed interaction pattern should follow. In giving attention to the dyadic interactive process, the worker needs to bear in mind the balance of relationships throughout the family. This avoids rearousal of jealousy between parents and children and prevents its appearance between family members and the worker or workers on the treatment team.

Teaching Communication

Wells (1981) draws attention to deficits of verbal communication in abusive families. Noting the earlier work by Polansky, Borgman, and DeSaix (1972) on "verbal inaccessibility" in neglect families, she says that abusive families manifest similar inaccessibility. Communication rates are lower. Behavior occurs as a substitute and elicits minimal comment. The need is for talk and verbal exchange of observations, thoughts, feelings, and reactions instead of nonverbal communication. Worker effort promotes conversation, no matter what the topic. Conversation between parent and child conveys interest and caring. The worker stops nonverbal interaction to label actions and talk about them. Explanations by the parent to the child, which are often lacking, are encouraged and serve to provide instruction and structure. Expressing feelings and being listened to offer relief and provide understanding. Since feelings of futility, depreciation, and powerlessness lie behind the noncommunicativeness, the opening of communication stimulates hope and frees energy. Increased conversation between spouses can have similar effects. Listening as well as talking may be difficult, and worker effort may be needed to enable other family members to be attentive, to take seriously what has been said, and to respond with relevant verbalization of their own. Clarity of messages can be facilitated by worker suggestions for rephrasing when needed or by proffering verbalizations when the individual is having difficulty in finding appropriate words. These need to be confirmed by asking the individual whether the worker's words convey accurately what he or she intended to say.

Communication problems other than verbal inaccessibility may be present. Interruptions, simultaneous talking, irrelevant remarks, or a general escalation of noise require worker regulation of verbal behavior so that family members listen to each other and convey respect and affirmation through their listening behavior. When noise levels are high it may also be necessary to be clear about who is talking to whom and to require members to talk *to* each other rather than *about* each other.

We have placed this discussion of communications in the context of parent/child relationship treatment where it is clearly needed and useful. Regulation of communication may also be necessary with other family pairs and, in some aspects, more applicable when more family members are in conjoint sessions.

Encouraging Parental Acceptance of Responsibility

Parents also can be helped to move from a defensive denial of responsibility for the child's injury to ownership of responsibility, to concern for the child's welfare and recognition of their own wish to be better parents. In the context of a giving and nonjudgmental relationship, it becomes possible for them to do so. They are often relieved to reveal the assault and to talk about their emotions at the time and how they felt afterward. These sessions, timed rightly, can be individual with one parent or conjoint with both. Ounsted, Oppenheimer, and Lindsay (1974) found that parents can set for themselves the task of breaking the cycle of violence that has been characteristic of their families for generations. The worker's questions about their own childhood family experiences help them become aware of this cycle and make it more possible for them to break the hostile identification with their own parents. Increasing the individuation of the parents and their own separateness from their own parents helps to establish a separate identity and increases confidence and competence. In instances in which the child is scapegoated because in a parent's eyes he or she is representative of some other hated person in the life of the parent, the displacement has to be recognized and the original feelings about those persons need to be resolved.

These interventions, which are of a psychotherapeutic nature, may occur in individual or conjoint sessions with parents. Group treatment has also been found to serve this purpose productively. But they may also occur when time is allowed in visits to daycare centers, in sessions in which plans are made for visiting a child who is separated from the home, or interspersed in parent skills training sessions.

The mix of the various interventions with parents—nurturance, parent skills training, and psychotherapy—will be different for different parents. The readiness of the parents to engage in parent training or emotional abreaction will come at various stages of contact, depending on their ability to trust the worker's acceptance and caring for them. The mix of interventions depends also on the family's material status and needs and the agency's ability to provide services such as daycare, parent aides, and other needed services in support of the parents and their parenting efforts. Worker assessment and reassessment of needs and readiness must be continuous.

Treatment of the Abused Child

We have described the great amount of effort devoted to nurturing abusive parents as family leaders, which enables them to fulfill themselves and their functions as parents. The children also need help, of course, and for some of the same reasons as the parents. Beyond immediate physical care, their emotional needs must be met, and their interaction with their parents needs to be changed.

The child's need to be given to and attended to can take many forms. At a minimum, physical injuries and health problems must be cared for. When the child feels physically well, the demands on parents for care are reduced, and child and parents can feel more friendly to one another. Caring attention can release the child from "frozen watchfulness," unresponsiveness, or withdrawal, and from the opposite behaviors of hyperactivity and unregulated or hostile responses. New behaviors appear first with substitute caretakers while the child is receiving residential or daycare, and only tentatively in contacts with the child's own parents. But as parents learn to respond to the child's changed responsiveness, the child's responsiveness to parents continues to improve. The changed interaction between parents and child is made possible initially through meeting each party's individual needs, and then through the more reasonable and explicit structure provided by the parents. Jeffrey's (1976) effort to teach children how to respond shows promise of promoting positive interactions between parent and child.

Beyond these efforts, play therapy or psychotherapy may enable abused children to cope with their feelings about injuries and illnesses, and about their parents and siblings. The hurts and rejection they have experienced will no doubt be alleviated by the changed behavior of the parents and the new interaction pattern that will result. But play therapy or psychotherapy can remove further blocks to children's growth and development and make it possible for them to behave in relationship-seeking ways that are rewarding to them and to the parents.

Marital Treatment

The treatment of the parents and the abused child described thus far is designed to help them as individuals and to change their interactions. However, the dyadic interaction between parent and child occurs in the context of other relationships, some of which do not involve the child's participation but which nevertheless result in child abuse. These relationships also need correction and alteration.

While we agree that a focus on marital problems in general may be out of place in the early stages of treatment, marital relationships as they affect behavior toward the child can be considered early in the contact. Once the parents have acknowledged their violence to the child, the relationship between spouses may be considered as a situational element in the *specific* act of abuse—what was going on at the time, how the spouse behaved, and how the abuser felt about these events. The parents can be encouraged to express not only feelings of anger and rejection, but also their views of what was wanted from spouses and others and what would have been helpful. These feelings and the responses of the spouse to the abusing parent can be elicited in conjoint sessions. The worker is in a position to acknowledge the needs of each, to note the expectancies of the other that give rise to disappointment, jealousy, and scapegoating behavior. The spouse's ability or inability to respond, his or her wish or unwillingness to do so can be made explicit and can then be taken into account in the further development of the child care plan and of the marital relationship.

The problem to be solved at this stage of treatment is the occurrence or avoidance of further abuse. The task of the family adults is to find a way, if they can, of helping each other to achieve avoidance of further abuse. At this stage of the treatment the parents can learn what each needs from the other to achieve this goal.

These efforts may move them, over time, to deal with many aspects of their relationship, so that in the long run they can depend on each other rather than on their child for positive responsiveness and affirmation. Alternatively, they may have to accept the knowledge that the dependability they seek will not be forthcoming, and they can learn to avoid further disappointment by looking to their own strengths or elsewhere for the support they need.

In addition to the clarification of roles and expectations, couples can benefit from help in learning how to communicate in ways that promote positive relationships. Communications that are vague or ambiguous, and sequences of communications that do not result in clarity, can be corrected by means we have suggested elsewhere. (See especially Chapter 10 on income loss and poverty.) Work on communications not only facilitates the clarification of roles and expectations; it can also help to resolve differences and disagreements so that they do not build into reservoirs of ill will that might eventually spill onto spouse or child.

For many parents, work in couples groups offers an added advantage in that they can often respond better to other parents than to professionals. The group can bolster both the parental and marital roles. McNeil and McBride (1979) have reported success with couples groups that covered such subject matter as parenting, discipline, finances, sex, communication, sensitivity, and decision making. The group offered support for both partners, especially the overtly abusive parent. A male-female therapist team was seen as particularly useful as a model for working together.

Our underlying assumption is that solid relationships between the parents or between a single parent and other supportive adults or agencies reduce parental dependence on positive responses from the child as a means for affirming parental identity and self-worth. These adult relationships, therefore, ought to be fostered and enhanced. The relationships of one or both adults to external systems may also need to be encouraged, changed, or enlarged, so that these systems can be supportive of the nuclear family group.

We commented earlier that the mothers of abused children may themselves concurrently be battered, in which event it may be necessary, in addition to the work with the parent figures just described, to work on ending the abuse of the mother. Douglas (1991) offers a framework for understanding and assessing the parent interaction and the cycle of violence that occurs between them, providing a basis for work on the battering behavior. We cannot here do more than offer a brief outline of an approach to treatment of that aspect of family violence.

A dominant view is that the basic approach to the couple should be in separate groups for the battered women and their battering partners. Conjoint sessions tend to get stuck on the airing of complaints and accusations, which leave the abused woman in a more vulnerable state and thus not free to make maximum use of such sessions. Initial conjoint sessions may be used for establishing each partner's willingness to participate, to contract an agreement not to resort to violence, for defining what the wife should do, and for stating the consequences for treatment if violence occurs. Conjoint sessions may be useful later after group sessions have induced some change and some assurance that there will not be further resort to violence.

Leeder (1994) takes a contrary position, insisting that conjoint work is preferable and that the therapist can, being aware of such risks, move to forestall the danger. One way to do this is to ask, at the end of each session, given the revelations and attributions of blame of the session, what the partners expect to happen on their way or at home; then, to work out a constructive plan for handling of feelings. Leeder is also of the opinion that the same therapist can work effectively with both spouses.

Treatment groups for the men work on developing a greater awareness of their own emotional processes, on restructuring the way they see women, women's roles and their own role, and on managing their anger by thinking before acting, by time-outs, and through the development of communicational skills (Gondolf, 1988).

Shelters are a much needed resource for women and the children, whether they choose them or to return to their partners. Women work on their sense of entrapment and their "learned helplessness," on the costs and benefits of staying in or leaving the relationship, and on developing the skills and resources needed if they decide not to stay.

Treatment for the Family, Including Siblings

The literature on child abuse is almost totally silent on family therapy, except to note that it is strange in a field in "which the focus is on the family, that so little family therapy is offered" (NIMH, 1977). The net result of all the previously described aspects of treatment should be improved family relationships and functioning. While work on any part of the system can and should help the family as a whole, work with the whole system is still important and offers added advantages.

Work with the family as a whole has been undertaken in all-day programs for groups of families (Alexander, McQuiston, and Rodeheffer,

1976), on a full-time residential basis (Bentovim, 1977), and in regular sessions in the home (Cautley, 1980). Other formats of varying duration and intensity may be developed. Such extended and more intensive contact with the entire family around a variety of activities and circumstances allows workers to observe interactions between all family members, including siblings of the abused child, and to focus attention on interactive processes as they occur. In the residential and all-day programs multiple-family participation promotes interaction around work, food, and play as well as talk, and work in split groupings of children, couples, mothers, and fathers as well as whole-family meetings. In these situations, action is live and attention can be directed to changing interpersonal transactions, using many of the procedures described above for changing parent-child or spousal relationships, such as learning to respond to good behavior, improving communications, and sharing feelings.

Cohesiveness can be fostered by whole-family participation. Family structure can become more firm and clear. Individual isolation and blame is minimized. Children and their parents may be helped to negotiate behavior changes and the rewards that follow. Boundaries between parental and child generations may be strengthened through worker support of the parental subsystem. Multiple-family groups in all-day, residential, or outpatient programs allow families to see how other families work and to learn from each other.

Work with the Extended Family

In some cases it is useful to help an abusive mother work on her relationship with her own mother, to resolve the disappointment, fear, and ambivalence that characterize the relationship (Steele and Pollock, 1972). We see the need for both parents to achieve greater separateness and detachment from their families of origin and to define an identity of their own. This work on differentiation of self is characteristic of the family therapy field. It may be accomplished by direct work on these relationships in contacts with members of the extended family or by asking individuals or couples to describe relationships in their families of origin. In these ways they may become aware of the origins of their expectations for current relationships, and this awareness can relieve them of the need to continue these relationships and enable them to negotiate new kinds of interaction.

In instances in which the parents' relationships with their own parents and with siblings are characterized less by hostility, ambivalence, and lack of differentiation and more by simple lack of contact, it may be possible for the worker to enable the extended family to be more of a resource for the parents. This can provide the parents with avenues of social contact or, in some instances, emotional or tangible support.

Coping with Situational Stress

While relationships with spouses, paramours, and the extended family are one form of situational stress, other crises may also require intervention. These stress situations include pregnancy or birth of another child, loss of employment or other change in financial situation, illness of an adult or child, or loss of an immediate or extended family member. Any of these stresses can disrupt whatever balance has existed in the give-and-take of family relationships. They may overwhelm a child-caring parent or thrust the parent into an undesired role. New expectations can arise for all family members.

Workers should be available at such times to family members, either individually or as a group, to help them deal with feelings and find ways of coping. Tasks must be defined and agreement reached as to how they are to be accomplished and by whom. Where external resources are needed, the worker needs either to make arrangements for them, with family members' consent, or to serve in a broker or advocate role for the family. The worker's availability at times of crisis seems particularly important in this group of families, where the balance of relationships and personal and social resources is often precarious.

The social isolation of the family is another aspect of situational stress or, more specifically, a factor in the lack of relief from situational stress. Inputs from the extended family are, of course, one way of reducing the isolation. Initially, however, the treatment agency is the chief avenue for reducing social isolation. The agency provides the family with new feedback about its operations and supplies it with specific means of support and help. Treatment in groups, in residential settings, or even in weekend camps (Oppenheimer, 1978) can open up new personal contacts for the family. These new experiences can provide them with the skills needed in interactions with individuals outside the immediate family group and offer them a bridge to relationships in the larger community. Referral to Parents Anonymous, a self-help group of abusive parents, can serve to reduce isolation and provide support.

A NOTE ABOUT THE ORGANIZATION OF SERVICES

The kind of connectedness of the agency to the family that we have described requires considerable outreach, substantial time in contact, and a variety of modes of helping and giving. These are not always available. Certainly, it is not enough to assign a single worker to a huge caseload of families. The literature refers repeatedly to the necessity for interdisciplinary teamwork, for both diagnosis and treatment. This provides a variety of modes of helping and meets the need to work with all members of the family, not only with the person who has physically inflicted the abuse.

There is a great need to broaden and strengthen the range and availability of services to include all of these elements if families in which abuse has occurred are to be successfully helped. Treating agencies will increase their effectiveness to the degree that they are organized toward these ends.

McKay (1994) notes that agencies serving cases of conjugal violence and those providing child welfare services are not always alert to the abuse of other family members. Child welfare service providers should be alert to clues that suggest battering. Mothers with bruises, mothers who seem evasive about injuries and tend to attribute them to accidents, who seem sad or lethargic, who have somatic or emotional complaints, or who exhibit anxiety in the presence of their partners should arouse the worker's concern about possible abuse. Similarly, cues are offered whereby social workers with battered women may become aware of special situations of children. And both workers with battered women and with abused children need to be aware that the child welfare goal of protecting and perhaps rescuing the child may at times be at odds with the conjugal worker's goal of preserving the marriage, or that it may be hard to determine the mother's ability to care for children if she is being battered.

SUMMARY

In this chapter we have taken a brief look at various forms of family violence and offered a frame of reference for analyzing and understanding it. Further, we have taken note of some specific characteristics of abusing parents and abused children and have observed how these characteristics give rise to negative patterns of interaction. We have noted that the interaction of abusive parent and abused child does not take place in isolation but is affected by other interactions in the family and events in the family's situation. The relationship between the parents is seen as particularly crucial, perhaps as crucial as the relationship between parent and child. There has been relative neglect in the field of the experiences of siblings of the abused child, and the family as a whole is seen as likely to be isolated from external supports, or in difficult relationships with extended family. Unlike other writing on child abuse, which focuses primarily on the abused child and the overt perpetrators of the abuse, we have emphasized the transactions between family members and with the larger family system.

We also find useful the techniques identified by Star (1983) in helping the abuser—supportive confrontation, enhancement of self-esteem, problem solving, providing structure and direction, honesty, modeling desirable behavior, role-playing (perhaps with an empty chair to represent an absent other), and the use of a buddy system.

The treatments described are designed to strengthen individual identity and competence, to improve interpersonal transactions, and to alter relationships within and beyond the immediate family. The efforts include nurturance of the parents, imparting skills and knowledge for parenting, help in dealing with feelings, and recognition of reactions to members' own behavior and that of others. These activities are useful in interrupting old patterns and initiating new behaviors, and thereby altering interactional patterns. Enabling the parents to alter their relationships so that they can support each other in child-caring and parenting activities is an important means of helping the child, as well as providing greater satisfaction for the parents themselves. Where other situational stresses affect the balance of family relationships, agency action is needed to provide relief and support.

The range of services encompassed requires comprehensive care that cannot be provided by a single worker assigned to a huge caseload. Thus, the interdisciplinary teams that are widely noted in the literature, and services to the entire family, are valued and needed in effective programming for families in which abuse of the child occurs.

REFERENCES

Alexander, H., McQuiston, M., and Rodeheffer, M. 1976. "Residential Family Therapy." In *The Abused Child*, ed. H.P. Marten. Cambridge, MA: Ballinger Publishing Co.

Avis, Judith. 1992. "Where Are All the Family Therapists? Abuse and Violence within Families and Family Therapy's Response." *Journal of Marital and Family Therapy* 18(3):225–32.

Baldwin, J., and Oliver, J. 1975. "Epidemiology and Family Characteristics of Severely Abused Children." *British Journal of Preventive and Social Medicine* 29:205–21.

Beezley, P., Martin, H., and Alexander, H. 1976. "Comprehensive Family Oriented Therapy." In *Child Abuse and Neglect*, eds. R. Helfer and C. Kempe. Cambridge, MA: Ballinger Publishing Co.

Belsky, Jay. 1980. "Child Maltreatment: An Ecology Integration." *American Psychologist* 35(4):320–35.

Bennie, E.H., and Sclare, A.B. 1969. "The Battered Child Syndrome." *American Journal of Psychiatry* 125:975–79.

Bentovim, A. 1977. "Therapeutic Systems and Settings in the Treatment of Child Abuse." In *The Challenge of Child Abuse*, ed. A.W. Franklin. New York: Grune and Stratton.

Blumberg, M.L. 1974. "Psychopathology of the Abusing Parent." *American Journal of Psychotherapy* 28:21–29.

Bograd, M. 1984. 1990. "Why We Need Gender to Understand Human Violence." *Journal of Interpersonal Violence* 5(1):1332–35.

Bolton, Frank, and Bolton, Susan. 1987. *Working with Violent Families*. Newbury Park, CA: Sage Publications.

Cautley, P. 1980. "Treating Dysfunctional Families at Home." *Social Work* 25(5):380–86.

Cichetti, D., and Rizley, R. 1981. "Developmental Perspectives on the Etiology, Intergenerational Transmission and Sequellae of Child Maltreatment." In *New Directions for Child Development: Developmental Perspectives on Child Maltreatment*, eds. C. Cichetti and R. Rizley. San Francisco: Jossey-Bass.

Cirillo, Stefano, and DiBlasio, Paola. 1992. *Families That Abuse*. New York: W.W. Norton & Co.

Dobash, R.E., and Dobash, R. 1979. *Violence Against Wives*. New York: Free Press.

Douglas, Harriet. 1991. "Assessing Violent Couples." *Families in Society* 72: 525–33.

Erickson, Beth. 1992. "Feminist Fundamentalism: Reactions to Avis, Kaufman, and Bograd." *Journal of Marital and Family Therapy* 18(3):263–67.

Gaensbauer, Theodore, and Sands, Karen. 1980. "Distorted Affective Communications in Abused/Neglected Infants and Their Potential Impact on Caretakers." *Journal of the American Academy of Child Psychiatry* 18:236–51.

Galdston, R. 1965. "Observation on Children Who Have Been Physically Abused and Their Parents." *American Journal of Psychiatry* 122:440–43.

Gondolf, Edward. 1988. "How Some Men Stop Their Abuse: An Exploratory Program Evaluation." In *Coping with Family Violence*, eds. Gerald Hotaling, David Finkelhor, John Kirkpatrick, and Murray Straus. Newbury Park, CA: Sage Publications.

Goodwin, D. 1978. "Dwarfism: The Victim Child's Response to Abuse." *Baltimore Sun,* September 24.

Hampton, Robert L. 1991. *Black Family Violence*. Lexington. MA: Lexington Books.

Holland, C. 1973. An Examination of Social Isolation and Availability to Treatment in the Phenomenon of Child Abuse." *Smith College Studies in Social Work* 44:74–75.

Jeffrey, M. 1976. "Practical Ways to Change Parent/Child Interaction in Families of Children at Risk." In *Child Abuse and Neglect*, eds. R. Helfer and C. Kempe. Cambridge, MA: Ballinger Publishing Co.

Johnson, B., and Morse, H. 1968. "Injured Children and Their Parents." *Children* 15:147–52.

Kadushin, A., and Martin, J. 1981. *Child Abuse: An Interactional Event*. New York: Columbia University Press.

Kagan, Richard, and Schlossberg, Shirley. 1989. *Families in Perpetual Crisis*. New York: W.W. Norton & Co.

Kinney, J., Haapala, D., and Booth, C. 1991. *Keeping Families Together*. New York: Aldyne-deGruyter.

Leeder, Elaine. 1994. *Treating Abuse in Families: A Feminist and Community Approach*. New York: Springer Publishing Co.

Levinson, David. 1989. *Family Violence in Cross-Cultural Perspective*. Newbury Park, CA: Sage Publications.

Lynch, M. 1975. "Ill Health and Child Abuse." *Lancet* 2:317–19.

McKay, Mary. 1994. "The Link Between Domestic Violence and Child Abuse: Assessment and Treatment Considerations." *Child Welfare* 73(1):29–39.

McNeil, J., and McBride, M. 1979. "Group Therapy with Abusive Parents." *Social Casework* 60(1):36–42.

National Institutes of Mental Health. 1977. *Child Abuse and Neglect Programs: Practice and Theory*. Washington, DC: NIMH.

Newberger, E.H. 1973. "The Myth of the Battered Child Syndrome." *Current Medical Dialogue* 40:327–34.

Oppenheimer, A. 1978. "Triumph over Trauma in the Treatment of Child Abuse." *Social Casework* 59:352–58.

Osnes, Pamela, and Stokes, Trevor. 1988. "Treatment of Child Abuse and Neglect: The Role of Functional Analyses of Observed Behavior." *Journal of Child and Adolescent Psychology* 5(1):3–10.

Ounsted, C., Oppenheimer, R., and Lindsay, J. 1974. "Aspects of Bonding Failure: The Psychopathology and Psychotherapeutic Treatment of Families of Battered Children." *Developmental Medicine and Child Neurology* 16:447–56.

Pardeck, John. 1988. "Family Therapy as a Treatment Approach to Child Abuse." *Child Psychiatry Quarterly* 21(4):191–98.

Polansky, N., Borgman, R., and DeSaix, C. 1972. *Roots of Futility*, San Francisco: Jossey-Bass.

Post, S. 1982. "Adolescent Parricide in Abusive Families." *Child Welfare* 61(7):445–55.

Roy, Maria. 1988. *Children in the Crossfire*. Deerfield Beach, FL: Health Communications, Inc.

Russell, D. 1984. *Sexual Exploitation: Rape, Child Sexual Abuse, and Sexual Harassment*. Beverly Hills, CA: Sage Publications.

Sargent, D. 1962. "Children Who Kill." *Social Work* 7(1):35–42.

Smith, S. 1984. "Significant Research Findings in the Etiology of Child Abuse." *Social Casework* 65(6):337–46.

Smith, S., and Hanson, R. 1975. "Interpersonal Relationships and Child Rearing Practices in 214 Parents of Battered Children." *British Journal of Psychiatry* 127:513–25.

Stacey, W., and Shupe, A. 1983. *The Family Secret*. Boston: Beacon Press.

Stanley, Janet, and Goddard, Christopher. 1993. "The Association Between Child Abuse and Other Family Violence." *Australian Social Work* 46(2):3–8.

Star, Barbara. 1983. *Helping the Abuser*. New York: Family Service Association of America.

Stark, E., and Flitcraft, A. 1988. "Women and Children at Risk: A Feminist Perspective on Child Abuse." *International Journal of Health Services* 18(1):97–118.

Steele, B., and Pollock, C. 1972. "A Psychiatric Study of Parents Who Abuse Infants and Small Children." In *Helping the Battered Child and His Family*, eds. C. Kempe and R. Helfer. Philadelphia: J.B. Lippincott Co.

Straus, M., Gelles, R., and Steinmetz, S. 1980. *Behind Closed Doors: Violence in American Families*. Garden City, NY: Doubleday.

Tracy, J., Ballard, C., and Clark, E. 1975. "Child Abuse Project: A Followup." *Social Work* 20:398–99.

Van Soest, Dorothy, and Bryant, Shirley. 1995. "Violence Reconceptualized for Social Work: The Urban Dilemma." *Social Work* 40(4):549–57.

Vogel, E., and Bell, W. 1968. "The Emotionally Disturbed Child as the Family Scapegoat." In *A Modern Introduction to the Family*, eds. N. Bell and E. Vogel. New York: Free Press.

Watzlawick, P., Beavin, J., and Jackson, D. 1967. *Pragmatics of Human Communication*. New York: W.W. Norton & Co.

Wells, S. 1981. "A Model for Therapy with Abusive and Neglectful Families." *Social Work* 26(2):113–18.

CHAPTER 14

Helping the Family with Alcoholic and Substance-Abusing Members

Family members are increasingly involved in the treatment of alcoholics and abusers of other drugs (AAOD). They come to the agency for help with or without the abuser. The help provided may do much for the family and may or may not resolve the drinking problem. We are concerned to help the family whether or not the drinking problem is resolved. From our systems orientation we expect that resolving family problems and reducing the abuse go hand in hand. While the ensuing discussion is phrased in terms of alcoholism, the description and concepts apply as well to abusers of other drugs and to their families.

There is no doubt that alcoholism is a family problem whether the family is seen as victim of the alcoholic or the alcoholic is seen as victim. Given that one or more additional members of the family may feel the consequences of the drinking problem, help for the family seems justified whether the alcoholic changes or not. Some treatment programs do not seem to be as strongly committed to the family as that implies and retain their focus on the alcoholic alone. The evidence suggests, however, that help to the family is also help to the alcoholic (Janzen, 1977) and that helping the alcoholic to change is clearly also help to the family.

Our position about alcoholism and the family is thus a systems position. Change in one part of the family system necessitates response or adaptation of some kind in other parts of the system. The drinking member's behavior, whether the drinking is increased or reduced, has family impact. Members are affected and adjust their behavior one way or another. Their new behavior is experienced by the alcoholic who responds with either more of the old behavior or some new behavior. The family's response to the drinking may neither have been helpful in reducing the drinking nor in alleviating the family's distress about it. The alcoholic's response to family behavior may have done little to alter the behavior of other family members. They seem locked in a repetitive cycle that results in no satisfaction for either party. There is no way of establishing where this cycle starts, and it seems fruitless, for treatment purposes, to seek first causes. The concern in treatment is to find ways of interrupting the destructive cycle. It seems evident that both the family and the alcoholic are, by their behavior, seeking to relieve distress and that the means they use to do so serve to increase rather than decrease it for both parties. If either the family or the alcoholic can find other means to relieve their distress, this serves to elicit new ways of coping on the part of the alcoholic or the family. Helping family and alcoholic to find new ways of coping in response to the distress they experience is the essence of our treatment approach.

Our definition of family treatment, given this point of view, is an intervention in any part of the interactive system. It is not contingent upon seeing the family members together. The essence of family treatment is that the social worker thinks of the family as a system and keeps in mind, whatever part of the family is being seen in a given treatment session, that changes occurring as a result of treatment will have impact on other parts of the system. Such impact needs to be anticipated and forecast, helping the members present to prepare for possible responses. Our interest in treatment is in changing the interactive process. Though we are saying here that it is not necessary to have all family members present to understand and change the interactive process, we do note that there may be advantages to having them present, both for the purpose of understanding how the interaction works in the here and now of behavior and also for promoting a change in it.

Our discussion will proceed initially in relation to the adult male family member's alcoholism. Practice and experience have focused on him as the identified alcoholic. We will devote some discussion later in the chapter to the situation in which the wife/mother or an adolescent is the identified alcoholic. We will direct our attention first to the interaction between spouses and the relationship between the marital interaction and the alcoholism and then to the functioning of children in the system.

MARITAL RELATIONSHIPS AND ALCOHOLISM

Several different views have been held about the relationship between the wife and her husband's alcoholism. In earlier writings the wife was seen as disturbed, struggling with strong feelings of inadequacy and dependency, which prompted her to relate to the alcoholic in a controlling and aggressive manner. These behaviors would be intended to perpetu-ate the relationship in a way that would be sure to meet her needs but instead had the opposite effect of burdening the alcoholic and thus pro-moting the drinking or at least giving him an excuse for drinking, a view that he might himself be prone to take.

Later studies have seen the behavior of wives as responsive to and varying with the alcoholic's drinking, and not as a personality feature. Thus, though her behavior affects the alcoholism, the alcoholism affects her behavior as well.

Other studies note the presence of marital difficulties apart from the alcoholism. Orford, Oppenheimer, Egert, Hensman, and Guthrie (1976) note the lack of cohesion in alcoholic marriages. Spouses are likely to refer to each other in derogatory terms. There is little giving or receiving of affection and minimal participation by the alcoholic in family activi-ty. Increased participation and expressions of affection are needed, as is a change in the negative picture each holds of the other.

Esser (1968, 1971) also advances this view. Spouses in alcoholic rela-tionships have difficulty admitting marital problems, and drinking serves to avoid facing them. If marital problems are mentioned in a treatment session, drinking episodes often follow, and subsequent ses-sions revert to focus on the drinking.

Al-Anon Family Group (1967) also notes that alcoholics and their wives have trouble seeing their difficulties as marital, whether the alco-holic is still drinking or is sober. Al-Anon asserts that alcoholism does not create all their problems, nor does sobriety cure them.

Even though the case for the complete independence of marital prob-lems and alcoholism may be made, it is still possible that there is a func-tional relationship between them. The possibility of a functional relationship between the alcoholism and family interaction has been demonstrated in yet another way. Steinglass and others (1977) observed families while drinking and also during nondrinking times. He notes,

> A family that claimed drinking by their "identified alcoholic" caused de-pression, fighting and estrangement, was observed to show increased warmth toward each other, increased caretaking, and greater animation when the alcoholic was permitted to drink. (p. 105)

Cadogan (1979) writes that in some instances drinking can strengthen family bonds and provide a sense of purpose—that of helping sick mem-bers—and gives the family a sense of meaning and importance that is otherwise lacking. The behavior serves a function for the system in such cases but is obviously dysfunctional for the alcoholic and also in a larg-er sense for the family. These observations may not be generalizable to all families with alcoholics, but they do support the idea of a functional relationship between family interaction and the alcoholism. They also suggest that discontinuance of the drinking would still leave the family with other interactional problems and that treatment would need to be attentive to them.

Our understanding of the relationship between the alcoholic and the spouse is furthered by attention to the role-taking of the two actors, to their struggle for power and position, and to the payoffs for both that result from the interaction. The role-taking of each is seen as being driven more by the behavior of the other than by personality. Role-taking changes over time as the participants' views of each other's behavior and of their own predicament changes.

From this standpoint, alcoholic and spouse are reciprocal roles. (See Straussner, Weinstein, and Hernandez, 1979; Black, 1980; Wegscheider, 1981.) In beginning phases of the drinking problem, both alcoholic and spouse collude in denial of a drinking problem. Typically the spouse excuses the drinking as a response to stress, as something occasional or temporary. When the drinking reaches more problematic proportion and becomes harder to deny, it may still be disguised in an effort to avoid embarrassment, save the alcoholic's job, or avoid family conflict and potential breakup. The spouse thus serves a supporting role in the alcoholic's denial. Still later, when the problems caused by the drinking can no longer be overlooked or excused, she may seek to control the drinking in various ways such as by drinking with him, by limiting money supply, by disposing of alcohol on hand, or by limiting affection, attention, or care. The alcoholic opposes such resistance to his behavior. He denies his wife such control. He asserts his independence by not changing in the way she desires. The more she tries to control, the more he defies. Whether the wife is denying or controlling, she is, unintentionally, an actor in a self-perpetuating exchange. Both are stuck in the pattern.

Gorad's (1971) investigation, in which he compared alcoholic and nonalcoholic spouse pairs, supports his view. He says that spouses in alcoholic marriages compete with each other more than those in nonalcoholic marriages. Sharing and self-revelation, which are suggestive of more openness and less manipulation of others, are less frequently exhibited.

Bepko (1986), views the husband-wife relationship from a feminist orientation, as well as from the position just described that the use of alcohol serves a function within the family (Steinglass, Davis, and Berenson, 1977). Traditionally, women in our society are taught to be overfunctioners—to be for others and to do for others. When the husband is an alcoholic, he does less, and the wife does more: as the wife does more and acquires greater control over family life, the husband does less. The alcohol allows the couple to maintain the sex role status quo, because the husband can avoid acknowledgment of his increased dependency and the wife can avoid acknowledgment of her increased power, independence, and psuedo autonomy.

The irresponsible behavior or dependency of the alcoholic may not seem controlling, but they do require action and response on the part of the spouse, and they imply resistance to doing the spouse's bidding, manifesting his part in the struggle for control of the relationship. Thus, neither spouse dominates more than the other. The control struggle continues with the only variations being variations in intensity. Thus, whether the spouse's participation occurs by collusion in denial or by efforts to control, the drinking persists.

The control struggle we have outlined implies that the spouses in alcoholic marriages view each other as instruments of their own bidding, as extensions of self, and not as separate persons. Al-Anon notes this conception and goes on to point out that it is destructive to believe that "being married to a man puts us in charge of him. We are so deeply involved that we treat those closest to us as though they were part of ourselves" (Al-Anon Family Group, 1967). Bowen (1974) talks of failure of differentiation to refer to that same condition. Individuals are not individuals in the sense of having a clear sense of being a separate self. If one partner is less responsible, the other becomes more responsible. If one (the alcoholic) underfunctions, the other compensates by overfunctioning, and the underfunctioning spouse becomes even less functional. Independence and autonomy are clearly lacking. Bowen sees the overfunctioning spouse as more capable of change, that is, of assuming less responsibility and becoming more autonomous, and works with that spouse for change in the relationship.

It seems evident that there is some advantage to the spouses of the role reciprocity we have described. There are "certain interpersonal payoffs" that motivate the behavior of each. A clear example can be seen in Ward and Faillace (1970, p. 686):

> If the wife is forgiving, the husband has learned that forgiveness for being drunk can be obtained, provided he is appropriately remorseful and very sick. If she punishes him for his behavior by criticizing him, his guilt and shame are relieved and he feels considerably less anxious. In either case the pattern cannot be understood except in terms of the total sequence.

And in either case the sequence recurs because it is reinforcing to both spouses.

Problems in communication go hand in hand with these relationship problems. Cadogan (1979) notes that communication between spouses is one-directional, going from spouse to alcoholic, who responds with silence or by leaving. Conversations are filled with blaming statements; defensive and counterblaming statements are the response. Old conflicts and resentments surface repeatedly and are left unresolved. Family members, particularly children, hesitate to share interests, bring concerns, raise issues, and to voice doubts, questions, or differences for fear of being responded to with impatience, hostility, or retaliation. Capacity to listen and respond empathically to another's description or point of view is minimal. Maintaining a conversation that leads to understanding, resolution of conflicts, or problem solving has become next to impossible. Assistance in engaging in constructive communication is sorely needed.

The conceptions discussed in this section clearly apply to the relationships between male alcoholics and their wives. A later section on female alcoholics will suggest that these conceptions hold when the sexes of the participants are reversed. Role reciprocity and communication problems exist as well between alcoholics and other members of the family, including children.

CHILDREN IN ALCOHOLIC FAMILIES

Children are affected by and may affect relationships in alcoholic families. Cork (1969) was the first of many who have documented a variety of effects on children over the years. Effects have been noted over the life span of children beginning prior to birth as manifest in the prenatal alcohol syndrome (Young, Wallace, and Garcia, 1992). Goldman and Rossland (1992) note higher absenteeism and lowered achievement in school, the frequency with which they become abusers of alcohol and other drugs, and the tendency to marry alcoholics. Different problems may occur at different ages, including stuttering, fears, bed-wetting, tantrums, and fighting. Similar problems have been noted in children of drug-abusing parents (DeCubas and Field, 1993). Incest is not uncommon (Yama, Fogas, Teegarden, and Hastings, 1993). El-Guebaly and Offord (1977) conclude that difficulties in the research efforts result in inability to conclude that these children have more problems than children in other kinds of problem families, but there is no doubt that they do suffer. They also say that the problems these children have may not be solely attributable to alcoholism, since other problems such as poverty or family disorganization were also present in the families studied. And it is not clear exactly how these problems interact with the alcoholism. Problems continue into adulthood and have resulted in the formation of support groups for adult children of alcoholics (ACOA) (Sheridan and Green, 1993; Goglia, Jurkovic, Burt, and Burge-Callaway, 1992).

Children are affected by the general atmosphere of unhappiness, by parental quarreling and fighting, and by lack of their parents' interest in them. These factors, more than the drinking itself, serve to create their problems. Even when parents do concern themselves with the children, they are inconsistent, sometimes spoiling, sometimes punishing. Uncertainty and unreliability undermine their growth and confidence. Denial of the alcoholism confuses them and mars their reality testing. The nonalcoholic parent is often no more helpful than the alcoholic because of her own confusion and unmet needs and is unable to provide structure and nurturance. If both parents are alcoholic, children have to assume complete responsibility for themselves and often for their parents as well.

Children in alcoholic families are often caught in triangular relations with their parents (Goglia, Jurkovic, Burt, and Burge-Callaway, 1992). The mother may seek the child's support and understanding in her difficulties with her husband, forming an alliance against him. Or she may involve the child in her attempts to control the drinking. Likewise, the alcoholic may air his complaints to the child about being misunderstood and abused by his wife. The child, caught in the tug-of-war, is put in the position of having to decide between the parents or take the role of peacemaker. Taking sides loses the support of the other parent. All three get locked into their respective roles, and nothing happens to diminish either the conflict or the alcoholism. In addition to the psychological suffering, the child may even be physically hurt in attempts to interfere when conflicts between the parents become physical. Efforts to mediate parental conflict require more maturity than the parents themselves possess and puts the child in a parental role with them. The phenomenon of an overfunctioning member compensating for underfunctioning members is thus evident in this even more inappropriate manner. In taking any of these roles in the family interaction, the child is not only experiencing the effects of parental behavior but unwittingly serving to perpetuate the problematic interaction as well.

Different children take different roles in these family situations, depending on age, sex, and sibling rank as well as on other factors. The specific influence of each of these factors has not been identified and has received only limited comment, except in the review by El-Guebaly and Offord (1977). Our foregoing discussion has inferred victim, peacemaking, and parental role-taking. Black (1980) identified additional roles such as responsible one, placator, or adjustor. Straussner, Weinstein, and

Hernandez (1979) and Wegscheider (1981), in addition to the role of primary enabler, who is usually the spouse, identify still other roles taken by children such as hero, scapegoat, lost child, and mascot. These roles are also seen as enabling of the alcoholism, since each in a unique way contributes to its perpetuation. The consequences for the role-player are different in each case but similar for the alcoholic in that they serve an enabling function. Sex, age, or sibling rank of the various roles is not to be inferred from the following sequence description.

The hero child takes a great deal of responsibility for himself, stays out of trouble, and achieves in school. He is good, is successful, and parents his parents. He may have a favored position with one or both parents. He gives no clue that anything is wrong and thereby serves to perpetuate the denial of the alcoholism along with his parents. His behavior has a positive function for him as well in setting a lifelong pattern of doing well but, carried to the extreme and accompanied by compulsion to achieve and by denial of any dependency, can result in serious adjustment problems. Black (1980) comments that this responsible and self-denying role sometimes sets the individual up to become alcoholic in later life.

The scapegoat child performs in a negative, acting-out manner, seeking attention by negative behavior, since outdoing the hero child by good behavior seems impossible. Parental attention is of necessity turned to him, distracting them from the alcoholism and their problems with each other and defining him as the problem instead. It perpetuates their denial and interferes with their attention to resolution of their problems. The child can feel more certain that the home will not be broken, but at the same time faces increasing difficulty in life if his behavior becomes entrenched in a delinquent pattern.

The lost child is shy, a loner, and stays out of the way. He or she is unnoticed, the neglected child in the family. Since the child causes no trouble for the family, the parents' denial of the alcoholism and their difficulties with each other is maintained. The danger in this role for the child is the extent of retreat into isolation and fantasy. Black's (1980) "placating" child may be similar—a child who is totally adaptive to anything that happens. Such flexibility and attentiveness are assets for the family but do deprive the child, whose needs and wishes are worthy of attention, of an adequate sense of a self.

The mascot takes the role of family clown, relieving tension for self and family by humor, antics, and distraction. Here too the parents can feel that all is well, and the child himself or herself can bask in the approval of others. Yet, though these qualities seem useful in this situation, and may even be so in some gainful occupations, the disguising of their pain may in the long run create difficulty for them.

These roles may not be taken only by children in alcoholic families but are often present in them. They are illustrative of the systemic properties of the family in that the role serves a function for the family as well as for the person taking the role. It is adaptive for the individual and serves to stabilize the system. As long as this is the case, the system is locked in, with no change either in relationships or in the alcoholism.

BEYOND THE NUCLEAR FAMILY

Where alcoholic families do not live in isolation from extended family, parents or siblings of the alcoholic and/or the spouse may become participant in the alcoholic family interaction in ways similar to those described for immediate family members. They may assume an enabling role similar to the spouse. They may be drawn into a triangular relationship with the marital pair either as a peacemaker or ally. They may divert attention to themselves by argumentativeness, dependency, or demandingness. The parent of an alcoholic may seek to defend him by efforts to excuse, explain, or harbor him at critical times, and then blame and criticize the spouse. Similarly, the parent of the nonalcoholic spouse may join her in blaming or criticizing the alcoholic, or shelter her or encourage her to separate. Members of the extended family thus do not separate themselves and stand apart from the problems of the nuclear family's interaction.

In Bowen's (1974) terms, such extended family participation represents the failure of the couple to achieve a sufficient degree of differentiation from each other and from their family of origin. When tensions between the spouses are high, they may seek parents or sibs as allies, asserting their disdain and independence of one another, and returning to each other when the tension subsides or when tension with family of origin increases. Family interaction problems persist, as does the drinking.

TREATMENT

The systems view of the nuclear and extended family and its relation to the alcoholism that we have outlined lead clearly to the importance of the family's participation in treatment. Participation may be seen as benefiting the family in any event, especially in those cases in which the alcoholic is not initially motivated for help or change. Change that begins with the family will affect the alcoholic and may lead to change on his part. Conversely, if change begins with the alcoholic, it will affect the family and necessitate adjustments on the part of other members. In the paragraphs that follow we will focus on work with the family and its consequences for the alcoholic, and also demonstrate how the family needs to change if and when the alcoholic changes.

Family members, in their desire to be helpful to the addicted member, often operate in ways that do not contribute to a solution and, in fact, are enabling the perpetuation of the addiction (dePeyer, 1990). Such behavior may arise also out of their denial that a problem exists. Making excuses, explaining or justifying behavior, and calling in sick for the symptomatic member are examples of family behaviors that do not require that member to face the consequences of his or her substance abuse. As we pointed out earlier, it is the abuser's problem. Family members who feel that they caused it and attempt to take responsibility for it are allowing the addicted member to avoid responsibility. In some instances, family members take on such responsibility and neglect their own well-being. They may at first experience feelings of superiority and a satisfying sense of being needed. But they may also come to the point of feeling exploited and victimized. Helping family members to see the aspects of such behaviors as unhelpful and destructive for both the substance abuser and for themselves is one of the tasks of the middle phases of treatment.

The fact of and the extent of family participation appear to be a more crucial variable for the alcoholic's improvement. Attendance of a family member at even one session of a treatment program has been associated with the alcoholic's continuance in treatment. His continuance in treatment is lengthened by lengthening family participation. O'Farrell (1989) says that intervening at the marital/family level with nonalcoholic members can motivate an initial commitment in the alcoholic to change. Further, marital/family therapy alone or with individual treatment produces better marital and/or drinking results than approaches that don't involve the family.

The many literature references to family involvement convey a great enthusiasm for family treatment. Regan, Connors, O'Farrel, and Jones (1983) have shown, however, that services to the family are often limited in scope and follow-through, especially for children. The needs of the family are viewed as secondary to the help that the family can offer to the alcoholic. Janzen's (1985) survey confirms that finding and notes frequent lack of understanding of the needs of the family and lack of clarity in conception of the relation of the family's operations to the alcoholism. Nevertheless, many programs did describe themselves as having a family systems view of these situations and viewed help to the family as help to the alcoholic as well.

Some treatment programs for families of alcoholics can be clearly identified as using specific theories of family treatment. Bowen (1974) used the same theoretical orientation with these families as he does with other problem families. Berenson (1976) and Carter (1977) also employ Bowen theory, though Carter also makes use of structural family therapy techniques in early stages of treatment. Esser (1968, 1971) implicitly and Wegscheider (1981) explicitly use Satir's (1983) communications approach to treatment. Transactional analysis conceptions have been used by Ward and Faillace (1970) to understand the interpersonal transactions within these families. Each of these theories appears to be productive in achieving understanding of the relationship of the alcoholism and family interaction and in planning treatment.

Our approach to treatment draws on several theoretical orientations, as the earlier part of the chapter suggests, and on multiple possibilities for ways to involve the family. Our discussion has not meant to imply that the family causes the alcoholism, only that family interaction may be a factor in its perpetuation. In this conception it becomes important to interrupt the interaction that enables the continuance of drinking and which defeats the family in solving its problems. As a first step, it is necessary to deal with the denial of alcoholic and family of the drinking problem. Then the family's efforts to regulate and control the drinking need to be interdicted. In these steps there can be relief for them and possibility of change for the alcoholic member.

The first step has already been taken when alcoholic and/or family seek treatment. Next steps may be accomplished in several ways. One way is to teach the spouse that alcoholism is a disease over which she has no control and therefore cannot cure. She can therewith be relieved of her guilt for causing it and the burden of being responsible for helping her husband with it. This method has been used in numerous instances and has been found to be helpful. Cohen and Krause (1971) have shown that spouses treated by workers using the disease concept were able to help the spouse to change and to function more effectively in the family and that this often served to draw the alcoholic into treatment. Workers not using the disease concept, however, were also able to produce the same effect using their general treatment theory of individualizing and valuing clients as persons, supporting them in the idea that they could only be responsible for their own well-being, and demonstrating that they did not really have the power to regulate the behavior of others. Thomas and Santa (1982) also demonstrate that unilateral work with the spouse can be helpful to the spouse, to the alcoholic, and to the relationship between them. Mueller (1972) describes how this works. He says that the wife needs to recognize that she did not cause the illness and that she is not capable of or responsible for curing it. Once freed of that burden, she can drop her ineffective coping and rescue operations. She can learn to stop nagging, making threats without carrying them out, and protecting her husband from the consequences of his drinking....Her consequent lack of action should not emanate from anger and retaliation but rather, so far as possible, from a sense of objectivity and detachment...surrender and release. (p. 82)

Thus, she makes herself to be a separate person from her husband and becomes a stronger person within the family.

The wife and other significant adults are also well served by a referral to Al-Anon, which provides a peer-group experience as a complement to the help provided by professionals (Gorman and Rooney, 1979). Davis (1980) sees such referral as not only helpful but necessary. These groups share with family therapists the idea that family members suffer if they only react to the behavior of the alcoholic. Al-Anon members learn in their groups, as they do in family treatment, that being only reactive does not alleviate the drinking but may indeed serve to perpetuate it as we have described above. They also learn that they can only be responsible for themselves, that they are not only "justified" for such "selfish" behavior but that it can have a positive effect on the alcoholic. Continuity and long-term membership in these groups can provide a long view that may not be available in therapy groups and which will help new members persevere in the initial stages of change.

The concern in our method is for the well-being of the spouse and for that of the alcoholic, though we have described only work with the wife which, we note, may be done on a one-to-one or group basis. The alcoholic may see the wife's new behavior as a loss of interest and caring and may respond by increased drinking, greater dependency, or belligerence. The wife must be helped to see this as a phase. Since the alcoholic can no longer accuse his spouse of running his life, he must begin to assume responsibility for his own behavior. He can begin to see himself as someone free from the direction of others and as more of a person over whom he may come to develop some control. Such positive results from the family's unilateral action may be more likely if the family seeks help early in the alcoholism career. However, if the situation is of long duration or severely deteriorated, more drastic action on the part of the family may be needed before the alcoholic will change or enter treatment.

When the family no longer denies the problem, family members may be prepared for more direct approach to the alcoholic (see Wegscheider,

1981). They are encouraged to recall their many instances of disappointment, the money shortages caused by the drinking, the lack of love and relationship, the abuse they have experienced, the shame they have endured, and the isolation of the family and alienation from friends. When they are ready for confrontation, a meeting with the alcoholic is arranged as is admission to a treatment program for the alcoholic should he decide to seek it as a result of the confrontation.

Liepman et al. (1989) report that alcoholics who were confronted were significantly more likely to enter an alcohol detox or rehabilitation program and to remain continuously abstinent more than nonconfronted alcoholics.

Success of this method in getting the alcoholic to change is not guaranteed. Though willingness to confront is clearly based on a wish to restore a positive relationship, this step may need to be undertaken with the recognition that the further step of threatening to end the relationship through separation or divorce may be necessary. The spouse's willingness to consider such a possibility depends on her confidence in herself and her ability to survive, both psychologically and materially. If financial or employment resources are lacking, worker support in obtaining these as well as the psychological support must necessarily be a part of the treatment offered.

The alcoholic may respond positively to these drastic actions if his relationship with his family is still meaningful to him. Here again it is evident that earlier action on the family's part, before relationships deteriorate beyond the possibility of restoration, seems more likely to produce positive response than delay. Where relationships are still valued and the change in the drinking behavior occurs, both the alcoholic and the family gain.

If the alcoholic stops drinking or enters treatment as a result of the family's effort, family interaction has to change to adapt to his new behavior. The recovery phase has its own tasks. If he now seeks to assume a more responsible role, family members will need both to learn to trust that he will actually do so and to relinquish some of the role responsibilities they had undertaken in his place. Children may need to learn to count him into their activities. The wife may need to relearn to consult him about discipline or other family decisions. Everyone's hypersensitivity will likely show in verbal exchanges. Meeks and Kelly (1970) and Esser (1968) have demonstrated the usefulness of conjoint sessions at this phase to promote constructive family communication, problem solving, and conflict resolution. Additional work during the recovery phase should address the communication and marital difficulties we noted above.

Beginning with the Alcoholic

Helping the alcoholic to accept treatment has never been considered easy. Berg and Miller (1992) differentiate three groups of referred alcoholics: those who acknowledge their problem and their need for help; those who do not admit to a problem and come with complaints about others; and those who may be helped to identify something they either need or want for themselves and who become willing to accept help.

Focusing on the latter two groups, workers treat the alcoholic, alone or with the family group, to identify problems or dissatisfaction, which either category of subjects can easily do. The worker may suggest that the alcoholic's presence in the interview may mean that he is dissatisfied or looking for something to improve his situation or possibly himself. Therapists move quickly from what is wrong to how the alcoholic would like things to be. Some alcoholics are able to acknowledge that they have bad days, on the job or at home, maybe or maybe not due to or resulting in drinking, or for other reasons. In many instances, though not in all, the referred person is able to identify something or some way that he or she would like to be or have different, or a goal toward which to work.

Questions follow. What have you tried to do about the bad days? What has worked? What has not worked? If good days happen, what made them happen? Can you predict when you will have a good day? Could we make them happen more? When "things that don't help" have been identified, the effort is to stop doing them and do more of the kinds of things that do help.

The approach does not dwell on the past; it is present and future oriented. It fits well into the problem-solving approach, drawing out client motivation in relation to goals that are important to the client. It identifies what strengths the client has and does not focus on his having or being a problem. The problem identified may be one in family relationships, but may nevertheless bear on drinking behavior. In either case, whether done in the family's presence, or not, there should be gain for the alcoholic and family. Work with the family in ways identified in the previous and following sections is still important in view of changes in the alcoholic's behavior. Berg and Miller have found that this approach is relatively short term, contrary to the thinking about most efforts with alcoholics.

CHILDREN IN THE TREATMENT PROCESS

As we have described them, children are both victims of the alcoholism and unwitting participants in its continuance. As victims, they need treatment for their own sake to help them with their fears of abandonment, neglect, or violence, their sense of shame, and their feelings of guilt about having contributed to the family difficulties. They need also to be freed from the side-taking alliances into which they may have been drawn and from age-inappropriate role behavior such as their sense of responsibility for comforting or parenting their parents. Some of this may come as a result of their mother's change and her ability to assume stronger parental responsibility, unless she, too, is alcoholic. In that instance, extra supportive measures will be needed, and if the parents are not responsive to treatment, removal from the home may be warranted.

Children may also be helped in the same manner we have outlined for the spouse by education in disease concepts and by the idea that they can and need be responsible only for themselves. By freeing them in these ways, they may be released from the roles we have described and thereby from their unwitting functions as secondary enablers in the family. Some of this learning may come as a result of separate treatment for the children. Individual treatment may be appropriate for some. Richards (1979) says that group treatment is preferable for most children. Conjoint family sessions are certainly valuable for all the purposes just mentioned. Participation in family sessions can enable them to join in family communication processes in a new way, helping them to learn that it is again safe to ask questions, give observations, and express feelings. They can come to contribute in a positive way to family problem solving. Beyond this they will also benefit from referral to Alateen, which operates by principles similar to Al-Anon and which is organized especially for children of alcoholics. This is especially important if treatment programs that include children are limited in scope.

More recently there has been an expanding movement to services for adult children of alcoholics (Sheridan and Green, 1993). Professionals providing therapy for adults have long known that the problems of children of alcoholics continue into adulthood. There is now an expanding self-help movement within this population that is becoming more accessible with expansion in numbers of groups and which is providing an extremely useful service. Referral to such groups can supplement therapy.

HELP WITH SOCIAL ASPECTS OF ALCOHOLISM

Many consequences for the family's social situation arise as a result of the alcoholism. Money spent on alcohol can leave the family without essential food, clothing, and sometimes shelter. Physical assault and abuse sometimes occur along with the alcoholism. Concern for safety as well as needs for food, clothing, and shelter are often what prompt the family to request help (see Flanzer, 1978). Simple withdrawal or escape from abusive behavior and denial of the neglect the family experiences no longer suffice. The spouse may need support of family, friends, and eventually social agencies in the form of material assistance or alternative shelter. Her (and the children's) needs must be met while she is also given the psychological encouragement to protect and care for herself and the children. She has taken a long time in coming to the conclusion that she needs or will accept outside help. It is obvious that she is no longer relying on the alcoholic to be responsible. Our support of her during this is again based on the position that she can only be responsible for herself and that he must be responsible for himself. If he also can recognize this as a result of her focus on her own needs, this is all to the good, but she is supported in proceeding to meet her own needs whether he recognizes the change or not.

ALCOHOLIC WOMEN AND THEIR FAMILIES

Alcoholic women are typically described as suffering from depression, low self-esteem, social anxiety, guilt, and a sense of inadequacy (Bepko, 1986). Drawing from other sources, Bepko notes also a preoccupation with femininity and overevaluation of the wife and mother roles. They have been socialized to be caretakers, selfless, and dependent. To be independent and powerful is unfeminine, and they thereby risk rejection from their spouse, who has been their source of self-validation. This bind is oppressive.

When she drinks, "she is similarly allowed to avoid acknowledgment of anger and potential rebellion against her responsibilities; the husband, who typically becomes the overresponsible caregiver and protector of the wife, is allowed to avoid acknowledgment of his more 'feminine' care-giving behavior. When both spouses drink, each is alternately overresponsible and under responsible" (Bepko, 1986, p. 69).

Contradictory views about these women's relationships to their spouses and children are reported, as was the case for the male alcoholic. On the one hand, it has been reported that the spouse of the female alcoholic is less likely to attempt control of her drinking and more likely to be either passively receptive of it or to separate himself from her. Corrigan and Anderson (1978) and Dahlgren (1979) have presented data that shed doubt on that view. Corrigan (1980), relying on the reports of women alcoholics, reports that most of the husbands of the women she studied had considered separation, but few of the women reported that their husbands had actually threatened it.

The issue of the husband's personality type has also been raised as it was with the wives of alcoholic husbands. According to Fox (1972) some are long-suffering and controlling; some alternate ambivalently between leaving and begging to return; others are dependent or hostile and sadistic. Wolin (1980) notes that many have psychiatric problems, and Corrigan (1980) reports that many of the husbands are also alcoholic. At a minimum, it seems possible to conclude that there is no single personality-type husband of the female alcoholic. Clemmons (1979) draws attention to the fact that men leave their wives after they have stopped drinking because "she's changed...boring" (p. 141), an observation suggesting that her drinking serves some function for the man.

Wolin's (1980) research also shows that the marriages are characterized by a higher frequency of unsettled arguments, of disturbed communication patterns, and of a poorer match of self-perceptions of the spouses than in nonalcoholic marriages. Similar points have been made, as shown above, about the marriages of male alcoholics. Babcock and Conner (1981) view them as more stressful for the woman than for the man, since the basic cultural expectation is for the woman to adapt to her husband's role and position. There is in this position the suggestion of a power differential in favor of men generally. In these marriages, the struggle for control may be even more severe, and the female alcoholic may need more specific support in treatment.

Babcock and Connor advocate marital treatment for alcoholic women who are still in marriage because the marital role is so stressful. Page (1980) supports this position.

> Success (for her) should need to be not only related to drinking consumption but also to personal, family and mental health. For women it is clear that this definition of success is inevitably intertwined with their own cure. They are more inclined than men to be influenced by and dependent upon their husband's view of their health and progress. (p. 170)

In her view, marital treatment is more likely than individual treatment to result in rapid improvement. The sharing and participation of the spouse diminish guilt and rage and serve to open channels of communication. These factors seem similar to those noted earlier when the wife participates in the husband's treatment. However, Dinaburg, Gleck, and Feigenbaum (1980) caution that research demonstrating support for marital treatment of women alcoholics suggests that marital treatment by itself is insufficient to assure successful outcome. They advocate additional referrals to Alcoholics Anonymous, Al-Anon, and Alateen, and so do we.

As many as three-fourths of women alcoholics live with and care for their children in some way. The impact on them would likely vary according to their age, sex, and sibling rank, as was the case with children of male alcoholics, and with the time of onset of her drinking. The male spouse's ability to nurture and protect them from the consequences of her behavior is also likely to vary. Wilson (1980) suggests that the problems for the children may be due more to the marital conflict than to the mother's drinking. She also contrasts the situations of children of alcoholic fathers and mothers in reference to family coalitions. Whereas children of alcoholic fathers have been observed to coalesce with mothers against the fathers, "no equivalent coalition exists between fathers and children (of alcoholic mothers) and that the woman's isolation ends when she sobers up" (p. 109). Beyond this, Wilson's discussion cites family dynamics and problems for the children that are similar to those described here for families of male alcoholics. Clemmons (1979) also describes problems and adjustments for children in the same way. Morehouse (1984), working with alcohol-abusing children of alcoholic mothers and fathers, also does not differentiate problems for children of alcoholic mothers from those of children of alcoholic fathers. She does point out that when parents stop drinking and resume more responsible, limit-setting roles in the family, children often complain.

Corrigan's (1980) research found that the women themselves acknowledged giving too little attention and too much responsibility to their children. Their husbands agreed with this evaluation. Richards (1979) cautions that therapists must resist the tendency to supplement the alcoholic mother in her child-rearing tasks, since this will alienate her, but should instead work to strengthen her in her parenting role. She also suggests that in separate work with the children care be taken not to overidentify with the children against the mother. Page (1980) says that a family systems orientation is needed for effective treatment of the woman alcoholic. Treatment should include the family and be goal specific in changing the system. Just "seeing the family" and "being supportive" are not adequate orientations to the tasks of treatment. Family participation in problem solving in conjoint interviews will serve to lift the woman's self-esteem. Page says that centered and highly structured work will likely lead to positive results in a short term of treatment.

Davis and Hagood (1979) describe a program of homemaking and child-care assistance to help in situations where the female alcoholic's ability to care for her children is extremely limited. When her limited capacity is coupled with that of a spouse who is also impaired by alcoholism or personality limitations, protective services intervention on behalf of the children may be needed.

Programs concerned about the protection of children of substance-abusing women (Reed, 1987; Straussner, 1989) have drawn attention to the advantage of a family focus in treatment. Finkelstein (1994) sees as inadequate an individual approach to treatment that insists that the woman needs her own space and cannot concentrate on her own recovery with children present. Since women develop sense of self in relationships, involving important others in treatment facilities recovery. Azzi-Lessing and Olsen (1996) also support this family-oriented approach and point to the need for more programs that include concurrent attention to the woman's mothering activity.

Burman and Allen-Meares (1991) report that women alcoholics are often stranded by their spouses who are not expected to "stand by them" as is the expectation of women with their husbands. Further, they are often scorned by their children. The woman alcoholic is lacking in support in carrying her various roles. She is overloaded in the sense both of expectation of others and of her own expectations of herself. She is subject to situational stress.

In addition to the stress she experiences, the woman alcoholic is likely to be burdened by her own internalization of society's depreciation of women. In direct work with her, a focus on her internal problems is thus seen as misplaced. The goal of work is to enable her to see herself operating as a valued, competent independent individual. She can be helped to see where the environment is a source of stress, where she has assumed a dependent role and felt unable to deal with the stress and to meet her own needs. Seeing this and where she has let others define her role for her, putting others' needs before her own, she can learn and be helped to try out new role behaviors that can serve to give her a sense of control over her situation and reduce the drinking behavior.

As these efforts to strengthen the woman alcoholic as an individual affect her positively, they can be expected to have an impact on the family system. Her reduced drinking and generally more adequate functioning may, as noted above in the husband alcoholic situation, require some adaptation on the part of other family members. Her taking a more independent and responsible role is likely to be valued and appreciated. On the other hand, such new behavior may be experienced as a threat to the power or control the spouse or older children had been exercising. Both she and the family may benefit from conjoint sessions in making the transition to the new sets of relationships.

WHEN CHILDREN ARE THE SUBSTANCE ABUSERS

What is known about adolescents who are abusive users of alcohol and other substances suggests their similarity to each other and to adolescents who manifest other behavior problems. It also suggests similar ties and problems within the family network.

While adolescent alcoholism and substance abuse frequently result in hospitalization, our discussion here will center on working with them and their families on an outpatient basis. Some interventions we mention imply that the adolescent is still living at home. For others no longer at home and perhaps somewhat older, family ties and family work are nevertheless real and relevant.

It is important to obtain as part of the assessment a detailed picture of the pattern and kind of substance use (Kaufman, 1986). This can come out by way of a family genogram, as we suggested earlier, and/or as part of the inquiry about the efforts already attempted to cope with the problem.

Stanton's (1982) report from the joint effort with Todd to provide family treatment for substance abusers indicated that they had anticipated work with the current family rather than the family of origin. Their assumption had been that current relationships were a more important element both in perpetuating the problem and in possible contribution to its solution. They found that less than half of their subjects were married and that 86 percent had at least weekly contact with their family of origin.

As in the case of the parent's abuse, denial is evident. Parents may be oblivious to signs of substance use. Lee (1988) found this to be the case in households where both parents were employed. He bases a strong case for family treatment, as opposed to traditional individual treatment. Even when educated to the signals, parents may minimize their significance as a passing phase. Depending on rank among siblings, brothers and sisters may be reluctant to tell, even if they know of the abuse. Denial becomes more difficult to maintain when the abuse puts the abuser in contact with police or school authorities.

Involving the family in treatment may be resisted by both the family and the substance abuser. At this stage of the family life cycle it is usual for them to be thinking about the child's emancipation, movement out of the family. The adolescent tends to deny need for the family. The family, depending on how long or how difficult their endurance of the behaviors related to substance abuse has been, may feel guilty or that they have tried everything possible and are totally at a loss. Some may wish to bow out and be no longer bothered; others may be willing to keep trying.

In fact, the continuing abuse serves to throw the abuser back to the family for periods of time. The obvious reasons may be need for care, housing, or financial support. These periods of dependency may help the abuser to deal with anxieties of becoming independent while at the same time making it more difficult to achieve a satisfactory degree of separateness. Aside from the function these periods of dependence serve for the child, there may be advantages to the family system.

The substance-abusing child may be the scapegoated and rebellious child in an alcoholic family as described above. Lee (1984) notes that the adolescent's drinking serves to distract attention from his or her parents' marital problems. In that sense, it is functional for the family, serving to contain and minimize anxiety. It also serves to diminish the adolescent's anxiety about the pain in the family, though it is destructive to him as well. Shifting alliances are observable in the family triangle. A parent may ally himself or herself with the drinking adolescent, thereby meeting a need of the parent and protecting the adolescent from the other parent's knowledge of his difficulty. Ultimately, parents may ally themselves against the adolescent, blaming him for all family problems. These shifts may be abetted by the alcoholism of one or the other or both parents.

An adolescent whose drinking creates problems for him in the community draws parental attention and engagement, leaving him more dependent and family-involved. The problems of separation and independence typical of adolescence are exacerbated and make it more difficult for both adolescent and parent to achieve a satisfactory degree of separateness.

Engaging the Family

The principles outlined earlier in this chapter for engaging persons who don't see the need for treatment apply here also. For the parents who have tried to end the adolescent's substance abuse, it is soon evident that what they have tried has not worked and something new is needed. Therapist efforts need to be directed to joining them and the adolescent so both can sense therapist support. Rather than looking for answers to "why" questions about the behavior of either adolescent or family, questions pertain to goals and what they would like to have happen (Quinn et al., 1989). This can provide a basis for their engagement around emotional issues and hope for their resolution. For the parents, the apparent goal is ending the substance abuse. The child may share that goal or seek something different, for example, establishing separate residence or getting the parents to stop "running my life." The emotional exchange may also help to overcome the denial, without which treatment would be sabotaged (Wynne, 1984).

Where parents are themselves substance abusers, the difficulty in helping the child to change is amplified and will need to be treated if change in the adolescent is to occur and be stable.

Parents need to take charge of regulating the abuser's substance use (Quinn et al., 1989). They need to agree on this as a goal, to agree on the means to achieve it, and to be willing to take needed action by setting rules for behavior and specifying the consequences for noncompliance. Where medical supervision is not required, a "detox" can be carried out at home. Though it may be difficult to arrange, taking of urine samples should serve as a check for times when behavior cannot be observed or other accurate reports obtained.

If these measures are insufficient, they need the backing of what Quinn and associates call the "bogeyman threat." In some cases, the bogeyman may be a probation officer with the implicit threat of detention; in others it may be referral for inpatient care. Where the legal system is or should be involved, both therapist and family need to be informed of the possibilities for action and willing to follow through if necessary to end the substance abuse.

Attention to the adolescent substance abuser's peer network generally reveals that it consists mainly of other substance abusers. Development of a nonabusing network is important. Quinn has found it useful to invite non-substance-abusing friends into family treatment sessions. Selekman (1991) reports that, in this way, peers can serve to facilitate trust between adolescents and parents and can also serve as a relapse prevention group.

SUMMARY

We have defined alcoholism as a family systems problem in that there is a functional relationship between alcoholism and the problems of the family. While family problems may not be viewed as the sole cause of alcoholism, they may exacerbate the alcoholism and alcoholism exacerbate family problems. Our effort was not to determine causality but to focus on the interactive characteristics of the system. All family members, including children, may be unwitting contributors to both the alcoholism and the family problems, and all members are obviously affected by both.

We have discussed individual work with adult family members of both sexes, as well as treatment when an adolescent is the substance abuser, assuming in the case of the adolescent little difference in approach as compared to that for alcoholics and abusers of other substances. We have also drawn attention to both the kinds of work the family, as a group, needs to do in confronting the substance abuser to get him or her to stop and the work they all need to do when the drinking or abuse of other substances has stopped.

The approach described in this chapter emphasizes that family treatment is any form of treatment that meets the needs of the family, whether it does or does not solve the problem of the alcoholism or substance abuse. At the same time, treatment that serves the family is seen as contributing to reduction of alcoholism and other drug abuse, or at least as a means of promoting the abuser's participation in treatment. Once the alcoholic does begin to change, continuing work on family communications and problem solving is required to deal with problems in family relationships, since the drinking is not the only problem the family has to solve.

Our base in the structural treatment approach should be evident to the reader. Our discussion of the individual work with the adult male alcoholic is based more in the solution-focused approach of Berg and Miller. We note that Todd (1991) has also identified the value of both of these approaches in work with substance abusers.

REFERENCES

Al-Anon Family Group. 1967. *The Dilemma of the Alcoholic Marriage*. New York: Al-Anon Family Group Headquarters.

Azzi-Lessing, Lennette, and Olsen, Lenore. 1996. "Substance Abuse-Affected Families in the Child Welfare System: New Challenges, New Alliances." *Social Work* 41(1):15–25.

Babcock, M., and Connor, B. 1981. "Sexism and the Treatment of the Female Alcoholic." *Social Work* 26(3):233–38.

Bepko, Claudia, 1986. "Alcoholism as Oppression." In *Women and Family Therapy*, ed. Mariann Ault-Riche. Rockville, MD: Aspen Systems Corp.

Berg, Insoo Kim, and Miller, Scott. 1992. *Working with the Problem Drinker: A Solution Focused Approach*. New York: W.W. Norton & Co.

Berenson, D. 1976. "Alcohol and the Family System." In *Family Therapy Theory and Practice*, ed. P. Guerin. New York: Gardner Press.

Black, C. 1980. "Children of Alcoholics." *Alcohol, Health and Research World* 4(1):23–27.

Bowen, M. 1974. "Alcoholism as Viewed Through Family Systems Theory and Family Psychotherapy." *Annals of the New York Academy of Sciences* 233:115–22.

Brown-Mayers, A., Seelye, E., and Brown, D. 1973. "Reorganized Alcoholism Service." *Journal of the American Medical Association* 224:233–35.

Burman, Sondra, and Allen-Meares, Paula. 1991. Criteria for Selecting Practice Theories: Working with Alcoholic Women." *Families in Society* 72:387–91.

Cadogan, D. 1979. "Marital Group Therapy in Alcoholism Treatment." In *Family Therapy of Drug and Alcohol Abuse*, eds. E. Kaufman and P. Kaufman. New York: Gardner Press.

Carter, E. 1977. "Generation After Generation." In *Family Therapy: Theory and Practice*, ed. P. Papp. New York: Gardner Press.

Clemmons, P. 1979. "Issues in Marriage, Family and Child Counseling in Alcoholism." In *Women Who Drink*, ed. V. Burtle. Springfield, IL: Charles C. Thomas, Publisher.

Cohen, P., and Krause, M. 1971. *Casework with Wives of Alcoholics*. New York: Family Service Association of America.

Cork, M. 1969. *The Forgotten Children*. Toronto: Addiction Research Foundation.

Corrigan, E. 1980. *Alcoholic Women in Treatment*. New York: Oxford University Press.

Corrigan, E., and Anderson, S. 1978. "Training for Treatment of Alcoholism in Women." *Social Casework* 59(1):42–50.

Dahlgren, L. 1979. "Female Alcoholics IV: Marital Situation and Husbands." *Acta Psychiatrica Scandinavica* 59:59–69.

Davis, D.I. 1980. "Alcoholics Anonymous and Family Therapy." *Journal of Marital and Family Therapy* 6(1):65–73.

Davis, T., and Hagood, L. 1979. "In-Home Support for Recovering Alcoholic Mothers and Their Families: The Family Rehabilitation Coordinator Project." *Journal of Studies on Alcohol* 40(3):313–17.

DeCubas, M.M., and Field, T. 1993. "Children of Methadone-Dependent Women: Development Outcomes." *American Journal of Orthopsychiatry* 63(2):266–76.

dePeyer, Janine. 1990. "The Family." In *Cocaine Solutions*, eds. Jennifer Rice-Licaare and Katherine Delaney-McLoughlin. New York: Haworth Press.

Dinaburg, D., Gleck, I., and Feigenbaum, E. 1980. "Marital Therapy of Women Alcoholics." In *Alcoholism in Women*, eds. C. Eddy and J. Ford. Dubuque, IA: Kendall/Hunt Publishing Co.

El-Guebaly, N., and Offord, D.R. 1977. "On Being an Offspring of an Alcoholic: An Update." *Alcoholism Clinical and Experimental Research* 3:148–57.

Esser, P.H., 1968. "Conjoint Family Therapy with Alcoholics." *British Journal of Addiction* 63:177–82.

_____. 1971. "Evaluation of Family Therapy with Alcoholics." *British Journal of Addiction* 66:86–91.

Finkelstein, Norma. 1994. "Treatment Issues for Alcohol and Drug Dependent Pregnant and Parenting Women." *Health and Social Work* 19(1):7–15.

Flanzer, J. 1978. "Family Management in the Treatment of Alcoholism." *British Journal on Alcohol and Alcoholism* 13:45–59.

Fox, R. 1968. "Treating the Alcoholic's Family." In *Alcoholism: The Total Treatment Approach*, ed. R. Catanzaro. Springfield, IL: Charles C. Thomas, Publisher.

_____. 1972. "Children in the Alcoholic Family." In *Problems in Addiction: Alcoholism and Narcotics*, ed. W.C. Bier. New York: Fordham University Press.

Goglia, L.R., Jurkovic, G.J., Burt, A.M., and Burge-Callaway, K.G. 1992. "Generational Boundary Distortions by Adult Children of Alcoholics: Child-as-Parent and Child-as-Mate." *American Journal of Family Therapy* 20(4):291–99.

Goldman, B.M., and Rossland, S. 1992. "Young Children of Alcoholics: A Group Treatment Model." *Social Work in Health Care* 16(3):53–65.

Gorad, S. 1971. "Communicational Style of Alcoholics and Their Wives." *Family Process* 10:475–89.

Gorman, J.M., and Rooney, J.F. 1979. "The Influence of Al-Anon on the Coping Behavior of Wives of Alcoholics." *Journal of Studies on Alcohol* 40:1030–38.

Janzen, Curtis. 1977. "Families in the Treatment of Alcoholism." *Journal of Studies on Alcohol* 38(1):114–30.

_____. (1985/1986). "Use of Family Treatment Methods by Alcoholism Treatment Services." *Alcohol Health and Research World* (Winter) 10(2):44–45, 60.

Kaufman, Edward. 1984. *Substance Abuse and Family Therapy*. New York: Grune and Stratton.

_____. 1986. "A Workable System of Family Therapy for Drug Dependence." *Journal of Psychoactive Drugs* 18(1):43–50.

Lee, J. 1984. "Adolescent Alcohol Abuse." *Focus on Family and Chemical Dependency* 7(3):22–25.

Lee, Robert. 1988. "Employed Couples and Substance Abuse: The Tip of the Iceberg." *Contemporary Family Therapy* 10(1):44–52.

Liddle, Howard, and Diamond, Guy. 1991. "Adolescent Substance Abusers in Family Therapy: The Critical Initial Phase of Treatment." *Family Dynamics of Addiction Quarterly* (1)1:55–68.

Liepman, M.R., Nirenberg, T.D., and Begin, A.M. 1989. "Evaluation of a Program Designed to Help Family and Significant Others to Motivate Resistant Alcoholics into Recovery." *American Journal of Drug and Alcohol Abuse* 15(2):209–21.

Meeks, D., and Kelly, C. 1970. "Family Therapy with the Families of Recovering Alcoholics." *Quarterly Journal of Studies on Alcohol* 31:399–413.

Morehouse, E. 1984. "Working with Alcohol Abusing Children of Alcoholics." *Alcohol, Health and Research World* 8:14–19.

Mueller, I. 1972. "Casework with the Family of the Alcoholic." *Social Work* 17:79–84.

O'Farrell, T.J. 1989. "Marital and Family Therapy in Alcoholism Treatment." *Journal of Substance Abuse Treatment* 6(1):23–29.

Orford, J., Oppenheimer, E., Egert, S., Hensmen, C., and Guthrie, S. 1976. "The Cohesiveness of Alcoholism: Complicated Marriages and Its Influence on Treatment Outcome." *British Journal of Psychiatry* 128:318–39.

Page, A. 1980. "Counseling." In *Women and Alcohol*, ed. Camberwell Council on Alcoholism. London: Tavistock Publications.

Quinn, William, Kuehl, Bruce, Thomas, Frank, and Joanning, Harvey. 1988. "Families of Adolescent Drug Abusers: Systemic Interventions to Attain Drug-Free Behavior." *American Journal of Drug Alcohol Abuse* 14(1):65–87.

Quinn, William, Kuehl, Bruce, Thomas, Frank, Joanning, Harvey, and Newfield, Neal. 1989. *American Journal of Family Therapy* 17(3):229–43.

Reed, B.G. 1987. "Developing Women-sensitive Drug Dependence Treatment Programs: Why So Difficult?" *Journal of Psychoactive Drugs* 19:151–64.

Regan, J., Connors, G., O'Farrel, T., and Jones, W. 1983. Services for Families of Alcoholics." *Journal of Studies on Alcohol* 44(6)1072–82.

Rice-Licaare, Jennifer, and Delaney-McLoughlin, Katherine. 1990. *Cocaine Solutions: Help for Cocaine Abusers and Their Families.* New York: Haworth Press.

Richards, T. 1979. "Working with Children of an Alcoholic Mother." *Alcohol, Health and Research World* 3(3):22–25.

Satir, Virginia. 1983. *Conjoint Family Therapy.* Palo Alto, CA: Science and Behavior Books.

Selekman, Matthew. 1991. "With a Little Help from My Friends: The Use of Peers in the Family Therapy of Adolescent Substance Abusers." *Family Dynamics of Addiction Quarterly* 1(1):69–76.

Sheridan, M.J., and Green, R.G. 1993. "Family Dynamics and Individual Characteristics of Adult Children of Alcoholics." *Journal of Social Service Research* 17(1/2):73–97.

Stanton, M.D. 1982. A Review of Reports on Drug Abusers Family Living Arrangements and Frequency of Family Contact. In *Family Therapy of Drug*

Abuse and Addiction, eds. M.D. Stanton and T.C. Todd et al. New York: Guilford.

Steinglass, P., Davis, D., and Berenson, D. 1977. "Observation of Conjointly Hospitalized Alcoholic Couples During Sobriety and Intoxication: Implications for Family Therapy." *Family Process* 16:1–16.

Straussner, S.L. 1989. "Intervention with Maltreating Parents Who Are Drug and Alcohol Abusers." In *Clinical Social Work with Maltreated Children and Their Families*, eds. S.M. Ehrenkranz, E.G. Goldstein, L. Goodman, and J. Seinfeld. New York: New York University Press.

Straussner, S.L., Weinstein, D.L., and Hernandez, R. 1979. The Effects of Alcoholism on the Family System." *Health and Social Work* 4(4):111–27.

Thomas, E., and Santa, C. 1982. "Unilateral Family Therapy for Alcohol Abuse." *American Journal of Family Therapy* 10(3):49–59.

Todd, Thomas. 1991. "The Evolution of Family Therapy Approaches to Substance Abuse—Personal Reflections and Thoughts on Integration." *Contemporary Family Therapy* 13(5):471–95.

Tracy, E.M. and Farkas, K.J. 1994. "Preparing Practitioners for Child Welfare Practice with Substance-Abusing Families." *Child Welfare* 73(1):57–68.

Ward, R., and Faillace, L. 1970. "The Alcoholic and His Helpers." *Quarterly Journal of Studies on Alcohol* 31:684–91.

Wegscheider, S. 1981. *Another Change: Hope and Health for the Alcoholic Family*. Palo Alto, CA: Science and Behavior Books.

Wilson, C. 1980. "The Family." In *Women and Alcohol*, ed. Camberwell Council on Alcoholism. London: Tavistock Publications.

Wolin, S. 1980. "Introduction: Psychosocial Consequences." In *Alcohol and Women: Research Monograph No. 1*. Rockville, MD: National Institute on Alcohol Abuse and Alcoholism.

Wynne, M. 1984. "Teenage Chemical Dependency Treatment." *Focus on Family and Chemical Dependency* 7(3):20–21.

Yama, M.F., Fogas, B.S., Teegarden, I.A., and Hastings, B. 1993. "Childhood Sexual Abuse and Parental Alcoholism: Interactive Effects in Adult Women." *American Journal of Orthopsychiatry* 63(2):300–05.

Young, N.K., Wallace, V.R., and Garcia, T. 1992. "Developmental Status of Three to Five Year Old Children Who Were Prenatally Exposed to Alcohol and Other Drugs." *School Social Work Journal* 16(2):1–15.

CHAPTER **15**

Treatment During Family Dissolution

Disruption of marital relationships as well as separation of one or the other of the partners and children to different residences are increasingly facts of everyday life. Data from 1990 suggest that about four out of ten first marriages may eventually end in divorce, a rate slightly lower than the five out of ten that had been reported earlier, but higher than anywhere else in the world (U.S. Bureau of the Census, 1993). Four out of ten marriages are remarriages for one or both partners. Data from 1990 show that over three million women aged 15 to 65 ended their first two marriages in divorce. Figures also suggest that the failure rate of second marriage is no higher than that of first marriages, though it had earlier been shown to be higher. About one in every twelve two-parent families that existed at the beginning of a typical two-year period in the mid 1980s no longer existed two years later. Family finances seem to play a large role in this: Two-parent families were more likely to break up if the father was unemployed, if both parents worked full time, or if the family was poor rather than nonpoor.

Marital separation and the consequent disruption of family life are stressful and painful, no matter how stressful and painful the family's life together had been or whether the separation had been earnestly sought or strenuously resisted. Both partners suffer, as do the children. Although there may be relief for the partners, and in some instances for the children too, breakdown of family relations to the point of separation of family members is still seen and experienced as deviant because of the pain, loss, increased difficulty in relationships, and the new and unknown complexity of the ensuing years. Yet, because of its frequency and the fact that so many lives are affected, it must also be seen as a family life experience that needs to be understood, so that it can be normalized, perhaps even ritualized, in order to give people the ways and means to cope when they come face to face with such a major transition in their lives. A massive amount of experience, research, and publication has been devoted to understanding the formation of families, giving guidance for that life transition. By comparison, relatively little guidance, and consequently little support, has been available for the transition out of the nuclear family group. People have been left to suffer and cope alone and on their own as best they can. Professionals have similarly been at a loss for knowledge and the best ways to help.

Nevertheless, as the rate of marital dissolution continues unabated, there has been an increasing tendency to recognize serial monogamous relationships as a common form of the family life cycle. Hunter and Schuman (1980, p. 447) note that the fact that families dissolve and reconstitute shows "the low level of commitment by parental members of the household group to maintain any particular household as a stable unit over an extended period of time." This has come to be an increasingly accepted standard. A period of life with one partner ends. It may or may not have brought with it the arrival of children. It is followed by a period of singlehood and/or single parenthood that ends by remarriage and the constituting of a new household, which may include children from one or both previous marriages as well as births to the current marriage. The family in the phase of dissolution, or of single parenthood, and of remarriage is a different kind of organization from the first family. Each family stage needs to develop its own rules, relationships, and place in the community.

This chapter will be devoted only to the family in the dissolution phase. Chapter 16 will look at the family formed out of two prior families. We see the dissolution phase as a transitional crisis for the family in which psychological and social stresses place severe demands on individual adjustment and interpersonal relationships, and during which personal and social resources may be lacking. Within the dissolution phase there are smaller identifiable phases, which we will describe in terms of their impact on family members. We will also suggest goals for treatment. Without doubt, research on what helps most, for what kinds of situations, and for which phase or dissolving family type is still in short supply.

UNDERSTANDING FAMILY DISSOLUTION

Our overall objectives in working with dissolving family units are to help the couple achieve a successful psychic separation and to enable them to continue a positive parental role and relationship with their children. Achieving an understanding of how the relationship failed and defining the kind of relationship that had been dissatisfying to the partners can facilitate the detachment and also forestall the possibility that the ex-spouses will repeat a bad relationship with a new partner. In initial stages of treatment, reasons for breakup are put forth in justification for it and need to be put in perspective.

Our emphasis is on situations in which the spouses/parents decide for reasons of their own not to continue the marriage. Other circumstances prompting family breakup will not be part of our discussion, such as instances of physical or sexual abuse, which often result in the removal of the abuser or the victim of the abuse from the family.

Reasons for Divorce

Causes of difficulty in marriage are many, but they do not always lead to complete breakdown of marital relationships and divorce. The combination of factors leading to a decision on the part of one or both partners to separate is not clear for marriages in general or often even for a particular marriage.

The decision may be seen as the product of a formula that on one side of the equation includes the sum of dissatisfactions to be endured if one remained in the relationship minus the remaining satisfactions in the relationship. On the other side of the equation are the satisfactions to be gained by leaving minus the additional stresses that would come into play if one left the relationship. Some of the specific reasons for seeking divorce have been identified in various studies. Levinger (1966) noted that husbands and wives do not give the same reasons. In his study, wives cited, in order of frequency, physical abuse, financial problems, mental cruelty, and neglect of home and children. Husbands most frequently cited sexual incompatibility, followed by neglect of home and children, infidelity, in-law troubles, and mental cruelty. For both husbands and wives there were variations due to social class.

Subjects in a study by Kincaid and Caldwell (1995) gave a slightly different set of reasons. They cited emotional abuse, communication difficulties, and excessive demands most frequently as reasons for separation. Somewhat surprisingly, initiators did not have a larger support network for assistance in coping during this stressful phase, and non-initiators did not have more emotional support available to them than initiators.

Little (1982) suggests the possibility that the actual behavior of the partners may be less of a factor than the fact that there is a disparity between an ideal image of others as partner and parent and the actuality of the partner's performance. What might be reason for divorce in one relationship may not be sufficient reason in another relationship. Little identifies clusters of role images that seem to be important. Closeness, companionship, and intimacy were ranked high as characteristics of ideal husbands and wives by both husbands and wives; yet, both saw themselves and their spouses as failing to meet these expectations. A second cluster pertaining to caring for, and modeling behavior for, the children was not ranked quite as high. Both husbands and wives rated themselves as well as their spouses better than on the previous cluster. They were more satisfied with their own than their spouse's performance. The third cluster, income production and family management items, ranked lower in overall importance to the marriage. Both spouses scored themselves and their spouses higher in meeting expectations on these items. In this study, then, men and women put highest priority on companionship, sharing of feelings, and listening and caring. It is in this area that they are most disappointed, and for deficits in this area that they are most likely to divorce. Of interest also in Little's study is her report that 65 percent of the women and 70 percent of the men identified the wife's going to work as a factor leading to separation. Husbands being too involved with work was also frequently cited.

Lyon, Silverman, Howe, Bishop, and Armstrong (1985) identified additional specifics such as extramarital relationships, drug or alcohol abuse, poor communication, money problems, and the spouse's failure to accept personal change in the partner. In their study 57 percent of the respondents blamed the spouse for failure of the marriage. In this and other studies it is interesting to note that substantial numbers of respondents thought that their own behavior as well as their spouse's contributed to the failure of the marriage. They did not put sole responsibility on the partner.

Levinger (1965) in a speculative review posits that a change in the combination of bonds and bars leads to a shift from cohesiveness in marriage to its dissolution. Cohesiveness in the marriage is "a direct function of the attractions within and barriers around a marriage and an inverse function of such attractions from other relationships" (p. 20). When the cohesiveness is due more to barriers to dissolution than to bonds between the partners, the marriage may be seen as an empty shell but still hold together. Attraction may be for intrinsic reasons such as genuine affection, esteem, and companionship, or for extrinsic reasons such as financial or social status. Barriers to dissolution may consist of feelings of obligation, moral proscriptions, community pressures, or legal bars. Promoting dissolution are such things as alternate affections (toward lovers or kin loyalties), differing religions, or alternate sources of income. Levinger cites research that has demonstrated the importance of all these factors, but the relationship between them and the exact combination of them that would lead to dissolution are left to be determined.

Some of these factors suggest the impact of broad social forces such as the changing place of women in society as factors in marital dissolution. Their entry into the work force, whether for reasons of financial necessity or personal gratification, as a factor draws attention to this larger picture. Another such broad social factor is our society's emphasis on individual freedom and satisfaction. Whitaker and Keith (1984) draw attention to this when they say, "In our 'do your own thing,' 'preserve your freedom' culture a person has to be crazy to get married" (p. 53). Achieving individuality is often emphasized in seeking separation and divorce. There is the pervasive concern that individual identity will be lost in commitment to the family. Making interpersonal relationships work and endure always involves struggle, negotiation, and effort. The part of each individual that does not want to make the effort is reenforced by the cultural norm to which Whitaker and Keith draw attention. We have noted at other places in this book that the balance between separateness and connectedness, between individual goals and the goals of the family group is constantly shifting. It may be that in the emphasis on "doing one's own thing" one may lose sight of the possibility that in struggling for relatedness one's individuality may also be enhanced.

Decisions to leave or stay in the relationship will also be affected by the cultural context of the couple/family. The position of women, their prerogatives and their power in the culture of which the spouses are a part, and the degree to which they are embedded in it will be factors in the decision process. The influence of their religious group will be a factor of greater or lesser importance. Helping each partner to evaluate where they are in comparison to other couples in their ethnic group is an important aspect of treatment.

However intense the struggle for individuality has been, attachment has also come to be of great importance. It is the remaining attachment that makes for part of the difficulty in separation. Furthermore, one is never left unchanged by a relationship. In Whitaker and Keith's words "It is impossible to go back to being single. Marriage is like a stew that has irreversible characteristics that the parts cannot be rid of. Divorce is leaving part of the self behind," and that adds to the difficulty and stress of separation and divorce. Todorski (1995) attests to the importance of this in the helping process.

We do not suppose that in the foregoing material we have exhausted the discussion of reasons for divorce. The specific impact of each differing cause on the way the divorce proceeds remains to be understood for each situation. However, awareness of at least some of the reasons can give the social worker an idea of the issues the partners will bring to the help-seeking effort. Conceptually framing the specifics as role-image disparities and as a balancing of bonds of cohesiveness and bars to dissolution also provides the worker with a way of looking at the specifics. In some instances the specific reasons will also influence the ease or difficulty with which the divorcing process flows.

Divorcing Types

Therapists will encounter a variety of behaviors from separating couples, all of which may serve to characterize their relationship and which require different therapeutic strategies. Several relationship typologies of divorcing couples have been identified. While the studies from which these typologies are drawn have not firmly established that they were also the type of the marriage, there is the suggestion that type is related to the way in which the disengagement of the partners proceeds as well as to the subsequent adjustment of family members. Knowing these should help the worker know what to anticipate. Understanding the relationship the couple has had may also make it more possible for the partners to let go of the relationship and to avoid entry into another similar and unsatisfying relationship.

Little (1982) identifies six types of dissolving relationships in which the nature of the relationship was in itself reason for the divorce. She also sees the character of the relationship as a determinant of the post-divorce adjustment of the couple and of the kinds of decisions made about custody for the children. In the *fragile-bond marriage* the spouses replayed without question the patterns in their families of origin. They did not communicate feelings, lived in separate worlds, and never struggled to create a common world. They eventually withdrew from each other and parted company completely. In the *fractured family* the couple also initially played out patterns from families of origin. However, in addition to withdrawing, they began to appeal to, attack, or try to coerce each other into new behavior. Conflict and competition developed and led finally to dissolution.

In the *doll's-house marriage*, the husband initially controlled a very submissive wife who later became more assertive. Both partners then resorted to posturing, rewarding, persuading, depreciating, and inflating tactics, which finally led to moves to end the relationship. A *stalemate-marriage* type was devoid of emotional expressiveness, particularly on the part of the man, who never invited or demanded expressiveness from his wife. The woman, however, demanded it from her husband and was seen as more striving and achieving.

The *perfect-model marriage* is so labeled because the relationship started as the picture of success with outside careers of both partners, healthy children, and a relatively egalitarian relationship. However, the man expected deference, discounting his wife and making her needs secondary. A sixth marriage-type was *unformed families*, in which adequate bonding had never occurred and in which the partners lacked self-awareness. Little asserts that these ways of relating continued through divorcing and divorce periods and profoundly influenced the adjustment of the children. As in the classification that follows, degree of individuation and levels of communication, conflict, and investment in the relationship are important variables.

Kressel, Jaffee, Tuchman, Watson, and Deutsch (1980) offer a typology of divorcing couples based on the degree of ambivalence manifested by the participants, the level and overtness of the conflict, and the frequency and openness of their communication. They were interested in determining whether type was associated with readiness to accept or benefit from divorce mediation efforts. They found all four types among couples who had, and couples who had not, sought mediation.

An *enmeshed type of couple* showed high levels of conflict, communication, and ambivalence. They stated explicitly their wish to divorce but manifested in many ways their inability to let go by continually taking opposing points of view and sometimes reversing their positions in doing so. Turmoil continued even after the divorce was finalized.

Autistic-pattern couples showed a low level of communication and overt conflict. The spouses avoided each other physically and emotionally. Expressed ambivalence was at a low level. There was a low level of communication of doubt and uncertainty about the divorce. A *disengaged-pattern group* similarly showed a low level of ambivalence but had had a much lower level of intimacy in their earlier relationship, so that the conflict at the time of divorce was much less. They showed a strong wish to avoid conflict, and the danger in working with them was excessive cordiality.

A *direct-conflict pattern group of couples* manifested high levels of conflict and open communication about the possibilities of divorce. Initially high ambivalence was resolved over the space of a year. This was the only group that the authors identified as having a good experience with mediation and as achieving a successful postdivorce adjustment.

Another classification of divorces is based on the characteristics of surprise and mutuality. Divorces that are sought by one partner and resisted by the other are characteristically more difficult than those in which both partners have concluded that divorce should be sought. Sprenkle and Cyrus (1983) see the divorce that is sudden and unexpected for one of the partners as a crisis situation. The initiating partner has often pondered leaving for a long time (ten years in one of our cases) before announcing intention and sometimes even before voicing dissatisfaction. The abandoned partner must recover from shock as well as other feelings attendant upon divorce. The surprise factor is indeed an added stress for the person being abandoned and creates greater difficulty at least initially than the situation in which thoughts of separation have been openly discussed by both spouses as the marital difficulties increased.

DIVORCE AS PHASES OF CRISIS

The frequency of divorce is seen as a result of developments in society that have changed the expectation placed on and the nature of family life (Ahrons and Rodgers, 1987). This being the case, divorce is seen as a crisis and a transitional stage in the family life cycle rather than as pathology of the partners. As with other transitions or crises with which family members have little or no prior experience, our approach to treatment is to assess the way the stress is being felt and the resources available for coping, and to provide needed direction and support.

The time span from awareness of hardly bearable dissatisfaction with the marriage to the completion of parting into separate households, legalization of the divorce, and a more or less stable pattern of singlehood or single-parenthood may be divided into distinguishable phases, each of which has its own set of stresses, feelings, and tasks. Each may be considered a crisis that requires successful resolution before the tasks of the subsequent phase can be fruitfully engaged. The work and use of treatment are tailored as much as possible to the needs of the phase. Though some things are more at issue in some phases, many will have residuals in subsequent phases and some work on them will likely have been done in phases prior to our placement of them.

Some features are applicable to all phases (Hunter and Schuman, 1980). Role ambiguity and role confusion abound. "How am I supposed to behave? What is expected of me? How do I want to be? What can I or should I say?" There are no guidelines for what to do and likely no one else who can give the benefit of their experience. And even if there were someone, resistance to seek out such a person is great because of the accompanying feelings of failure. In all phases there are also boundary problems for the family system. What can be taken outside the family system? Whom can we tell? To what extent are problems and feelings shared across generational boundaries, or how much should they be? How much can parent and child confide and rely on each other for solace and support? Conflicting loyalties also arise. How much do I owe myself? How much to my spouse? To my children? And for the children there is the question of siding or not siding with one or the other of the sparring parents.

Feelings of loss and grief are ever present for the spouse who seeks the separation as well as for the one who resists it. Mutual suspicion is strong, as is wariness that the other will take some advantage and be unfair. Self-blame, lack of self-worth, and uncertainty about who one really is add to difficulties in adjustment and coping over the entire span of the divorcing process.

Many factors contribute to the level of stress experienced at this time and to the ability to cope with it. The spouse who is opposed initially to separation and divorce will experience greater stress. Suddenness and unexpectedness of the action add to stress. Length of the marriage and the degree of intimacy once achieved in the marriage may make separation more difficult. Numbers of children in the family and any problems they have can make a difference. Loss of friends, changes in residence, and limited finances all add their burden.

Level of coping depends on personality strengths and social resources. Persons may be limited in coping by residual effects of past losses and separation (see Counts and Sachs, 1985). Another loss is even more devastating when grief over past relationships is unresolved and the capacity for new attachments has not been developed. Remaining overclose attachments to family of origin indicate a limited capacity to detach and achieve independence and will result in ambivalent holding on and letting go during the separation period. These characteristics suggest a limited degree of individuation and separation and a limited capacity for independent living.

Social resources can complement personal coping resources. Friends and family may be supportive both psychologically and with material resources and advice. Availability of material resources may also enhance coping capacity.

Predivorce Phase

Disillusionment with the marriage evolves eventually into a decision to separate and divorce. In Spanier and Thompson's (1984) research it took less than six months for over half of the women and for almost two-thirds of the men studied for that evolution to end with filing for divorce. But it took as long as two years for a third of the men and 43 percent of the women. Kressel and associates (1980) say that the "leavers" had been considering leaving for 11 months, on the average, before seeking mediation. The "abandoned" spouse may have had only a month. Disappointment becomes disillusionment when one partner recognizes that the other is not what had been hoped for. Love erodes, and the tenderness of earlier attachment disappears (Kessler, 1975). In the midst of this come efforts to restore the relationship, and the assistance of marriage counselors is sometimes sought. When efforts to restore fail, the public facade of marital bliss is shattered and energies shift to consideration of separation and divorce (Kressel and Deutsch, 1977). Decisions are made and unmade. Most permanent separations are preceded by at least one trial or temporary separation.

Actual consideration of divorce is devastating for both partners. Intensity and difficulty vary. The "initiator" may have handled many feelings and developed a fairly clear picture of what it was all going to be like before announcing intent, but for the "abandoned spouse" the announcement comes as a shock. "I am being rejected, I am a failure, You are being unfair. I am hurt. I am angry. You can't, you shouldn't do this to me." Or "What have I done? What do you want me to do? Please stay! I'll do anything. Don't leave me alone." Sprenkle and Cyrus (1983) suggest that in the offer of the "abandoned one" to change is the implicit recognition that he or she has in some way previously been the abandoning one. In any event, ambivalence runs high. Fighting alternates with clinging when the anxiety level engendered by the prospects of the future is raised or when self-confidence flags and doubts occur about whether this is really the best course to take.

Grief is strong. Loss of the love relationship is no doubt central. An important someone no longer cares. And separation also means loss of familiar routines, familiar environment, and familiar associations outside the family with friends and kin. The experience is emptiness, and no prospect of filling it or the confidence that one would even know how to go about it and loss of prospects, disruption of hopes and plans.

It seems initially strange to consider that the "initiator" would also grieve. That is an emotion one tends to attribute only to the "abandoned one." It is nevertheless a loss. It is the loss of investment in the relationship. It is leaving a part of oneself. It is loss of an image of what might have been and of what one had waited for, the end of hope that what was desired will ever be attained.

There is also the loss of outside relationships for both spouses. Friends have often been friends of the couple, rather than of one or the other, and are uncertain how to relate, whether with sympathy or congratulations. They too feel a loss and tend to withdraw. Further, they are unwilling to be caught in taking sides. The latter may be less true for kin than for friends. It is not unknown for kin to side with their in-law rather than with blood relatives. Research by Kitson, Moir, and Mason (1982) concludes that even relatives are not inclined to be helpful if they disapprove of the divorce. All these losses serve to leave the parting couple with minimal sources of support at a time when support is most needed and could be most helpful.

For both partners, loss engenders anger, blame, and fighting. Elkin (1977) calls it "angerism—a deep-seated unresolved anger, dependency, anxiety, fear, and at times a degree of irrationality and an inability to set aside the anger long enough to do what is necessary for all concerned, especially the children" (p. 56). It can continue five or ten years. It needs to be resolved.

Evaluations of the helpfulness of treatment are not always definite about the phase at which treatment occurred or the reasons for seeking it. In some instances the search for treatment during this phase has the objective, at least on the part of one of the partners, of seeking to restore the marriage. Sometimes the other spouse comes along to make a last effort to save the marriage, though it is sometimes also evident that coming along is only for show when in reality they have made up their minds to separate. Spanier and Thompson (1984) said that 70 percent of their research sample had sought help at some point during the process, though it was not clear whether the purpose was to save the marriage or to ease the process of divorce. About a third of these couples had sought help from clergy persons and another third from marriage and family counselors. Of the sample, 30 percent found their counseling to be extremely helpful, and another 51 percent thought it was somewhat helpful.

Though separation, or even contemplation of separation, may be considered a crisis, as the preceding discussion would suggest, the crisis may also be an opportunity for growth. A general goal for all the succeeding phases of treatment is for a quality of emotional detachment that frees the partners from a need to continue to fight or blame or pressure each other to change, which eliminates their using the children as pawns or allies and which leaves them clear about their own contribution to the difficulties. Aside from the increase in individual well-being, the outcome should enable each partner to have a fairly clear understanding of the relationship and why it didn't work, thus reducing the likelihood of moving into another identical relationship, an oft-observed occurrence, in our experience.

Marek (1989) identifies similar goals—increased self-understanding, a mourning of the now-disrupted relationship, a balanced view of the marriage, the ability of the partners to work together regarding the children, and a satisfactory resolution of terms of legal settlement.

An early decision about whether to meet jointly or separately needs to be made. Storm and Sprenkle (1982) suggest that during the predivorce or decision-making stage and the next restructuring stage, conjoint interviews can be very useful. We, and likewise Marek (1989), tend to agree that beginning with joint sessions is advisable, that the frequent result of beginning individual sessions has led to the unilateral decision to separate.

Goals of treatment in the decision-making phase are to help the partners become clear about the nature of their relationship and whether there is any possibility that either partner could or would make the changes needed for the relationship to become satisfying. If one of the spouses has already decided to separate, the contact can demonstrate whether the decision can be reversed and/or help the other spouse to make a case for reversal or to accept the inevitable. Communication can be promoted in conjoint sessions that identifies the issues and the capacity of the partners to respond to them. Each can evaluate the importance of the issues and the possibilities of change. Clients differ in their wishes for the conduct of the treatment sessions. Some simply want to hear what their spouses have to say or to have their spouses listen to what they have to say. Others seek more active help in resolving as well as in clarifying issues.

Couple type may be a factor in the ability to benefit from either individual or conjoint treatment during this phase. The types we have mentioned have been only briefly sketched by their developers, and diagnosis is most certainly difficult. However difficult, a relationship diagnosis is helpful. The couple with low rates of communication, such as Little's "fragile-bond" type, may particularly benefit from an increased flow of information and exchange of feeling that is possible in conjoint sessions. A couple diagnosis of the enmeshed pattern (Kressel et al., 1980) may suggest limiting the expression of feeling and an emphasis on cognitive grasp of the situation or a focus on the difficulties of letting go. Couples of the enmeshed type achieve neither harmony nor separation until one of them is strengthened for greater assertiveness and independence. On the other hand, their "direct-conflict" type would seem likely to benefit from conjoint treatment at this stage as well as from mediation at a later stage.

Each spouse also begins at this stage to deal with feelings of badness and failure, with their sense of loss, and with what lies ahead. They also begin to develop ways to present themselves to the outside world and to anticipate how friends and kin will respond to them. They begin to hear how the other is thinking about who will move, who will have the children, what their financial situation will be. All of these considerations enter the basic decision to be made at this stage—whether to stay together or to part.

One issue that arises during this decision-making stage is posed by the partner who has edged into another relationship and is ambivalent about giving up either the marriage or the extramarital one. Continuation of the affair generates strong reaction in the spouse and needs to be dealt with by both. We have come to the conclusion that that is not a workable arrangement for therapy and that what is likely to be more productive in resolving the ambivalence and/or improving the marriage is for the partner to make a decision to work on the marriage and give up the other relationship. This may still lead to a resolution to terminate the marriage, but at least the effort will have been made and forestalls the feeling that not all alternatives have been tested. Suggestions that the third person be brought into the treatment are generally opposed.

When therapy has included individual sessions along with the conjoint ones, extramarital affairs, current or past, are sometimes revealed to the therapist but are unknown to the other spouse. Such secrets create a dilemma for therapists. How they are handled depends on what has been said about confidentiality, and on the goals of the partners at the time the secret is revealed.

Negotiating and Restructuring

Once the decision to separate and divorce has been made, the central task is to restructure the family. This means achieving an end to the marriage that is as constructive as possible and at the same time recognizing that a family continues to exist if children are involved and making workable plans for that family. Ahrons (1980) points out that divorce creates new households of single parents, but it results in a single-parent family only when one of the spouses is or becomes unavailable. A parental coalition must be preserved, or created, while the marital coalition is dissolved (Goldman and Coane, 1983). For constructive resolution for the children, and for themselves as well, the former spouses must achieve an ability to cooperate in responsible care for the children and in continuing their own separate relationships to them. Housing, financial support, property settlement, child custody, and visiting arrangements must all be negotiated. Lyon and associates (1985) call this the litigation phase. It is indeed litigious, even if it does not come to legal litigation. The issues are highly charged emotionally.

Restructuring has an emotional and a rational practical component. For the crisis of divorce to be resolved successfully, both components must be addressed. Rational planning and handling of reality matters cannot be completed if the emotional issues are unresolved. And unless reasonable plans are made, emotional tension will remain at a high level. Skill for assisting the couple with both aspects should be part of the social worker's repertoire, though, as we suggest later, referrals to mediators for financial and custody mediation may be useful.

Emotional Issues

Work on emotional issues will have begun in the initial phase. The couple's efforts to arrive at a decision about dissolution of the marriage expose feelings of rejection, pain of loss, anxiety about the future, guilt over past behavior, feelings of inadequacy, and the hostility and anger directed at the other for being incompetent, irresponsible, or unfair. Tension and anger levels may still be high. The "abandoned one" may still be defending against "narcissistic injury" (Rice, 1977) by projecting all blame and attempting to instill guilt in the leaving spouse. In some instances attacks, retaliatory behavior, and even suicide threats are made in efforts to keep the other bound to the relationship. These may be based on a concept of self as unlovable and unworthwhile and a conviction that "no one else will ever want me." Limits on such behavior need to be set. Drawing attention to the incendiary results of threatening and "get-even" behavior may help. Interventions need to be designed to build confidence in self and one's ability to survive. Praise for small achievements and reassurances of one's worthwhileness conveyed through worker interest and caring contribute to that end. Teaching practical skills needed for survival such as cooking or banking or organizing will not only aid survival but build confidence and hope as well.

Separate individual as well as conjoint sessions are useful to enable each spouse to express feelings and to be listened to and understood. Even though there may be cognitive recognition that the marriage is over, opportunity to mourn the loss, to consider one's own and the other's contributions to the breakdown of the marriage, and to let go of the relationship are provided in the treatment process. In this connection it may be useful to wonder why the reluctant spouse is not more dissatisfied. Achieving an understanding of one's own behavior in the marriage and of the responses of the spouse should lead to an acceptance of self and a reasonable degree of toleration of the spouse, enough at least so that they do not continue efforts to fight and destroy each other and so that they do achieve the ability to cooperate on behalf of the children. Each partner should also gain a sense of his or her strengths and individual rights to enable him or her to put in some perspective their feelings of inadequacy and guilt. Hopefully each spouse will be able to acquire a greater sense of separateness and wholeness as a person as a result of these crisis resolution efforts and achievements.

Practical Matters

Resolving practical issues becomes easier as the treatment succeeds in diminishing anger, building self-respect, and achieving mutuality of conviction about the inevitability and advisability of divorce. The spouses, if at this phase one can still call them that, can begin to cooperate better in deciding who is to move and who is to stay, how to divide possessions, what degree of financial self-sufficiency is possible for each, and who will need the support of the other. Decisions about custody of the children and visiting rights should also be easier.

When couples on their own are unable to resolve these issues and seek help for them, the worker's primary task is to elicit facts about what has been, what resources there are, and what the persons involved want to have happen. The information provided can suggest what the range of possibilities might be. While the acquisition of information may be difficult, due to enduring anger and reluctance, an even greater difficulty lies in achieving agreements about all of these matters that are fair to all concerned. Workers need to be as attentive to the possibility that one or another of the participants has been insufficiently assertive in stating expectations or making demands as to the possibility that the other has been overly demanding.

Some therapists have been reluctant to be involved in these matters and feel that their role should be limited to establishing a favorable climate for negotiation so that other mediators can help the couple achieve a settlement (Kressel and Deutsch, 1977). Kelly (1983) distinguishes between treatment and mediation by saying, "The role of the therapist is to encourage exploration of the meanings and levels of dysfunctional psychological reactions. In contrast, the role of the mediator is to manage and contain emotional expression so that the process of reaching a settlement can proceed" (p. 44). Chandler (1985) sees a similar distinction between mediation and social work helping processes. Workers who do not feel comfortable or who lack skills in negotiating practical aspects may profitably refer to mediators for such negotiation. Workers may be encouraged to acquire mediation skills, since they are so closely related to good treatment practices (see Barsky, 1984). It is helpful for therapists, even if they do not handle negotiations themselves, to encourage reasonableness, to suggest what might be equitable, and most of all to discourage vengeance.

Both therapists and mediators have contended that involvement of lawyers in divorce and custody disputes have often aggravated the difficulty of settlement by single-minded pursuit of individual advantage. They nevertheless affirm the validity and necessity of having lawyers review agreements achieved by counseling or mediation processes to assure that all possible consequences and aspects have been considered and that individual rights have been protected.

Sprenkle and Storm (1983) in a review of the reported research on divorce and custody mediation conclude that mediation and counseling are superior to adversarial approaches in resolving divorce-related issues such as custody of children (to be discussed below) and financial settlements. Agreements are more likely to hold and be less subject to later dispute and court action. Some of the variables related to the success of mediation and counseling are the level of intensity of the conflict, the number of issues involved, and the capacity for reasonableness of the disputants. These suggest that a combination of issue-focused mediation and psychologically focused treatment may both be necessary to successful resolution.

Reestablishing Phase

By this time in the course of events the active steps of dissolution of the marriage have occurred. New households have been established, and the financial picture is fairly clear. The families are settling into a new life and continuing the task of recovery. Reports vary about the length of time involved, but periods of one to five years are mentioned. The ex-spouses have the individual task of developing new lives for themselves and the joint task of co-parenting. We will address the first of these tasks here and defer discussion of the co-parenting tasks to the subsequent section on children.

The absence of rituals of induction into the divorced status has been frequently noted. Ceremonies to solemnize entry to marriage are deemed useful in assuring newlyweds of community consent and support. Such consent and support are markedly lacking for divorcing family members. Some couples, when both are convinced that divorce should occur, have made public announcement of the event in newspapers and even sponsored receptions to honor it. Lewis (1983) reports a variety of rituals that have been used, including religious ones to pronounce the end of a relationship and the commencement of a new life. While rituals may not be necessary or may not do the job, what does seem necessary in this day of dissolving marriages is the gaining of acceptance, support, encouragement, and direction for the new life ahead.

The emotional issues of the previous stages are still alive, though possibly less intense. Working through positive and negative feelings continues. Self-doubt and guilt, feelings of loss and rejection continue to surface but are put into perspective by increasing acceptance of self and more or less successful adaptation. Emotional release and cognitive restructuring facilitate this process. Coping with loneliness and the absence of another adult are added to the stress of this period.

Questions continue to arise about relationships with the ex-spouse and with one's own and the ex-spouse's family. Management of the children and the effects of the divorce on them are of ongoing concern. Movement to enter new relationships begins and with it new fears and doubts—fears that the new relationship will repeat the old, that rejection may be experienced anew, that unwanted demands may be made. People often feel as if they are adolescents again when it comes to forming new relationships. They have questions about their identity, handling themselves socially, the rules of the dating game, and handling sexual matters.

Development of skills in management of everything that one now has to do is another aspect of the overall adjustment task. Depending on the person and who did what in the marriage, the individual may lack skills in such things as food preparation, caring for the car, or getting/making minor repairs on the house. It is not only a matter of learning to get all these things accomplished, but also a matter of not being overwhelmed by them.

Mitchell-Flynn and Hutchinson (1993) found that, for men, different problems took priority over the space of a year. At first, finances, social relationships, and loneliness were primary concerns. A year after the separation, there was a significant decrease in concern about loneliness and about the reactions of friends and relatives. Garvin, Kalter, and Hansell (1993) found that divorced women experienced more stressful events than a normative comparison sample and had more psychiatric symptoms and poorer social adjustment. The strongest mediating factor in their difficulties was their social support system.

The tasks in this phase are individual ones, and if treatment is sought, it is usually provided on an individual rather than a conjoint basis. Several authors (Granvold and Welch, 1977; Shelton and Nix, 1979; Thiessen, Avery, and Joanning, 1980) report successful progress on divorce adjustment through group work. A series of five to seven sessions is offered. Each session begins with a didactic presentation on topics such as problems of communication with the ex-spouse, effects of divorce on children, handling finances, responding to curious family members or friends, unfulfilled sexual needs, effects of divorce on future relationships, and needed supports and social isolation. Group members then share experiences and insights, providing both cognitive grasp and emotional support and working through the various issues. These authors report that the groups have been well received and that members have shown improvement on measures of adjustment and self-esteem.

DIVERSITY IN DIVORCE

We have thus far made only passing reference to the relationships the partners of the dissolving marriage have with others in the kin network and how this may affect their decision making. In general the extent and makeup of the partners' support network changes over time. We have noted that initiators of the breakup do not necessarily have larger support networks. In some instances, kin take sides with the spouse, whom they see less at fault, rather than with their own family member.

The organization and views of the family in different ethnic and cultural groups also have an impact on the experience and decision making of the respective partners. Among Asian-Pacific families, where family commitments take priority over individual goals, divorce is seen as unacceptable. That suicide is frequently considered preferable to the shame of marital breakup (Ho, 1987) is an element of concern for therapists in the decision-making phase. Consideration of the possibility of divorce should come as a last resort. Efforts to connect persons at this stage to family members who might be supportive and to respected members of the cultural group need to be parts of the therapeutic effort. Reframing of the divorce process as necessary to end the indignities or to protect the children from the anxiety of the marital discord may also be useful.

While persons from other ethnic groups, especially Hispanics and African Americans, will have experienced a similar emphasis on family as over against individual goals, consideration of divorce may not seem as threatening. Nevertheless, an important aspect of treatment will include a review of the clients' awareness of how marital breakup and divorce are viewed in their culture. Connecting with kin and others in their network who can be supportive in this stressful phase will still be an important aspect of treatment.

CHILDREN IN THE DIVORCE PROCESS

As divorce is difficult for the spouses, it is also hard on the children. Their short-term and long-term adjustment is affected by the level of stress and by how their parents handle their relationship to each other and to the children. We have noted earlier that, though the marriage ends, the family does not. The parenting relationship continues, and if both parents wish to continue a relationship with the children, they must learn to work together in doing so. To the extent that they can do so the children's adjustment will be bettered. Noble (1983) cautions, however, that while parental cooperation enhances child adjustment, such cooperation may cause the child to wonder why they can't all live together again. It is not unknown for children to try to bring their parents back together, such as the child who insists that the former spouses hug and kiss when one of them picks up or returns the child to the other.

One of the first issues the parents must resolve is custody and domicile for the children. Unfortunately, in early stages of the dissolution, children can become objects for barter. "If you leave, I'll keep the children and you won't get to see them." Or, when anger is strong, "You are not a fit parent, and I will see that you don't get them." Children can get drawn into taking sides. They can also come to feel that they are the cause of their parents' problems with each other and that they are not really wanted.

In the past, custody of the children was usually acquired or assigned to one parent or the other. Most generally in recent times this has been the mother, though fathers are increasingly seeking it. Legal custody means that the parent to whom custody is assigned has all rights and responsibilities for the child (Bernstein, 1982) and that the noncustodial parent has none, except for the privilege of visitation and the responsibility of support or whatever else is granted by a custody agreement or court decree. Joint custody means that responsibility is shared and that contact between the parents over many issues (Bernstein lists 23 kinds of issues) will need to be frequent. Though it does not differ greatly in outward appearance from single-parent custody with extensive visitation rights for the other parent, it is increasingly sought and agreed to by both parents.

Custody disputes that are not resolved by the parents end with court investigations and decisions about which is the most fit parent. Charnas (1983) notes in this connection, "Although a child may have a qualitatively different relationship with his or her mother and father, it is absurd to posit that after a divorce the courts must change this by designating one parent as more psychologically valuable to the child than the other" (p. 548). Such decisions are often unsatisfactory to one of the parents and frequently result in reopening of the dispute at a later time. Mediation and custody counseling are beginning to show themselves as superior to such adversarial approaches. Joint custody and custody counseling are increasingly advocated. The general goal of custody counseling is to facilitate joint decision making and parental cooperation. Each parent must come to understand and accept the other's approach to the children and allow their separate relationships to flourish and grow. They must be able to negotiate responsibilities and decisions, such as medical care, vacations, and schooling. Since initial decisions come during the worst heat of the divorce process, it is evident that the progress they make in handling other emotional issues will bear upon their ability to cooperate in parenting. Custody counseling is a conjoint effort, and the children may be productively involved at times to allow expression of their observations, feelings, and wishes.

Stress and tensions for children in divorcing families manifest themselves in anxiety, depression, and conduct. Many factors affect their adjustment to the situation. A study by Lengua, Wolchick, and Braver (1995) identifies three groups of factors and looks at the contribution of each group on childrens' adjustment. The first set of factors, which they call the ontogenic system, are child variables: their age, sex, internal locus of control, and misconceptions about divorce. Did they cause it? The family will get together again. It is mom's fault. Group two factors are microsystem variables: quality of parent-child relationship, parental conflict, social support from nonparent adults, and so forth. Group three variables (exosystem) are place of residence, change in residence and school, financial hardship, and the residential parent's own adjustment. The three sets altogether and sets two and three separately accounted for significant amounts of variance in the child's self-report of adjustment, but not in parents' report of child adjustment.

Most reports of child adjustment have been of white, middle-class children. Wolchick, Ramirez, Bandler, Fisher, Organista, and Brown (1993), using a similar set of variables, studied the reaction of poor inner-city children to divorce. Their sample was 51 percent Hispanic, 17 percent African American, 25 percent Caucasian, and 5.7 percent American Indian. There were no significant differences between different ethnic groups. Children's adjustment was positively related to negative divorce events—for example, parents acting worried, missing visits, saying bad things about each other, hurting each other. One factor, fear of abandonment, also positively related to child adjustment. Beliefs involving maternal blame were marginally related. Not related were hope for reunification and paternal blame. Findings about divorce-related events—resident parent acting worried, nonresident parent missing a visit, parents arguing, saying bad things about each other—and beliefs about divorce replicate findings of previous studies of white, middle-class children.

Wallerstein (1985) has engaged in intensive study of the adaptations made by a clinical population of children of divorce. She groups them into several categories. The common feature is that they are all over-burdened with care and responsibility. Children in one group take complete responsibility for themselves and make minimal demands, a manner of role-taking that taxes them beyond their capacity. Another kind of child feels responsible for the parent and serves "as arbiter, pro-tector, advisor, parent, sibling, comrade in arms against the other parent or the world, confidante, lover or concubine" (p. 119). Children in a third group are overburdened by the continuing custody battle that rages around them. While some of the custody conflicts embody gen-uine concerns about adequate care for the child, others are more reflec-tive of the parent's intense need for the presence and companionship of the child.

Morawetz and Walker (1984) categorize the behaviors of parents that put children into those overburdened roles. They say that single (we are saying, divorced) parents create problems for their children when they see them as an embodiment of the absent parent, when they put the child in the role of spouse, when they see the child as an overwhelming burden, when guilt impedes their own functioning, and when the par-ent's reentry into the social scene is experienced as a return to adoles-cence. It is of obvious importance to help the parent with these issues if the child is to make a successful adjustment.

Bonkowski, Bequette, and Boomhower (1984) report that only 25 per-cent of the children of divorce as compared to as many as 90 percent of the parents receive professional help. Our impression is that many more children could benefit from professional help than actually receive it. Kalter (1984) reports that individual work with adolescent girls from divorced families resulted in frequent dropping out of treatment and that conjoint work with girls and their mothers promoted continuance. The conjoint sessions served to mediate mother-daughter conflicts and opened the way for the girls to address issues of separation, self-esteem, lovability, and femininity. Bonkowski describes a successful group ex-perience for six- to seven-year-old children. The group enabled the chil-dren to deal with changes in family structure, the causes of divorce, and their feelings about it. They could also talk about the predivorce family, the losses they experienced, and how they saw themselves in the fu-ture. Farmer and Galaris (1993) also report that support groups for chil-dren serve an important function in lessening the negative effects of divorce process on them.

These treatment group achievements address the tasks that Waller-stein says need to be accomplished by the children of divorce. Children need to acknowledge the reality of the marital rupture, to disengage from the parental conflict, to resume normal pursuits, to resolve their loss, anger, and self-blame, to accept the permanency of the divorce, and to achieve a realistic hope regarding future relationships and to become willing to take a chance on loving and closeness. In Wallerstein's view, children do have their own working through to do and should have the benefit of treatment. They tend to be referred for help not during the divorce process, but only when serious difficulties manifest themselves. Yet, help during the divorce process should be available and could be naturally and beneficially provided when their parents seek help by seeing them at times together with their parents and sometimes referring them to groups of children experiencing the same crisis in their lives.

SUMMARY

Family dissolution is an increasingly common phenomenon. Because it has been considered a deviant form in the family life cycle, there are no firm pathways for the participants to follow to guide and support them through it. But because it is so common, it is important to understand what happens and what is needed for all family members to survive the process and make postdissolution adjustment that is as successful as possible.

The time span between marital dissatisfaction and postdivorce adjustment may be seen in three phases. The predivorce phase focuses on the decision to continue or end the marriage. Treatment may begin with an effort to rescue the marriage and end in this phase with a decision to separate and divorce. A restructuring phase centers on the planning needed to reorganize the family, who is to move or to stay, where the children will go, what the financial situation will be, what each parent's relationship to the children will be like. A resettlement phase completes the work of resolving all the issues raised in the dissolution and the work of developing an ongoing lifestyle.

Divorce is a crisis for family members and engenders great emotional pain for them. Coping with the crisis is facilitated by enabling family members to handle their emotions and to achieve a cognitive grasp on what is needed to reorganize their lives. Personal and interpersonal issues must be dealt with through all phases of the crisis. Individual goals for the adults are to achieve a constructive dissolution of the marriage in as humane a way as possible and to enable them to regain their self-respect and confidence so that they can build their future lives as stronger and more capable persons. While ending the marriage constructively is necessary, it is also necessary, if there are children, to enable the ex-spouses to develop and continue a constructive co-parenting relationship because the family of parents and children continues to exist. Success in achieving a constructive divorce is crucial for the subsequent adjustment of the ex-spouses. Their ability to be constructive also enables better adjustment of the children.

Substantial numbers of divorcing spouses do seek treatment at some point during the divorce process. Children are brought to treatment less frequently during the divorce process, but from knowledge gained about children from divorcing families who have been brought to treatment, it is clear that the divorce has not been adequately handled in their adjustment. Individual treatment has in the past been seen as the treatment method of choice for the divorce process. We have taken the position that in the predivorce, decision-making phase and in the restructuring phase, conjoint family sessions can serve very usefully. In addition, particularly during the restructuring and resettlement phases, support groups for the adults and for the children have been shown to be helpful in facilitating change.

REFERENCES

Ahrons, C. 1980. "Redefining the Divorced Family: A Conceptual Framework." *Social Work* 25(6):437–41.

Ahrons, Constance, and Rodgers, Roy. 1987. *Divorced Families*. New York: W.W. Norton & Co.

Barsky, M. 1984. "Strategies and Techniques of Divorce Mediation." *Social Casework* 65(2):102–08.

Bernstein, B. 1982. "Understanding Joint Custody Issues." *Social Casework* 63(3):179–81.

Bonkowski, S., Bequette, S., and Boomhower, S. 1984. "A Group Design to Help Children Adjust to Parental Divorce." *Social Casework* 65(3):131–37.

Chandler, S.M. 1985. "Mediation: Conjoint Problem Solving." *Social Work* 30(4):346–49.

Charnas, J. 1983. "Joint Custody Counseling—Divorce 1980's Style." *Social Casework* 64(9):546–54.

Counts, R., and Sacks, A. 1985. "The Need for Crisis Intervention During Marital Separation." *Social Work* 30(2):146–50.

Elkin, M. 1977. "Post Divorce Counseling in Conciliation Court." *Journal of Divorce* 1(1):55–66.

Farmer, S., and Galaris, D. 1993. "Support Groups for Children of Divorce." *American Journal of Family Therapy* 21:40–50.

Garvin, V., Kalter, N., and Hansell, J. 1993. "Divorced Women: Individual Differences in Stressors, Mediating Factors, and Adjustment Outcome." *American Journal of Orthopsychiatry* 63(2):232–40.

Goldman, J., and Coane, J. 1983. "Separation and Divorce." In *Helping Families with Special Problems*, ed. M. Textor. New York: Jason Aronson.

Granvold, D., and Welch, G. 1977. "Intervention in Post Divorce Adjustment Problems: The Treatment Seminar." *Journal of Divorce* 1(1):81–92.

Ho, Man Keung. 1987. *Family Therapy with Ethnic Minorities.* Newbury Park, CA: Sage Publications.

Hunter, J., and Schuman, N. 1980. "Chronic Reconstitution as a Family Style." *Social Work* 25(6):446–51.

Kalter, N. 1984. "Conjoint Mother-Daughter Treatment: A Beginning Phase of Psychotherapy with Adolescent Daughters of Divorce." *American Journal of Orthopsychiatry* 54(3):490–97.

Kelly, J. 1983. "Mediation and Psychotherapy: Distinguishing the Differences." *Mediation Quarterly* 1(September):33–44.

Kessler, S. 1975. *The American Way of Divorce.* Chicago: Nelson-Hall.

Kincaid, Stephen, and Caldwell, Robert. 1995. "Marital Separation: Causes, Coping, and Consequences." *Journal of Divorce and Remarriage* 22(3):109–28.

Kitson, G., Moir, R., and Mason, P. 1982. "Family Social Support in Crisis: The Special Case of Divorce." *American Journal of Orthopsychiatry* 52(1): 161–65.

Kressel, K., and Deutsch, M. 1977. "Divorce Therapy: An In-Depth Survey of Therapists' Views." *Family Process* 16:413–43.

Kressel, K., Jaffee, N., Tuchman, B., Watson, C., and Deutsch, M. 1980. "A Typology of Divorcing Couples: Implications for Mediation and the Divorce Process." *Family Process* 19(2):101–16.

Lengua, Liliana, Wolchik, Sharlene, and Braver, Sanford. 1995. "Understanding Children's Divorce Adjustment from an Ecological Perspective." *Journal of Divorce and Remarriage* 22(3/4):25–47.

Levinger, G. 1965. "Marital Cohesiveness and Dissolution: An Integrative Review." *Journal of Marriage and the Family* 27(1):19–28.

———. 1966. "Sources of Marital Dissatisfaction Among Applicants for Divorce." *American Journal of Orthopsychiatry* 36(5):803–07.

Lewis, P.N. 1983. "Innovative Divorce Rituals: Their Psychosocial Function." *Journal of Divorce* 6(3):71–82.

Little, M. 1982. *Family Breakup.* San Francisco: Jossey-Bass.

Lyon, E., Silverman, M., Howe, G., Bishop, G., and Armstrong, B. 1985. "Stages of Divorce: Implications for Service Delivery." *Social Casework* 66(5):259–68.

Marek, Terry. 1989. "Separation and Divorce Therapy—A Struggle to Grow for Clients and Therapists." In *Treating Couples*, ed. Gerald R. Weeks. New York: Brunner/Mazel Publishers.

Mitchell-Flynn, C., and Hutchinson, R.L. 1993. "A Longitudinal Study of the Problems and Concerns of Divorced Men." *Journal of Divorce and Remarriage* 19(2):161–82.

Morawetz, A., and Walker, G. 1984. *Brief Therapy with Single Parent Families.* New York: Brunner/Mazel Publishers.

Noble, D. 1983. "Custody Contest: How to Divide and Reassemble a Child." *Social Casework* 64(7):406–13.

Rice, D. 1977. "Psychotherapeutic Treatment of Narcissistic Injury in Marital Separation and Divorce." *Journal of Divorce* 1(2):119–28.

Shelton, S., and Nix, C. 1979. "Development of a Divorce Adjustment Group Program in a Social Service Agency." *Social Casework* 60(5):309–12.

Spanier, G., and Thompson, L. 1984. *Parting: The Aftermath of Separation and Divorce.* Beverly Hills, CA: Sage Publications.

Sprenkle, D., and Cyrus, C. 1983. "Abandonment: The Stress of Sudden Divorce." In *Stress and the Family*, Vol. 2, eds. C. Figley and H. McCubbin. New York: Brunner/Mazel Publishers.

Sprenkle, D., and Storm, C. 1983. "Divorce Therapy Outcome Research: A Substantive and Methodological Review." *Journal of Marital and Family Therapy* 9(3):239–58.

Storm, C., and Sprenkle, D. 1982. "Individual Treatment in Divorce Therapy: A Critique of an Assumption." *Journal of Divorce* 6(1/2):87–98.

Thiessen, J., Avery, A., and Joanning, H. 1980. "Facilitating Post Divorce Adjustment Among Women: A Communication Skills Training Approach." *Journal of Divorce* 4(2):35–44.

Todorski, Jane. 1995. "Attachment and Divorce: A Therapeutic View." *Journal of Divorce and Remarriage* 22(3):189–204.

U.S. Bureau of the Census. 1993. Current Population Reports. Population Profile of the United States.

Wallerstein, J. 1983. "Children of Divorce: The Psychological Tasks of the Child." *American Journal of Orthopsychiatry* 53(2):230–43.

_____. 1985. "The Over-Burdened Child: Some Long Term Consequences of Divorce." *Social Work* 30(2):116–23.

Whitaker, C., and Keith, D. 1984. "Counseling the Dissolving Marriage." In *Counseling in Marital and Sexual Problems*, eds. R. Stahmann and W. Hiebert. Lexington, MA: Lexington Books.

Wolchick, S.A., Ramirez, R., Bandler, J.N., Fisher, J.J., Organista, P.B., and Brown, C. 1993. "Inner-city Poor Children of Divorce: Negative Divorce Related Events, Problematic Beliefs and Adjustment Problems." *Journal of Divorce and Remarriage* 19(2):1–20.

CHAPTER **16**

Problems and Adjustments of the Reconstituted Family

When considering the family created by the coming together of two people, one or both of whom have experienced a previous marriage or cohabitation with a partner, the first concern is what to call the new family. Since these families are made up of individuals from various lifestyles and experiences, we have chosen a definition with sufficient breadth to include people from all walks of life. We believe the reconstituted family is an appropriate definition for families formed under these conditions. Therefore, throughout our discussion we shall refer to this union of individuals as the reconstituted family. We also realize there are other definitions applicable to this group—for example, blended family, stepfamily, remarried family, and recoupled family—and our choice in no way denies the appropriateness of different definitions used by other authors. While our discussion may not always reference all the different types of reconstituted families specifically, we wish to point up the fact that the skills, techniques, and processes we discuss are generally applicable to a wide range of different families, including the nontraditional family constellation consisting of a union of two adults of the same sex. This family composition is becoming more prevalent in contemporary society, yet it continues to struggle for acceptance of the right to serve as parents. We believe the suffering of all families deserves the full attention of professional helpers, and this will be reflected in our discussions. We will also refer to all relationships involving cohabitation by adults as unions instead of identifying their existence by legal definition.

When two people, one or both of whom have experienced a previous union with other partners, join to form a new family, it sets into motion a system that is structurally and psychologically different from the intact nuclear family that normally results from the first union. This suggests to social workers and to other professionals encountering this type family the necessity of viewing the structure and functioning of this unit in a different way than they view the family generated by the initial union. Many aspects of this new family will have a beginning that is different from the nuclear family of the first union and will likewise present a different set of problems. However, understanding the structure of this new family and the manner in which it develops and functions as it struggles to reach a cohesive existence is most important (Smith, 1991). We agree with Kent (1980) that all families, regardless of how they are constituted, operate as a system and the best understanding of the structure and functioning of reconstituted families is reached by the application of a family systems approach when considering the adjustment problems of this group.

In keeping with this position, the remainder of the chapter will present the reconstituted family from a family systems perspective, with consideration given to various family patterns, the problems family members are likely to experience, and the adjustments necessary for appropriate functioning in contemporary society.

FAMILY COMPOSITION

The complexity of the reconstituted family is reflected in the many different compositions resulting from the joining of individuals who bring to the new family various preestablished and continuing nuclear and extended family relationships. To consider a few patterns of the reconstituted family organization, there are divorced men and women who have children from previous marriages, all of whom live together in a single household; divorced men without children married to women with children; women without children or previous marriage married to men with children; men without previous marriages and divorced women with children from the previous marriage; reconstituted families composed of widows and widowers, both with children, who live together part or all of the time; same-sex couples who have experienced previous unions; and, finally, divorced parents with children from previous marriages and children from the present marriage.

While all reconstituted families go through varying periods of adjustments, a number of situations can be anticipated. For example, the household with children from previous unions will most likely have to struggle with sibling jealousies centering around attention from the biological parent, resistance to the authority of the new parent, and turf battles over sharing space and possessions. In the case of the woman without children or a previous union who joins with a divorced man with children, the lack of experience in being a mother may well be a handicap, as she does not know what to expect from children—who are likely to react in a hostile manner to what is perceived as her intrusion into their lives. Visher and Visher (1979) found that a similar handicap also existed with men who entered a reconstituted family situation without parenting experience. Children who spend time with both a stepparent and a divorced biological parent might experience some difficulty with a perception of divided loyalty, or, in most cases, struggle with feelings of resentment toward the stepparent, especially in the early phase of reconstituted family development.

IMPACT OF PAST EXPERIENCES

Reconstituted families are created out of a past union experience. Many of these experiences have been unhappy due to incompatibilities between partners, which have ended in dissolution of the partnerships, and other unhappy experiences have come as the result of losing a mate by death. In any case, a reconstituted family begins under the weight of what might be described as "a long cast of characters." This is to say that a number of people are likely to be involved. Both partners may bring positive or negative relationships from a previous union as well as friendships developed in different contexts over time. Children from previous unions bring to the new family current relationships with grandparents, aunts, uncles, cousins, and other acquaintances (Hobart, 1990). Stuart and Jacobson (1985) refer to beginning a reconstituted family under these conditions as not joining just a mate, but joining a family, and this can put a strain on new relationships. This is especially so as there are new sets of grandparents, in-laws, and other relatives with whom to interact, which increases the possibility of conflict around divided loyalties, jealousies, and inappropriate expectations. For example, the biological grandparents may think they have first call on the grandchildren's attention and behave in such a way as to discourage the development of an amicable relationship with the stepparent or stepgrandparents. On the other hand, the new "step-relatives" may embrace the new family and expect its members to become a part of their network. This places the children in the uncomfortable position of being expected to maintain loyalty to established relationships while, at the same time, entering freely into new relationships with "step-relatives."

Children are not the only ones affected by previously established relationships. In cases where members of the family of origin enjoyed good relationships with the former spouse, the new spouse may find acceptance difficult. Instead of being accepted by reason of position in the family, by becoming the partner of a family member, the new partner may be required to earn his or her way into the family, and comparison with the former partner is likely to make this a very difficult process. Past experiences may also contribute to the reconstituted family in positive ways. If both partners have parenting experience, they will enter this new situation with knowledge of what it is like to be a parent as well as some understanding of the behavior of children and the strategies they use to gain attention and protect themselves against the hurt of rejection. This should be useful in negotiating some of the conflicts they are likely to encounter.

MYTHS AND OTHER EXPECTATIONS

Perhaps the most prevalent myth associated with the reconstituted family is the "wicked stepmother." The belief that stepmothers do not function in the best interest of stepchildren is exemplified in the case of the biological parent who always manages to find a way to interrupt all efforts on the part of the stepmother to discipline the children or have sustained meaningful interaction with them. In this case, the belief regarding the "wicked stepmother" has been internalized and will likely remain as part of the couple's interaction until change in the biological parent's belief system is effected. However, it should be noted that most stepmothers do not fit the wicked and cruel model that has been perpetuated nor do they experience serious problems in relating to stepchildren. If the stepmother has sufficient ego strengths and is supported by her mate, a wholesome and satisfying stepmother-stepchild relationship can develop (Schulman, 1972).

Another common myth about reconstituted families is that of "instant love" (Wald, 1981). This is predicated on the belief that stepparents are no different from natural parents and, therefore, feel no differently toward stepchildren than they do toward their own natural children. In other words, when one takes on the role of stepparent, he or she is expected to feel instant love for children with whom there is no shared history or bonding experience, and, in return, these children will show love and admiration for the new stepparent. This is certainly a myth because it implies an instant relationship between people who are for the most part strangers. Relationships between them will require time to build and grow. To expect anything different from people who suddenly find themselves living together as the result of a union by two adults is to invite feelings of insecurity, disappointment, and anger (Visher and Visher, 1982). It is well to remember that building new relationships between stepchildren and stepparents will involve adjusting to new rules and new roles as well as adjusting to each other over time. And this process is usually made easier if the stepparent can refrain from forcing himself or herself on the children. Stepchildren must be given the opportunity and time to test out the new situation and move closer to the stepparent at their own pace.

In contrast to the myth of instant love, some stepchildren hold a belief that "step is less" (Wald, 1981). This means that the stepchild cannot be loved in the same way as a natural child can and the child cannot love the stepparent as he or she loves the natural parent. As in the case of all myths, these allegations about the reconstituted family are unverifiable and should not be taken as a logical starting point from which to view this new family. In addition to the unverifiability of myths, to hold on to these beliefs denies the presence of individual strengths and the fact that positive relationships can be developed within the structure of the reconstituted family.

RECONSTITUTED FAMILY STRUCTURE

The organization of the reconstituted family can be best understood when viewed as a social system in the same manner as the nuclear family. It operates from a set of functional demands that determine and guide the interaction of its members. It adheres to a power hierarchy that gives different levels of authority to parents and children. It is composed of subsystems and protected by boundaries, and it passes through stages of development, all of which is common to the nuclear family formed by the initial joining of two adults for the purpose of creating a family. However, the reconstituted family frequently encounters difficulty in its development because of a number of circumstances peculiar to its origin. Among the things that interfere with the various developmental tasks is the composition or makeup of the family, which brings together individuals with different lifestyles, different values, and different world views (Hobart, 1989). In spite of the prevalence of reconstituted families in society, we have not established a clear set of guidelines that can be applied to this family. This handicaps not only family members, but also practitioners who seek to help this group negotiate developmental tasks. If we are to be successful in this undertaking we must be informed of the makeup of the subsystems and something of the history of those who participate in them.

COUPLE SUBSYSTEM

As architects of the reconstituted family, the couple subsystem carries major responsibility for family development. As mentioned earlier, these two people may come together from a variety of statuses to form the new family. For example, the union may bring together two people who are divorced from previous marriages; one divorced and the other single; one widowed and one divorced; both widowed; one widowed and the other single; or a couple of the same sex who have ended their previous relationships. This is important information for practitioners, as it provides a history and some notion of where knowledge and common experiences may or may not exit.

To these unions, each partner may bring children, only one partner may bring children, or neither may bring children. In some cases, children may become permanent members of the stepfamily or divide time between the stepfamily and the natural parent. This is also useful information for the practitioners, as both partners must accommodate each other and differentiate the couple subsystem by developing clear boundaries. These tasks may become more difficult when children from previous unions are brought into the family. The presence of these children may stress the functioning of the couple subsystem, which exists primarily as a workplace for the couple in negotiating a complementary relationship. Under normal conditions of beginning a nuclear family, children would not be present, and the boundary of the couple subsystem would allow the couple an opportunity to focus on their own interest as it pertains to sharing space, developing mutuality, and establishing individuality within this new relationship. The presence of children from the beginning limits the time the couple can spend together in defining what their relationship will be, as some time must be spent involving the children within the context of the parent/child subsystem. Further, complication is likely in the relations of the stepchild and stepparent around a number of experiences. For example, if both parents bring children from previous unions, there is the potential for a "we/they" complex, with children vying for the attention of their biological parent to the exclusion of the stepparent and his or her children. There is also the problem of how much and in what ways the demands of children affect the perception both parents have of each other. If one parent perceives the other as caring more for his or her natural children at the expense of neglecting the stepchildren, this will create tension within the couple subsystem, which will interfere with the normal processes of this subsystem. As a result, each parent may not only be drawn closer to his or her natural children but see the other parent as disliking the stepchildren. And, out of a need to protect his or her own, a parent will allow the children to invade freely the boundaries of the couple subsystem, thereby preventing the development of an appropriate (permeable) boundary that controls the children's access to this subsystem.

In cases where only one parent brings children to the reconstituted family a satisfactory adjustment may well depend on the experience of the other parent in child-rearing and the expectations these parents have of each other and the children. This understanding can be quite helpful in negotiating with the child in relation to developing trust and gradually giving up some of the closeness to the natural parent and moving into a relationship with the stepparent. This is not to say parents with child-rearing experience are always successful in effecting an adjustment in a reconstituted family situation with children. If the experience causes the parent to assume expert status in dealing with children, leaving no room for error, the stepparent will likely behave in such a way as to demand too much from herself or himself and, in turn, expect too much from the child. In this case, the stepparent must be helped to reassess his or her role and allow the child to remain closer to the natural parent while gradually developing trust and comfort in relating to the stepparent.

The stepparent who has no experience in parenting may find the stepparent role very frustrating. The lack of knowledge of how to proceed in fulfilling a role already established with the child, who is likely to resent an outsider attempting to take the place of the natural parent, can reinforce feelings of inadequacy and cause the stepparent to withdraw or, in some cases, react negatively, toward the child. Such experiences often create tension within the couple subsystem. The natural parent is not likely to understand or accept the stepparent's negative reaction, while failure in relating to the child causes the stepparent to feel inadequate and in need of support from his or her partner. However, to ask the natural parent for help would further damage the stepparent's self-esteem, and if support is not volunteered, he or she usually chooses to remain silent and resentful of the other's failure to come to the rescue. In this situation, priority should be given to work on improving communication between the parents and helping the stepparent to a better understanding of the parenting role.

PARENTAL SUBSYSTEM

This subsystem is composed of the same two people as the couple subsystem. However, it is child-focused and requires the parent to reach a delicate balance between exercising control and promoting independence among family members. When compared to the parental subsystem of the nuclear family, this subsystem in the reconstituted family clearly deals with some of the same problems, but also deals with a set of problems quite different from those experienced in the initial family.

In the first place, the parents in this new family do not have the opportunity to experience the couple subsystem role and effect a beginning adjustment to each other. Instead, they are faced with the necessity of moving into the couple and parental subsystem roles at the same time. This is to say that at the same time the couple is undertaking an initial adjustment to each other they must also be concerned with responding to the demands of a sibling subsystem composed of individuals without kinship ties or shared experiences. As a result, the parental subsystem is likely to be stressed in carrying out executive responsibility for the reconstituted family.

Among the areas of stress are the likely violations of boundary structures. For example, children should experience freedom in moving back and forth across the boundaries of a parental subsystem to receive guidance in developing a self and assimilating into the wider society. However, in the case of reconstituted families, care must be taken to prevent children from seeking and receiving unilateral guidance from the natural parent (except perhaps in cases where unalterable dislike exists between stepparent and stepchildren). In any case, unilateral guidance by the natural parent tends to divide family authority and create tension within the parental subsystem. And with increased tension, boundaries between natural parent and child may become blurred and lead to involvement of the child not only in the functioning of the parental subsystem but in problems of the couple subsystem as well. Such involvement may seriously interfere with the carrying out of appropriate parental subsystem tasks.

Adolescence is a time at which balancing control and promoting autonomy is perhaps most difficult for parents of the reconstituted family. This is the point at which parents' demands are likely to be in conflict with the children's desire for age-appropriate autonomy (Minuchin, 1974). Parental demands in the reconstituted family are not always the results of consensus between the parents. In many cases the marital pair have not discussed their likeness or difference with regard to what represents appropriate behavior or responsibility for the children. Nevertheless, failure to communicate does not mean an absence of firm conviction on the part of each parent about how children should behave and how much autonomy they should be given. In the absence of agreement about what will be expected of the children different messages are likely to be given that will reflect the past experiences of each parent. For example, a parent from a family that tended toward enmeshment would likely be reluctant to allow children to move freely outside family boundaries, which would increase opportunities for developing autonomy. In contrast, the parent from a family that tends to be disengaged would not be comfortable with close family ties, but interested in the development of independence. These opposite views signal the need for increased communication within the parental subsystem, and change efforts should be directed toward open discussion of parenting issues and mutual accommodation between parents on the matters of child-rearing, and between parents and children with regard to effecting a healthy balance between autonomy and control.

SIBLING SUBSYSTEM

In this subsystem within the natural family, children are customarily afforded their own turf and the opportunity to develop and experiment with behaviors in learning to relate to peers and adults in the larger contexts of the family and society. This subgroup is normally composed of individuals with kinship ties who share common parentage, rules, and values. The sibling subsystem in the reconstituted family may exist in many forms. Children from one union may be joined by children from another union, only the children of one parent may be included in the subsystem, or the children from the new marriage may be born into the family and join children from previous unions of one or both parents. In each case a complex group is brought into existence, and a crisis may be precipitated by the failure of old roles and old boundaries, defined within the context of a previous family structure.

If the reconstituted family assumes residence in the home of a parent with children from a previous union, these children may perceive the children of the other parent as intruders into their territory and react by attempting to exclude these new members. From a systems perspective, rejecting the new members is their way of safeguarding the boundaries of the old subsystem by closure—which will control the input of new energy from the new group. If this new energy is allowed to enter the system, it may threaten the existence of the old subsystem in which the previous occupants have found comfort and wish to preserve.

Sibling rivalry, common to all sibling subsystems, is likely to be more stressful in the reconstituted family as members seek changes in coalitions and alliances generated by losses experienced in the breakup of the nuclear family. Jealousies may be acted out in rather destructive ways as children attempt to hold on to natural parents and reject stepparents and siblings. For example, children with a natural parent living elsewhere may attempt to move back and forth between this parent and the reconstituted family whenever they choose not to abide by the rules established in either household.

The development of the sibling subsystem in the reconstituted family is not always characterized by continuing conflict. If the parents of this family have sufficiently resolved their own adjustment problems and are able to pursue relaxed relationships with the children, their behavior will serve as a role model for the children and help them join together and develop a sibling subsystem that will promote the growth and development of its members. However, when intervention is necessary, attention must be given to what the children bring to this new subgroup experience from past associations. Losses and expectations should be dealt with and assurance offered, where possible, that further losses are not likely to occur as a result of developing new relationships with stepsiblings, and old relationships that are important to children need not be abandoned.

PARENT/CHILD SUBSYSTEM

This subsystem is characterized by interaction between parents and children. Clarity of boundaries and lines of authority is an important factor in the successful functioning of this subsystem. In the nuclear family, the parents have shared with each other in a relationship before children are born or adopted into the family. And all children in this case belong to the couple, forming a nuclear family that customarily lives together until the children reach the appropriate age for separation. This is not the case with the reconstituted family. At least one parent has shared a relationship with the children, who are now a part of the new family, before joining the other partner in this union. In many instances both parents have experienced ties with some of the children, but not with others, prior to joining and forming the new family.

For these reasons the stepparent begins at a different point than the natural parent in interacting with children. The parent who brings children to the reconstituted family has close ties with this part of the sibling subsystem but must begin to establish new relationships with everyone else. Such an entry into the family system may cause an imbalance in relationships. One of the difficulties in building relationships is that stepparents are often cautious in attempting to establish a relationship with stepchildren out of concern for how they are perceived in this role by these children as well as by other members of the family. At the same time, the parent/child relationship from the previous union is in place, and the interaction within this relationship is likely to be viewed by others as closing the boundary around this part of the subsystem and denying entry to others. As a result, tension increases and family homeostasis may be disrupted until an understanding is reached regarding new roles and new ways of relating among family members.

The perception of the parenting role by stepparents and stepchildren is an important factor in determining how they will interact in forming a viable family relationship. Some adults who enter into a new union after the breakup of a previous one expect too much of themselves and other family members. For example, many stepparents try too hard to be exceptionally good parents in order to please their mates and expect in return to gain love and respect from the children. Yet, stepchildren are likely to be hesitant in responding to the overzealous efforts of these "superparents" who want to receive instant love from them and immediately enjoy a happy family. Stepparents must learn to relax and allow positive interaction with stepchildren to occur gradually. Immediate acceptance of a stepparent is difficult for stepchildren who are likely to be grieving the loss of the natural parent. In most cases of children of divorced parents, accepting a stepparent is further complicated by the fact that there is an ongoing relationship with the natural divorced parent. And the thought of replacing this parent with another creates feelings of guilt and disloyalty. In the case of deceased parents, many children experience similar feelings, especially in the early stages of the stepparent relationship, as interacting with the stepparent is likely to rekindle painful feelings of this previous loss.

Another problem in the parent/child relationship in reconstituted families may be brought on by the stepparent's immediately attempting to assume the authority formerly held by the absent natural parent relative to family rules and discipline. In most cases this not only causes anger and rebellion among the children, but also creates tension between the parents. If the stepparent continues to carry the instant authority role, the natural parent and his or her children will likely be drawn together against the stepparent, and professional help is usually needed if the family is to become a viable unit. Change efforts should be directed toward the natural parent's taking a more active role in setting rules, disciplining the children, and sharing his or her thoughts and wishes about parenting with the stepparent. At the same time the stepparent should be helped to accept a lesser role in parenting until appropriate rules governing family conduct are established and the role of the hierarchical structure is agreed upon.

TASKS AND ISSUES IN RECONSTITUTED FAMILY DEVELOPMENT

The tasks and issues facing the reconstituted family are slightly different from those faced by the natural family as it proceeds toward realization of basic goals. Visher and Visher (1982, p. 343) point up the need for the new family to address previous losses, develop new traditions, preserve important old alliances and form new ones, achieve integration within the current family unit, and deal with such issues as financial power and sexual boundaries.

Recognizing Losses

Members of a reconstituted family have experienced a number of losses that may prove devastating in establishing the new family if they are not recognized and dealt with by each individual. The partner who has experienced a previous union and has lost a mate experiences a sense of loss. In the case of divorce, regardless of how unsatisfactory the relationship may have been, there is a sense of loss over failure to have made the marriage the success that was envisioned at the beginning, and the personal investment in trying to make it succeed cannot be recovered. There are always feelings of sadness and loss associated with the death of a mate; the good times spent together and many old friends that were a part of that experience will not continue to be a part of the new life being fashioned. As for the children, the death of a parent is one of the most painful losses possible. And disruption of the parent/child relationship by divorce is also a serious loss, together with the disappearance of familiar surroundings such as friends and extended family members who may no longer be readily available due to relocation to the reconstituted family.

These losses contribute to feelings of sadness and anger that may be displaced in the reconstituted family relationships. In this case, help is usually needed to assist family members in sorting out feelings, identifying sources of sadness and anger, and looking at the new family as an opportunity to develop and share meaningful relationships, without being disloyal to friends and relatives or desecrating pleasant memories from previous experiences.

Establishing New Traditions

Reconstituted families may come together from very different places, bringing values, goals, and traditions established through previous experiences. Although reconstituted family members may have been served well by these structures in the past, it is highly unlikely that they will work effectively to bind the new family together. It is well to remember that family relationships are built around shared experiences, and reconstituted families have usually had few, if any, shared experiences. Therefore, it is necessary for family members to establish new goals and traditions through engaging in activities of interest to the new family and deciding together what the family likes and values and how it will go about realizing desired objectives.

Forming Alliances

We agree with those who suggest a relaxed and gradual formation of alliances in the reconstituted family. Forming a new family from members who bring experience and traditions from a previous nuclear family always reactivates old memories and often introduces conflict. Efforts to expedite this process by exerting pressure on family members, including showing excessive amounts of affection or increasing interaction within the family at the expense of eliminating contacts with friends and relatives outside of the new family, will most likely fail. It is appropriate for the parents to spend time together without interference from real or imagined demands of the family. Stepparents also need to spend some time with stepchildren. This should be done without the natural parent being present; however, care must be taken to keep this time between step-members of the family casual and of short duration in the early stage of family development (Visher and Visher, 1982). A useful strategy might begin by complimenting the child on something he or she likes to do such as coloring pictures or working with building blocks and later participating briefly in this activity with the child whenever the opportunity is presented.

It is very important while developing new alliances to allow reconstituted family members to continue important old alliances established through previous associations. For example, children should be expected to continue communication with grandparents with whom they share close relationships and with friends whose company they enjoy. Stepparents should also continue to be in touch with relatives and friends whose associations they value. By continuing important old alliances, the pressure to become totally engaged in the immediate development of a new family is lessened. And with this lessening of pressure to become completely involved in the processes of the reconstituted family, both stepparents and stepchildren can gradually move toward getting to know each other, which sets the stage for development of a viable reconstituted family. When there is total commitment to "instant success" in becoming a new family, the members experience tremendous pressure to interact positively, and this often leads to anger, frustration, and failure.

Integration

Integration within the reconstituted family is an important task that is facilitated by knowing what to expect. The primary responsibility for achieving integration rests with the parents, who must create conditions conducive to family organization. Since the parents are the architects of the family, they must clarify what is expected and reach consensus on important rules before attempting to involve the children in forming a new family. The relationship of the new couple will need to be strengthened, and new relationships must be developed between parents and children. This will enhance the development of a sense of membership in the new family (Visher and Visher, 1990). This is supported as well by Duncan and Brown (1992) who also posit a necessary family connection with supportive institutions in the community. This agreement between the parents should help with involvement of the children and provide some support for the stepparent in dealing with them around the issues of roles and expectations.

In addition to arriving at an understanding between the parents, integrating the reconstituted family requires nurturing children and setting limits that will allow them to continue appropriate development while the parents remain in control. This is not an easy task for the natural family and a very difficult one for a new family. Stepparents inherit a family already in existence, where controls are needed, without having carried out the nurturing elements of child-rearing of the stepchildren. As a result, these children are without the experience of having received, at an earlier age, the "giving" aspects of a relationship with the stepparent but are now faced with accepting the limits this stepparent imposes. This is tantamount to having missed the initial phase of the parent/child relationship in which a basis is established for the child's wish to please the parent. Therefore, stepchildren are likely to resent limits imposed by the stepparent, and this will complicate integration of the family.

Time is also a factor in achieving integration, as members of the reconstituted family must get to know each other before the trusting and sharing needed for the family to function as a cohesive unit can develop. A time period of up to two years is sometimes required before a satisfactory state of integration is reached. And stepparents should not become discouraged by the gradual pace at which relationships are developed.

Complex Issues

The development of the reconstituted family involves a number of roles, tasks, and issues related to family relationships that preceded the start of this new family. It begins with the coming together of the couple, at least one of whom has experienced this process before. In many cases, both have experienced it previously. One of the most important considerations for those repeating the process is how well they have resolved issues relating to their experience in the previous family. It is not uncommon for individuals to enter a reconstituted family with very strong positive or negative feelings about his or her former mate, which may be reflected in a number of ways. Feelings of guilt over the breakup of a relationship may interfere with the sharing of one's self with the other or cause one to invest too much in trying to make up for past mistakes by becoming "the perfect partner." In some situations, unresolved positive feelings may surface as divided loyalty between past and present mates. On the other hand, unresolved negative feelings may contribute to distrust in relating to the new mate or an overinvestment in trying to make life difficult for the former partner.

Visher and Visher (1982) speak of the exaggeration of power issues in reconstituted families. For example, if the wife is divorced and successfully carried family responsibility as a single parent prior to joining the family, she may enter the new family with confidence in her capability to provide for herself and her children. This self-sufficiency represents power and control of her own life, and sharing these through a union with someone new may threaten a return to an unsatisfying pattern of dependency. Divorced men who remarry after experiencing difficult financial settlements with previous mates may feel they have unjustly lost their power and control and become vulnerable to future attacks on their finances, ergo their power. In such cases they may be unwilling to share information about finances with the new mate or live in a miserly fashion in order to prevent further erosion of their power and control.

Sager and associates (1983) suggest that in-laws and former in-laws sometimes have strong influence on the reconstituted family system. If in-laws have played a major role in the life of a partner, especially between the breakup of the previous relationship and uniting with a new partner, during which time the support and assistance they gave was crucial, they may find themselves seeking a decision-making role in helping to establish the new family. This is likely to prove disruptive to forming appropriate relationships in the new family system. Former in-laws who enjoy good relationships with their grandchildren may have difficulty accepting the replacement of their son or daughter by someone else who will assume the role of parent.

When children from previous families are brought into the reconstituted family, there is a parent/child relationship that precedes the relationship of the new parents. This prior parent/child attachment is likely to create an emotional imbalance in family relationships, with the child favoring the natural parent while having only minimal contact with the stepparent. In many cases, children brought into the reconstituted family also cling to the hope that their natural parents will reunite and reestablish the nuclear family, thereby making it unnecessary for them to adjust to the stepparent. The need to balance old ties with children and new ties with the new partner is one of the most important issues with which stepparents must deal (Wald, 1981).

Unlike the family situation where the couple has time to accommodate to each other before turning their attention to the needs of children, the presence of children in the reconstituted family makes it necessary for the parents to assume both couple and parental roles simultaneously. This makes it more difficult to accomplish marital tasks, as it limits the time, privacy, and energy available to stepparents (Wald, 1981).

In all families, boundaries play a significant role in family development and family homeostasis. In reconstituted families, issues around boundaries take on a special significance due to the unique structure of these families. Boundary violations may occur at many levels, as indicated earlier in our discussion of subsystems. Children may violate the boundary around the couple subsystem as a result of the previous close association with the natural parent and the lack of experience in relating to the stepparent. This makes it easy for children to turn to natural parents for support and guidance in the same manner as before the new family was established. If the natural parent is ambivalent about the stepparent's relations with his or her children, a closer relationship is likely to be encouraged by the natural parent's own reactions to this situation. Repeated transactions between these principals while excluding the stepparent will interfere with the performance of normal couple tasks and represent a violation of the boundary that should limit the children's access to the private domain of the parents.

A blurring of boundaries may also occur when children share the homes of both the reconstituted family and the other natural parent. This often centers around arrangements for the children visiting and spending time in both households. Each household must recognize and respect the boundary of the other, thus allowing for a clear separation of the households, with each unit free to exercise control over what takes place within its domain (Visher and Visher, 1982). In this way, boundaries remain clear and children are able to function within the boundaries established by each household.

Another problem facing practitioners who work with reconstituted families is the issues of sexual boundaries. Sager and associates describe a loosening of sexual boundaries in the new family that is related to "the heightened affectionate and sexual atmosphere in the home during the new couple's early romantic bonding period" (1983, p. 293). The inclusion of teenagers of the opposite sex in the new family tends to intensify the sexual climate. This, together with the fact that members of reconstituted families have not shared close emotional ties and are without biological ties, makes possible a complete breakdown of sexual boundaries. The extremes of a breakdown of sexual boundaries may be reflected in sexual relations between stepsiblings and sexual abuse, usually between stepfathers and stepdaughters. If this point is reached, someone in the reconstituted family is likely to ask for help, as the members of this family are less likely to reinforce a breakdown in sexual boundaries through the conspiracy of silence and unconscious collusion often found in natural families (Wald, 1981).

One of the mistakes frequently made is to assume there is no difference in family functioning between the reconstituted family and the natural family. This occurs largely out of a lack of knowledge about the complexity of this family, its structure, and its functions in carrying out various tasks. The confusion begins with the variety of names used to identify this family unit, which we have chosen to refer to as the reconstituted family. Neither society, by tradition, nor research efforts have as yet developed a widely accepted set of norms for this family. Many myths, some of which we discussed earlier in this chapter, still exist relative to what should be expected from the members of a family that begins without biological ties. Nevertheless, research and experience in working with this type family have provided some information regarding the processes in which it engages that should be recognized by family members and social workers engaged in helping with family adjustments.

The couple who joins to establish a reconstituted family should realize that adjustment among all family members will not automatically occur as a result of bringing family members together. Adolescent children are likely to be resentful of the stepparent and openly demonstrate preference for the natural parent. Efforts to force the development of relationships between step-members of the family will result in frustrations and defeat. In most situations, children will be relating to at least the biological parent outside of the reconstituted family, and in many cases extended natural family members as well. This does not mean a problem will develop; however, the potential for family boundary disputes and conflicting loyalties is always present in these interactional processes.

When both parents bring children into the reconstituted family, they should be aware that a difference in feeling toward biological children and stepchildren may exist and that a display of this difference in affection might create tension throughout the family. Disciplining children is another potential area of tension, and unless there has been prior discussion and agreement on how authority will be used in this respect, problems are likely to develop.

Disagreement over the use of money is not uncommon in the reconstituted family, where alimony and/or child support payments are likely experiences. In many instances new couples have never discussed such expenditures, and in such cases misunderstanding regarding old and new responsibilities may occur. And finally, as previously indicated, it must be recognized by everyone involved in dealing with reconstituted family processes that good family relationships are not an instant accomplishment and must be given an opportunity to develop over time.

SUCCESSFUL RECONSTITUTED FAMILY FUNCTIONING

In spite of the difficulty under which this family begins, not all of them struggle for identity and adjustment in relationships throughout the family life cycle. Some families are able to develop sound relationships between family members early in the new family's existence. There are a number of conditions that contribute to successful development of reconstituted family structure and functioning. For example, the ages of children who are brought into the family may have impact on the stepparent/stepchild relationship as well as on the functioning of the sibling subsystem. The younger child usually has less difficulty in forming intrafamilial relationships in the new family than the adolescent, who is more likely to have a stronger attachment to the biological family by reason of a longer association and a deeper appreciation of the fabric of this family and his or her role in it. Another factor is the individual life cycle of the adolescent. This stage of development is characterized by the adolescent's struggle with issues to identify and the desire for independence, which are demonstrated by rebellion against authority and disagreement with measures of control. The preferred posture of the adolescent is freedom and autonomy rather than forming a new attachment to a stepparent with whom, in most cases, he or she is totally unfamiliar. This would involve not only giving up freedom, but also being placed in the position of being controlled by an unfamiliar adult who is taking the place of the natural parent. This usually contributes to the difficulty in establishing relationships that is experienced in many reconstituted families. When the stepchildren are adults who do not occupy the reconstituted family household, the possibility of establishing acceptable working relationships is usually good.

Parenting experience by the new couple is useful in developing the family in cases where children from previous families are involved.

Parents with experience in dealing with children bring to the new family some knowledge of what to expect from children and how to relate to them in a number of circumstances. While this does not guarantee instant adjustment, it adds a positive dimension to the process.

Good Relationship Between Partners

As architects of the family, the couple must maintain a good relationship if they are to guide the development of the family successfully. This takes on added importance in the reconstituted family, where bonding between the couple is more difficult to achieve than in the case of the natural family. In order to achieve and maintain a good relationship, the new couple must be able to communicate with clear messages that spell out their wishes, expectations, joys, and fears as related to their lives together and the establishment of the new family. There must be agreement on matters pertaining to family functioning and their roles in this process. They will also need to support each other in the performance of their respective parental roles. A good relationship between the parents, together with mutual support and cooperation, are among the necessary ingredients for successful family functioning.

Relaxed Atmosphere for Children

Children from previous marriages who enter the reconstituted family often resist establishing relationships, especially with stepparents. A major factor in this resistance is their attachment to biological family networks and the difficulty they experience in relating to a reconstituted family network at the same time. The greatest conflict is experienced in relating simultaneously to biological and stepparents. This problem can usually be overcome if the stepparent does not insist on instant positive relations with the child and allows the relationship to develop gradually. It is also important that children be given the opportunity to continue relating to both natural parents. In this kind of relaxed atmosphere children usually learn to respond positively in reconstituted relationships, which enhances the functioning of the family.

Mature Relationship Between All Parental Figures

Much of the difficulty experienced in reconstituted family functioning can be ameliorated if a mature relationship exists between the parental adults. Such a relationship requires abandoning attempts to both avenge previous wrongs and to compete for the affection of children. For example, no adult should demand total loyalty from children who must divide their time and attention between two sets of parents. Instead, they should be encouraged to relate to both natural parents and stepparents. Children's visits with the natural parent outside of the reconstituted family should be made as easy and convenient as possible. If negative feelings still exist between the natural parents, this should not be a topic for discussion with children nor should family boundaries be interfered with by criticism of rules and expectations of stepparents or natural parents. If these adults can relate in a civil manner, children will enjoy their time with them and the families will more likely function in a satisfactory manner.

TREATMENT CONSIDERATION

The practitioner who has worked primarily with the traditional intact nuclear family will need to understand what is different about the reconstituted family. We can safely say that a family systems approach is recommended for work with all families regardless of the stage of development or the nature of composition. And while the same therapeutic skills used in treating the nuclear family are also used in work with reconstituted families, the dynamics underlying reconstituted family problems are often quite different from the dynamics of nuclear family problems. An understanding of the difference and a few specific guidelines for intervention will add to the likelihood of success when family maladjustment is the object of change.

Social workers and other professionals who work with these families should be careful not to approach them as if they fit neatly into the traditional pattern of the nuclear family. This is a family whose members do not share a common history, and one needs to be aware of what is unique about the structure of this type family and the common feelings and situations its members experience. When the reconstituted family seeks professional help with problems related to family functioning, Johnson (1980, p. 307) suggests, "The starting point for assessment and intervention planning should be the exploration of those dynamics inherent in the institution of the reconstituted family." For example, it is useful to learn what family members expect from each other, as this is likely to be "a well-kept secret." It is not unusual to find that no one in the family has ever made his or her expectations known, in which case there are no guidelines for a family member's behaving in a manner that is totally satisfactory to other members. Helping family members express what they desire from each other introduces a new way of relating. This is especially true with stepparents, who usually enter into a new union without having addressed many important issues such as role expectations and disciplining of the children. Stepparents do have ideas about these things, and practitioners should assist them in clarifying and formulating these ideas and expectations, supporting what is realistic and helping them to understand and eliminate that which is related to fallacious beliefs often held by these couples. This includes such preconceived notions as believing that all family members will love each other and immediately adjust to each other, which will allow the family to go forward with its various tasks without difficulty.

It should be kept in mind that members of the reconstituted family often bring different lifestyles to the task of developing a new family. These differences may center around such things as dress codes, entertainment preferences, disciplining children, attitudes toward sex or the use of alcohol, rules governing the conduct of family members at home and in interaction with others outside of the family, and so on. These differences may result in conflict between family members and should be evaluated as possible sources of difficulty in family functioning when the family comes for help.

Contrary to the myth that "instant love" should exist between stepparent and stepchild, in some cases the relationship is characterized by competition or even a strong dislike for each other. When no basis for improving this situation can be found, we concur with Johnson (1980), who suggests accepting the fact that, in reality, a family does not exist and movement in this direction is not likely to occur in the near future. As a result, the ensuing process is usually one of waiting for the child to grow up and leave the family. In working with this situation, we also agree with her strategy and support intervention in the direction of the stepparent and stepchild spending as little time as possible together, with the natural parent assuming the major parenting responsibilities.

Sager and his associates (1983) suggest caution in setting goals for reconstituted families. Many couples come together with specific individual goals in mind, including the hope that this union will be a positive answer to all of the disappointments experienced in their previous unsatisfactory relationship. When failure to realize unrealistic goals brings the couple into treatment, they frequently try to achieve the same goals through the treatment process. In such cases it is necessary to clarify the situation and establish realistic goals on which the work might be focused.

It may be useful at times to work separately with different subsystems of the reconstituted family in the same manner as do many practitioners when working with the nuclear family. For example, when helping the new couple resolve issues around discipline and consolidating parental authority, work with subsystems at some point in this process might offer some advantages. The use of support groups for parents and children has also been found to be a profitable undertaking.

Finally, it is important for social workers and other professionals to be aware of their own attitudes toward the concept of reconstituted families and the impact this unit might have on them and vice versa. There is always the potential for emotional reactions that will prove counterproductive, depending on the practitioner's position relative to a number of factors surrounding the institutions of the reconstituted family. Sager and others refer to value conflicts around the ending of a union and forming a new one that are held by some practitioners as having the potential for interfering with treatment. Others may be concerned that their own mates might behave in a similar manner as one of the partners in the reconstituted family, or be uncomfortable in exploring specific aspects of a previous union or family experience that is viewed as negative by a family member. This can result in the practitioner's acceptance of the anxiety and denial underlying the client's perception of the experience, which will diminish the probability of a successful outcome of the treatment experience. And practitioners who have ended a previous union but have not resolved their own ambivalence about their former partners are likely to find it difficult to allow clients to resolve similar problems in their lives.

SUMMARY

The breakup of couple relationships for various reasons, resulting in creation of a new family, is by no means a novelty in contemporary society. However, it is still viewed by some as a departure from the accepted norm. As a result, society has failed to define norms for the reconstituted family to establish guidelines for the appropriate behavior of its members. This has contributed to the confusion surrounding this new family, which responds to several different titles.

This family has a number of unique features, most of which do not make for a quick and easy adjustment among family members. The family is frequently seen in treatment as it struggles to stabilize its processes and become an organized unit. It is generally accepted that a family systems approach is most applicable to assessing and treating reconstituted family problems. The use of support groups is also effective. It is helpful for practitioners who engage these families in treatment to be aware that the dynamics underlying reconstituted family problems are not always the same as those associated with the nuclear family. Therefore, this family cannot be viewed in exactly the same manner as the nuclear family. And practitioners must be aware of their own attitudes as well as their personal experiences as they relate to the family as a functioning unit.

It is difficult to visualize the future relative to the place of the reconstituted family and how it will be viewed as an entity among other groupings in society. Nevertheless, it is a family form that will continue to be with us, and we must strive for the most effective ways of understanding and dealing with these adults and their children.

REFERENCES

Duncan, S., and Brown, G. 1992. "RENEW: A Program for Building Remarried Family Strengths." *Families in Society* 73:144–58.

Hobart, C. 1989. "Experiences of Remarried Families." *Journal of Divorce* 13:121–44.

_____. 1990. "Relationships Between the Formerly Married." *Journal of Comparative Family Studies* 21:81–97.

Johnson, H.C. 1980. "Working with Stepfamilies: Principles and Practice." *Social Work* 25(4):304–08.

Kent, M.O. 1980. "Remarriage: A Family Systems Perspective." *Social Casework* 61(3):146–53.

Minuchin, S. 1974. *Families and Family Therapy*. Cambridge, MA: Harvard University Press.

Sager, C.J., Brown, H.S., Crohn, H., Engel, T., Rodstein, E., and Walker, L. 1983. *Treating the Remarried Family*. New York: Brunner/Mazel Publishers.

Schulman, G.L. 1972. "Myths That Intrude on the Adaptation of the Step Family." *Social Casework* 53(3):131–39.

Smith, T. 1991. "Family Cohesion in Remarried Families." *Journal of Divorce and Remarriage* 17:49–66.

Stuart, R.B., and Jacobson, B. 1985. *Second Marriage*. New York: W.W. Norton & Co.

Visher, E.B., and Visher, J.S. 1979. *Step Families: A Guide to Work with Stepparents and Stepchildren*. New York: Brunner/Mazel Publishers.

_____. 1982. "Step Families and Stepparenting." In *Normal Family Processes*, ed. F. Walsh. New York: Guilford.

_____. 1990. "Dynamics of Successful Stepfamilies." *Journal of Divorce and Remarriage* 14:3–11.

Wald, E. 1981. *The Remarried Family*. New York: Family Service Association of America.

Part III

The Social Work Agency

Part I presented theoretical perspectives relative to family functioning, and Part II suggested social work strategies for intervention with selected populations of families with problems. Extrapolations of theory and strategy can be made to work with a wider variety of families with different backgrounds and problems. Emphasis has been on the family as a system and its interactions with the social worker, and on the interrelatedness of the family's problems and its problem-solving efforts.

An important part of effective family treatment is the context in which the social worker provides the necessary services. Many social workers and practitioners are successfully engaged in family treatment in private practice, but the context we consider here is the social work agency. Part III focuses on the role of the agency organization and its staff in planning and providing treatment to families.

This section endeavors to bring the social work agency more directly into the treatment process by presenting various aspects of agency operations that impact on service delivery to families as clients. Among the issues addressed are treatment within the interdisciplinary agency; colleagial involvement and responsibility in treatment; the responsibility of agency administration; and implications for training social workers to engage in treating families.

In Part III, while not an exhaustive presentation of the impact of agencies, we nevertheless hope to increase awareness of the mutual responsibilities of social workers, agency administrators, and other staff members in engaging the family as the unit of treatment.

CHAPTER **17**

The Agency and the Worker in Family Treatment

Unless families seek private practitioners for the solution of their problems, agencies provide the setting for their contact with the social worker. In many instances, such as the hospital or school setting, the family could not get the services it needs outside an agency context. Were it not for its need for other services, it might not of its own initiative seek contact with the worker.

A multitude of factors in the relations between family members and workers come into play because of the agency context for family treatment. Of central interest among these many factors is the way the agency conceptualizes the problems of individuals and families that come to its attention. A corollary and closely related factor is the congruence (or lack of it) between agency views and worker views of the client and the family. These views have consequences for the way the agency organizes itself for services to the family, and consequently also to the way the worker engages with the family when they are referred.

These conceptions of agency impact on family treatment have clear implications for the kind of training needed by social workers. They imply that if workers are to "think family," the agency must provide them with support. All staff, not only those in direct contact with the family, need orientation and training in order to "think family." Without such orientation, staff and agency practices may impede or prevent effective work with the family.

THE IMPORTANCE OF THEORETICAL
CONCEPTUALIZATION OF FAMILY PROBLEMS

At the core of agency impact is the way in which the problems brought to the agency by individuals are defined. Two basically different

394

conceptualizations are possible. One orientation sees the problems as resident in the individuals. The other, which we have presented, sees them as resident in family relationships and in the family's relation to the external world.

Working from the individual orientation, helping systems have readily understood that physical or mental illness, delinquency or crime, and the loss or gain of a spouse, parent, or child are problems for the individuals who present them. They are the ones who have the problems and need to cope with them. In many instances this problem definition has been used even if the problem has been defined by someone, be it family member or person in the community, other than the individual who supposedly has the problem. Diagnostic procedures are designed to illuminate the problem the individual has, and diagnostic staff are recruited accordingly. Treatment procedures are oriented to work with one individual, and staff with skills in individual treatment are recruited.

This orientation may run into difficulty when the individual who supposedly has the problem does not accept the idea that it is his problem but sees it rather as a problem that others, especially family members, impose on him. Individually oriented agencies have responded to such client positions in two ways. Either the client's view is seen as a distorted perception of others, or the problem is viewed as lying in the way the individual responds to family behavior. Family members are not included in treatment and sometimes are specifically excluded. Workers are not permitted time for contact with family members. The treatment focuses on changing the client's perceptions or ways of coping with the family. The need for change in the family is not recognized. While some of these clients may be able to accept such a redefinition of their problems, others will participate in treatment only to convince the helper of their views. Or they may discontinue treatment.

Agencies oriented to treating individuals, however, sometimes see the need to "do something about the family" of a primary client or patient. The family is seen as having a detrimental effect on the patient, creating anxiety, frustration, or rage in the patient, allowing no relief and providing no support. Frequently, in this view, "family" does not mean the entire family but refers primarily to a parent or spouse. A separate worker is assigned to help that family member with his or her problem, or the same worker might see the other family member at a separate time. The problem created by the family member is not seen as "appropriate" for service in the agency serving the identified primary client and is therefore sent to some other agency or another department or branch of the same agency. These separate workers may see the value of consultation among themselves about what is happening in the family, but their good intentions are often foiled by lack of time or their supervisors' lack of understanding of the need for such consultation. Family members may be divided up between agencies for individual treatment. Treatment is for the patient *and* for the family. Another possible consequence of this view is that it can prompt hostility toward the family by agency staff, who see them as at fault. This can result in a need to defend the patient to the family.

This orientation is not, in our view, a family systems conception of the situation. The "patient *and* the family" view, as contrasted to "the family *as* the patient," attends to the effects of the family on the patient but gives insufficient attention to the effects of patient on family and their continuing efforts to influence each other. It also seems to be a dyadic view that does not account for the participation of third persons and alliances that may arise.

We have taken pains in this book not to define family systems treatment as the use of conjoint family sessions. Nevertheless, it does seem possible that the greater use of individual sessions is associated with the position that the problem resides in the individual or separately in client and family members.

If problems are defined by the agency as problems in family operations, as they have been in this book, very different agency procedures follow. There is insistence that other members of the family participate in the diagnostic process and in some or all of the treatment. Different diagnostic procedures are used. Home visits and whole-family interview sessions for observation of family interactions serve as the basis for assessment. These take the place of a lengthy social history or psychological or psychiatric examinations. Current transactions are more important than historical developments and psychological introjects.

When the problem is presented by the individual or the family as a family problem, family assessment procedures pose no difficulty for the family. The procedures seem ultimately sensible to them. When the individual who presents his own or someone else's problem as a problem of the individual is confronted with the family orientation of the helping system, however, the encounter may be experienced as an affront. This can easily give rise to hostility and uncooperativeness toward the helping system. Consent to participate will come only when the individual is convinced of the relevance of the family's participation and its use to him.

Social workers are prepared to cope with such hostility and resistance when they and the agency have a thorough grounding in family systems theory. They must be able to see readily the ways in which the family system impinges on the problem-solving ability of the person presenting the problem. Several brief examples from our own cases will illustrate the issues.

A mother and her 14-year-old daughter were seen on a walk-in basis at a community mental health clinic. The mother complained that her daughter was not investing herself in her school work and was only doing passing work, when she could be doing much better. Also, her daughter neglected her household responsibilities and had to be constantly prodded to do them. Both home and school problems resulted in frequent conflict between mother and daughter. Mother's request was that the clinic find out what was wrong with her daughter and change her.

In this instance the social worker did not agree that the problem presented was the problem of the 14-year-old daughter alone, though her lack of cooperation and apparent stubbornness would in some agencies have been defined that way. In that event efforts would have been made to interest the girl in individual or group treatment and to offer, but not push upon the parents, the "opportunity" to be seen. Instead, the social worker expressed concern about the difficulty that the mother and the father were having in gaining their daughter's cooperation, suggesting that all three needed to be seen in order to understand and solve the problem.

While the mother expressed some awareness of the need for her to be involved, her resistance was expressed in terms of her husband's unwillingness to be involved. She felt that he saw the children as her responsibility. Though this left her feeling unsupported in child-caring responsibilities, she saw no way of gaining his cooperation. At this point she had given up on her efforts to involve her husband. Her agreement to try to bring him for the following appointment was seen as an attempt to reengage him. While the focus remained on the presenting problem, there was also the simultaneous emphasis on changing the family system and its way of coping with the problem.

This brief case description includes only the initial impact on the family. But even in the initial efforts to work on the problem there is a redefinition of family roles, of the images that family members hold of each other, and of the means they use to negotiate and communicate about their problems. The focus on the roles, expectations, and images of family members and their effort to communicate about and change them is also central to the continuing treatment process.

Unintentional consequences may arise in the family system even when all parties concerned—agency, client, and family—initially agree that a given person has the problem. In the following example all three systems defined the problem as resident within the individual. Unfortunate consequences arose because they did not define it as a family problem.

A middle-aged, married male was admitted for psychiatric hospital treatment on the basis of complaints of severe depression and inability to work. In his conversations with hospital staff, the patient began to air negative feelings about his marriage and to express a wish to proceed for a divorce. The hospital staff had experienced the wife as extremely managerial and dominating and had observed that the patient was upset after his wife's visits, being more depressed and manifesting a great deal of body twitching. Given their view of the problem as one individual coping with a difficult relationship, they accepted as realistic the patient's efforts to distance himself in this relationship. They saw this distancing as crucial and valid treatment in his recovery from depression. They supported him by limiting his wife's visiting and by encouraging consideration of divorce.

The wife's response was to employ their adolescent son to tell both his father and the hospital staff how much the father was needed in the family. The wife also got her minister to talk to the hospital chaplain about how she was being deprived of the opportunity to visit her husband. Finally, she cruised the hospital grounds in a car, waiting for her husband to leave the ward so she could visit him.

While it is evident that the hospital staff saw themselves as helping the individual patient to cope, it is also clear that they did not anticipate the impact on family relationships of a change in the identified patient. They were unrealistic in the amount of or kind of separateness achievable in this instance and in their means for achieving it. The wife clearly had not counted on distancing as a consequence of the help that she wanted the hospital to give her husband. Relieving depression did not mean to her this kind of a change in their relationship. The wife's response was to attempt to change the hospital system rather than permit change in the relationship.

A "family is the patient" response on the part of the staff to this problem would have engaged both husband and wife in solving the problem of the depression, recognizing that some alteration in husband/wife roles and expectation of each other might be necessary to the achievement of that goal. Awareness of the transactional qualities of the relationship would have led the staff to see that the patient's withdrawal behavior was a stimulus for the wife's managerial behavior, and vice versa. The focus would have been on their transactions, and this would have resulted in a different experience for both patient and spouse.

CONSEQUENCES OF MIXED THEORETICAL POSITIONS

When individual treatment orientations exist side by side with a family orientation in a given agency, or during a time of changeover from one orientation to the other, cases such as the one just described may become more complicated. A given worker may hold to an individual problem definition in contrast to the agency's family orientation, or vice versa. Staff disagreements may arise over philosophy and procedure. An individual-problem-oriented intake worker may tell client and family of the need for individual treatment, and a family-oriented continuing worker may at a later point have difficulty engaging the family. Staff may be confronted with the same difficulties in solving the problem of how to deal with the client that the family group faces in solving its problems.

Staff therefore need to agree on a common value or theoretical perspective about families. They must find ways of resolving their differences if they are to function and agency service is to be effective. Otherwise client or family contacts with staff will produce different interpretations of the problem, inconsistent treatment, confusion instead of help, and frustration of the family's own efforts at problem solution. Foster (1965), using experience in a medical hospital, makes the more positive suggestion that the social worker has a specific dual role in the midst of such difficulties. The first is to enable the resolution of staff differences. The second, which follows from the first, is to make it possible for agency system and family system to work together. In order to do this in the hospital setting, the problems of the patient in the family as well as the problems of the family need to be taken into account.

There is therefore a need for clarity and consistency in the theoretical perspective in both worker and agency. In an agency that is family systems oriented, procedures, starting at intake, are used to engage the family as a group in the assessment and treatment process. All staff who have contact with any member of the family are sensitive to the way in which family relationships affect work on the family problem and to the way in which a particular staff person's interventions influence family relationships. Time is available to meet with members of the family other than the identified problem person, either separately or as a group with the patient. Solutions to problems that other family members are having are seen as relevant to the solutions of the problems of the person for whom agency contact originated. There will be less likelihood of dividing the family up between agencies or workers.

SPECIAL PROBLEMS OF INTERDISCIPLINARY AGENCIES

Social workers are not always the ones that determine agency policies, and thus they are not totally in control of the decision about whether or how to engage the family in treatment. This is true in psychiatric, medical, school, and residential settings. The family-oriented worker, therefore, not wishing to stand alone or to leave families unassisted, may have to take a position of advocacy for the family and for a family systems view. The worker's primary approach in this regard is to orient other staff members or disciplines to the needs of the family and to the way in which agency procedures interfere with or support the family's own efforts at problem solving.

This orientation is likely achieved initially on a case-by-case basis (see Foster, 1965), but it may require more systematic training. Beyond this, it may entail considerable effort to change agency procedures and budget to allow more time for work with family members and to minimize the referral of family members to other agencies. And it may entail considerable worker effort to moderate staff reactions to family members or to lessen differences among staff members about how to intervene in the transactions between client and family members.

SPECIAL PROBLEMS OF MULTIPLE-PROBLEM FAMILIES

A variety of forms of intervention is needed for multiple-problem families (for example, child abuse, problem poverty, and alcoholism families) due to their relatively closed nature and their isolation from the larger community. A one-worker-to-family relationship that emphasizes talking appears to be insufficient for their needs and provides only limited support and access to the larger community. More contact hours per family and the possibility of home visits need to be made part of the agency repertoire. Doing with, being with, going with in relation to everyday activities and specific needs of the families are important aspects of worker activity. The simultaneous provision of information, ideas, and access are all conditions of contact that enable family members to relate to the worker, the agency, and other available services in the community, and to each other in a new and meaningful way.

Earlier chapters have cited the assignment of co-therapists or teams of workers for simultaneous attention to separate problems or different parts of the family, as well as varying worker patterns and time commitments (Whittaker, Kinney, Tracy, and Booth, 1990). We have drawn attention to these in our discussion of work with poor, multi-problem families (Chapter 10) and note that these may be necessary agency adjustments for effective service.

Tracy and Parkas (1994) draw attention to the situation of agencies serving abused children whose parents have problems with alcohol and other drugs. They point to the need for broad agency capacity and worker training to be able to see connections and provide services across a variety of problems.

Agency willingness and capacity to relate to such family systems on these terms is predicated on the kind of understanding about modes of operation that has been put forth in this book. Where agencies persist in seeing such families as unmotivated, additional services and different modes of engaging the families will not be available, and the families will continue to be viewed as hopeless and hard to reach. A change in agency thinking and operations is required before change in the families will be possible. Such a change in the agency may not guarantee success with the family, but it will make it possible or more likely.

Where agencies have continued to define problems as problems of individuals rather than of families, the tendency to divide families up among agencies has persisted. The adult with problems is seen at one agency, the children at another, and workers from still other agencies providing special services are also involved. Each worker in each separate agency sees only part of the problem and gets only an individual member's report of what is happening. Decisions are made with or about the family member that do not take into account the reactions of, or consequences for, other family members.

At a minimum, all workers involved with the family should confer enough to come to a common understanding of the family's structure and process. This understanding should reveal the effects the family has on individual capacity and performance, the effects of individual performance and capacity on family operations, and the changes required in the family's process and structure if performance is to change. One worker must be enough of a case manager to be in regular contact with all the workers involved and keep them abreast of needs and changes. Additionally, case conferences involving all workers are imperative. Joint meetings between family members and their various workers serve to promote the exchange of information, improve communication, and facilitate decision making in the family. Multiple-service agencies that can provide service to all family members are better able to promote such interaction than single-service agencies serving only one family member. The crucial factor, however, is not where the service is provided but whether case analysis is done on a family systems basis.

ISSUES OF CONFIDENTIALITY

The difference between an individual and a family orientation in an agency is also revealed in the way in which confidentiality in the client-worker relationship is handled. Initial assurances of confidentiality between family members are less likely to be given by the family-oriented worker and may indeed be moot in the worker's way of structuring the initial contact. In a situation that is seen as a problem for the family system and in which all members are affected in one way or another, whether as leaders, opposers, followers, bystanders, perpetrators, or victims, and in which change between persons rather than within persons is an objective, workers structure the situation to increase the exchange of information and feelings between family members. The worker frames the situation as one in which significant others need to be involved in the problem-solving process right from the beginning by providing information needed to understand the problematic situation.

By contrast, where the individual is seen as the primary client, worker assurances are given that client communications to the worker will not be revealed to others, including family members, without client consent. This is seen as necessary to enable clients to deal more directly and openly with thoughts and feelings of anger, anxiety, or guilt, to experience some relief from ventilating those feelings in a nonthreatening relationship, and to reorient their thinking and feelings in a more realistic way.

The feelings and reactions revealed in individual treatment often arise in transactions with significant others. The fact that they have not been resolved with those significant others suggests an impediment in the communication and relationship between the individuals involved. It is a problem not only of having the thoughts and feelings, but of how these might be expressed to another and how they might be received by another. What is discussed between worker and client in individual treatment must eventually be surfaced and resolved in intrafamily relationships. In that sense it is not subject matter that can be held in confidence between worker and client if the worker is to be at all helpful. Adherence to usual rules of confidentiality would limit the worker's ability to be helpful.

> Treatment for a child's behavior problem was initially structured to provide separate workers and individual treatment for the child and the mother, who was divorced from the child's father. Both child and mother were given assurances of confidentiality. The child's worker received a phone call from the father in which he said that the child was complaining to him of maltreatment by his mother, but he did not want the mother to know that he had called. It seemed to the worker that he may have been exaggerating to make a case for himself as a better parent because he also said he was suing for custody. Hemmed in by rules of confidentiality, the workers in this situation had difficulty in obtaining needed facts to assess the validity of the father's complaint.

A family-oriented worker would likely have viewed the child's problem as a function of his life situation and sought participation of both parents at the beginning of contact. Conjoint sessions with all family members would have implied open exchange of information and thus minimized the problems of confidentiality that appeared here. If parents had not agreed to conjoint sessions, the worker could still structure in the necessity of sharing information among all family members.

When confidentiality is offered at the time of initial contact, the worker leaves himself or herself vulnerable to becoming a keeper of secrets between family members. When separate sessions are sought by a family member, they are often sought for the purpose of enlisting the worker's understanding of the member's particular view of a situation, which is biased against another member. This not only puts the worker in an uncomfortable position, but also creates a collusion or an alliance between the worker and that particular family member that may foster other family members' suspicion and distrust in the worker and prevent their constructive involvement in the treatment effort. They may see the worker as siding with the other family members against them and become resistant to participation.

It is sometimes useful to accede to requests for separate interviews to enable the family member to open up subject matter they would otherwise hesitate to deal with directly with others in the family. However, the worker in acceding to separate sessions frames them as sessions in which the family member will not be encouraged to bring up anything that they would not subsequently want to have surfaced with relevant other family members, and in which they would be helped to find ways of doing so.

This is not to say that everything needs to be privileged to all family members. Some matters, for example, may concern only members of the parental generation. Our purpose here is not to offer detailed guidelines about confidentiality, but to stress that in a family systems view of problematic situations, in which the family is seen as the client, information pertaining to the system is not appropriately secreted between one member of the system and the worker. The inability to communicate openly and directly may in itself be the core of the family's difficulties.

IMPLICATIONS FOR TRAINING WORKERS

A family-oriented way of conceptualizing presenting problems in agencies has implications for training and staff development. Social workers need to have knowledge of the way family systems work and of the ways in which problems and external systems affect the workings of the family and the individuals in it. Based on this theoretical understanding, they need to have skills that will guide family members in more constructive approaches to problem solving and which will involve them jointly in the problem-solving effort. These needs clearly should influence the training of the worker who meets the family.

Where there is unanimity between the agency and the worker about his way of viewing the problems of individuals and families, the worker and the agency support each other in the provision of services. Where other staff members are at odds with the worker, some effort must be made to orient or train other staff members, including those who are not in direct contact with client and family.

A family systems approach is not merely the addition of a treatment technique such as conjoint family interviewing (though that technique may be used) to another conceptual base and set of skills. It is a different way of thinking about presenting problems. Knowledge about intrapsychic dynamics and skills in individual treatment is, therefore, not always a prerequisite for engaging families. Workers who have no knowledge of individual dynamics often learn just as easily about the way families work, and they need not face the problem of having to dispense with previous learning. Workers who shift from thinking about individual dynamics to the family orientation sometimes have just as much to learn about family dynamics as those who have no knowledge of individual treatment.

The individual-treatment orientation of many social work students and staff members accounts in part for the persistent lack of family contact in agencies. Levande (1976) notes,

> Many social work students are hesitant about becoming involved with the family as a whole as the designated client. Part of this reluctance may stem from having a theoretical frame of reference which provides understanding of the individual as the unit of treatment, but having only a limited knowledge when confronted with the possibility of conceptualizing the family system or any of its sub-systems as the unit of intervention. (p. 295)

Yet another aspect of professional development in family treatment needs to be mentioned. Throughout our writing we have emphasized the knowledge base and skill needed for work with families. As workers acquire these, their effectiveness with families will be enhanced. However, we have little noted the tensions the worker may experience in family work. Workers will be involved with families different from those in which they grew up, with greater or lesser degrees of awareness of the difference. The need for knowledge about many kinds of families and family problems and how to work with ethnic and social-class differences is evident.

Biases, unfavorable or favoring particular family types, need to be surfaced and dealt with. Situations in which family members are in conflict result in attempts by each side to influence the worker. While side-taking at some points may be necessary, workers need the capacity to be aware of and resist pulls to judge or be partial. Workers need to become aware of other biases such as tendencies to identify with and favor a parent or a child, or to prefer less rigidity, fewer rules, or a lower or higher level of cohesion.

We have also given extensive attention to the worker's efforts to join the family in beginning the change effort. Ability to accept the family where they are is obviously enhanced by knowledge of various family types. The effort to identify with the family and individual members, while extremely important, needs to be coupled with the worker's capacity to maintain his or her own identity and separateness in order to be an effective change agent.

How training programs build this sort of attitudinal awareness and development into training of workers is varied. One useful means is the live supervision of sessions with families by means of observation through a one-way window, with telephone connections used during the session and with other students or trainees participating in the process. Aponte (1991) has discussed attitudinal awareness in relation to work with poor and minority families. He proposes a multi-faceted program in a group-training context in which each student develops a history and genogram of the student's own family, conducts a session in which other students role-play members of his family, and conducts sessions with actual client families. Hardy and Laszloffy (1995) also make use of a cultural genogram to enhance workers' awareness of their own cultural identification and that of others.

Many aspects and styles of supervision and training in family treatment have been identified. Research is under way to define a model for training (White and Russell, 1995). Agencies and schools may not have the facilities, the supervisors, or the number of students to implement such a training model, necessitating reliance on more traditional models of didactic instruction and individual supervision. However, the goals of awareness of the ways in which one's own family experience enters into family work and the development of appropriate attitudes would remain the same as in the more intensive experience proposed by Aponte.

Schools of social work are increasingly offering classroom training in the understanding and treatment of family systems. Skilled supervision in the field is often unavailable, however, because supervisors themselves lack the necessary conceptual base and experience. For the time being, therefore, continuing education courses and in-service training are needed for workers who wish to move in this direction. Both of these forms of training are open to workers, regardless of the kind or level of previous training. Thus, paraprofessionals, persons with bachelor's, master's, and doctoral degrees, and persons with training in psychiatry, nursing, psychology, guidance, and social work all can acquire family treatment skills.

In some instances, as Haley (1975) has noted, this has resulted in a blurring of the distinctions between professional backgrounds and levels of education. Since prior training often is less relevant in the family systems approach, the emphasis on family treatment puts staff members in a different relationship to each other. This creates or at least opens the possibility of staff rivalries and conflicts equaling those of the family, particularly between those of different disciplines but also between workers and supervisors. In such circumstances, the awareness and training of persons at supervisory and administrative levels are as important in the implementation of family treatment efforts as are those of the workers who have direct contact with the family.

SUMMARY

A family orientation needs to be built into the agency as well as into the worker. Thinking "family" means thinking differently about who the client is, putting in place a set of procedures—beginning at case intake—that allow for and expect family input, being open to different mixes and time allocations of workers in a given case, and educating referral sources to the agency's thinking and ways of working.

In many instances, workers may have had training for family treatment; but for those who have not, the agency needs to think about providing training and supervision. We have noted some special aspects of training family therapists, discussing briefly modes of supervision and training that have been successfully utilized. An important aspect of this preparation is the enhancing of workers' awareness of their own family experience and the resulting biases and preferences.

REFERENCES

Aponte, Harry. 1991. "Training on the Person of the Therapist for Work with the Poor and Minorities." *Journal of Independent Social Work* 5(3–4):23–39.
Foster, Z.P. 1965. "How Social Work Can Influence Hospital Management of Fatal Illness." *Social Work* 10:30–45.

Haley, J. 1975. "Why a Mental Health Center Should Avoid Family Therapy." *Journal of Marriage and Family Counseling* 1:1–14.

Hardy, Kenneth, and Laszloffy, Tracey. 1995. "The Cultural Genogram: Key to Culturally Competent Family Therapists." *Journal of Marital and Family Therapy* 21(3):227–37.

Levande, D.I. 1976. "Family Theory as a Necessary Component of Family Therapy." *Social Casework* 57:291–95.

Tracy, Elizabeth, and Parkas, Kathleen. 1994. "Preparing Practitioners for Child Welfare Practice with Substance Abusing Families." *Child Welfare* 73(1):57–68.

White, Mark, and Russell, Candyce. 1995. "The Essential Elements of Supervisory Systems: A Modified Delphi Study." *Journal of Marital & Family Therapy* 21(1):33–53.

Whittaker, James, Kinney, Jill, Tracy, Elizabeth, and Booth, Charlotte. 1990. *Reaching High Risk Families*. Chapter 3, "The Homebuilders Model." New York: Aldyne-deGruyter.

Name Index

Subject Index

FAMILY TREATMENT IN SOCIAL WORK PRACTICE
Third edition
Edited by John Beasley
Production supervision by Kim Vander Steen
Cover design by Jeanne Calabrese Design, Oak Park, Illinois
Composition by Point West, Inc., Carol Stream, Illinois
Paper, Finch Opaque
Printed and bound by McNaughton & Gunn, Saline, Michigan